A HISTORY OF
GREAT IDEAS IN
ABNORMAL PSYCHOLOGY

ADVANCES IN PSYCHOLOGY

66

Editors:

G. E. STELMACH

P. A. VROON

NORTH-HOLLAND
AMSTERDAM · NEW YORK · OXFORD · TOKYO

A HISTORY OF GREAT IDEAS IN ABNORMAL PSYCHOLOGY

Thaddeus E. WECKOWICZ

Professor Emeritus of Psychology and Psychiatry
University of Alberta
Edmonton, Alberta, Canada

Helen P. LIEBEL-WECKOWICZ

Professor of History
University of Alberta
Edmonton, Alberta, Canada

N·H
P&C

1990

NORTH-HOLLAND
AMSTERDAM · NEW YORK · OXFORD · TOKYO

NORTH-HOLLAND
ELSEVIER SCIENCE PUBLISHERS B.V.
Sara Burgerhartstraat 25
P.O. Box 211, 1000 AE Amsterdam, The Netherlands

Distributors for the United States and Canada:
ELSEVIER SCIENCE PUBLISHING COMPANY, INC.
655 Avenue of the Americas
New York, N.Y. 10010, U.S.A.

Library of Congress Cataloging-in-Publication Data

Weckowicz, Thaddeus E.
A history of great ideas in abnormal psychology / Thaddeus E.
Weckowicz, Helen P. Liebel-Weckowicz.
p. cm. -- (Advances in psychology ; 66)
Includes bibliographical references.
ISBN 0-444-88391-6 (Elsevier)
1. Psychiatry--History. I. Liebel-Weckowicz, Helen P.
II. Title. III. Series: Advances in psychology (Amsterdam, Holland)
; 66.
RC438.W43 1990
616.89'009--dc20 90-31159
CIP

ISBN: 0 444 88391 6

Printed in The Netherlands

Preface

The present book: *A history of the great ideas in abnormal psychology* is a sequel to an earlier book by the senior author, *Models of mental illness* (T. Weckowicz, 1984). The previous book discussed different perspectives, or models, in the field of abnormal psychology and psychiatry. The ideas found in these systems are currently in competition with one another and each is trying to establish itself as paradigmatic for the psychological discipline.

Space limitations in the previous book did not allow a detailed presentation of the historical background of the various approaches (models) to the subject. A cross-section of contemporary views on mental illness was the result. This seemed to make necessary a further work in which an in-depth historical analysis could be presented. The purpose of this work has been to make an ingress in the history of ideas and to treat the history of psychological ideas as valid in their own right. There is thus an agreement with the view expressed by Baker, Hyland, Van Rappard, and Staats (1987) in *Current issues in theoretical psychology* (Amsterdam: North-Holland):

> The history of psychology is important for our understanding of theory since history informs our understanding of theoretical development.

The above quotation is even more applicable to the field of psychiatry and abnormal psychology, and also to that of medicine since the latter disciplines are concerned with theory as well as with practice and public policy.

The senior author's 1984 book distinguished the following models (systematic beliefs) about mental illness: (1) biological (medical), (2) psychological, (3) socio-cultural, and (4) philosophical-moral ones. These four categories could be sub-divided further into sub-categories. The present book is concerned with tracing the history of these models of mental illness throughout the development of Western thought and Western medicine. However, even greater emphasis has been placed on distinguishing the emergence of the disease and constitutional models of illness and their influence in shaping ideas about human psychopathology and the problems of mental illness.

Psychiatry has more than other fields of medicine been influenced by the prevailing philosophical views on the nature of mind and of man. It has also been confronted with the dilemma of making a distinction between "mad" and "bad." Consequently, psychiatry has been influenced by the prevailing theories of ethics, which involved the definitions of virtue and sin. As a result of these considerations, the present work deals with the history of ideas in psychiatry, psychology, and medicine, and also with the influence of some of the prevailing philosophical ideas. These represent cross-currents found in the successive epochs of thought which marked the development of Western Civilization. The understanding of the human mind and of human behaviour must of necessity involve considering them against the background of contemporaneous philosphical beliefs about human nature. It seems inseparable from the conditioning influence of the surrounding culture and its accepted philosophical assumptions. These have always exerted an important influence in shaping the development of psychiatry and of ideas about madness.

This book has been the joint effort of a psychiatrist who has also been trained as a psychologist, and of an historian with a strong interest in the role of psychological ideas in the general progress of the history of ideas. A shorter version of this book has been presented on several occasions as a series of lecture-seminars to psychiatric residents in the Department of Psychiatry at the University of Alberta. Some material has been presented in lectures in the History of Ideas in the Department of History at the same university. The authors are grateful to the psychiatric residents and to their colleagues for comments on the lecture notes which contained some parts of the book. Further, we thank those students and colleagues who have commented on material presented during historical lectures. This work is intended as a history of ideas. It is not concerned with the detailed biographies of prominent psychiatrists, psychologists and physicians, although these have been taken into account. Nor have we been concerned with a detailed chronology of historical events. An analysis of the emerging ideas has been preferred where possible, and the interested reader may, we trust, find the references in the bibliography a guide to further studies of the subject.

Acknowledgements

The authors would like to acknowledge the sources of the graphs and quotations used in this book as follows: Ronald Press, for the diagram on p.57 of *A Short History of Medicine* by Erwin Ackerknecht. Mentor Books for the quotation from Plato's *Republic*, pp. 369-370. The University of Chicago Press for the quotations on pp. 7-8 from *Hysteria, the history of a disease* by I. Veith. Random House for the quotation on p.158 from *The rise of experimental biology* by E.B. Gaskin. Princeton University Press for the quotations from pages 178, 309 and 313 from *Concluding Unscientific postscript of philosophical* fragments by S. Kierkegaard. Baillière, Tindal,& Cox Ltd. for the quotation, p. 1, from *Lectures on clinical psychiatry* by E. Kraepelin. The Citadel Press for quotations from pp. 141-142 of *One hundred years of psychiatry* by E. Kraepelin. The Viking Press for quotations on pp. 462-463 from *The Vital balance* by K. Menninger. Harcourt Brace for the quotation on p.255 from *Physique and character* by E. Kretschmer. Dover Press, for the quotation on p.34 from *Beyond psychology* by Otto Rank. Norton Publishers for the quotation on p.104 from *Behaviorism* by J.B. Watson. C.C. Thomas Publishers for the quotation from p.118 in *Psychobiology:A science of man* by Adolf Meyer.

The authors would like to express their gratitude to Professors William J. Baker, Director of the Center for Advanced Study in Theoretical Psychology at the University of Alberta, and to Leendert P. Mos of the Center and of the Department of Linguistics for computer text formatting of the manuscript. They would like to thank Mrs. Evelyn Murison and Ms. Jan Zielinski for secretarial and text formatting assistance, and Mr. John Butterfield of Elsevier Publishers in Amsterdam for expediting the publication of the book. Further, the junior author would like to thank the University of Alberta for granting a half-year study leave during the fall of 1986 in order to facilitate research in West Germany, at the library of the Max Planck Institut fuer Psychiatrie in Munich, and also at the library of the New York Academy of Medicine. Thanks are due also to the archive of the University of Vienna for sending biographical information about former members of staff.

The senior author would like to thank Dr. William Dewhurst, Chairman of the Department of Psychiatry of the University of Alberta for his support and help. He would also like to thank Professor Richard Jung of the Department of Sociology of the University of Alberta for offering the use of the desk at the Center for Systems Research at the University of Alberta and for stimulating discussions of phenomenology and the history of science at the Center seminars. The junior author would like to thank Patricia Clements, Dean of Arts of the University of Alberta for her encouragement. Many thanks, as well, are owed to the Center for Theoretical Psychology where from an historian's perspective, the lectures presented by prominent scientists and psychologists during the past twenty years, have exerted a most stimulating influence on the shaping of this work.

T. E. Weckowicz
Helen Liebel-Weckowicz
September, 1989, Edmonton, Canada

Table of Contents

1

Introduction

Psychiatry more than any other medical specialty has been influenced by ancient metaphysical ideas about the nature of man, his mind, and his behaviour (Altschule, 1965). A history of ideas pertaining to mental illness is extremely important for understanding the background of contemporary thinking about the subject. It is not intended to present a systematic recapitulation here, of the history of psychiatry and abnormal psychology. The interested reader is referred to the standard texts of the history of psychiatry, such as those of Kirchhoff (1912; 1921-1924), Zilboorg (1941), Leibbrand and Wettley (1961), Alexander and Selesnick (1966), Mora (1967), Ellenberger (1970), and Ackerknecht (1985). Also, texts in the history of medicine are of interest, such as those of Garrison (1929), Siegerist (1932/1951), Meyer-Steinegg and Sudhoff (1950), Leibbrand and Leibbrand-Wettley (1964), and Ackerknecht (1968). The present book attempts to present certain perennial issues in the history of psychiatry and abnormal psychology. It seeks to discuss the concepts and the ways of thinking which have been underlying the theories of causation and treatment of mental diseases throughout the ages.

There is a great danger inherent in the approach of taking ideas and concepts out of their historical and cultural context and forcing them into the mould of contemporary ideological issues. In spite of a superficial similarity with modern ideas, the ideas of primitive and ancient peoples have a meaning which is different in their historical and cultural contexts. Nevertheless, there is a continuity of thought and ideas in religion, philosophy and medicine, particularly in the history of Western thought. Also, if one takes an evolutionary rather than a functionalist point of view, there is a similarity between differrent cultures, past and present, which are at the same level of technological development (Liebel-Weckowicz, 1982). Thus, magical beliefs and shamanism are associated with hunting and gathering bands, and with preliterate, primitive agricultural societies. At this level, magic, religion, science and technology are not separated from one another (Malinowski, 1948; Lynn Thorndike, 1923-58, 1967). The supernatural is inseparably blended with the natural. Magical practices cannot be separated from technological activity. Dead ancestors, ghosts, demons and deities inhabiting the mountains, trees, rivers, and lakes are as real as living people, real animals and geographical features. Together they constitute the total reality with which the individual has to come to terms.

One of the earliest specialists to appear in primitive societies is the shaman or witch doctor. He combines the functions of the priest, the medical doctor, the psychiatrist and the fortune teller. He mediates between the supernatural agents causing calamities and their victims. Illness is believed to be produced by sorcery (black magic), by evil spirits or demons entering the body or stealing a vital part of it. Sometimes deities send an illness in the form of a curse or of an evil demon, because the victim has broken a taboo and offended a deity. Madness is often regarded as caused by demoniacal possession. The strange, incomprehensible behavior of the victim is caused by an indwelling demon. However, it may also be due to an evil spell inside the body by means of which a sorcerer controls the behaviour of the victim. Madness may also be due to a loss of the vital part of the soul. Fears like these may still be found among primitive peoples. In the twentieth century, contemporary Andean Indians continue to display a fear of being photographed because they are afraid that their soul is being taken, and that they will fall ill.

According to Ellenberger (1970) and Oesterreich (1930), the belief in possession by an evil or even by a benign spirit, originated in Western Asia and became part of the folklore of the peoples who came from that part of the world. It became deeply ingrained in the world view of both Semitic and Indo-European peoples. Victims of possession appeared to lose their identity and to become incarnations of other beings, whether evil or benign spirits, sometimes of the spirits of dead ancestors. Ellenberger distinguishes two types of possession; the somnabulic, and the lucid. In the somnabulic type, the individual goes into a hypnotic trance and assumes the incarnated personality. In lucid possession, the individual is constantly aware of himself as well as of another personality dwelling within his body. There is a struggle between the personality of the victim and that of the invading spirit. At times, an individual induces a state of possession by himself, as exemplified by the shamans of Siberia, or by the priestesses of Delphi in ancient Greece. At such times, the shaman acquired the supernatural power of the possessing spirit and was capable of healing illnesses, of forseeing the future and of pronouncing oracles (as in the case of the Greeks).

Possession by a spirit may be overt or latent. In the latter case, an individual may suffer from a mental or physical illness without realizing that it is caused by an indwelling spirit. Exerorcising that spirit by incantations and by pitting the will of the exorcist against that of the spirit, may bring about a cure. The possessing spirit may be an evil demon, as in the case of the several raving demoniacs (both male and female) cured by Jesus Christ. The evil spirits are always described as "unclean." They originate in the heart of man, not from his stomach or from food ingested, and are mostly referred to as "devils." (Matt.9:32-34; 12:22-29). The Egyptians too believed that melancholia meant that a man "tasted" his heart. Yet they ascribed cases of mental illness to organic disease, despite the fact that theirs was still a demoniac system of medicine (Ghalioungui,1963). In Indo-European cultures, however, it is a benign deity which takes possession, as in the case of the Delphic priestness who is possessed by the earth-mother. Or, a bard may be possessed by a muse. It might be observed that the benign possession comes from a psychic, godlike influence, while the evil ones are viewed as unclean and emanating from the emotional center of man in the heart. The Greeks called it the thymos, in order to distinguish it from the psyche which related more to the divine forces of the universe (Ballard,1971). Finally, the possessing spirit may be a mythical animal, as in the Japanese folk belief in possession by a fox.

Modern scholars have interpreted the classical symptoms of possession as similar to those of schizophrenia, or those of a hysterical dissociation which results in the syndrome of multiple personality. Possession by a benign spirit was made responsible for a "divine", prophetic, or creative madness. Possession by an evil spirit, or by a devil, was associated with destructive madness. The latter notion became prevalent in the western world during the middle ages and persisted until recently. This tradition is responsible for the perception of madness as intrinsically evil and as being caused by moral corruption and sin. This led to the rejection of the mad man by his society, and to a superstitious fear of him, something which was true in ancient times as well (Luke 8:26-39). Beliefs about demoniacal possession are important for understanding the history of abnormal psychology.

All these theories imply that diseases, both physical and mental, are conceived as being extrinsic and alien to both the body and the mind of which they take possession. Disease is then believed to be caused by an external agent which enters the body and which plays havoc with its normal functions, or steals some vital part of the body or soul. Some beliefs of primitive people suggest a recognition of psychodynamic factors. Already at the level of magical medicine, two conceptions of mental illness may be recognized: one, to use modern psychiatric terminology, is a "disease process," which causes madness or physical illness; the other is a "personality disorder."

The first may be illustrated by the shamanic practices of the Northwest Coast Indians as described by Franz Boas (1925). The shaman worked himself into a state of frenzy by druming, singing and dancing. Then he went into a trance in which he consulted the ancestral spirits as to the cause of the illness. When he had ascertained the causal agent and its location, he sucked the affected part of the victim's body and spat out a little tuft of down or a pebble covered with blood. Thus the disease was literally "removed" from the inside of the body.

The idea of blood sucking also occurs in European culture in a quite different context. Louis Lavater of Leiden in 1570 included a species of demons called striges or blood suckers, in a group between laren (old Roman household gods), and demons who caused illnesses. (Leibbrand & Wettley, 1961). By the eighteenth century, a belief in vampires emerged in Danubian regions. In these beliefs, an permanent illness entered by the bite of the external agent, the vampire, who hoped to live forever as a result. These are more modern versions of the primitive belief in possession.

The modern idea that mental disease is a personality disorder is also found among primitive people. An early psychodynamic "personality disorder" theory of mental illness is illustrated by the beliefs about mental illness of the seventeenth century Hurons, an American Indian nation. These were described by Father Paul Ragueneau, S.J., in *Jesuit Relations for 1647 and 1648 (1898)* (Thwaites, 1896- 1901/1980; Altschule, 1965). The Hurons believed that all illnesses were either natural or accidental. If natural, then such physical and mental diseases were caused by inborn, concealed desires coming from the depths of the soul which had not been satisfied. These desires could be uncovered by analyzing the dreams of the patients. Once uncovered, they could be satisfied. Dream analysis could also reveal other causes of illness such as spells or charms. Such an analysis was carried out under the supervision of the village chief and council of elders who called for a community festival and brought in the medicine man (Campeau,1987). According to the *Jesuit Relation,* he was sometimes called a *Saokota* among the Quebec Hurons. He tried to discover the cause of the illness while the community feasted, and brought gifts to the sick person.

The Huron shaman much like the Greek Asclepian physician (Krug, 1985), tried to determine the nature of the illness from a dream. If it was a demon, then the festivals helped to chase it away. Here a fire dance could be employed, although only the specially gifted could perform them. Nervous ailments were more clearly diagnosed under the supervision of the tribal chief. Here a three day cure called the urn of the head or *ononhouaroia* was performed.

Surrounded by violence, primitive man imagined himself to be possessed by demons which caused it. Relief from these tensions came through religious frenzy of the kind expressed in games and festivals. Trances, bacchanalian feasts, beliefs in possession, and even an escape into schizophrenia became characteristic of such cultures (Campeau,1987).

Huron, shamanist medicine believed that once concealed desire was revealed, it could be gratified. In addition to exorcism of demoniacs and the removal of disease causing objects, shamans could also treat diseases caused by the loss of the soul, by a breach of a taboo, and those caused by sorcery (Clements, 1932). Belief in the loss of the "soul" is common among tribes like the Negritos of the Malay peninsula, among Australian aborigines, and also in Peru, among the Quechua Indians. It is related to the notion that the soul leaves the body and wanders abroad during sleep. While it is wandering, the soul may be captured by a sorcerer, or it may be prevented from returning to the body by a sudden fright. When treating the loss of the soul, the shaman goes into a trance in order to track the lost soul and to guide it back to the body of the patient. If there is a breach of taboo, however, such a belief may actually cause death. Such cases have been recorded among Polynesian people. In such cases the shaman must encourage the patient to confess his transgressions publically.

The concept of disease as a punishment for sin was common among the Semitic tribes of the Middle East. The revelation of a shameful secret associated with suppressed guilt, also played an important role in the hypnotic method used in psychotherapy in the nineteenth century. A disease caused by an evil spell or black magic such as the "pointing bone" used by Australian aborigines, was treated by shamans with counter-magic (Clements,1932).

A consequence of the confusion of the natural with the supernatural, and of such an animistic conception of causality, is a lack of clarity in the separation of physical and mental diseases. This separation developed relatively late and was finally crystallised by Cartesian dualism in the seventeenth century. Did the peoples of the ancient world actually have a concept of madness as a disease, distinct from the more primitive idea of possession by spirits ? It may seem almost impossible to answer this question. Mora (1967) argues that the Bible (Deuteronomy) mentions madness together with blindness and the "astonishment of the heart" as the punishments meted out to those who violated God's commandments. The agency of a spirit is not mentioned. Mora points out that the Hebrew *Talmud* considered insanity and epilepsy as definite diseases rather than as supernatural phenomena. For pre-historic cultures one may only speculate about whether there is a true basis for drawing an analogy between these and contemporary pre-literate societies. It would seem that all cultures, including the primitive ones, have a concept of madness (Weckowicz, 1984). This may be illustrated from the case of the Bering Sea Eskimos who clearly distinguish the hallucinations and bizarre behavior of a shaman during a trance, and the behavior of a madman called by them *nuthkavihak*. The first occurs in a socially sanctioned situation and is in accordance with prescribed social roles and expectations. The second behavior is quite incomprehensible, it is contrary to social expectations, and is therefore socially defined as madness (Murphy, 1976).

In historical times, many authors such as Albertus Magnus, St. Thomas Aquinas, Felix Plater and Thomas Willis have in their classification of mental diseases, clearly distinguished mental diseases which were due to natural causes from those due to supernatural causes. By this, they have understood diseases caused by demoniacal possession or witchcraft. The feature which distinguished mental illness due to demoniacal possession from the one due to natural causes, was the "crisis." Such a "crisis" proved to be an initial exacerbation of the patient's affliction when it was treated by exorcism, although it afterward got better. Such a belief system was carried into modern times by the West's religious traditions. It was the unclean spirit which wandered in the desert in order to collect more evil spirits and cause a worse affliction (Matt.12:43-45). Such cases indicated an intense personal life crisis for the afflicted individual, a kind of ultimate situation in the sense that an existentialist psychiatrist like Karl Jaspers, used that expression. These are the "fundamental" and unchanging situations of life, death, suffering, chance happenings, and guilt. Despair, anguish, and dread are common human reactions. However, a rebirth of the personality is possible after the consciousness of existence has reached a higher level (Jaspers,1951). On the horizon of the ancient world, only prayer and faith could overcome a hopeless case (Mark,9:14-29). For the modern mind which rejects the supernatural, the known causal agents, whether intrinsic or extrinsic, would be understood as lying within the realm of natural law. They could then be treated by a medical knowledged based on an understanding of such laws of nature.

2

Antiquity

Early Period

The development of early civilizations, such as those of Egypt, Babylon and Assyria led to the rise of complex states ruled by god-kings. These societies were highly stratified, had well developed urban cultures, and quite an advanced division of labour. The attitude towards mental disease was shaped by the religious beliefs and by observations of behaviour.

The early civilizations of the Middle East emerged along the banks of large rivers; the Nile, the Tigris, and the Euphrates. The seasonal floods of these rivers produced a rich and fertile soil, and made food surpluses possible. This allowed the undertaking of grandiose projects such as the construction of the Egyptian pyramids and the building of monumental temples. The regular, cyclic and rhythmic changes brought about by the annual floods of the Nile, fostered a cyclical view of existence, a sense of the cycle of life and death. Life was viewed as a preparation for death which constituted a continuation of the journey of life on the flowing river of existence. Stability and regularity ruled the world. In Egypt, the goddess Nut daily swallowed the sun and expelled it again at sunrise. Human personality was controlled by internal forces which represented a balance against the external forces of the gods (Mora,1969). The internal forces centered on the heart which was both the seat of mood and emotion as well as of much physical activitity. The external world was deemed more important. It included deities like the sun god Re, who was later merged with the god of Thebes as Amon-Ra (National Geographic, 1978; Budge,1959). Osirus, the grandson of Re of his daughter Nut, the sky goddess, ruled the netherworld. Slain by his brother Seth, he was avenged by the "golden" god Horus, often depicted as a falcon. (Also as a bull). Osirus' wife was Isis. Bird-like, she had magical powers and became an eternal wife and mother figure. Most important was Geb, the god of the earth and of vegetation. Horus was also the god of "fertile Egypt," and Thoth the god of healing arts (Patrick,1972; Gardiner,1961; Brunner, 1989).

There were other deities, some benign and some evil. These internal and external forces balanced one another and maintained the rhythm of the universe and gave immortality to men. Mental health depended on this balance. Communication with the dead, interpretation of dreams, and healing sleep induced by incubation techniques, were used to restore mental balance when it was unhinged. Pharaohs communicated with the spirits of their dead ancestors seeking their advice in the conduct of the affairs of state.

The living pharaoh was identified with the god Horus and his dead father with Osirus. According to the theory of the bi-cameral mind proposed by Julian Jaynes (1976), the ancient Egyptians were still at the stage of an underdeveloped consciousness in their mental evolution. They were subject to auditory hallucinations which controlled their behaviour. Consequently, the pharaoh's communications with his dead father and with his *ka*, the guardian spirit, took the form of auditory hallucinations.

Mental illness in ancient Egypt probably took the form of demoniacal possession. In this condition, an individual was controlled by the voices of an evil spirit rather than by those of an ancestor or the *ka*. According to an Egyptian stele in the *Bibliotheque Nationale* in Paris, a royal princess of the twentieth dynasty was possessed by a demon. Incantations and prayers to the god Khons apparently cured her (Zilboorg, 1941). An earlier belief in demons and the efficacy of incantations seemed to co-exist with a more modern idea of medical treatment based on observation of patients. The physician seemed to use very few incantations in the later dynasties, and his practical medicine much influenced both the Persian and Greek conquerors (Kamal, 1967).

In *The Origins of Consciousness in the Breakdown of the Bicameral Mind* (1976), Julian Jaynes asserts that insanity, by which he means schizophrenia, did not exist at the stage of the bi-cameral mind of mental evolution before 1000 B.C. According to Jaynes, most people were controlled by auditory hallucinations. By the norm of modern standards, this would be considered schizophrenic. Whatever the validity of this assertion, the fact is, that there are practically no references to madness in the sources for Egyptian medicine, in spite of the fact that it was highly developed. There were many physicians or *swnw*, mostly above the social rank of commoners. Egyptian medicine was divided into many specialties in the earlier stages of the country's history. The history of ancient Egypt shows that there was increased bureaucratization, and that during such stages some of the medical specializations disappeared. Yet they reappeared in the last dynasties as the authority of the central government broke down, and medical specialists worked in the service of the local chieftains and lords (Ghalioungui,1963;1983).

The kingdom of Egypt centered on the Nile valley and its trade. An artisan class had a well developed and continuous existence, as did that of the priests and bureaucrats. There were priests who specialised in the practices of medicine, like those of Imenhotep, the founder of Egyptian medicine. As the natural causes of diseases became better understood so did therapeutic techniques, such as surgery. This is illustrated by the Edwin Smith papyrus which dates back to 1600 B.C. However, the medical system was still based on a belief in the supernatural the diseases were believed to be caused by the anger of gods who sent demons and curses which entered the bodies and minds of the transgressors and caused diseases. Several centuries later, the belief in magic tended to diminish, and an idea of the organic causes of diseases began to prevail (Ghalioungui,1963,1983).

Therapy was originally based on magic, incantations and purification rites. Diseases by and large were conceived as alien and extrinsic entities lodged in particular parts of the body. In Egypt this conceptualisation was, to a great extent, empirically justified by the fact that many diseases were caused by parasites which could be seen with the naked eye. The Egyptian doctor-priests knew, as documented by the *Ebers Papyrus* (1550 B.C.) that hookworm, filaria, taenia saginaeta and ascaris were the pathogenic agents of several diseases, hence there was a tendency to interpret many other diseases as due to an invasion by worms.

A notable exception to this extrinsic agent theory of diseases was the theory of hysteria which was believed, according to the testimony of the *Kahun Papyrus* (1900 B.C.) and the *Papyrus Ebers* to be caused by a wandering womb (Veitz, 1965). However, the womb was endowed with animistic properties and was regarded as a wild animal, autonomous of the host organism. The recommended cure was to fumigate the vagina with fragrant incense in order to induce it to return to its proper place. Subsequently, this theory was incorporated into Greek medicine and survived in an altered form into the seventeenth century, A.D.

The Mesopotamian cultures were similar to the Egyptian, except that city-states prevailed. Ur was probably the best known of these.

Commerce within the river regions as well as with the Persian gulf and with the Indus river delta was important. Both the Assyrians and Babylonians established empires on the ruins of the city-states. Babylonian and Assyrian medicine used methods of prognostication such as astrology and hepatoscopy, which was based on primitive scientific theories developed by these cultures. The art of astrology spread to the Greeks and later, for many centuries, came to play an important role in European medicine. The Mesopotamians as well as the Egyptians had a highly developed art of dream interpretation. Oppenheim (1956) reports that the Assyrians distinguished three types of dreams. (1) The dreams in which a deity appeared and gave instructions to the dreamer. (2) The dreams revealing the state of mind of the dreamer, which could have been hidden from him, and (3) prophetic dreams, foretelling the future (Mora, 1967; Oppenheim,1956).

The earliest Mesopotamian civilization, that of the Sumerians, had physicians, *a-zu,* who were diviners working under the auspices of the water god, *Ea* (Saggs, 1962). Disease usually represented a punishment of the gods for human sin or moral evils. However, possession by the devil or a demon could also account for specific diseases. The god *Sin* "caused" epilepsy to occur. (The Egyptians, however, described it naturalistically, as a disease). In Babylon, treatment of diseases caused by moral offences, lay in the hands of priests who divined the hidden causes. Still other priests exorcised the demons by incantations. The upper class physicians were professional men who were trained for years in special schools and apprenticed to physicians. Many of their prescriptions resemble the Egyptian ones. Fees were regulated by law as early as the Code of Hammurabi in the eighteenth century B.C. There was obviously a common kind of medical knowledge diffused throughout these lands. Some of it would seem to have been more advanced. The Mitanni sent their medical experts to Amenophis III of Egypt in the fourteenth century, and the Babylonians sent their experts to the Hittite ruler, King Hattusilis III in the thirteenth century (Roux, 1964).

Early Greek medicine and psychiatry was similar to that of the Middle Eastern cultures. It was a theorgic medicine based on the belief in supernatural forces and agents. An early God of medicine, Apollo, was replaced by his son Asclepius, a legendary hero-physician who was deified some time in the sixth or the fifth centuries B.C. He was also compared with Imenhotep, the deified Egyptian healer and vizier of Pharaoah Zoser, in 2800 B.C (Kamal, 1967). The Greek Asclepius had been born in Epidauros, and his sect had spread from there. The cult of Asclepius was practiced in a special temple, the *Asklepeion.* The best known of these was at Epidaurus. More prominent was the greater temple and theatre complex supported by the Roman emperors at Pergamon. (This one was associated with healing waters). Another Asklepian center was on the isle of Cos. The will power of the patient was enlisted in the healing process (Krug,1985). The priests of Asclepius, the *Asclepidaes,* treated diseases by incantation, suggestion, laying on of hands and potions made of hellbore or poppy seed extracts. As part of the treatment, patients underwent purification at the fountain of the temple of Asclepius, after which they slept in a chamber of the temple (incubation). During sleep, the god Asclepius was supposed to reveal the nature of their illness and the required cure in a dream. The *Asclepidaes* interpreted the dreams and even performed operations. Possibly they used anaesthetics. The curative powers of the mind were awakened by a further emphasis on the appreciation of the arts, on theatre, and on reading philosophy and literature. The Asclepian cult was popular with Roman emperors as well, and Pergamon and its great library were endowed by them. The Asclepian practice of medicine continued to the end of Antiquity, side by side with the more rational schools of medicine.

Snakes played an important part in the Asclepian cult. The Greeks and many other Indo-European and Semitic people believed them to be immortal, for they shed their skin, but did not die. Consequently, they were regarded as a source of health and general goodness, as well as messengers of the gods. During the cure, the snakes were handled and were trained to lick the affected parts of the body. Asclepius was also represented by a serpent when his cult was first introduced in Athens about 430, after the great plague (Ackerknecht,1968; Schmidt, 1989).

Since the causal agents of the disease were seen as being extrinsic to the organism, it was believed that madness was caused by the goddesses of dread and night: *Mania* and *Lyssa.* (*Lyssa* was also a product of Dionysian madness). They belonged to the godesses of madness, together with *Erinyes* known to the Romans as *Furies*, who avenged crimes and tormented dead souls (Grimal,1987). Sent by angry gods, they took possession of the minds of mortals. Not only mental illness, but also temporary moods and the emotional states of mortals were depicted in Homer's Iliad, as caused by the gods. The intrinsic motives of men played no role. Many forms of madness existed. There was the madness associated with possession by evil spirits and by the goddesses of darkness. There was also a divine madness. This was a state of ecstatic inspiration which resulted from being possessed by friendly deities. Thus, Plato tells us in his *Socratic Apology,* that there are two kinds of madness: one is the result of a disease, the other is a gift of gods. He develops further this theme in *Phaedrus* where he says that there are four kinds of madness: prophetic, telestic or ritual, poetic and erotic. All these kinds of madness, with the exception of the last, had a positive value. The first bestowed the gift of prophecy, as exemplified by the priestesses of Apollo at Delphi. The second induced a serene mystical, otherwordly experience during Corybantic religious rites which brought freedom from instinctual needs, purified the soul, and restored an internal calm. Poetic madness was attributed to possession by the muses and bestowed a state of artistic inspiration. Sexual madness could lead to a destructive passion.

Finally, the early Greeks believed that epilepsy was a "sacred disease," bringing a special status to the sufferer. Interestingly enough, in recent times, epilepsy was regarded as "sacred" in other, more remote, parts of the world as well. Among Siberian tribes it was interpreted as a calling to shamanhood. The Asclepian cult lasted till the end of Antiquity, side by side with the empirical-rational schools of medicine.

Other cults existed outside of the official religions of ancient Greece. These were the mysteries and the secret cults. Participation in them had a profound psychological effect and could be considered psychotherapeutic. One of them, the Corybantic cult, probably of Asiatic origin, mentioned in Plato's *Phaedrus*, was a mystic cult of the "Great Mother," which had its origins in the pre-Olympian religion of the Chthonic gods. In that religion, female goddesses played the central role. They derived, possibly from the Anatolian Kybele of the Phrygians and continued in the later Sybillines. In Greece, they were displaced by the Olympian male gods. The rites associated with this cult were of an orgiastic nature, expressing the Dionysian aspect of Greek culture (Nietzsche 1872/1967). Wild dancing was an important part of the ritual, and was supposed to have powers of healing mental illness. Corybantic dancers were usually depicted in Greek art as fully armed, and engaged in a wild dance. The cult may go back to pre-historic times and may have been associated with shamanistic practices. The Corybantic rites were used as a cure for madness. They served the function of an abreaction.

By an induction of Corybantic madness, the mind was purged, and its balance restored. The Aristotelian theory of *catharsis* as an explanation of the therapeutic effects of watching tragedies was another example of a cure by abreaction. However, Sophocles himself was an Asclepian priest and he attacked the *hubris* associated with too much reliance on human wisdom in his *Oedipus* (Schmidt, 1989).

Abreaction was also important to the Dionysian Bacchic rituals and to the Eleusian mysteries. They exemplified the Dionysian and Apollonian aspects of Greek culture in extreme forms. Apollo was, like Asclepius, also a healer God, whose worship was transmitted to Rome during the fifth century, B.C. The Dionysian cult came to Athens about the same time. Dionysios was a male god of Phrygian origin. He had been a god of vegetation, fertility and wine growing and wine drinking. Demeter, who had a similar cult, was associated with an expression of ecstatic violence. Dionysios, driving with a panther and a wagon, was usually accompanied by Maenads, or "crazy women." In some parts of Greece, female worshippers identified with the Maenads and worked themselves into a frenzy, even to the extent of attacking animals, eating raw meat, drinking blood, and resorting to cannibalism. The Bacchic rituals were associated with heavy drinking and sex orgies as well. These provided an expression to socially forbidden urges and desires. When the Dionysian cult became popular in Athens, the dramatists attacked it. Euripides depicted the Maenad possession as a personality disorder (Schmidt, 1989).

Eleusian mysteries aimed at a purification of the soul through a mystical experience. They were associated with the Orphic cult, which stresses the spiritual aspect of man, his immortal soul. Since the members of the cult were secretive not much is known about its details. Its worship became widespread in Athens. Cretan and Myccncan themes predominated with an emphasis on a mother-daughter theme. The daughter was kidnapped by a lord and then reunited with her mother (Leveque, 1968). Cult members strove to attain a higher level of spiritual being associated with a state of serenity and with the felicity of the blessed. Eleusian mysteries may represent a therapy based on spiritual healing, meditation, and religious conversion. This was similar to the practices of the Pythagoreans who established another Orphic cult.

Pythagoras lived 99 years and was born in 510 B.C. He left Samos, then much influenced by Egyptian trade and art, with the son of its ruler.

After learning from Greek teachers like Anaximander, he went to Egypt where at age 22 he was introduced into the secrets of the priests at Memphis. He gained the support of the aristocracy and established a private school in Crete. In his sixties, after political upheavals forced him to flee, he settled in Italy at Croton. His numerological science was both mysterious and cultic, musical, mathematical, and religious. Even moral virtues were symbolized by number symbolism. F.W. Hagen, a modern psychiatrist at Erlangen University has tried to dissect the brain according to the Pythagorean theory of the golden mean (Leibbrand, 1939).

The Pythagoreans became prominent during the third and second century, especially at Croton in southern Italy. In addition to studying mathematics, they were committed to asceticism and dietary (vegetarian) rules. They believed in immortality and in the transmigration of souls.

The Greek Philosophical-Scientific Revolution

In the sixth century B.C. a remarkable intellectual revolution took place in the Greek colonies in Asia Minor and in Italy. A phenomenon which, as far as we know, had no parallel in the previous history of the world. It may be called the first philosophical revolution or perhaps even the first scientific revolution, although a scientific method in the modern sense was not created. For the first time, the traditionalist explanations of reality in terms of the supernatural, animistic, and anthropomorphic forces were consciously questioned. Speculations were offered about the causes of the observed phenomena, and the origin of the world, in terms of natural physical forces. Thus, the foundation was laid down for a future development of science. The group of philosophers who were responsible for the first scientific revolution, between 600 and 400 B.C. are known as the pre-Socratic, cosmological philosophers. The most important representatives of this group were Thales, Anaximander, Anaxamines, Heraclitus, Parmenides, Empedocles, Anaxagoras, Pythagoras, and Democritus.

The first three were members of the Milesian school in Asia Minor. They speculated on the nature of a basic substance from which all things arose. For Thales it was water. For Anaximander it was the primary, boundless substance which he called *apeiron.* (This was counterbalanced by *peras* or limit). Both constituted a double first principle of existence (Kerferd,1967). For Anaxagoras and Anaximander the foundation of life was air or *pneuma*. Anaximander identified life with breath and believed that pneuma was the life and intelligence-giving principle. This notion became important in subsequent philosophical and medical theories during Antiquity.

The Pythagoreans rejected the notion of substance and believed that the universe was mathematical and musical in structure and ruled by harmony. The universe was characterized by certain invariant mathematical relations and by the equilibrium of opposites (*isonomia*). The Pythagoreans differed from the other Pre-Socratic philosophers. They were less concerned with cosmology and natural science explanations than the others. Medicine as well as music was one of their main concerns. They favored a "harmonic diet" over surgery, and opposed addictions because they represented an escape into an unlimited, disorderly sphere of existence. Human wisdom reached its apogee in the healing arts. The Pythagoreans believed in strengthening the memory and treated the body in a medical way. The immortal soul was treated by *catharsis* and the arts of the muses (Leibbrand, 1961).

The Pythagorean notion of balance and harmony was opposed by Heraclitus of Ephesus. For him, change or becoming (*pantarei*), constant flux, represented the state of the world. According to him, one could not step twice into the same river. The world was characterized by a constant strife of opposites, although, ultimately, the opposites flowed into one another. (This was the principle of *enantiodermia*). Heraclitus believed that the most important element of the universe was fire which he identified with life and intelligence.

Heraclitus' notion of constant change was opposed by the Elean School, located at Elea in southern Italy. Parmenides, the leader of that school believed that the perception of the changing universe was an illusion. In such an unchanging and immobile universe, there was no empty space in which movement could occur. An empty space was "something which was not." It was therefore in contradiction with the existing universe.

The monistic, one element, theories of the universe were opposed by Empedocles of Agrigento in Sicily. He believed that the universe was composed of four elements: water, air, fire, and earth. Hippocrates, the great Greek physician based his theory of humors on these four elements. According to Empedocles the four elements were combined in various proportions and were united by love, and separated by strife. Love and strife governed the universe. In a Pythagorean way, the principle of goodness was identified by him,with love, while strife was evil.

Finally, the atomists, Leucippus and Democritus of Abdera, believed that the universe was not composed by one or four elements, rather, by a countless multitude of atoms. These moved in empty space to form different aggregates and accounted for the physical characteristics of objects. Mind was composed of very small, extremely mobile atoms.

The Pythagorean and Elean philosophical theories influenced Plato and originated the tradition of philosophical idealism. The atomists may be regarded as the originators of the tradition of philosophical materialism. As will be seen, the ideas of pre-Socratic philosophers influenced medical theories in Antiquity (Leibbrand, 1961).

One result of this philosophical revolution was the emergence of a new empirical-rational medicine which developed at the same time. The characteristic feature of this new medicine was the naturalistic type of explanation of diseases and therapeutic processes. Physical forces and elements replaced supernatural agents as explanatory concepts. Thus, medicine became separated from religion and the medical practitioner was no longer a priest, but a philosopher-scientist. The two professions became separated. However, diseases of the mind, in contrast to diseases of the body, have remained for centuries and still remain a gray area staked out by both priests and medical doctors. When subsequently medicine, as an empirical science, became separated from philosophy, the dispute became a three- cornered one between the medical doctor, the priest and the philosopher. A few facts may be presented to support this statement. In Ancient Rome, both medical practitioners and philosophers made claims to the exclusive expertise in the area of mental health. Throughout the Middle Ages and well into the seventeenth century, priests claimed for themselves the field of mental disease and mental health. Immanual Kant, at the end of the eighteenth century, strongly opposed the medical man's intrusion into the field of psychopathology, believing it to be a prerogative of the philosopher (Zilboorg, 1941).

The break-through to a more rational way of thinking occurred in fifth century Greece. Here Hippocrates, the father of medicine, looms large, and is the central figure of the Greek "enlightenment." Demonology was seen as absurd, and the use of natural explanations prevailed.

The world of traditional religion with its belief in prophecies and oracles began to recede, although for centuries it continued to exist contemporaneously with the schools of rational explanation. The ideal man was wise and rejected *pados*, the irrational disturbance of the mind. This kind of Greek rationalism triumphed by the end of the fourth century (Schmidt, 1989).

In the Classical Greek period four important schools developed in the new empirical-rational medicine. The first was the school of Croton in Southern Italy, which was influenced by Pythagorean philosophy. The most illustrious member of this school was Alcmaeon of Croton, in the first half of the fifth century B.C. It is believed that he dissected cadavers. He claimed that the seat of the psyche was in the brain and that the sense organs were connected with it. He took from the Pythagorean philosophy the concept of a harmony or equilibrium of opposites (*isonomia*) and applied it to the concept of health. Alcmaeon considered the state of health as a state of equilibrium of opposites. This idea became quite important in the field of medicine and mental health and nowadays plays an important role in the modern guise of "homeostasis" and "adjustment."

The second school was the Sicilian school of the followers of Empedocles of Agrigento (490-430 B.C.), a philosopher, physician and poet, who was the originator of the theory of the four elements of the universe: fire, air, water, earth. One of the members of this school, Philistion of Syracuse (the fifth century), influenced by the ideas of Empedocles and Anaximenes of Miletus (the sixth century) about the importance of air for life processes, developed the theory of pneuma. Pneuma was a life-giving breath inhaled from the all pervading soul of the universe, which gave a vital energy to the organism and was responsible for its movements. This idea became very important in medical theories in later ages and in more recent times reappeared in the guise of Driesche's vitalistic "entelechy," Bergson's "elan vital" and Jung's "libido." It became the focus of controversy between the "Vitalists" and the "Mechanists" in the nineteenth century.

The two most important schools, or traditions of empirical-rational medicine, in the Greek Classical period were the Coan School, founded by Hippocrates of Cos (460-380 B.C.) and the Cnidian School, founded by Euryphon (the fifth century B.C.), the putative author of *Cnidian Sentences* (Ackerknecht, 1968). The two schools adhered to two different medical models. These two distinct conceptual medical models can be discerned throughout the course of the history of medicine. At some periods, one model was prominent, at other periods, the other. The two models are the *disease model* and the *constitutional model.*

The tension between the two models, between, to use Henry Siegerist's terms, the "ontology of the patient" and the "ontology of the disease" (Siegerist, 1932) has persisted throughout Antiquity, the Middle Ages and Modern times. Some medical systems stressed one model, some the other. The issue is whether to treat a disease, believed to be located in an organ or treat the whole patient. In the disease model, diseases are regarded as extrinsic and alien to the organism. A disease begins at a certain point in the history of the organism and interrupts the organism's natural development. It is caused by an extrinsic agent, has its anatomical locus, its own natural history and its end in the death or recovery of the affected organism. The disease model best fits the theory of infectious diseases. The constitutional model attributes ill health to an imbalance of certain basic components, or, "elements" of the organism. It considers the whole patient as a unique organism with a unique history and development.

The Coan school of medicine, founded by Hippocrates at the turn of the fifth and fourth centuries B.C., represented the constitutional model in the early history of medicine. Hippocrates and his followers, whose writings are preserved in the document called *Corpus Hippocraticum* developed a systematic theory of human constitution. The idea of four elements was borrowed from the pre-Socratic cosmological philosophers, namely the four elements postulated by Empedocles: water, air, fire and earth. These elements were considered to be the basic constituents of the four bodily humors: phlegm equated with water, blood equated with air, yellow bile equated with fire, and black bile equated with earth. Four seasons were also associated with the four humors: spring was associated with blood and air, summer with yellow bile and fire, autumn with black bile and earth, and winter with phlegm and water. There were also four qualities: hot, cold, dry and wet. Two of each of these was also associated with four humors. Thus yellow bile was hot and dry, blood was hot and wet, black bile was dry and cold, and phlegm was wet and cold. The Hippocratic humoral theory of human constitution is presented in Figure 1. In health, the humors were in a state of equilibrium (*eucrasia*).

In disease they were in a state of disequilibrium (*dyscrasia*). The idea of equilibrium or harmony and the importance of the idea of the number

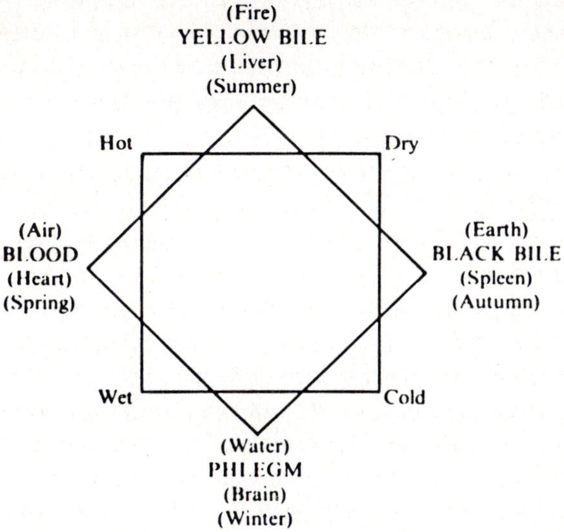

Fig. 1. Diagram illustrating the Greek theory of the four qualities, the four elements, four humours and four seasons. The elements were regarded as being related to qualities and these in turn governed the respective humours. Imbalance in the qualities and humours could be compensated by using drugs associated with opposite qualities. (From E. Ackerknecht, 1968, p. 57, by permission.)

four, were taken from Pythagorean philosophers. Hippocratic therapy was based on a presupposition that nature (*physis*) had strong self-healing forces and that a sick organism tended to heal itself naturally by restoring a state of equilibrium among the humors through a process of coction (*pepsis*). The coction, which means cooking, was produced by the so-called "innate heat." This process culminated in a *crisis* when a portion of an excessive humor was eliminated, and the balance was restored. Sometimes the process unfolded more slowly in the form of *lysis*.

The Hippocratic doctor treated the whole organism and not one disease, or a diseased organ. He assisted the natural healing process and did not direct it by an arbitrary intervention. The doctor had to make a prognosis regarding the eventual recovery of the patient rather than to diagnose a disease. In health the humors were not only in a state of internal equilibrium with one another, but were also in a state of equilibrium with the environmental forces, weather being the most important such force. Thus, it was not only the internal equilibrium which was important for the health and well-being of man, but also the equilibrium of harmony between him and his environment. In addition, to the humors, *pneuma,* played an important role in Hippocratic physiology and pathology. The concept was borrowed from the Sicilian school. *Pneuma* was a vital force or spirit which directed all the functions through the brain of the organism. It was responsible for consciousness and perception.

The members of the Coan school believed that mental disorders were caused by superfluous black or yellow bile rising to the brain and affecting the pneuma, causing melancholia in the case of black bile, and frenzy or mania in the case of yellow bile. Some mental condition such as a state of exaltation was believed to be due to an excessive warmth and dampness of the brain. In his famous treatise, *On the Sacred Disease,* Hippocrates denied that epilepsy was a "sacred disease" sent by the gods. According to him, it was the result of a brain disorder, and had natural and not supernatural causes. It was caused by the blocking of the blood vessels by phlegm, or by black bile, which prevented the intelligence-giving air (pneuma) from reaching the brain.

Similarly, Hippocrates' view of hysteria, followed the Egyptian theory, and believed that it was caused by a wandering womb. In spite of his theoretical speculations Hippocrates was basically an empiricist. (Actually he is considered the father of Empiricism, as well as of medicine). He eschewed dogma and stressed observation. He noted that mental illness could improve when the patient developed a fever, and that insanity might follow a childbirth, a direct observation of post-natal depression.

Hippocrates and his followers offered an early classification of mental illnesses into: (1) Phrenitis (delirium associated with fever) (2) Mania (delerium without fever). (3) Melancholia (chronic mental illness). (4) Epilepsy. (5) Hysteria. (6) Scythian disease (transvestism, apparently common amongst Scythians, the northern neighbors of the Greeks).

Another school of medicine flourished in Cnidus, a Greek colony in Asia Minor. This was the *Cnidian* school of medicine, under the leadership of Euryphon, and was contemporary with the Coan school. It stressed the importance of diseases, caused by external agents and localised in different parts of the body. Galen, a great physician of

Antiquity who lived six centuries later, wrote that the Cnidians had differentiated seven diseases of the bile, twelve of the urinary bladder, four of the kidneys, five of the foot and two diseases of the thigh. In addition, they differentiated three forms of vertigo and four of angina (Neuburger, 1910). The Cnidian physicians stressed in the treatment of patients the importance of diagnosis instead of prognosis. The Cnidian system of medicine, whose only surviving records are the fragmentary *Cnidian Sentences,* was influenced by the Babylonian, the Assyrian, and the Persian medical traditions. An important member of the Cnidian school, Ctesias, was for many years the court physician of a Persian king.

The Coan and Cnidian schools were representative of the two medical models: the constitutional and the disease model. The first model stressed the treatment of the whole patient, the second, the treatment of a disease. The Coan school had a greater influence than the Cnidian school on medical thinking in the Classical Greek and Roman periods. The constitutional model became the dominant one. However, the disease model has persisted . This may be illustrated by Plato's description of diseases in the *Timaeus* as living creatures, which have an independent existence and a naturally predestined form of life (Rather, 1959). These two medical models, two ways of thinking, are still with us. The proposed theories of mental illness by these medical models were organic.

When one turns to psychological models of mental illness, one finds that the psychodynamic model of human mind and of mental disease is also of considerable antiquity. Thus, Empedocles of Agrigentum (490-430 B.C.), from whom Hippocrates took the theory of four elements, stressed the importance of emotions of love and hate as the controlling agents of human behaviour and of physiological functions.

Plato (427-347 B.C.), in his philosophical writings, stressed the inner psychological reality in contrast to the reality of the external world. He believed that the human soul consists of three parts. 1) The rational soul, which resided in the brain. 2) The animal soul, controlling emotions and passions, was located in the chest. 3) The vegetative soul, controlling physiological needs, was located in the abdomen. When dreams occurred in sleep, the irrational souls reasserted themselves. The story is best told in Plato's own words in book nine of *The Republic:*

> I feel that some of the unnecessary desires and pleasures are lawless; they are born in everyone, it is true, but when they are chastened, by laws and the better desires, with reason's help, some people can get rid of them wholly, or only a few remain and weak, although in others

> they are stronger ... Those which are aroused in sleep, whenever the rest of the soul, all the reasonable, gentle and ruling part is asleep, but the bestial and savage, replete with food or wine, skips about and, throwing off sleep, tries to go and fulfill its own instincts. You know there is nothing it will not dare to do, thus freed and rid of all shame and reason; it shrinks not from attempting in fancy to lie with a mother, or with any other man or god or beast, shrinks from no bloodshed, refrains from no food— in a word, leaves no folly or shamelessness untried. (Plato, *Republic.* Book 9, *Great Dialogues of Plato*, Mentor Classic, pp.369-70).

This psychological interpretation of dreams was adumbrated by Hippocrates who believed that when man was asleep, his soul was awake and in motion. It was putting its house in order, and it was important for the physician to interpret the behaviour of the soul during dreams. Plato used the theory of the rational and irrational parts of the soul to explain insanity. In insanity, the rational soul was overwhelmed by the irrational. Plato offered a novel interpretation of the traditional Egyptian-Greek theory of hysteria, stating in *Timaeus* that:

> The womb is an animal which longs to generate children. When it remains barren too long after puberty, it is distressed and sorely disturbed, and straying about in the body and cutting off the passages of the breath, it impedes respiration and brings the sufferer into the extremist anguish and provokes all the manner of diseases besides. (*Timaeus*, 917c, quoted by Veith, 1965, pp.7-8).

Plato thus recognised that a repression of sex instinct could be harmful and he recognised the existence of psychosomatic diseases. A similarity of these ancient ideas to Freud's theories of the conscious and the unconscious, one of the life instinct and death instinct, of the Oedipus complex and his theory of dreams, is obvious.

The Post-Socratic Greek period

Starting with the Sophists, Socrates, and Plato, the Greek philosophers shifted the focus of their interest from the cosmos to the inner experiences and moral behaviour of man. Thus, Aristotle (384-322 B.C.), wrote works on psychology and this in addition to works on physics and biology. In contrast to Plato, Aristotle regarded the soul not as a separate entity made of a differemt substance, but as a form, or a form-giving principle, of a living organism. This did not apply to that part of the human soul known as active reason which was a divine transcendental entity, separate from the body. Aristotle located the center of the soul in the heart rather than in the brain. He also stressed the importance of "heat" as the mediating factor between the humors and the soul. The heat produced vapors which were cooled and condensed in the form of dew in the brain. Excessive vapors could produce mental illness. However, Aristotle also believed that disturbing passions could cause mental illness and had to be purged by *catharsis.* The latter was an emotional excitement produced by music, wine, aphrodisiacs or by watching the performance of a tragedy.

In his writings on ethics, Aristotle stressed the importance of following a middle course in conduct and avoiding extremes in the quest for *eudaimonia,* which is usually translated as "happiness," but which could be translated as self-fulfillment or actualization of human nature. Aristotle's student, Theophrastus of Ephesos (371-286 B.C.), the father of botany, developed a typology of thirty moral types based on the kind of classification given in Aristotle's *Nichomachean Ethics.* All these developments went in the direction of strengthening the constitutional model in medicine and psychiatry, and weakening the disease model, although the importance of psychodynamic factors was also recognized.

Other philosophical schools concerned with the way of life as well as with the nature of the universe were the Cyrenaic and Cynic schools of philosophy and their offshoots. These included the Epicurean school, founded by Epicurus (342-270 B.C.), and the Stoic school, founded by Zeno of Citum (336-263 B.C.) The Epicureans drew their inspiration from Leucippus and Democritus (fifth century B.C.) They had postulated that the building blocks of matter were countless atoms rather than a few elements such as air, water, fire and earth. Mind was just a refined variety of matter. As materialists, they advocated a pursuit of moderate pleasure. The Stoics, were pantheists and advocated an obedience to the natural laws of the universe. They stressed the importance of life-giving pneuma. Stoics, Epicureans, and also the Sceptics became very important in later antiquity. Scepticism was originated by Pyrrho (360-270 B.C.), and with the other two schools influenced the schools of medicine of the Hellenistic and the Roman periods. They offered an atomistic alternative to the doctrine of the four elements of Hippocrates. After the death of Hippocrates, the Coans abandoned their founder's empiricst orientation and became rigidly dogmatic.

Thus far we have discussed the Greek folk beliefs about madness, and about the medical and philosophical models of mental illness. However, there were also contributions of poets and playwrights on this topic. Bennett Simon discussed the ideas of mental illness found in

Mycenaean and Hellenic Greece in his *Mind and Madness in Ancient Greece* (1978). In addition to the theorgic ideas based on popular beliefs, the medical and the philosophical models, he distinguished a poetic one. Greek poetry and drama reflected changing conceptions of mind and madness which existed in the literature and philosophy in the fifth century.

In the course of his discussion, Simon compares the mental disturbance found in the Homeric epics with those of the Greek tragedies of the classical age. Homeric literature may be traced to the ninth century; the oral tradition behind it, to the thirteenth century B.C. or the Achaean (Mycenaean) period. Simon stresses the fact that the Homeric hero was a "pre-psychological" man. He had no conception of a clearly delineated self, and no clearly defined ego boundary. Man was an "open force field" to external social forces and supernatural influences. Completely embedded in his social group, he had no autonomy. His relations to gods and to people were not internalized. His conflicts were interpersonal rather than intrapersonal. He heard his gods talking to him. According to Jaynes' theory of the bi-cameral mind (1976), Homeric man heard his god speaking to him quite literally. He obeyed these voices which actually originated in the non-dominant right hemisphere, automatically. In Homeric times, man had not yet developed consciousness in the contemporary sense of the word. That is to say, man did not yet have an inner space representing the external space, and no analog to the ego or "I" that represented himself.

Perhaps it was in consequence of such an ego development, that the Homeric hero's temperament was tempestious. He was subject to violent outbursts of anger and grief. In comparison, the mental life depicted in fifth century tragedies of the classical period, showed a much greater internalization of motives, and a greater autonomy of the individual from external social and supernatural forces. Heroes were conscious of being separate selves and possessing minds distinct from those of other people. Their conflicts were internal ized. Some tragedies such as Aeschylus' *Oresteia,* Euripides' *Orestes* and *Bacchae*, as well as Sophocles' *Ajax,* portrayed madness as a frank psychosis.

As in the case of Greek folk beliefs, these playwrights attributed the causes of madness in supernatural forces external to man: *Mania*, *Lyssa*, the *Furies* or *Erinyes*. These dreadful messengers were sent by vengeful gods to inflict madness on transgressors for a breach of taboo, for the sin of *hubris*; the presumption of being equal to the gods.

However, on the deeper level, the real cause of madness were profound internal psychological conflicts experienced by the heroes of the tragedies. They were shown as torn between social obligations and incompatible loyalties. There were desires for revenge and there were erotic passions. Shame, guilt and disgrace were conspicuous causes of madness. Murder, suicide and madness are frequent topics of tragedies. In Aeschylus' *Oresteia,* Agamenon is murdered by his wife Clymenestra. Their son, Orestes is obliged to revenge his father's death. He is the subject of an acute conflict, and experiences extreme ambivalence of emotions. However, he eventually murders his mother, Clymenestra. As a punishment, he is afflicted with insanity, by the Furies sent by angry gods. His madness, however, is not seen as an alien intrusion. It has personal meaning, which stems from his character and from his emotional conflicts.

In the *Bacche*, of Euripides, the conflict of the hero is between the masculine and femine aspects of his personality. It drives him into madness. In Sophocles' *Ajax,* Athene drives Ajax mad to prevent him from killing Agamemnon. She deceives him by producing a hallucination which shows him actually committing such a grisly murder. In the end, Ajax is driven to commit suicide by his guilt feelings. The role of the gods reaffirms the piety of the viewers as well, for Sophocles was a traditionalist who wrote during a rationalist age. Since he was also an Asclepian priest, dramas of this kind may well have served to help the patients through a catharsis of their own aggressive emotions.

The torments of the heroes, and their emotional conflicts were described in metaphorical language rather than in the explicit psychological language of the philosophers. There were two threads weaving simultaneously through the plots of epics and tragedies. To use Nietzsche's phraseology, these were the Apollonian and Dionysian themes, which were rational and the irrational ones. Often, rational designs of the gods were implemented by them, provoking irrational behaviour in mortals. The interplay of the chorus and of the actors emphasized these double aspects of Greek tragedies.

Simon believes that recitation of Homeric epics by the bards, had a psychotherapeutic effect on their audiences and on themselves. This was caused by the fact that the situation emphasized the collective and the communal rather than the individual and the idiosyncratic aspects. This definition of the situation was congruent with the prevailing mentality. The experience could be compared to that of contemporary group psychotherapy or to a psychodrama. Simon believes that the intuitive perception of the psychodynamics of the heroes' behaviour in tragedies, had a psychotherapeutic effect. This belief is in agreement with Aristotle's theory of catharsis or release of pent up emotions in the viewers of a tragedy. One may assume that the poetic model of madness was not confined to classical Greece. It may also be found in Shakespeare's description of madness in *King Lear*, and in his character of *Ophelia* in *Hamlet.*

The Hellenistic Period.

Following the conquests of Alexander the Great (356-323 B.C.) and the formation of new kingdoms by his successors, the center of Greek learning and medicine shifted from Athens and the Greek Islands to Alexandria in Egypt. The names of Herophilus and Erasistratus became the symbols of the Alexandria medical school at the end of the fourth century and the beginning of the third century B.C. The schools of medicine in Alexandria and later on, in Rome, adhered to the constitutional medical model. The issues which were debated, were those of dogmatism versus empiricism. Both dogmatism and empiricism opposed scepticism. Humoralism opposed solidism. Humoralists followed Hippocrates and Aristotle in believing that the basis of the human constitution was in the four humors. Solidists believed that the human constitution was determined by the configuration of atoms. Thus, Erasistratus, as a consequence of his anatomical research, gave up Hippocratic humoral pathology, and regarded atoms as the essential body elements. According to Eristratus, the atoms were set alive by external air (*pneuma*), which circulated through the blood vessels. Humoral pathology was replaced by a more solidist view. Diseases were caused by a local *plethora* (congestion, or closing the pores between atoms), which interfered with the circulation of pneuma. However, the basic constitutional model remained the same in contradistinction to the disease model of the earlier Cnidian school. At the end of the third century B.C. the empiricist school, led by Philinos of Cos, became prominent in Alexandria. The empiricists eschewed the philosophical speculations. They observed their patients carefully. As a result of it, they left good descriptions of clinical symptoms and made many therapeutic discoveries in the fields of surgery and pharmacology. In the Ptolemaic Alexandria, the treatment of mental patients was progressive even by modern standards. Mental patients were placed in special hospitals and treated with kindness and respect, even given sedatives. Restraints were avoided. Music therapy and hydrotherapy, in the form of soothing baths, were widely used.

The Roman Period

With the rise of Rome and the decline of Ptolemaic Egypt during the second century B.C., many Greek physicians from Alexandria and other centers of the Greek world migrated to Rome. There, after an initial resistance, Greek learning and "know how" were held in high esteem. One of the early emigrants was Asclepiades (born c.124 B.C.), who was an adherent of the Solidist school of medicine in Alexandria. Asclepiades was an atomist who rejected Hippocrates' theory of humors and the passive therapeutics of the latter. He considered therapeutics practiced by the Hippocratic humoralists as a "meditation of death." Instead he advocated active intervention and more heroic therapeutic measures than those of the humoralists. From the subsequent writing of Caelius Aurelianus we know that Asclepides was interested in mental diseases. He believed that they were caused by emotional disturbances affecting senses and he differentiated delusions from hallucinations. He advocated humane treatment of mental patients by such measures as soothing baths, music therapy, rest and sedation.

The Methodist school of medicine was developed as an offshoot of the Solidist school, by Themison Laodicea about 50 B.C. Themison, a follower of Ascledpides and a Solidist, made the atomic theory of Democritus the basis of his methodism. The Democritean theory postulated that the human body was made of atoms with spaces (pores) between them through which pneuma circulated. According to Themison, diseases were caused either by *status strictus* - an excessive narrowing of the pores, or by *status laxus* - an excessive opening of the pores. Therapy consisted of counteracting these states by relaxing or astringent remedies. The Methodist school also advocated a more active involvement of the physician in the therapeutic processes than was customary with the Humoralist school. Thus, the Methodists subscribed to the constitutional model, although they made a greater allowance for localisation of pathology and for the active interventionism than the Humoralists did. Another important Methodist was Celsus Aulus Cornelius (first century A.D.) who was not a practising physician, but a Roman gentleman scholar. He wrote a treatise on medicine: *De Re Medica* (On Medical Topics). A large part of one volume of this book was devoted to mental diseases. He argued that mental diseases were diseases of the whole organism and not of a single organ. He advocated heroic therapeutic measures including shocks and production of sudden fright.

Thessalus of Tralles (first century A.D.), was a court physician of the Emperor Nero. He advocated a method of treatment which he called *metasyncrisis*. By means of some violent procedure a thorough commotion of the patient's fundamental constitution took place which led to a reestablishment of the equilibrium compatible with a state of health. The most illustrious representative of the Methodist school was Soranus of Ephesus (about 100 A.D.), an accomplished gynecologist and obstetrician who was also interested in mental diseases. His views were recorded by another Methodist, Caelius Aurelianus (second century A.D.). Soranus, who like other Methodist, had a somatic approach to mental diseases, was an advocate of a humanitarian treatment of mental patients. He opposed physical restraints and other violent procedures. Instead, he recommended rest, soothing warm baths and musical therapy. His approach to patients was individualistic, and he was against routine therapies used by other Methodists.

The second late Greek school of medicine, which was influential in Rome was that of the Pneumatists. Pneumatists were also Solidists, even if strongly influenced by Stoic philosophy. They explained human physiology and pathology in terms of pneuma, an important concept in Stoic philosophy. The founder of the school was Athenaeus of Attalia (first century A.D.) Two important members of the Pneumatist school were Archigenes and Aretaeus of Cappadocia (30 - 90A.D.). Of the two, Aretaeus was more important. He was a keen observer and a shrewd clincian who was first to suggest that depression and mania may be the same illness and that melancholia tends to reoccur in the same people. He abandoned the current typology based on the four humors of the Hippocratic school and was interested, instead, in individual personalities and came to the conclusion that certain mental diseases are extensions of premorbid personalities of patients. Thus, he was a supporter of what is now called the continuity view of mental illness and was therefore a supporter of the constitutional as against the disease model. Aretaeus was against attempts at localisation of disease processes and believed that in an illness many parts of the body, if not the whole organism, are affected by *consensus*.

Other medical schools flourished in Rome in late Antiquity, in addition to Methodists and Pneumatists. There were Humoralists, following the tradition of Hippocrates, the Empiricists, the Eclectics, an offshoot of the Pneumatist school, and the Sceptics. Sextus Empiricus (second century A.D.) was the most illustrious member of the sceptic school, who was interested in general philosophy and medical methodology.

The foremost medical thinker of the Roman era was Galen of Pergamum (A.D. 130-201) who undertook the daring task of synthesizing the views of all the medical schools of his age within the Aristotelian framework (Sigerist,1933; Freind, 1727). Galen was strongly influenced by the Humoralists and may be regarded as a continuator of the Hippocratic tradition. He was also influenced by Aristotelian philosophy, and also incorporated into his system concepts taken from the Methodists and the Pneumatists. Basically his system was a humoral one, an elaboration of the original system of Hippocrates. It was an extremely complex system of seven naturals elaborated into four elements, four humors, nine qualities, four members, three faculties, two operations, three spirits, four ages, two colours, five figures and two sexes. In addition to the four humors: blood, yellow bile, black bile and phlegm, Galen incorporated into his system the Aristotelian notion of "heat" and the Stoic notion of pneuma. He took from Plato the idea of a rational soul with its seat in the brain and two irrational souls located in the heart and liver. Galen maintained that food passed from the intestinal tract into the liver, and was transformed there into the blood by natural spirits. The natural spirits were carried by the blood into the lungs where the inhaled pneuma combined with the natural spirits to form vital spirits. The vital spirits passed into the brain and were transformed into animal spirits and passed back into the blood. The animal spirits controlled the body through the rational soul. According to Galen, individual bodily organs and the soul could be affected primarily, but usually they were affected by consensus, in sympathy with other organs. As a theory of physiological function, the idea of animal spirits was retained into the seventeenth century and used still, by Descartes.

Thus, diseases were not regarded as localised processes, but as disturbances of the harmony of the functions of the total organism. Galen was also influenced by the teleological way of thinking common to Aristotelianism. All the bodily structures, functions and processes were conceived in terms of their purposes and goals, rather than in terms of antecedent causes and independent variables. As far as mental diseases were concerned, Galen believed them to be due to physiological disorders such as rarification or reduction of animal spirits from the coldness and humidity of the brain. He believed that febrile delerium was produced through a consensus by an excess of yellow bile, melancholia was not produced directly by black bile, but by its byproduct which he called melancholic humor (*succus melancholicus*). He classified mental illness into: (1) humoral pathological types such as melancholia and mania; (2) psychopathological types such as paranoia, moria; (3) anatomopathological types such as phrenitis and hysteria; (4) clinical types such as epilepsy, catalepsy, lethargy, apoplexy and carus. Finally, Galen considerably modified the traditional theory of hysteria by rejecting the idea that hysteria was caused by a wandering uterus. Instead he maintained that hysteria in women was caused by sexual abstinence which led to a suppression of menses and a retention of menstrual fluid and hypothetical "feminine semen." These retained substances poisoned the bodily humors and through them affected the brain. True to his spirit of eclecticism, Galen did not disregard the emotional and psychological factors in the causation of mental diseases. In his treatise, *On Passions*, he stressed the importance of the proper harmony between the rational, irrational and lustful parts of the soul. He pointed to erroneous judgments, conscious or unconscious, as possible causes of mental disorders.

Galen was a prolific writer on various medical topics. Through an accident of history, Galen's system of medicine came to dominate the medical scene for about fourteen hundred years. This accident was due to the fact that in his writing, apart from Aristotle's biological views. Galen espoused also the latter's theological views, namely the monotheistic doctrine of the Primary Mover. Galen's monotheism appealed to the Moslem Arab physicians when they started studying Greek manuscripts. The humoral system of Hippocrates and Galen was taken over by the Arabs and became the basis of their medical science. It was further elaborated by such great Arab physicians as Al Rhazi (866-932 A.D.), Avicenna (980-1063 A.D.) and Najab ud din Unhamaad (the tenth century), who offered a description of thrity mental diseases classified into nine categories. Thus, the Najab, although steeped in the Hippocrates-Galen tradition, leaned towards the disease model of mental illness. In the eleventh and twelfth centuries, Arab treatises on medicine were translated into Latin. These were compilations and writings of Galen and other Humoralists and were translated by Constantinus Africanus (1020-1087 A.D.) and by Gerard of Cremona (1140-1187 A.D.). As a result of these developments, the Humoral medical system of Hippocrates and Galen spread from the Arab world to Christian Europe and became the basis of medical teaching at the famous Salerno medical school and the new universities such as Montpellier, Paris, Bologna, Oxford, and Padua. The humoral system of medicine was dominant in Europe until well into the sixteenth and seventeenth centuries when there took place the work of such medical scientists and clinicians as Andreas Vesalius (1514-1564), Girolamo Fracastorius (1484-1553), William Harvey (1578-1657), Sylvius of Leydea (1614-1672), Marcello Malpighi (1628-1694), Thomas Willis (1621-1675), and Thomas Sydenham (1624-1689), to name only a few. Their work laid the foundation for the new science of medicine.

What were the features of the Humoral system ? First, it stressed the whole organism in its total life span. Second, it stressed intrinsic organismic factors in causation of illness in contradistinction to extrinsic, extraorganismic factors. Third, in their thinking, the proponents of the system tended to base themselves on analogy and metaphor. For instance, yellow bile and fire were similar because they were yellow. Fire and summer were similar because both were hot and dry. Therefore, there was a family resemblance between the three and they were categorised as being the same. Fourth, the proponents of the system tended to apply teleological explanation to the observed phenomena. Fifth, the Humoralist system exemplifies the constitutional medical model. Sixth, the Humoralist system stressed the concept of balance and harmony as the characteristics of a state of health. If we think, for a moment, of the constitutional versus the disease models not as exclusive categories, but as a dimension along which various systems of medicine in Antiquity could be placed, the Humoralists would be placed close to the constitutional model; the Cnidian school would be placed close to the disease model. The Solidists and the Methodists also leaned towrds the constitutional model. Off center perhaps, not as close as the Humoralists. However, it has to be pointed out that the disease medical model was never completely abandoned in late Antiquity. The localisation of pathology in particular parts of the body and organ played an important role in the Solidist school and its successor the Methodist school. It had a place in the Galenian system. In addition, a relation between acute fevers and external agents was noticed by the Greeks and Romans. Thus, miasma, a hypothetical vapour-like substance was postulated as the causal agent of malaria to explain the geographical association of the incidence of this illness with swamps in the vicinity of Rome. Two Roman agriculturalists, Varro (116-27 B.C.), and Columella (first century A.D.), went further, and advanced a bold hypothesis that malaria was caused by small animals or insects coming out of the swamps. The miasma theory survived for many centuries until the beginning of the nineteenth century. In later ages, a distinction was made between miasma, an infection agent associated with locality, and contagium, an infection agent responsible for passing illness from one person to another.

The Humoralists, mainly Arabs, developed a typology of human temperament: they distinguished four basic temperaments: a) Chloric, due to an excess of yellow bile; b) Sanguinic, due to an excess of blood; c) Melancholic, due to an excess of black bile, and d) Phlegmatic, due to an excess of phlegm. This theory of four human temperaments was very influential for a long time. It survived as a theory of personality even after the theory of humors had been abandoned. It persisted until the end of the nineteenth century and, even in the twentieth century, Pavlov used the four basic temperaments taken from this theory, as the correlates of the individual differences in the functioning of the nervous system. The Humoralists, by and large, attributed the causation of mental illness to physiological factors. For instance, melancholia, as the name indicated, was believed to be due to an excess of black bile, delirium and furore to an excess of yellow bile. Other mental diseases were believed to be caused by disturbances of the temperature and the moisture of the brain, interfering with the circulation of the animal spirits. In the Middle Ages, the Humoralist theories of mental illness became purely academic, because the treatment of mental diseases was taken from the hands of physicians and placed in the hands of priests.

In late Antiquity, moral philosophers and the educated lay public showed a great interest in mental diseases and mental health. They refused to leave the field of mental diseases entirely to physicians. Whether mental diseases ought to be treated by physicians or philosophers was a widely debated issue. Marcus Tullius Cicero (106-63 B.C.), a Roman statesman, orator, writer and an amateur philosopher devoted his *Tusculanae Disputationes* (1878) to the problems of distress of mind, such as the fear of pain and of death. Cicero believed that mental illness was psychologically determined, that it was due to emotional disturbances in which strong emotions overruled rational judgment. He distinguished four groups of emotions or passions *(pate)*. These were: 1) *aegritudo* or discomfort; 2) *metus* or fear; 3) *voluptas* or pleasure; 4) *libido* or desire. When out of control, these emotions interfered with the function of reason and could drive an individual into madness. Yet Cicero believed that the mind controlled the body, rather than the other way around. This is why he opposed using a term like melancholia because it implied that mental illness was caused by black bile. He could ask why so much effort was put into treating the body and so little into treating the mind. Mental diseases posed a moral problem and as such should be treated by the patient himself with the help of a philosopher, but not by a physician who dealt only with the body and not the soul. This was an attitude close to that characterizing the cures practiced in the Asclepian hospital-theatre complexes during the Roman imperial period. The Pergamon centre which was perhaps the most famous of these, was visited and supported by the Roman emperors.

Roman medical writers did not share Cicero's views at all. Both Celsus and Caelius doubted that philosophers had the ability to treat mental patients; physicians ought to treat them. Other lay writers such as Plutarch (46-120 A.D.), showed a profound humanitarian concern for mental patients. Plutarch left an excellent description of patients who were suffering from severe depression.

The Roman philosophical systems differed somewhat from the Greek. They were Hellenistic, rather than Hellenic. In Contradistinction to the Platonic and Aristotelian systems they approached the problems of living concretely. They provided a recipe for a happy life devoid of perturbations. Yet much Greek influence remained in the Stoic, Epicurean and Sceptic schools. These were all moral philosophies concerned with ethical problems and with defining the good life. The Stoic, the Epicurean, and the Sceptic philosophies not only represented abstract theories, they were also prescriptions for a proper way of life. The Stoic philosophy originated with Zeno of Citium (fourth century B.C.). However, the most important late Stoic writer in the Roman period, was Epictetus of Hierapolis (50-130 A.D.), who was concerned mainly with the problems of ethics and of emotial maladjustment. The Stoics believed that the universe was ruled by immutable, inexorable, deterministic natural laws which were also moral laws since the universe was identified with God. The Stoics were pantheists. It was the duty of man to accept these laws with equanimity since human society and the individual fell under the same laws as the universe. Man could then experience tranquillity of mind (*apatheia*), also moral autonomy and a life controlled by reason. Epictetus maintained that humans were distressed not by the events and circumstances around them, but by the way they perceive these circumstances. For the Stoics, the cure of mental illness was in correcting faulty perceptions and preconceptions.

The Epicurean school was based on Democritean Atomism. It had originated with Epicurus of Samos (341-270 B.C.). Just as Democritus had allowed a degree of indeterminacy in the movement of atoms, some freedom of choice was granted to men. The Epicurean was a materialistic philosophy which rejected the belief in an after-life. The purpose of life was a sagious pursuit of pleasures. If one enjoyed pleasure in moderation and avoided deep emotional involvement, then a peace of mind or *ataraxia* would result.

The Sceptics were also interested in reaching a state of *ataraxia* or peace of mind. This school of philosophers had been founded by Pyrrho of Elis (third century B.C.) who argued that any knowledge of ultimate reality, assumed to lie behind the world of appearances, was impossible. Sceptics, therefore, advocated an open-minded approach to all problems (*epoche*), without committing oneself to a particular theory, an ideology, or a cause. This attitude was supposed to lead to an *agoge,* a way of life in which peace of mind (*ataraxia*), was attained. Dogmatism was eliminated, a broad outlook on the world was secured, frustrations and emotional perturbations were avoided. Briefly, it was a way of life compatible with mental health. A very important exponent of Scepticism was Sextus Empiricus (third century A.D.) who was also a medical doctor interested in psychiatry. The writings of Cicero, and the philosophical prescriptions of the Stoics, Epicureans, and Sceptics were interested in the good life and avoidance of emotional perturbations. Their work shows that a psychological-philosophical model existed alongside of the medical model of mental disease in late Antiquity. The ethos of all these moral philosophies may be characterised as Apollonian, to use Frederick Nietzsche's designation. (Nietzsche, 1872/1967). All three schools preached moderation if not Aristotle's golden mean. They all believed in submitting to one's fate, in being reasonable, and in avoiding strong emotions. A philosopher of history as pessimistic as Oswald Spengler, would probably argue that their *Weltanschauung* characterised a dying culture.

In the declining years of the Roman Empire, the social climate was subject to profound changes. The rationalistic outlook of the Hellenistic era had been abandoned. New occult, mystical cults such as that of Mithraism, spread throughout the empire. These as well as the new religion of Christianity came from the East and undermined existing Roman beliefs and values. As the older, Apollonian values had been increasingly eroded, they were replaced by Dionysian extremism. Debauchery and profligacy were common, and also excessive asceticism and self-mortification. A rising tide of belief in mysticism swept through the declining empire and replaced the older, mor urbane rationalism. This seemed true also, of the teachings of the last important philosophical school of ancient times; Neo-Platonism. Founded by Plotinus (205-270 A.D.), the Neo-Platonists writings were permeated with mystical ideas and allegories. The increased quest for faith and emotional security led also to superstition and to a new faith in magic. The old, Asclepian cults still flourished. So did astrology. (Veith, 1965). In times of trouble, people turned to all sorts of quacks who offered advice based on wisdom mixed with the old religion, and with ideas stemming from the new Oriental esoteric cults. Here we find fragments of the old philoso- phies, and above all, many magical beliefs. These developments set the stage for the Dark Ages, for what Zilboorg (1941) called a "great decline" in medical and psychiatric science.

Christianity: The Transition from Antiquity to the Middle Ages

The change from the classical to the medieval world did not occur overnight; it was gradual. Some Greco-Roman ideas were abandoned, others were incorporated into the Christian world view. The conversion to Christianity with its emphasis on faith and its condemnation of sensual pleasure, led to a rejection of Greco-Roman science, medicine, and philosophy. A few examples might demonstrate this clearly. Origen (A.D. 185-254), one of the fathers of the Church, was himself a scholar before his conversion. He believed that the Archangel Raphael took care of the sick and attacked the pagan Celsus. For him, different parts of the body were protected by different angels or gnomes. Ideas such as these represented a regression to the earlier Egyptian medical beliefs, according to which different parts of the body were controlled by different divinities. In his thinking Origen, who lived in Alexandria, was influenced by the teachings of the Gnostics, a Christian theosophic sect which combined Christian with Oriental occult beliefs stemming from the old Egyptian religion. The Gnostics in their beliefs populated the world with spirits and demons. Other Christian Church fathers sought to reject the classical heritage entirely. St. Basil (A.D. 330-379) regretted that in his youth he had studied classical literature. St. Jerome (fourth century A.D.) took a vow never to read pagan books. St.Gregory of Tours (sixth century A.D.) believed that all diseases, physical and mental, should be treated by miraculous cures effected by an exposure to prayers and to the relics of saints. Consequently, he rejected lay medicine. Cyprian, the Bishop of Carthage (third century A.D.) believed that fractures of the limbs were caused by devils. *Credo qua absurdum est.* (I believe it because it is absurd.) This became the motto of the age. Several of the patristic writers showed considerable psychological insight. John Cassian (360-435), who was interested in asceticism, described the sorrow and melancholia of young monks who carried on ascetic practices. Gregory the Great (540-604) advocated psychological counselling of parishioners who were distressed. (Mora, 1967).

Although Christianity was a monotheistic religion, it was influenced by some of the prominent mystical beliefs of the East, especially as these were exemplified in the Gnostic heresy. An animistic world view revived. As in the early stages of Antiquity, the world was once again populated with benign and with evil spirits who haunted certain localities. They either worked miracles or caused mischief.

3

The Middle Ages

The Early Period (Dark Ages)

The ancient world collapsed in the spasms of wars, social upheavals and general unrest. Barbarian tribes, themselves uprooted and fleeing before Asian conquerors, rampaged and looted Roman and Greek cities. Disease epidemics swept the land and decimated the population. As a result of these disasters, evil spirits and their master, the devil, loomed large in the popular imagination. These demonic forces were blamed for most calamities. The world was perceived as a stage on which the forces of good battled against evil. In their fear of the supernatural world of evil spirits, the populace turned for comfort and cure to religion.

As Christianity became firmly established, the protection of saints was invoked against diseases. St. Sebastian protected one against plagues, St. Job against leprosy, St. Anthony against fractures. Cures were sought at the shrines and graves of saints. Prayers and bodily contact with relics of saints became the favoured remedy provided by the priests. Thus, the separation of the role of the doctor and the role of the priest which had become common at the end of the Roman Empire, had disappeared in the early Middle Ages as urban civilization declined, and the church became prominent in rural areas (Dawson, 1945). After the invasions and the fall of the Roman Empire, a new culture arose to the north and west of the Alps. The Germanic tribes as well as the Celtic Druids now combined the offices of priest and physician (Leibbrand & Leibbrand-Wettley, 1964).

The collapse of the Roman Empire in the West meant that a great many people were forced to seek refuge from the maurading tribesmen who attacked at the frontiers and then established their own kingdoms, like the Franks, the Goths, and the Alemanni. This development resulted in the rise of a feudal and monastic culture (Painter, 1953; E.Peters, c1983, 1989). Schooling, learning, the preservation of books, libraries, and the medical arts that had survived the disappearance of the ancient world, now concentrated in the monasteries. It was a mission of the monks to spread medical knowledge. The most important representative of the new monastic medicine was St. Benedict of Nursia (A.D.480-543), the founder of the Benedictine Order of monks in the monastery of Monte Cassino. As Western culture revived (Boussard, 1968; Bullough, 1965), it experienced a new integration during the era of Charlemagne (A.D.768-814). During the reign of Charlemagne, the first emperor in the West since the fifth century, a general cultural revival took place (Einhard, 1960; Peters, 1983,1989). As schools were established and scholars like Alcuin brought from England, a uniform administration for the monasteries was introduced as well. The rule of St. Benedict as well as Benedictine practices were transmitted to the Carolingian Empire (Farmer, 1968). A dual system of health and education developed. The great monasteries and monastic schools at St. Gall in Switzerland, and Reichenau in Germany, produced doctor-priests and maintained hospitals and herb gardens. Frankish, and Jewish secular physicians also practiced independently of the Church. The tradition of lay medicine emerged once again in the secular medical school at Salerno between the ninth and thirteenth centuries. Here the medical lore of Hippocrates was continued and Arab medicine was introduced by Constantinus Africanus by the eleventh century (Leibbrand & Leibbrand-Wettley, 1964)).

In the monastic and feudal world, the monk-doctors did not rely completely on miraculous cures. The medicine they practiced contained a mixture of the supernatural and the natural. The natural component was taken from Greek and Roman medicine, and from the folk medicine of the invaders. Hospital treatment could take place in the monastery itself. Many kinds of medicine were prepared from the many herbs which were cultivated in the gardens of the main buildings (Price, 1982; Horn & Born, 1979).

Mental illness was believed to be caused by demoniacal possession and was to be treated by exorcism. However, some early fathers of the Church like Tertullian (A.D.160-230), believed that sometimes insane persons were possessed by the Holy Spirit and had prophetic powers. Tertullian recognized the demoniacal and the divine forms of insanity. Others of the early Church fathers like St. Cyprian, an early bishop of Carthage, believed that states of religious ecstasy were produced by demoniacal possession. This did not mean that one could not also believe that some types of insanity might result from natural causes rather than from demonic possession. St. Augustine (A.D. 354-430) referred (Augustine,1954), to many examples of demonic possession and miraculous cures. Yet he believed in a more modern way, that some cases of insanity resulted from diseases which were similar to physical afflictions. He believed that basically the human flesh was heir to diseases because of man's original sin.

St. Augustine has to be mentioned in another context. In the *Confessions* (1961) his argument emphasized the subjective nature of the human psyche. He gave a subtle analysis of his own inner experiences and of his motives of conduct. He showed an uncanny psychodynamic insight into the workings of the human mind. In this he anticipated both psychoanalytical and existential psychologies. He also became the originator of a more naturalistic approach to understanding human behaviour than that of the early fathers of the Church. Many of his interpretations were analyzed also by Thomas Aquinas and became characteristic of the medieval idea of the soul.

St. Augustine told the story of his childhood and of his conversion to Christianity in his *Confessions.* The son of a devout Christian mother, Monica, and of a pagan, Epicurean father, he was exposed to the conflicting values of Epicurean sensuality and Christian spirituality. A sickly child, he was torn later in life, between the temptations of the flesh and the demands of chastity. His conversion to Christianity gave him a new purpose in life as well as a new understanding of his own past (Guardini, 1960). He recognized that his childish motives were selfish and spiteful. Nor did he believe in the "angelic" innocence of infants. He came to recognize the dark and evil side of his own nature and exposed it, mercilessly. Augustine believed that frankness with oneself and the acknowledgment of one's own sinful motives would allow one to gain mastery over these motives. For his salvation, St. Augustine relied on self-understanding and on his own strength of will. God had given man free will, yet He also knew what choices men would make, since history followed a divine plan of eternal salvation.

In contrast to other fathers of the church, St. Augustine's faith in God was not based on blind faith: *credo qua absurdum est.* Instead, he favored a rational understanding. In book eleven of the *Confessions*, St. Augustine offered a subtle analysis of the meaning of time. He stressed the subjective aspect of time experience as a way of ordering the remembered and presently experienced events, a veritable extension of mind itself. The stress on the subjectivity of the time experience and on its intimate link with personal existence brings St. Augustine close to contemporary existential philosophers. The idea that the soul has a direct knowledge of itself has been termed the "principle of interiorization." Together with the subtle analysis of his inner experiences and of his early memories, this makes St. Augustine the "great introspective psychologist before Freud" (Alexander & Selesnick, 1966). The work of Aristotle is often seen as epitomizing the objective psychology of the ancient world. In contrast, St. Augustine's theories represented the opposite pole of a subjective psychology.

Although the idea of demoniacal possession became the generally accepted theory of mental disease in the early Middle Ages, the victims were not blamed for their fate. Instead, they were an object of pity and were treated by exorcisms. The association of demoniacal possession with sin and a willful collusion with the devil was a belief common in the later Middle Ages, and was linked to the Holy Inquisition and to witch hunts.

The early medieval picture of psychiatry and medicine which has been presented thus far, applies to Western Christendom. The Byzantine Empire, then the sphere of Eastern Christendom, escaped foreign conquest until the seventh century when the Arabs conquered the southern part of the empire. When they captured Alexandria in A.D. 604, they burned the greatest library amassed in ancient times. It had actually been sent there, at one time, from Pergamon, the site of a large Asclepian treatment center. Yet Greco-Roman medicine survived for a few more centuries in the Byzantine Empire. The two most famous Byzantine physicians were Alexander of Tralles (525-605), and Paul of Aegina (fl. sixth century A.D.). The system of medicine which they followed was that of Hippocrates and Galen with an admixture of oriental medical lore. They applied themselves to the practical problems of patient treatment, since the times were not propitious for scientific research. As was mentioned earlier, the Arabs conquered Alexandria in 640 A.D. By the beginning of the eighth century they had established an empire which stretched from Spain to Persia.

Arab Medicine

Although zealous in their religious beliefs, the Arabs showed a greater tolerance than did contemporary Christians to classical scholarship and science. Greek and Roman literature as well as the works of great Greek physicians were translated into Arabic, sometimes via Syriac (Aramaic) and Hebrew. As was mentioned before, the Moslem

Arabs were particularly attracted by the theories of Galen because of the latter's monotheistic theological orientation. Several medical centers developed, especially in Persia and Spain. The names of two great physicians, Al Rhazi (A.D.860-932) and Avicenna (A.D.980-1063) have already been mentioned. The Arabs made some important practical and original contributions. However, by and large, they followed the constitutional model of Hippocrates and Galen. In Mohammedanism, the role of the clergy and of the physician, were clearly separated. The *mulla* was a man learned in the religious laws, not a physician. The social and political status of the physician could be very high. This may be illustrated from the life of Chasdai ibn Schaprut, who in 900 became the physician-in-chief of the Cordoban caliph, Abd ar-Rahman III, and was also his minister as well as head of the Cordoba school of medicine (Franke,3,1967). Even more important was Moses ben Maimon (Maimonides) (1135-1204), a Cordoban Jew who had fled to Cairo and become the personal physician of Sultan Saladin. He wrote Aristotelian books influenced by the ideas of ibn Ruschd, better known as Averroes (1126-1198). The German Hohenstaufen Emperor Frederick II ordered Averroes' works translated, as well as of Maimonides. Thus a more accurate rendering of Aristotle's ideas was made known in Europe, especially as the emperor sent copies of the translations to the universities of Bologna and Paris (van Cleve, 1972).

Since mental illness was believed to be the result of natural causes, it was the field of expertise of the physician. The treatment of mental patients was quite enlightened. The patients were placed in special hospitals and treated with kindness. Therapy included special diets, soothing baths, and music specially composed for its beneficial effects on the patients. The enlightened attitude of the Arabs probably stemmed from a Moslem belief that insane persons were especially loved by God, and were chosen by him to tell the truth. Consequently they were often worshipped as saints.

The Late Middle Ages

In the eleventh and twelfth centuries, changes took place in Western Christendom which brought in their wake a separation of physical medicine and religion. In 1130, the Council of Clermont forbade the practice of medicine to monks as being incompatible with monastic life. Only the lay clergy was allowed to practice medicine. This decision paved the way again, for the separation of the priest's role from that of the doctor. While the treatment of physical illness was passing into the hands of physicians, the treatment of mental diseases remained in the hands of priests. About the same time, contacts between the Christian and the Arab worlds were increased because of the crusades. Scientific and medical treatises were translated from Arabic into Latin. There were two important translators active during this era. They were first, Constantinus Africanus (1020-1087), who worked at Salerno and at the Monte Cassino monastery in Italy. Second, Gerard of Cremona (1140-1187) who worked at Toledo in Spain. Salerno in Southern Italy, and Toledo in Spain, were situated in regions in which the European Christian culture and the Arab Islamic culture came into contact with each other.

Constantinus Africanus had brought Arab medicine to Salerno. Later, he spent his last years at Monte Cassino. Africanus' major treatise on melancholy (*De Melancholia*), attributed this ailment to an imbalance of bodily humors. He distinguished two forms of melancholia. The site of one form was in the brain. The site of the other, was in the stomach (*hypochondrium*). Salerno, the first lay medical school was devoted to the empirico-rational medicine founded by Constantius Africanus. It was for a long time under Arab influence. Soon afterwards, the Universities of Paris (1110), Montpellier (1181), and Bologna (1113), Oxford (1167), and Padua (1222), were founded. The faculty of medicine at these universities was independent of the theology faculty. By the thirteenth century, medicine flourished as an independent discipline, even if, for many years, the physician was often still a cleric. This development was further enhanced by a law introduced by the Hohenstaufen Emperor Frederick II (1194-1250) who was also King of Sicily. It established the standards a physician had to meet before he was certified by the Salerno medical school to practice medicine. According to this law, medical doctors were required to complete, besides a three year arts degree, a five year study of medicine and a one year practice with an experienced physician. After that, they had to pass an examination. It was at the Salerno school that the medical lore of the Middle Ages was rendered into verse in a long poem which was reprinted in 141 editions up to 1841.

In these uneasy times, the new Arab and Aristotelian learning encountered a hostile reaction from the Church. Pope Gregory IX banned the teaching of Aristotelian philosophy and Arab science early in the thirteenth century. In 1233, the same pope inaugurated the Office of the Holy Inquisition. In these circumstances physicians tried to reconcile Arab medicine with official theology. One of the more prominent medical thinkers, Arnold of Villanova (1240-1311) even tried to reconcile Galenian humoralism with demonology. He claimed that the devil was attracted by the warmth produced by disturbed humors, and could thus take possession of the patient's body. As a result, illness, both physical and mental, became associated with sin and with the workings of the devil. Villanova also tried to synthesize humoral theory with astrology. He believed that various humors were influenced by different planets. Mars thus influenced black bile and "caused" melancholia. Notwithstanding his attempts at a reconciliation of humoralism and astrology on the one hand, and demonology on the other, Villanova was excommunicated by Church authorities.

At the end of the thirteenth century, Aristotelianism became more acceptable because of the new theology of St. Thomas Aquinas (1225-1274) (Aquinas, 1955). The ban on Arab learning was eased. The gradual acceptance of Aristotle's philosophy reawakened an interest in psychology. Aquinas commented extensively on Aristotle's *De anima* (Aquinas, 1951) and made the Greek philosospher intelligible to a Christian world. Aristotle had established the important idea that the soul was actually the form-giving principle of life. As part of the world of natural phenomena, its essential feature was movement. Yet it also had cognitive functions. Human thought depended on the intellectual part of the soul which received form impressions in the mind. Apart from a sensitive or sensing (animal) soul, there was also a nutritive one which was tied to the life and death cycle of the organism (Aristotle, 1961). These basic ideas became important to the entire Western psychological tradition and influenced the modern age. The Aristotelian revival of the thirteenth century mediated the medieval under standing of the structure of Aristotle's psychology. All subsequent psychological thinkers had to contend with its main features. The writings of St. Thomas Acquinas and of his teacher, Albertus Magnus (1193-1280), exemplified the importance of the revival of this ancient philosopher's ideas. Both followed Aristotle in establishing the structure of the "soul." Both divided the psyche into three parts as he had done: the rational (*anima intellectiva*), the sensory (*anima sensitiva*), and the vegetative (*anima vegetativa*).

For Aquinas the vegetative soul also had three powers; these were nutritive, generative, and augmentative. It was thus organic in its functions. In addition to the intellect, the rational part of the soul contained the will (*appetitus intellectivus*), while the sensory part contained desires (*appetitus sensitivus*).

Aquinas disagreed with the idea of some of the ancients, notably Plato, that there was more than one soul. Although it had several parts, it was a united, single soul which was becoming more perfect. As it did so, the corruptibility of the sensitive (animal) part of the soul tended to disappear, for it merged with the intellectual soul which was immortal and incorruptible. Besides these parts, the soul also had appetities or ends, and locomotion or movement (Aquinas, 1948).

Both Albertus Magnus and St. Thomas envisaged voluntaristic, dynamic or connative aspects of the mind. Aquinas did not write on the subject of mental disorder in any extensive way, although his understanding of a healthy soul, made necessary a consideration of those illnesses and malfunctions which interefered with its proper operations. Insanity was viewed by these authors as primarily a somatic disorder. It resulted from a deficiency of reason caused by organic pathology. It could also be the result of strong passions. In *vesania*, the heart contained an ill will according to St. Thomas. He also believed that the natural sense was defective in cases of *hebetudo* or dullness (stupefaction). Demons were acknowledged to exist, but little was said about them. (Deferrari et al.,1948). The soul itself could not be touched by the external imperfectibility of maladies. Mental disorders arose from weaknesses in the body's organs.

These writers also described various psychiatric syndromes such as melancholia, mania, epilepsy, organic psychosis, psychopathic personality (*stultitia*), mental deficiency (*hebetudo*), and educational backwardness (*ignorantia*). For Aquinas God was the all powerful physician and Jesus was the physician of souls. The operation of the soul was impeded by sadness, which must be viewed as a kind of melancholia here. Much emphasis was placed on the power of the will which functioned weakly when sadness was present. Yet Aquinas had faith in the efficacy of reason in overcoming the bad effects of passions (Pegues,VII,1912).

Magnus and St. Thomas both believed that most cases of mental illness were due to natural causes, and that mental patients were not responsible for their acts. As treatment procedure, this age recommended soothing baths and plenty of sleep (Mora,1967). Similarly enlightened views were held by Petrus Hispanus (1200-1277) who became Pope John XXI, and by Pietro d'Albano (1250-1316). The latter anticipated some features of modern psychotherapy. He believed, first, that suggestion played an important role in the treatment of mental illness. Second, that dreams were related to the moral character of patients. Thus, in that period, in addition to the theory of demoniacal possession, natural explanations of mental illness were also offered. However, these thirteenth century thinkers including St. Thomas, were not entirely free of beliefs in demoniacal possession. They also continued to believe in astrological influences.

In addition to astrology, a new "science" of alchemy also emerged during this era (Bacon, 1975). This science, taken from the Arabs, was influenced by mystical Neo-Platonic ideas. It was half-accepted, but also condemned as sorcery and witchcraft by Church authorities. Yet it was to play an increasingly prominent role at the close of the Middle Ages. During the Renaissance, ideas borrowed from astrology and alchemy were incorporated into medical theory. Consequently, at the end of the Middle Ages, this theory was expressed in diverse ways which combined the elements of Galenian humoralism, astrology, alchemy, and demonology. However, on the whole, the notion that physical illnesses were due to natural causes, and mental illnesses to supernatural ones, became more clearly delineated. Some physicians even proposed diagnostic tests in order to distinguish between a stupor attributed to demoniacal possession and one caused by physical illness. It was believed that if one could shout a passage of the Bible into the ear of a patient and get an angry response, it showed that the person was demoniacally possessed (Zilboorg, 1941).

It was often believed that demoniacal possession was brought on by the sins of the patient. Treatment of mental patients was in the hands of priests who performed exorcisms in order to expel the devil from the body of the possessed person. This was a highly ritualistic practice. It consisted of invoking the names of various saints, of saying special prayers, of the laying on of hands, of washing with holy water and wine, and of touching the afflicted with sacred objects and relics. However, the exorcists were usually relegated to the lower ranks of the clergy. Some exorcists, like Father Johann Joseph Gassner in the eighteenth century, became quite famous.

Earlier in the Middle Ages those who were possessed were treated with kindness. Later on, the attitude changed as the victims came to be regarded as evil and were branded with diabolical stigmata. As a result they were often whipped and maltreated. Of course, a few isolated thinkers like Roger Bacon (1214-1294) and Bartholomew of Salerno (fl.13 century), maintained that mental disease had natural causes, but they were largely ignored. On the whole, the medieval model of mental illness was largely based on the theory of possession by an extrinsic, evil, and supernatural agent, the devil.

The model of physical illness remained basically a constitutional one throughout the Middle Ages. However, it had begun to incorporate in increasing proportions extra-organismic, astral, and alchemic influences. In physical medicine, the pendulum was swinging away from the purely constitutional model towards the disease model. Frequent epidemics, particularly the Black Plague in the fourteenth century, wiped out a large proportion of the population of Europe. (Between 30% and 60%, depending on the region). (Gottfried, 1983). The epidemics influenced medical thinking so that they were instrumental in shifting the focus of medical thinking from the intra-organismic constitutional factors to the extra-organismis environmental factors which caused disease epidemics. Frequent feuds, wars, plagues, and famines produced a general feeling of insecurity, bordering at times on mass psychosis. This accounts for epidemics of "mass hysteria," which swept across Europe in the late Middle Ages. Sometimes these were characterized by a denial of fear and manifested themselves in an ecstatic excitement visible as mass dancing epidemics. The famous "dance of death" much described in German engravings, the *Totentanz* is a case in point. At other times, they were characterized by mass guilt feelings for sins committed and were expiated by self-flagellation, as occurred during the Black Death in the fourteenth century. Certain of these madness epidemics could have been caused by mass poisoning by rye bread contaminated with the ergot fungus (*claviceps purpurea*). Finally, some mass hysterias were characterized by the search for a scapegoat. Such movements had particularly pernicious social effects and led to the death of countless innocent victims.

The belief in witches had existed since ancient times. It had receded somewhat during the enlightened centuries of Classical Antiquity, but re-emerged at the onset of the Middle Ages. In the beginning, witchcraft was not specifically associated with the female sex. St. Augustine (Veith, 1965), wrote about both male and female sorcerers. In later years, however, as the status of women was less equal in European feudal society than it had been in Roman times, there was an association of witchcraft predominently with the female sex. Witches were accused of having sexual relations with devils (*incubi*), and of being in collusion with Satan. They were blamed for a host of misfortunes raging from crop failure to cow's milk drying up. The first known instance of organized persecution of witches occurred in the ninth century when Charlemagne banished all women suspected of witchcraft practice. However, massive witch hunts did not occur until the end of the Middle Ages. The best known one was initiated by Pope Inocent VIII in 1484. He issued a Papal Bull on the subject and commissioned two Dominican monks, Fathers Heinrich Kramer and Jacob Sprenger to investigate the matter. The two Dominicans in due course submitted a report which was published as a book: *Malleus Maleficarum* (Hammer for the Witches, 1494/1971). The book was widely distributed because of the newly invented printing press and became a standard manual for dealing with witchhunting (Sprenger, et al., 1986).

It described procedures for interrogating a suspect, and for determining whether or not she was a witch. If so, she was to be turned over to the secular authorities and disposed of at the stake. The story is well known and does not have to be retold in detail. It suffices to say that untold thousands of women were burned at the stake both in Catholic and Protestant countries. Burning of witches continued, even if on a diminished scale, into the eighteenth century.

During the sixteenth century, certain enlightened men opposed the indiscriminate burning of witches. These included the jurist Cornelius Agrippa von Nettesheim (1486-1535) who wrote *On the Nobility and Preeminence of the Female Sex* in which he attacked mysogyny, and Johann Weyer (1515-1588), a physician. Deemed the father of modern psychiatry, Weyer was the author of *De prestigiis daemonum et incantationibus ac venefiis* (Basel, 1563). (On Demonic Manifestations, In cantations, and Magicians). Weyer argued that the majority of women accused of witchcraft were really mentally deranged. Even though they confessed to witchcraft, their confessions were a product of their deranged minds. According to Weyer, witchcraft did not exist. It was only imaginary. He admitted, however, that some accused women might be poisoners and evil doers, but he maintained that the belief in witchcraft was based on a superstition. He gave an excellent clinical description of women who suffered from mental illness and who were accused of witchcraft.

Johann Weyer also provided an excellent description of various psychiatric syndromes such as senile psychosis, epilepsy, toxic psychosis, hysteria, epilepsy and anorexia nervosa. He stressed the importance of a psychotherapeutic approach to mental patients. This was to be based on kindness, understanding, and a proper doctor-patient relationship. For this reason he may be regarded as a pioneer of psychotherapy, since he anticipated psychodynamic psychiatry in an age still dominated by mass hysteria and a belief in witches. These sober views were not accepted and were repudiated. Jean Bodin (1530-1596), a prominent legal scholar, political writer, and a founder of mercantilist economics, condemned Weyer for presenting witches as mentally ill. Bodin published this work in Paris in 1580, as: *De la demonomanie des sorciers aveque la refutation des opinions de Jean Wier.*

At the beginning of the seventeenth century, King James I of England opposed the supporters of Weyer and so ordered Reginald Scot's *Discovery of Witchcraft* (1584) to be burned. His own work on *Demonologie*, published in 1603, took a "hard-line" stand on witches and witchcraft. There is no doubt that numerous conditions now defined in psychiatric terms were perceived as witchcraft. *Malleus Maleficarum* provides ample indication that many signs which distinguished witches, such as cutaneous anesthesia, would nowadays be considered a manifestation of hysteria. Many women accused of witchcraft confessed to having sexual relations with the devil, to being witches and to committing other heinous crimes. In terms of modern psychiatry, most such women could be diagnosed as suffering from a severe psychotic depression. Many of the afflictions of the victims of witchcraft would also be defined in medical psychiatric terms today. Some conditions such as the delusion of the loss of the phallus does not occur any longer in Western culture. It does persist in Southeast Asian cultures where it is called *Koro* (Arieti & Meth, 1959).

The intensified preoccupation with witchcraft was accompanied by the excesses of demonology. Devils and black magic were seen everywhere. Devils multiplied. St. Fortunatus, allegedly, on one occasion cast out 6,670 devils from a man (Zilboorg, 1941). At the beginning of the seventeenth century, Zacchias, the personal physician of Pope Innocent X is quoted as having said that "the devil rejoices in a bath of the melancholoy humor" (Zilboorg, 1941; Heinemann, 1986).

Some of the leading medical scientists of the early scientific revolution (Hall,1956) remained rooted in the traditional demoniacal beliefs.

Ambroise Pare (1510-1590), the great surgeon who made surgery an independent profession by moving it out of the hands of barbers and assistant executioners, strongly believed in demons and demoniacal possession. Even Felix Plater (1536-1614), a great Swiss physician, one of the pioneers of modern psychiatry, also believed in demonology. Yet he was able to develop a classification of mental diseases, believing that most of them were caused by a "dryness" of the brain. Those which were not, were caused by demoniacal possession.

Plater was a professor of anatomy and medicine at the University of Basel. He became interested in mental patients to the extent of spending some time in the dungeons where the patients were kept. He carefully observed these patients and listened to their mad ravings. He concluded that the majority of mental patients suffered from organic brain disease. On the basis of many dissections, he attributed this to an excessive dryness of that organ. This was the old theory of Hippocrates and Galen (Zabarella, 1606-07/1966). Plater recorded some excellent case histories and clinical descriptions in his *Praxis Medica*. His fame rests on the taxonomic system which he developed in order to classify these diseases. He described mental patients as: idiots, morons, cretins, mutes, and melancholics. According to him, the patients whose insanity was caused by demoniacal possession were obsessed with vivid erotic fantasies, and experienced blasphemous hallucinations.

During the transitional period between the Middle Ages and the Renaissance, the intensification of witchhunts and of demonology, was associated with an increasing hostility toward, and rejection of the mentally ill. One reason for this, may have been the decline in the incidence of leprosy. According to Michael Foucault (1965), in the early Middle Ages, lepers were the pariahs of the society, the most feared and shunned of all the undesirables. They had been shut away, isolated in leprosoria. For an unknown reason, leprosy had almost disappeared at the end of the Middle Ages in Europe. The authors might venture the guess that as the crusades ended and contacts with the East diminished, the sources of infection were removed. Another supposition might be that since leprosy is a tropical disease, the increasing coldness of the European climate by the fourteenth century, might have helped to eradicate the disease. Nevertheless, Foucault believed that as a result of this development, the role of the outcast lepers was filled by the mentally ill. They were no longer regarded as objects of pity, but were feared, rejected, and ridiculed. The mentally ill were disowned by their families, chained, put in prison, driven out of cities and put on the "ships of fools," which sailed from one port to another with their despised human cargo while trying to unload it. (This was particularly true of the Rhine river ports. The local authorities would take their mad captives right down to the ships). Foucault points out that the rejection of the madman by the populace went hand in hand with a fascination of him, and a morbid curiousity about him. Sane people were perceiving, as it were, in the insane, the suppressed irrational side of their own psyche. Foucault believes this led to the practice of confinement of those who were mad in institutions, certainly by the eighteenth century. During the Renaissance the insane were at times believed to have a better insight "into reality". They were "speaking the truth." This belief found its expression in *The Praise of Folly* written by Desiderius Erasmus (1466-1536). The age of humanism dawned before 1500 and coincided with the end of the Renaissance, and the beginning of a new scientific age. It was to be one of the greatest epochs in human history since that of the ancient Greeks as Sir Francis Bacon was to note soon after 1600. It brought a new enlightenment to the understanding of human dignity on the whole. This attitude seems to have influenced the new and more enlightened attitude towards the mentally ill as well. The Renaissance was to broaden the scope of this new understanding of man.

4

The Renaissance

The Renaissance was a period of reawakened interest in man and in his surrounding world. Man was no longer only a soul preparing for the next world in order to be saved from the machinations of the devil; he was an individual in his own right. Man not only had a soul, but he had also a body which was not intrinsically wicked. This new *Zeitgeist* gave an impetus to the development of art, literature, science and medicine. In the literature there was a revival of interest in classical Greek and Roman culture. The scholastic concern with God and theology was replaced by an interest in man and his worldly affairs. The dignity of man, his closeness to the angels as Pico della Mirandola observed at the end of the fifteenth century, helped to define the new image of a rational creature who stood at the apex of the God's creation.

The Renaissance began with a new emphasis on humanistic studies. The philosophical and literary movement known as Humanism was born in Italy at the end of the fourteenth century, and came into maturity in the fifteenth and the beginning of the sixteenth centuries. Francesco Petrarch (1304-1374), is regarded as the originator of the movement, and is one of the first Renaissance personalities. The Florentine nobleman, Pico della Mirandola (1463-1494), and the Dutch monk, Desiderius Erasmus (1466-1536) are among the most outstanding humanist thinkers of the Western tradition. In contrast to the medieval attitude, the humanists did not regard man's life on earth as only a preparation for life in the next world. Human life became endowed with intrinsic meaning. The freedom and dignity of man was stressed. The medieval emphasis on asceticism was rejected, not in favor of a new sensualism, but in favor of the study of literature and language. The rebirth of classical learning also produced a new appreciation for the sculpture of the ancient world, and with it, for the naturalism of the human body. There was an interest in the whole man and in his spiritual and bodily needs. The uniqueness of each man was to be discovered and was glorified. Man ceased to be viewed as a stereotyped representative of a social status: as a king, a knight, or a peasant. There was an adulation of greatness and genius. Renaissance thinkers liked to emphasize the fullness of life, the fulfillment of human ambitions and talents. These new literary and scientific pursuits became the hallmark of the Renaissance man. The evidence of the senses and experience was accepted as the foundation of knowledge and of arts in contrast to the medieval reliance on the authoritative texts and models (Bernal, 1965-1972).

During the Renaissance, scientific ideas were still imbued with elements of neo-Platonic mysticism and the magic of alchemy. However, there was a considerable loosening of the authority of religious dogmatism as well as of Aristotle's science and Galen's medicine. Human cadavers were dissected and the dogmas of Galen challenged. Yet these dogmas did not die easily. When Vesalius (1514-1564), the great Renaissance anatomist and the author of *De Humani Corporis Fabrica* (The Machinery of the Human Body), demonstrated that Galen's ideas of anatomy were wrong, his teacher Jacques Dubois (Sylvius, 1478-1555) allegedly remarked that the human anatomy must have degenerated since the time of Galen, because the great physician from Pergamon could not have been wrong.

The man who proposed an alternative medical system to that of Hippocrates and Galen was Theophrastus Bombastus von Hohenheim, usually called Paracelsus (1493-1540). He was born in Einsiedeln in Switzerland where his father was the monastery physician. By 1502 the father had become the town doctor in Villach in Carinthia where the young Paracelsus learned much about chemistry and mining. His father's library provided the medical knowledge of the late medieval tradition, and included works by Albertus Magnus, Acquinas, and Roger Bacon. Both he and his father were Platonists rather than Aristotelian (Paracelsus,I, 1926, 1981).

Paracelsus became engrossed in the study of alchemy and of astrology. He regarded the human body as the alchemist's "kitchen," and replaced Galen's traditional humoral theory by his own theory based on concepts taken from astrology and alchemy. For him, the human body was dominated by a special integrative spiritual force called the *archeus*. Paracelsus replaced the four humors of Galen with the various minerals, salts, elements and *arcana* of alchemy. He sought to combine internal medicine with surgery, the latter, a field much neglected in the medieval Salerno school. Paracelsus considered himself persecuted by the orthodox physicians of the profession and often had to move his abode. The Basel University professors rejected him because of his radical approaches and because he lectured in German, not Latin. He eventually found refuge in Salzburg. Even if he discarded the traditional humors theory, he believed in the existence of life fluids and often refers to them as life juices (*Saefte*).

Paracelsus' explained the causes of disease by astral, cosmic and supernatural forces which he combined with both the constitutional and the psycho-physical model of disease. Thus there were five major forces at work and the astrological configuration at birth remained important. But God's will played its role, as did poisons and the human constitution. The psychological forces included the view that damage to the mind could exert a negative influence, and that distorted ways of thinking could also cause illness. Some of the ingredients of the Galenian humoral pathology which explained diseases as an imbalance of humors remained. Paracelsus advocated an improvement in the basic "liquids" or humors, as well as a "cleansing of the blood." This could be done by rejecting Galenic-Arab medicine with its many prescriptions, and by applying modern medicines which were tested more empirically. These were known as the *arcana*. If saltpeter cured some diseases, they became known as saltpeter diseases. If wolf's milk worked, then such ailments were classified as wolf's milk diseases. Many ointments and potions were composed of minerals like mercury [quicksilver], iron, and antimony. Mercury, and tinctures of alcohol played an important role in his therapeutic armamentarium.

Thus Paracelsus conceived of diseases as autonomous entities produced by specific etiological factors. This initiated a shift in the medical theory away from the constitutional model towards the disease model. The new development culminated in the seventeenth century in the ontological noslogy of Thomas Sydenham. Paracelsus believed that various human organs were in sympathetic contact with various celestial bodies: the heart with the sun, the brain with the moon, the kidneys with Venus, the lungs with Mercury, the liver with Jupiter and the gall bladder with Mars. He also believed that the human organism constituted a micro-cosmos which reflected the macro-cosmos. Man was under the influence of mysterious forces emanating from the sun, the moon, and the planets. On earth, these came from magnets. These were the primordial forces, guiding human behaviour and destiny. Yet man also possessed an individual life-directing principle which he called an *archeus*. The *archeus* was not unlike Aristotle's concept of entelechy. But it was less universal, and was unique for each individual. A wise man could free himself from celestial influence and become master of his own destiny. We see in the theories of Paracelsus an anticipation of general systems theory for he placed the micro-cosmos within the astral macro-cosmos. He also anticipated the principles of self-actualization and individuation described by C.G. Jung (1939, 1953, 1957).

Paracelsus made important innovations in therapeutics. He introduced the use of metals as therapeutic agents. This constituted a new development and anticipated the twentiethcentury interest in the role of trace minerals in human nutrition. Previously, it was believed that only organic substances coming from plants or animals had therapeutic properties. As a result of this new development, mercury became an important remedy in the treatment of syphillis, a new disease introduced from the Americas, which reached epidemic proportions in sixteenth century Europe. Another innovation was the insistence by Paracelsus that therapeutic procedures such as bone setting had to be carried out by the physician himself and was not to be delegated to his assistants.

Paracelsus was interested in mental illness and wrote *On the Diseases which Deprive Man of Reason*. He tended to reject demonology and hinted at the possibility of unconscious mental forces as causal factors in pathology. Paracelsus believed that mental diseases were due to a disturbance of *spiritus vitae*, a mysterious vital force. He offered a classification of mental disease into four basic types: (1) *Lunatici* or lunatics who were made ill by the fullness, oldness, or newness of the moon. (2) *Insani* or those with hereditary mental disease. These could be the result of birth defects as well. (3) *Vesani* or those made mad by poisoned food, drink, or potions (intoxification). (4) *Melancholics* or those whose reason left them because of the constitution of their own nature. A fifth type (5) was mentioned as *Obsessi* or possessed by the devil. (Preternatural disease). Each type had its own unique cause. These were all types of *Wahnsinn* or delusional insanity. There had been a shift towards a clearer definition of each kind of madness, however, for during the thirteenth century, Aquinas had defined vesani, for example, as an ill will of the heart. Paracelsus implied that the administration of potions, including love potions, led to an intoxification which produced the insanity.

In addition, human personality types were divided according to the four original humors or life fluids as melancholic, choleric, sanguine, and phlegmatic. There were another group of mental diseases not included in his original taxonomy. Epilepsy, which he considered to be a spiritual disease was amenable to medicines which could penetrate the brain and which included powdered horn of a putative unicorn, and camphor. Paracelusus also made an important contribution to the theory of hysteria, which he called *chorea lasciva*, and believed to be caused by sexual fantasies. In actual fact he did not distinguish it from St. Vitus' dance, which was very common during the Middle Ages. It was similar to mania, which could be healed by drawing the illness out through the skin or by making tiny holes in the fingers and toes in order to do so. Poultices soaked in vinegar were to be applied for five hours, mercury and also arsenic plasters were to be used. However in healing the varieties of insanity described above, he believed that the physician had to apply the hidden properties of seven metals and to work against the moon. Paracelsus seemed to be using the ancient Egyptian idea of the magical properties of the number seven as important to healing a mental disorder in this case. Sadness was to be healed with laughter and too much laughter with sedatives. In the approach to the treatment of mental patients, Paracelsus advocated kindness and a humane attitude (Paracelsus,II, 1928,1976).

For Paracelsus as for Freud and the physicians of the Asclepian school, dreams had a special meaning. Of course, Paracelsus did not yet have the insights of psychoanalysis. Physical events had more influence on dream content than they do in modern psychoanalysis. The weather could affect dreams, and dreams could be about personalities which were those of independent persons, and did not reflect the personality type of the dreamer. (Paracelsus, II, 1928, 1976).

Paracelsus replaced the constitutional model of Hippocrates and Galen by his own model which combined constitutional and disease features. He added two new dimensions to the old model. First, he introduced the psychological individuating principle of *archeus*. Second, he viewed the human organism as a system within a larger system of the macro-cosmos. He transcended a simple constitutional model in the direction of a general systems model. Some of his ideas such as that of the mysterious, universal force, emanating from planets and magnets were transmitted by J.B. van Helmont (1577-1644), a seventeenth century physician, to Franz Anton Mesmer (1734-1815). These ideas then gave rise to Mesmer's theory of animal magnetism. Other scholars of the Renaissance period had similar ideas. Nicholas of Cusa (1401-1464) put forward a theory, which defined the living world as constituted of a hierarchy of general systems containing lower systems and partially mirroring higher systems. This was similar to Paracelsus' idea of a micro-cosmos within a macro-cosmos.

Girolamo Cardano (1501-1576), a physician and mathematician wrote an autobiography in which he described his own emotional disorders in his childhood and in his adolescence. He rejected demonology and believed that the mentally ill were not responsible for crimes committed by them. Cardano believed that each man has a unique personality which was expressed in his physiognomy and that each man can actualize himself in a unique way.

Another scholar interested in human physiognomy was Giambattista della Porte (1538-1615), who wrote *De Humana Physiognomia*. He drew attention to the similarity between men and animals, and argued that different facial and physical characteristics might be associated with different personalities and types of behaviour. Both he and Juan Huarte (1530-1592) contributed a pioneering effort to constitutional psychology. Their ideas on individuality and on diversity in intellectual capacities and temperaments were anticipated by Aretaeus of Cappadotia, a Greek physician and a pioneer of psychiatry during the first century A.D. The contribution of Johann Weyer, another great Renaissance physician were discussed in the previous chapter.

One of the most important thinkers of the Renaissance was Juan Luis Vives (1492-1540), a friend of St. Thomas More. He wrote extensively on a variety of philosophical and social subjects. Two of his books are important for the purpose of the history of psychiatric ideas: *De Subventio Pauperum* (Support of the Poor), and *De Anima et Vita* (Soul and Life). In the first book, Vives discussed the social aspects of physical and mental diseases. He believed that poverty and stressful social conditions could lead to a physical and mental breakdown. Vives was an advocate of social welfare measures which included proper hospital facilities for the sick and a more just distribution of wealth. He believed that it was important to prevent mental illness and that the mentally ill ought to be treated in special hospitals. Kindness and understanding were considered by him to be the two most important features of the treatment of mental patients.

In his work on *The Soul and Life*, Vives left the metaphysical aspects of the human soul to the theologians, and discussed the principles of human psychology. His main interest was in empirical psychology as the study of sensation, association, and memory, not theology. Vives described human motives such as egoistic drives, appetites, active and passive love, and the various mixtures of these emotions. He realized that love is very often mixed with hatred. This foreshadowed the idea of ambivalence later developed by Sigmund Freud and Eugene Bleuler. Vives proved to be a pioneer of mental hygiene and an inaugurator of the social model of mental illness.

The experiential aspects of mental disturbance were described by Robert Burton (1577-1640), a scholar and Oxford don, but not a medical man. The famous *Anatomy of Melancholy* of 1621 (Burton,1948) has been often reprinted. Burton himself suffered from bouts of melancholia and was able to give an autobiographical account of his own experiences. His book emphasized the importance, to the unhappy individual, of confiding in a kind and understanding friend. Burton thus understood the importance of psychotherapy and a positive transference in the treatment of mental diseases.

If Renaissance science shattered the ancient conception of the universe, its renewed interest in the dignity of man continued to enrich the evolution of medical practice into the modern age. Beliefs in animal spirits were to continue to the end of the seventeenth century. Yet the great advances in biology and in microscopy in the Netherlands after 1600 were to revolutionize the understanding of the biological universe as much as Copernicus had transformed the theories of the cosmos.

5

The Scientific Revolution and the Beginnings of Modern Philosophy

The sixteenth, and to a greater extent, the seventeenth century, were periods of the rapid development of science. The ancient geocentric theory of the universe was gradually replaced by the heliocentric, even though Copernicus' work was banned. The startling new cosmography of Nicholas Copernicus (1473-1543), Tycho Brahe (1546-1601), and Johannes Kepler (1571-1630) opened the path to a modern scientific world view. The discoveries of Galileo Galilei (1564-1642) and Isaac Newton (1647-1727) laid the foundation of the new physics, with its focus on a universe ruled by the general laws of nature and its zest for the useful technology of the new mechanics. Chemistry flourished as well. The corpuscular theory had already been suggested by Galileo when he stated a belief in the different sizes of the particles of matter. Robert Boyle (1627-1691), continued the corpuscular ideas and laid the foundations of a theory of molecular structure. The work of Jean-Baptist van Helmont (1577-1644), and George Stahl (1660-1734), transformed alchemy into the science of chemistry.

New instruments such as the telescope and the microscope proved to be just as revolutionary in their impact, as the new cosmography. It was the telescope which gave Galileo his demonstrable evidence of the movement of the planets (Redondi, 1987). Anton van Leewenhock's (1632-1723) microscopic techniques opened the world of cellular biology. All of these scientific discoveries had a profound effect on the conception of man and his place in the universe and led to a new paradigm of science (Kuhn, 1962). Writers like Sir Francis Bacon (1561-1626) believed that the world was experiencing a rare and unique period of scientific advance, unknown to most cultures except for the ages of the Greeks and the Romans. It was the ancient authorities in particular whose still dominant ideas came under attack. Aristotle and his followers, the Peripatetics, had maintained the paradigm of teleogical explanation and essentialism. These were now questioned. The Aristotelian paradigm, for science based on teleological explanations and essentialism, as well as the neo-Platonic one based on ideal forms, were replaced by the new analytical paradigm of Galileo and Newton. It described the physical world in terms of independent and dependent variables related to one another by mathematical functions. It conceived the world in dynamic rather than static terms. The idea of constant change replaced that of immobility.

These developments also had a profound effect on philosophy, leading to the establishment of new criteria of knowledge and truth. Francis Bacon in *Novum Organum* (1620) laid the foundations of knowledge based on inductive thinking, observation and experiment. He opposed common sense stereotypes, or idols, whether individual (idols of the cave), or communal(idols of the tribe and of the marketplace) (Bacon, 1620). He thus became one of the founders of the tradition of British empiricism (Burtt, 1939). John Locke (1632-1704), who was both a philosopher and a physician, not only further developed empiricist philosophy, but laid down the epistemological foundations of modern science and of associationist psychology (Locke,1959).

In France, meanwhile, Rene Descartes (1595-1650) established a rational philosophy based on deductive, rather than on inductive reasoning. His *Discourse on Method* (1628) still ranks as a classic in philosophy and science. Like Bacon, he tried to offer a scientific method of inquiry based on a quest for the "clearness of ideas," and on an analysis of complex phenomena into elementary units. He concluded as a result of his meditations, that the only certainty he could infer was that he existed, and that he was a conscious, thinking being; *cogito ergo sum* (Descartes, 1628/1931).

Descartes continued the attack on Aristotle in those of his works which presented a theory of man, especially in his *Meditations*, the *The Passion of the Soul*, and the *Discourse on Method* (Descartes, 1931/1979). Aristotle's teleology and the organismic theory based on final and formal causes was abandoned. Only Aristotle's conception of antecedent, efficient causes was retained. The physical world was to be analyzed into elementary events and the observed complexities were reduced to a concatenation of these elementary events. Cartesian metaphysics separated two substances, that of mind (*res cogitans*), and that of matter (*res extensa*), as absolutely different, thus laying the foundations for the assumption of a mind-body dualism which profoundly influenced the subsequent development of biology, medicine, psychology, and psychiatry (Reeves,1958; Lovejoy,1955).

Descartes proposed a machine theory of human and animal organisms. The workings of human and animal bodies was explained in mechanistic terms. These were based on the same principles as those applied to explain the workings of man-made, hydraulically powered, mechanical figures in royal and public gardens.

The only difference between men and animals was that the bodies of men were in contact with, and were controlled through the medium of the pineal gland by the conscious soul, the witness of its own existence. Descartes believed that the human body was machine-like, with a ghostly homunculus having no location in space, but miraculously using the pineal gland as a rudder to steer the machine and to receive sensory information. For Descartes, animals were just machine-like without a "ghost", a consciousness or a mind.

As far as the theory of soul or mind was concerned, Cartesianism marked a radical departure from the Aristotelian idea of holism which had been so dominant in an attenuated form in the teachings of St. Thomas Aquinas throughout the Middle Ages. It represented a return to Pythagorean-Platonic ideas of the soul, viewed as an entity separate from the body. In his description of the body mechanisms, Descartes anticipated the theory of the reflex, even if he retained the ancient view that the muscles contracted because of the intervention of animal spirits. The theory was given a modern form and was developed further by physiologists at the end of the seventeenth and throughout the eighteenth centuries. The reflex theory adumbrated Pavlov's reflexology and the S-R (stimulus-response) behaviourism of the twentieth century (Weckowicz & Liebel-Weckowicz, 1982).

While psychology and psychiatry in English and French speaking countries were influenced by the rationalism of Descartes and his followers, as well as by the empiricism of Locke, Berkeley, and Hume, the paramount influence in the German speaking countries was the philosophy of Gottfried Wilhelm Leibniz (1646-1716). The son of a Saxon law professor in Leipzig, he studied both law and mathematics and was at first active as a diplomat in the service of the Elector Archbishop of Mainz who sent him to Paris in 1672. He met the great scientists of the age and travelled widely, even to England to visit Newton, to the Netherlands to meet Spinoza. After he became the general science adviser, librarian, and mining specialist to the Duke of

Hanover in 1673, his influence spread. He was later active in encouraging the foundation of royal science societies modeled after the French and English ones, in 1700 in Berlin (where the queen was a Hanoverian princess), and in Vienna in 1714 (Kiefl, 1913; Totok & Haase,1966). His views defy an attempt at a brief presentation, and only some aspects of his philosophy will be mentioned here. While Rene Descartes put forward the theory of interactionist dualism, as the explanation of the body-mind relationships, Leibniz' theory was that of parallelism and of pre-established harmony. He believed that mind, a mental substance, and the body, a physical substance, could not interact directly. Their activities were autonomous. However, these activities were synchronized by a "pre-established harmony." The basic unit of the universe was a windowless monad. Each monad was a potential psyche, striving to attain a maximum clarity of consciousness. The monads were also part of the plenitude of the universe, ranking from the lowest to the highest forms of life in a God-given order (Lovejoy, 1936, 1964).

Monads represented an entelechy, a primitive, active force which was tied indisolubly to primitive, passive forces. They were atoms of nature, perhaps not as discrete as in Greek thought, yet simple substances and mirrors of the universe. The created monad had perception, however, and appetition. Different laws influenced body and soul, and the soul remained indestructible existing according to a pre-established harmony which fitted it to the body and which existed among all substances of the universe. The monad that attained the highest level of consciousness in an aggregate of monads became a vital force (*vis viva*), which organized the aggregate of monads into an organism and became its psyche. While mental monads were striving to attain the clarity of consciousness, their physical counterparts were also characterized by dynamic properties (Leibniz, 1973; Frankfurt, 1972).

In contra-distinction to Locke and Descartes, Leibniz believed that the essential (primary) properties of matter were not extension and form, but activity (effort). Matter was not inert, but was endowed with a driving force. It was endowed with "conatus," a motive force which corresponded to will in human minds. The motive force was not blind, but had the intended goal of trying to attain perfection.

Leibniz did not agree with Locke's empiricist doctrine of "tabula rasa," or blank-mind. According to this belief, all the contents and the apparatus of the mind originated entirely in the perception of material reality. Leibniz was a strong critic of John Locke's *Essay on Human*

Understanding (1700/ 1959), in which Locke argued that there was nothing in the intellect which had not been before in the senses. In his own *New Essays* , Leibniz replied that there was nothing in the intellect except the intellect itself (Leibniz, 1765/1949). The Leibnizian concept of man was quite the opposite of the Lockean. It envisaged man as a creative, striving agent rather than a passive one, only reacting to and reflecting his environment.

The Leibnizian ideas were popularized in eighteenth century Germany by Christian Wolff (1679-1754), a professor at the university of Halle. Wolff tried to reconcile the Leibnizian philosophy of dynamic monads with Cartesian rationalism and with Aristotlian metaphysics. His purpose was to create a new system of rationalist philosophy which included a theory of two mental faculties: those of cognition and of conation. The components of the faculty of conation were (1) the will, as well as (2) feelings of pleasure and pain. Wolff's empirical and rational psychologies became very influential in Germany. They were scorned by the Prussian soldier king, Frederick William I, but his more famous son, Frederick the Great made them part of the Berlin enlightenment. Immanuel Kant's philosophy teacher at Koenigsberg, Martin Kuntzen, was a Wolffian. Consequently, Kant was quite early exposed to the ideas of Leibniz and of Wolff. Voltaire mocked them in his famous novel, *Candide*, written after a stay in Prussia. The Leibnizian idea behind the Wolffian optimistic philosophy, that this is the best of all possible worlds, was especially questioned because of the direct evidence of misfortune and misery in the real world.

The Leibnizian influence in the German world may also be detected in the writings of the Philosophers of Nature (*Naturphilosophen*), of the early nineteenth century. Their contemporaries, the *Psychiker*, psychiatrists, were influenced by Leibnizian philosophy. So were the psychodynamic psychiatric theories of the twentieth century. It may be detected in the transcendental philosophy of Kant, and of German idealist philosophy.

The seventeenth century scientific and philosophical revolution had a far-reaching effect on contemporary physiology and medicine. The humoral theory of Hippocrates and Galen was finally abandoned. This occurred gradually. In 1628, William Harvey (1578-1657) published *De Motu Cordis* (On the Motion of the Heart), in which he disproved Galen's by then quite hoary theory of blood circulation. Harvey based his theory on the principles of the pump and hydro-dynamics, and these were consistent with the new physics. In his *De Generatione Animalium* (On the Origin of Animals), published in 1651, Harvey opposed the then dominant theory of preformism, which held that the organs were already in the sperm at the time of conception. They only grew in size. He substituted for it, the theory of *epigenesis* which held that the embryo developed gradually. Francesco Redi (1626-1697) disproved the spontaneous life generation theory. He showed that a life can come only from another life.

Robert Boyle, the pioneer of chemistry, discovered by his experiments that animals used not the whole air in respiration, but only a particular component of it. Robert Hook (1636-1703) cast further light on the physiology of respiration when he demonstrated that an animal with a paralyzed thorax can be kept alive by blowing air into the lungs by bellows. Marcello Malpighi (1628-1694) discovered capillary circulation. Jean-Baptiste van Helmont (1577-1644), a follower of Paracelsus, did pioneering work in chemistry and in animal digestion. He showed that digestion was due to a series of fermentations and was an essential process of life. Van Helmont placed the Paracelsian *archeus* in the pylorus of the stomach. He developed Paracelsus' theories about astral influences further, and also suggested a theory of animal magnetism. According to this theory, "magnetic fluids" emanated from men and animals. These could be concentrated by magnets. They could also be guided by the wills of men in order to influence the minds and bodies of others. The theory of animal magnetism was taken up, more than one hundred years later. It was developed further by Franz Anton Mesmer at the end of the eighteenth century. Sanctorius of Padua (1561-1636) was interested in the heat produced by an organism and was able to measure body temperature with a thermometer. These applications of the new physics and the new chemistry to human physiology influenced medical theory.

The humoral theory was abandoned and replaced by the iatero-mechanical and iatero-chemical theories. The iatero-mechanical theorists came to perceive the human body as a system of mechanical levers or hydraulic pumps. They sought to base medical theory and practice on Newtonian mechanics and on the Cartesian conception of the human body as a machine. A prominent iatero-mechanist was Giovani Borelli (1608-1679), who explained the functioning of the muscles by the mechanics of pulleys and levers. Friedrich Hoffman (1660-1742), also belonged to this school. He regarded the body as a hydraulic machine and hypothesized that a fluid circulated in the hollow nerve tubes. Another iateromechanist was Giorigio Boglivi (1668-1706), a professor of medical theory in the Collegio della Sapienza in Rome. Boglivi combined the iatero-mechanical theory of the bodily functions with Cartesian dualism. This philosophical doctrine assumed a body-mind interactionism. The body could influence the mind and the mind, the body. In his *De Praxis Medica* (Medical Practice), Boglivi discussed the malfunctioning of the body caused by emotional disturbances. The "passions of the mind," could cause hysteria and somatic disorders. Boglivi may be considered a pioneer of psychosomatic medicine.

Other contemporary physicians tended to attribute hysteria to somatic causes. Some advanced beyond the idea of the ancients, that the locus of pathology was in the uterus, and placed it in the brain. Thus Charles Lepois (1563-1633), otherwise known as Carolus Piso, believed that hysteria was a disease of the brain. He also described postpartum psychosis. Thomas Willis (1622-1675), the great neuro-anatomist who described the *circus Willisi*, was a member of the iatero-chemical school. He believed that mental disorders, including hysteria, were caused by pathological agents located in the brain. Willis did admit that some mental diseases could be caused by demoniacal possession. The pathological mechanisms which caused mental illness, were, according to Willis, "explosions" of the animal spirits, which blocked nerve juices. Another mechanism which caused such illnesses, was the excessive acidity of nerve juices, and their effervescence in different parts of the brain. Hysteria resulted from explosions of animal spirits which blocked the nerves leaving the brain. Epilepsy was caused by other explosions of animal spirits in the midbrain. Mania was the result of acidity of the nerve juices.

The great clinician of English medicine, called the "English Hippocrates, Thomas Sydenham (1624-1689), also placed the locus of the pathology of hysteria in the brain, and attributed it to a disorder of animal spirits. Hysteria was caused by an imbalance between the mind and the body. However, he believed that hysteria was always accompanied by emotional disturbances and that the male equivalent of hysteria was hypochondria.

The iatero-chemical theory of medicine considered the human body to be a chemical laboratory where various juices were mixed and produced chemical reactions. In addition to Van Helmont and Willis, an important iatero-chemist was Francois de la Boe (1614-1672), known as Sylvius (not to be confused with another Sylvius, a sixteenth century anatomist and Vasalius' teacher). De la Boe classified diseases into two categories: those due to "acidosis" and those due to "alkalosis."

In the seventeenth century, the focus had shifted from the patient to the disease. To use the expression of Henry Sigerist (1951), the pendulum had swung away from the "ontology" of the patient to that of disease. The constitutional model of Galen and Hippocrates was replaced by the disease model. There were several reasons for this.

First, there were epidemics which suggested the possibility of contagion. Already Girolamo Fracastoro (Fracastorius) of Verona (1484-1553), wrote a famous poem about syphilis. He postulated that epidemic diseases were caused by minute germs which passed from one person to another. He recognized that smallpox, measles, bubonic plague, phtisis and syphilis were contagious diseases. Fracastorius was also interested in psychiatry, and described such mental ailments as melancholia and anxiety. He made suggestions about methods of suicide prevention.

More than a century after Fracastro, the Jesuit father, Athanasius Kirchner (1602-1680) claimed to have found microscopic worms in the blood of patients suffering from infectious diseases. However, the link between bacteria and infectious disease was not definitely established until the middle of the nineteenth century.

Secondly, the more analytical attitude of the clinicians tended to isolate the symptoms of diseases from the total patient and to treat them as entities in themselves. Thirdly, there was a growing interest in morbid anatomy. The bodies of dead patients were dissected, the diseased organs were examined, and the pathology of the organs was linked with the symptoms of the patients. Theophile Bonet of Geneva (1620-1689) compiled all the existing knowledge of pathological anatomy in his work *Sepulchretum*.

Thomas Sydenham attempted to classify all diseases as if they were species of plants. He stressed the importance of nosology in his work on *Medical Observations Concerning the History and Cure of Acute Diseases* (Sydenham, 1848). This affirmed the ontology of diseases as real entities. Each disease was an entity with its own natural history and its own essential features. He believed that each disease should be treated by the specific remedy for it. Thus Sydenham came out firmly on the side of the disease model and against the constitutional model.

Sydenham was mainly concerned with description and classification of fevers. However, he also wrote on gout, chorea, and hysteria. He believed that half of the patients who did not suffer from fevers suffered from hysteria. Thus Sydenham may be regarded as a pioneer investigator of psychoneurosis.

Felix Plater, who was discussed in chapter three, and Thomas Willis offered a tentative classification of mental diseases. The former divided mental patients into idiots, morons, cretins, mutes and melancholics. Willis classified these as melancholics, maniacs, idiots, and apoplectics. Both attributed mental illness to brain pathology. It is true that the causal factors of disease which were suggested, were not extrinsic, but intrinsic.

Seventeenth century physicians viewed diseases as disorders of animal spirits. These hypothetical substances were responsible for the functioning of the organs. Yet Sydenham put forward a theory of "epidemic constitution," a Hippocratic concept. This was to explain why only certain people contracted fevers. His emphasis, however, was on the disease entities which were associated with pathological changes localised in certain organs. It was thus that the disease model returned to medicine in the seventeenth century. This model had first emerged in Egyptian medicine and been adopted by Greek physicians of the Cnidian School. It then became firmly established in medical thinking and this led to a quest for essences underlying the manifest symptoms of disease. The new medicine had a preoccupation with classification systems as well. Nosology and nosography became important medical enterprises.

An important pioneer of legal psychiatry was Paolo Zacchia (1584-1659), the court physician of Pope Innocent X. He was mentioned previously in connection with the theory of demonology. In his *Questiones Medico-Legales* he addressed himself to the legal aspects of insanity. He distinguished three kinds of mental disorders: (1) *fatuitas* or personality disorder; (2)*insania*, or psychosis; (3) *phrenitis* or mental disorder due to organic cause. He insisted that only a physician can judge the mental state of an individual. He also proposed certain rules in regard to the legal responsibility of persons suffering from mental disorders which affected their competence to marry and to enter contractual obligations.

In addition to the emerging disease model of mental illness, the seventeenth century also saw a contribution from moral philosophy which anticipated the psychological model. Benedict (Baruch) Spinoza (1632-1677)' dealt with the psychotherapeutic implications of his ethical theory (Bernard, 1978). In part five of his *Ethics* (Spinoza, 1910), entitled "The Power of the Intellect," Spinoza stressed its role in transforming isolated, destructive, "passions" into constructive, intellect controlled "actions." Such transformations were achieved by an insight into the supreme law of logical necessity. Under the *sub quadam aeternitatis specie*, logic governed human behaviour and external events. The surrender to this necessity, and the understanding of the real nature of one's passions led to serene acceptance of one's fate. It further led to self-perfection, self-actualization, and self-fulfillment. Spinoza's prescription for mental health very much coincided with that of Stoic philosophy. His contribution may be regarded as an early version of the cognitive model of mental illness. It could also have influenced the views of Sigmund Freud on this point. (Bernard, 1946).

By the end of the seventeenth century, then, as the idea of animal spirits and the belief in witchcraft was gradually abandoned, the world was ready for the birth of the modern era. As the age of the enlightenment dawned, social attitudes towards the mentally ill were to change, and a natural science approach to the understanding of mental disease was to emerge.

6

The Eighteenth Century: The Age of Enlightenment and Reason

The preoccupation with disease entities and their classification became even more prominent in the eighteenth century, than it was in the seventeenth century. This was a century in which medical science focused on developing a classificatory scheme for diseases, nosography and nosology. More prominent than ever,was the interest in classification. Sydenham classified diseases according to their symptoms. His suggestion that diseases ought to be classified in the way of botanical and animal species was carried out by Carl von Linne (Linnaeus) (1707-1778), the great botanical taxonomist. Linnaeus, who was also a physician, treated diseases as plant species. His classificatory scheme grouped them in genera, families, and orders.

François Boissier de Sauvages (1706-1767) offered an even more complex classificatory system. In his *Nosologie Methodique* (Systematical Nosology), he distinguished twenty four hundred diseases which he divided into ten classes, each further sub-divided into several orders and genera. The whole eighth class and the order five in the sixth class were devoted to the classification of mental diseases. De Sauvages followed some of the classification system for mental illness already worked out by Linnaeus.

Both identified a condition of love-sickness accompanied by excessive day-dreaming as a form of mental ailment. Linnaeus also considered *vesania* as a form of quiet insanity, possibly schizophrenia. Both he and de Sauvages identified a type of insanity as mania. A third category was that of mind mood sicknesses (*Gemuetskrankheiten*) accompanied by an inability to form judgments, as defined by Linnaeus. In de Sauvages' system this type was categorized as a deliria. The latter also identified a kind of melancholia without feeling, as a partial psychosis. (Leibbrand & Wettley, 1961).

Boissier de Sauvages was a professor of medicine at the University of Montpellier in France. That university came under the influence of the vitalist theory of the German, Georg Ernst Stahl. His kind of vitalism tended to hypostatize and concretize the concept of disease. The other important vitalists at Montpellier were Theophile Bordeu, whose work anticipated the science of endocrinology, and Philippe Pinel.

The great Philippe Pinel (1745-1825) was the founder of the modern reform in psychiatric hospitals. This was the "moral treatment" movement in the treatment of the mentally ill. It had arisen out of the humanitarian ideology of the French enlightenment and from Pinel's personal study of ancient medical practices, especially of Asclepiades and others, who had advocated a kindly treatment of the mentally ill. The fervor for reform in all sectors of social life has remained one of the leading characteristics of the French Revolution. It is in part Pinel's acquaintance with some of the political leaders of the new government which brought him to Paris to direct the Bicetre mental institution for men in 1792. It was here that he proposed a daring experiment. He would remove all restraints from fifty-three allegedly dangerous patients. The date, August 25, 1793, when he removed the chains from these men, has become famous. Pinel's work was amazingly successful. His patients all calmed down and one became his faithful servant.

In 1795, Pinel also became director of the mental institution for females in Paris, Salpêtrière. Here he repeated his success by removing the chains from the female patients. The effectiveness of his new "moral treatment" policy was described in his work of 1801, *Medico-philosophical treatise on mania*. (English translation, 1806). With its appearance, the moral treatment movement, or moral management as it was called in English countries, soon became wide-spread throughout the western world (Deutsch, 1960).

Pinel established the foundations for a modern classification of mental disorders. This made possible, the more scientific researches of the nineteenth and twentieth centuries. The confused notion of madness was more thoroughly analyzed, and a new classificatory scheme of mental disease was offered in his *Nosographie Philosophique* (Philosophical Nosography), published in 1798 and 1813. Pinel described their essential characteristics, and divided mental diseases into : mania, melancholia, dementia, and idiocy.

Pinel's work marks the transition to a more modern system of classification. However, the work of many eighteenth century writers provided the foundation for the new schemes of classification. These in turn made a better form of treatment possible. During the earlier part of the century there was a special enthusiasm for creating nosological systems and for numbering types of diseases. A better kind of anatomical study and progress in the development of physiology, also made better systems of nosology possible. Thus, Giovanni Battista Morgagni (1682-1771) wrote a monumental book *On the Sites and Causes of Diseases* (1761) (Ackerknecht, 1968) in which he systematically discussed the pathological anatomy of various diseases, classifying them according to the location of their pathology in the human body. Diseases were also "caused" by the material they produced.

The iateromechanists and iaterochemists of the seventeenth and early eighteenth century, believed that mental diseases were organic in nature and were due to pathological changes localized in the brain. In the therapy of both physical and mental diseases they abandoned the conservative attitude of the Hippocratic physician. Like the Methodists of ancient Rome,they had recourse to heroic methods of treatment such as purging, cupping, and bloodletting. After Harvey's discovery of blood circulation (1628), they even attempted to transfuse blood from young animals into their patients in order to infuse them with animal spirits, and in so doing, to increase their vitality. Drastic measures, such as chaining, flogging and frightening were advocated in the treatment of mental illness. The patients were to be shaken out of their morbid preoccupations and restored to sanity. Such methods continued to be popular even after the iateromechanical and iaterochemical theories had been abandoned.

Michel Foucault has argued that the eighteenth century marked a transition to the modern concern with confining the mentally ill. This was what he called the "classical period" in the emergence of modern ideas of insanity. Disease entities were isolated and paired in "couplets." Thus "mania and melancholia" had been known before, but "hysteria and hypochondria" were twinned as well. In addition, Foucault believed that the break with the traditional belief in demonic possession, occurred by 1700. In ancient times the mad had seemed to be in touch with another world, but now madness was viewed as "non-being." (Foucault,1965/1973). This appears to be something of a misconception, for psychiatrists like Pierre Janet (1921) have argued that a lunatic is often regarded as a separate being, but not that he does not exist at all. Janet also listed the separate types of mental illness, but certainly did not maintain a narrow conception of pairing. Although Foucault acknowledged that mental asylums were opened to scientific medicine, he viewed such hospitals as having personalities, even as having a religious domain. They were not centers of research into the nature of organically caused diseases.

In England, Thomas Sydenham proved to be one of the few exceptions from the prevalent practices. In his treatment of patients, he adopted a conservative attitude, hoping, in keeping with the tradition of the Hippocratic physician, that *vis medicatrix naturae* (the healing forces of nature) would bring about the cure. The iateromechanical and iaterochemical systems turned out to be blind alleys in the development of medicine. The human organism was not a machine working on the principle of levers and pulleys, and although it could be regarded as a complex chemical system, the knowledge of chemistry in the seventeenth century was too rudimentary to be applicable to medicine. The application of science to clinical problems was premature. A reaction set in, with some physicians, like Sydenham, eschewing speculations and taking a purely empirical approach to medicine, and with others abandoning the mechanistic model of the human body, and replacing it by a vitalistic one, based on the unique properties of living matter.

The anti-mechanistic reaction was abated by the monistic philosophy of Baruch Spinoza (1632-1677) and the monadic philosophy of Gottfried Leibniz (1646-1716). The Leibnizian-Wolffian philosophy had become particularly influential in German speaking countries. It offered alternative metaphysical presuppositions about man to those of Cartesian dualism, and to those of British empiricism. According to Leibniz, the conscious or potentially conscious monads, provided the foundation of nature as they were striving to become fully conscious. Consequently, Leibniz equated Being with activity and consciousness. The boundary separating the mind from the body ceased to be important. This type of philosophy was conducive to vitalistic theories in biology and medicine. Such theories assumed the existence of vital, striving forces expressing themselves in physiological and psychological functions.

Francis Glisson (1597-1677) put forward a theory that irritability was a special property of living matter. This was the starting point of the vitalistic reaction which set in against mechanistic theories in medicine. The vitalists maintained that life phenomena could not be explained in terms of physics and chemistry. Some iaterochemists, for instance, J.B. van Helmont, used vitalistic as well as chemical concepts in their theorizing. This was in spite of their interest in chemistry.

The most important vitalist was Georg Ernst Stahl (1660-1734) of the university of Halle in Germany. In his *Theoria Medica Vera* (1708/1737) (True Medical Theory) he postulated the existence of a vital force which he called "soul." The vital force or *anima* lay behind all life phenomena. It prevented a disintegration of living matter, it was the driving force propelling the growth of organisms, and was at the root of instincts and emotions. Stahl was a pioneer of psychosomatic medicine. He believed that emotions could affect bodily functions and could even produce physical disease. Stahl also believed that dreams could reflect disordered bodily functions. They reflected the mental health of the individual and its impairment. This occurred when the life force (the "soul") was impeded or repressed.

He was interested in mental diseases and thought that they occurred when the vital force was impeded in its functioning. Stahl was not a mystic. He was quite scientific in his outlook, being one of the leading chemists of his time, and the inventor of the widely accepted phlogiston theory of combustion. He had a significant following, and vitalism became very influential in the eighteenth century.

Stahl's psychodynamic and psychosomatic theories captured the imagination of the *Psychiker* early nineteenth century German psychiatrists. One of them, K.W. Ideler, translated *Theoria Medica Vera* into German in 1831. Caspar Friedrich Wolff's (1733-1794) theory of epigenesis had postulated that the development, growth, and differentiation of an organism was controlled by vital forces. An important vitalist was Francois Boissier de Sauvages, known for his work on the classification of diseases (nosology). Although he believed that the vital force was responsible for all life phenomena, he also believed that all mental diseases were caused by anatomical lesions of the brain. Another important vitalist and a pioneer of psychosomatic medicine was Clement Joseph Tissot (1750-1826). He made excessive claims for the effect of the emotions on the body. The laughter produced by tickling children could, he claimed, cure children suffering from rickets. Such extravagant claims tended to discredit vitalism.

The vitalist theory became especially influential at the University of Montpellier where two important vitalists, Theophile de Bordeu and Paul Joseph Borthez were members of the faculty. Theophile Bordeu (1722-1776) believed that organs of the body secreted substances into the blood stream which influenced the functions of the whole organism. Thus it may be said that he anticipated modern endocrinology. Philippe

Pinel, the great humanitarian reformer of psychiatric treatment, studied medicine at that university and was influenced by vitalistic theories. This influence was responsible for the distinction he subsequently drew between the mental disease due to organic causes, and the functional mental diseases due to psychological causes. He believed that the latter disease did not respond to physical but to moral treatment. In the theorizing of many physiologists and physicians of the eighteenth century, the idea of vital forces became devoid of its psychological connotations. It became a type of physical energy, like electricity, which was unique for living matter. This represented a retreat from vitalism to physicalism.

The eighteenth century physiologists experimented with nerve and muscle preparations. The most important physiologist of that century, was Albrecht von Haller (1708-1777), who developed a theory of sensibility of the nerve fibers and the irritability of the muscle fiber. Robert Whytt (1714-1766) investigated the physiology of the nerve reflexes in 1763. This mechanism had already been anticipated in the writings of Descartes. Other scientists who investigated nerve reflexes were J. Astruc, who in 1736 coined the word "reflex," and Johann Unzer (1727-1799), a student of Haller and George Prochaska (1749-1820). In 1767 Whytt (1765) proposed a theory of hysteria. He believed, as his many contemporaries did, that the locus of the pathology of hysteria was in the uterus. However, the diseased uterus could affect the brain by "sympathy." This was a revival of the ancient notion of Galen that pathology in one organ affect the functioning of another by "sympathy" or consensus. The "sympathy" theory of hysteria became very popular, it soon spread to the continent and attempted to reconcile the uterine and cerebral theories of hysteria. At the beginning of the nineteenth century the "sympathy" theory was replaced by the reflex theory. The popularity of the second theory was brought about by the work of Prochaska and later of Marshall Hall (1790-1857) on reflexes. According to the reflex theory of hysteria, the brain and the spinal cord were affected by a diseased uterus. This came about because of a reflex of the nervous system (Shorter, 1985).

In the eighteenth century, in contrast to the seventeenth, medical research centered in the universities.There were three prominent centers of medical learning at the universities of Leyden, Edinburgh, and Vienna. The one at Leyden in the Netherlands, functioned under the leadership of a great clinical teacher, Hermann Boerhaave (1668-

1738), an iateromechanist. A student of Boerhaave, Alexander Monro (1697-1767), provided the stimulus at Edinburgh in Scotland. Another student of Boerhaave, Gerard van Swieten (1700-1772), the personal physician of the Empress Maria Theresa and later an influence in Russia as well, provided the leadership in Vienna. Van Swieten reorganized medical education and introduced the use of hospital training and observation, laboratory work in chemistry, and produced numerous successful students. Among them, George Prochaska pioneered the new understanding of nerve reflexes. In a 1755 memorandum to the Empress Maria Theresa, and as a social reformer, Swieten combatted superstitious beliefs such as the *Magia posthuma* (belief in vampires) which existed in places like Siebenbuergen, Banat, and Croatia. He also played a major role in securing the abolition of witchcraft trials and of torture (Lesky, 1979).

The enlightenment had a most profound influence on medical practices in Scotland. Edinburgh in particular became an important center for the study of neurology and nervous diseases. The Scottish enlightenment of the eighteenth century undoubtedly ranks with the French and the English ones which preceded it. The importance of Edinburgh University, deemed foremost in the world in science in 1789 by Thomas Jefferson, cannot be emphasized enough. Many contemporary students of the intellectual renaissance in Scotland have (1980) focused solely on the unique interest it showed in human social behavior. Sher (1985) has pointed out, that the developments in literary criticism, poetry, drama, science, and medicine also belong to it, and that these must not be overlooked. Further, the Scottish enlightenment did not decline at all, and its impulse carried over into the nineteenth century, particularly in the development of medicine and psychology. William Cullen (1712-1790), an Edinburgh physician, was one of the leaders of the enlightenment, and was identified with its moderate wing at the University of Edinburgh which in 1766 brought him into the chair of medicine. Edinburgh had become an important center for the study of neurology and nervous diseases, and was known for the researches of Robert Whytt who investigated reflexes and developed a theory of hysteria.

Cullen applied new neurological concepts to clinical medicine and neurology during the 1770s (Cullen, 1769). He finally rejected Stahl's concept of "soul" or vital force, and substituted for it the concept of nerve energy which was conceived in physicalistic terms, that is, it was a kind of electricity and no longer a "soul." The nervous system regulated other organs. Thus the vicissitudes of this nerve energy were responsible for all diseases - the physical, the nervous and the mental. These were due to an excessive or insufficient tension of the nerve energy affecting the total organism or individual organs. Cullen introduced the term "neurosis" to denote diseases caused by disturbances of nerve energy. He classified all diseases into these categories: fevers, cathexis, local disorders and neuroses. He further subdivided neuroses into: comata, adynamias (collapse), spasms and vesanias (insanity) (Cullen, 1792). Hysteria was categorized as a spasmodic condition which occurred predominantly in females. Thus, according to Cullen, mental illness was caused by an organic pathology of the nervous system. He also rejected the conservative Hippocratic approach to therapy, and advocated active intervention and heroic methods of treatment such as massive bleedings and purgatives. Cullen's views on therapy influenced psychiatric treatment in those days. Such methods as physical restraint, revolving chairs and ducking of unsuspecting patients into cold water, became popular.

Benjamin Rush (1745-1813), the American pioneer of psychiatry, studied at Edinburgh and was influenced by Cullen's ideas. He later became a signatory of the American Declaration of Independence (1776) and a leader in the development of hospital treatment of the insane at the Pennsylvania Hospital in Philadelphia. Rush believed that the "trinity" of psychiatric therapeutic remedies were "emetics, purgatives and bloodletting" (Zilboorg, 1941; Deutsch,1949,1960). He too used ducking into cold water as a treatment, and revolving chairs (Rush, 1972, 1981).

John Brown (1735-1788), still another member of the Edinburgh school and a student of Cullen, reduced all diseases to two basic states: the state of excessive tension or sthenia,and the state of deficient tension or asthenia (Brown,1780). Sthenia resulted from an excessive stimulation and an excessive tension of nerve energy, was to be treated by sedatives. Asthenia, due to lack of stimulation and a low level of nerve energy, was to be treated by stimulants or tonics. Because of its simnplicity, Brown's system of medicine was widely adopted at the end of the eighteenth and the beginning of the nineteenth century. The idea that the tonus of the nervous system could vary, caused a nineteenth century American physician, George Miller Beard (1839-1883) to reaffirm the existence of nervous energy. He described a clinical syndrome "neurasthenia," which he attributed to depletion of nervous energy. It was a state chracterized by low tension and exhaustion of the nervous system. This was manifested by chronic fatigue. Beard was also a pioneer of psychosomatic medicine; he maintained that many physical diseases were due to emotional causes. At the same time, the great American neurologist Silas Weir Mitchell (1829-1914), proposed "rest treatment" for neurasthenia and other neurotic conditions. Such ideas represented a retreat from both Hippocratic empiricism and Stahl's vitalism into an iateromechanistic way of thinking. Brown's system was reminiscent of the medical system of the Methodists of ancient Rome. It was they who also had a simple schema of causative agents and remedies, it was they who encouraged drastic methods of treatment. As far as the causation of mental illness was concerned, Brown's system offered an explanation in organic and mechanistic terms.

Iatermechanistic methods, at times quite brutal, were common in mental hospitals of the period. In addition to the generous use of emetics, purgatives and blood letting, cold shower baths were the standard treatment. Forty or fifty buckets of water were often poured on a patient. Maximilian Jacobi (1775-1858), a *Somatiker* psychiatrist of the early nineteenth century, reported on several occasions that up to three hundred buckets of cold water were dashed on the heads of patients (Kraepelin, 1962).

It was believed that a generous use of cold water would cool heads made feverish by blood congestion. A cold douche was supposed to make an obstreperous patient docile and orderly. It resorted speech to mute patients, awakened self-consciousness in motionless melancholics and disrupted their brooding. At times a powerful jet of cold water tore the skin and caused bleeding. Mason Cox (1762-1822), a British alienist, was responsible for the introduction of revolving machines and swings. The idea for this originated with Erasmus Darwin, the grandfather of Charles Darwin. The patient was strapped to a revolving chair and subjected to rapid rotations. A variant of the method was a revolving bed to which the patient was tied with his head pointing outward and subjected to rapid rotations. The centrifugal force pushed the blood to the brain, causing the feeling of suffocation, nausea, acute vertigo, vomiting, urination and defecation. The patients became panic stricken. Such contrivances were used for the treatment of delirious and melancholic patients in order to shake them out of their morbid mental state. The revolving machines were dreaded by patients who regarded them as instruments of torture.

The rationale for these methods of treatment was the belief of the alienists, that insanity was caused by abnormalities of blood circulation in the brain. This idea shows the significance of Harvey's discovery as well as the influence of the iateromechanical tradition of seventeenth century medicine. Physicians like Paracelsus had reflected the more ancient idea that the conduits to the brain had to be blocked to prevent the disturbing material from reaching it, for example, in epilepsy. That abnormalities of blood circulation in the brain might be among the causes of insanity, continued as a belief among the *Somatiker* psychiatrists early in the nineteenth century, and later, amongst the members of the neurological school in Germany.

The forms of treatment which emerged as a result of these beliefs combined some traditional practices with new ones. Skin irritants such as mustard plasters were applied to the skin of the neck and of the head to draw blood away from the brain and to relieve its congestions. Blood letting, the application of leeches and cups served the same purpose. Emetics and purgatives were believed not only to cleanse the body of harmful substances but also to "convulse" bodily organs, to stimulate the nerves in the abdominal region, and to calm the brain "antagonistically," by inducing vomiting. According to Kraepelin (1962), the medical armamentorium of a mid-nineteenth century German alienist, Schneider, included thirty-four kinds of emetics and fifty-four purgatives. The "nausea treatment" was used widely to control the unruly and riotous behaviour of excited patients.

That the eighteenth century had a great interest in mental diseases is attested by a great number of treatises which were written on the subject. The book by George Cheyne (1671-1743), *The English Malady, or a Treatise on Nervous Disease of all Kinds, as Spleen, Vapours, Lowness of Spirits, Hypochonriacal and Hysterical Distempers* (1733), may serve as an early example. Cheyne rejected the theory of demoniacal possession as an explanation of mental illness in favour of a theory of physical causation which was both organismic and environmental. He advocated a strict dietary regime as the cure (Cheyne, 1740). (Cheyne himself suffered from obesity). He also believed that the incidence of mental diseases was increasing and was due to the unhealthy conditions of life prevailing at that time in England. Cheyne was thus concerned, not only with the sick individual, but also with social and environmental conditions as possible causative factors of mental illness.

The idea that the complexity and stress associated with life in a highly civilized society, led to madness and corruption became quite popular. Jean-Jacques Rousseau (1712-1778) believed that civilization corrupted mankind and glorified the "noble savage." Immanuel Kant (1724-1804) believed that mental illness was a domain of philosophy and not of medicine. His *Anthropologie* (1789) discussed mental diseases and offered a classification schema. Kant believed that those mental diseases which were not organic, were caused by excessive demands made on man by his society. He believed that primitive man was relatively free from mental illness. These ideas are quite interesting because they indicate that, in addition to the medical organic model of mental illness, a socio-cultural model was already in existence.

Kant's theory of mental illness discussed the psychological factors as well as the socio-cultural aspects of such diseases. The framework for Kant's psychologicaal theory of mental illness was provided by Christian Wolff's faculty psychology. Wolff's theories influenced Kant's views on what philosophy was and how philosophical foundations had to support any classification of either normal or aberrant mental behaviour. Wolff had conceived of philosophy as the study of mental faculties or powers. These were abilities or *Vermoegen* of the human mind. They included cognition, the ability to know, and conation, the ability to exercise will.

Kant's interest in the human abilities to know (*Erkenntnis*) led to his renown critiques: (1) *The Critique of Pure Reason* (Kant, 1781/ 1966); (2) *The Critique of Practical Reason* (Kant, 1788/ 1949); (3) *The Critique of Judgment* (Kant, 1790/ 1949). These provided a reply to David Hume's scepticism about the possibility of human knowledge. It laid the foundation for the German transcendentalist tradition in its empirio-critical and idealist forms. The critiques of practical reason and judgment were concerned with practical knowledge and with empirical psychology, or as Kant called it,"anthropology."

Kant's interest in abnormal psychology was aroused by the claims made by the Swedish mystic, Emanuel Swedenborg (1688-1772), that he could communicate with the world of spirits. Swedenborg, who was trained as a philosopher, anticipated many of the ideas which were developed later, in the beginning of the nineteenth century by the German Philosophers of Nature. Among other things, he was concerned with the development of the finite world out of the eternal infinite world. According to him, the ideal mathematical point formed the connection between the two worlds. At this point, a motion originated which was built up into the Cartesian vortices. This was not a mechanical motion, rather a kind of Leibnizian conatus, a drive, which corresponded to the will in human minds. From this creative drive originated the great chain of being.

Swedenborg believed that the Cartesian spiritous fluid served as the means of communication between soul and body. It was also the formative force (*vis formatrix*) of the body. Swedenborg believed in the neo-Platonist conception of the world soul, a creative intellect from which the material world had emanated. According to him the human mind was composed of three parts: the soul (*anima*), reason (*mens mentalis*), and of the vegetative soul (*animus*). This was also in keeping with the traditional Aristotelian views continued by Aquinas and the medieval scholastics. Swedenborg identified reason with a *tabula rasa*, in Locke's sense of the word. Reason was void of any innate ideas. However, innate ideas as a treasure of inborn knowledge, were present in the soul (*anima*). As a consequence of the Fall of Man, the soul (*anima*) became separated from man.

Swedenborg believed that through mystical experiences, the lost knowledge stored in the soul could be regained. He maintained that there was a correspondence between the material universe and the spiritual world which could be elucidated by linguistic analogies. These speculations gave rise to Swedenborg's interest in theosophy, the novel interpretations of the scripture aiming at the understanding of its hidden meanings. Such meanings concerned the relation of God to man and to the material universe.

In 1745 Swedenborg had a profound mystical experience. As a result, he claimed that he could achieve higher spirituality and attain the understanding of the hidden meaning of scripture. Some of Swedenborg's subsequent theosophic writing became quite bizarre and cast some doubt on his sanity. Nevertheless he had a considerable following and influenced the Romantic poets as well as Baudelaire and Strindberg. Although there is no direct evidence for it, Swedenborg must have influenced the German Philosophers of Nature. However, there is direct evidence that Swedenborg's work had a profound influence on Carl Gustav Jung. As a young man, Jung was said to have been an avid reader of Swedenborg's books. Jung's notion of the collective unconscious may be compared with Swedenborg's notions of the *anima* and the world of spirits.

Swedenborg's philosophy and theosophy also influenced Jung's Austrian countemporary, Rudolf Steiner (1861-1925), a mystic and leader of the anthroposophic movement. The word "anthroposophy" was coined by Ignaz Troxler, a Philosopher of Nature. It referred to the psychological method by which man explored his own spiritual nature as well as the spiritual nature of the world. Jung's self-analysis, which could also be designated as his "creative illness," was influenced by the anthroposophic method. In his autobiography, Steiner reported several parapsychological and mystical experiences similar to those of Swedenborg.

Immanuel Kant found Swedenborg's assertion of the existence of a spirit world in the direct communication with human beings to be preposterous, even offensive to human rationality and common sense. Yet this was an ancient belief, and it persisted into the nineteenth century when even as important a historian as Leopold Ranke could claim to have encountered the image of a recently deceased person (Liebel-Weckowicz,1976). Kant represented an enlightenment trend in which the new scientific objectivity coincided with common sense beliefs. He believed that Swedenborg had created a private metaphysical world at variance with the one in which other men lived. He concluded that such a creation was probably the result of mental illness. He thus turned to a study of mental illness and its effect on the cognitive powers of the human mind. He was also concerned that the spread of mysticism would give a boost to the religious "enthusiasm" which he considered to be a sign of psychopathology.

Kant elaborated his beliefs in his 1762 *Essay on Mental Illness* (Versuch ueber die Krankheit des Kopfes), which was published in the *Koenigsbergische gelehrte und politische Zeitung.* In that essay, Kant offered a classification of mental illness based on the Wolffian faculty psychology.

Mental illnesses were divided into those of cognition, of affect, and of conation or will. The illnesses of cognition were further subdivided into those of perception, of judgment, and of reason. The illnesses of affect were subdivided into derangements of various passions. The illnesses of conation or will could be further subdivided into strongheadedness, and into the weakness of resolve and vacillation. Thus mental illnesses were disorders of mind and could be classified according to those faculties of mind which were deranged. Eighteenth century psychiatry and medicine were preoccupied with various nosologies or classificatory schemes of medicine.

Kant's classification of mental diseases was based on different principles from those of his contemporary nosologists such as Boissier de Sauvages, Linnaeus, Pinel, and Sydenham in the seventeenth century. Most of the other nosologies were based on disease entities considered as metaphysical essences. Kant's taxonomy was based on the mental faculties or powers and their disorders. It was more functional and less essentialist than the schemas of his predecessors and contemporaries.

In addition to the categorization based on the faculties of mind, Kant divided mental illness into two categories. The first constituted a class of mental defects which were primary and consisted of inborn disabilities of the brain. Here the cognitive faculties had never been developed. The second basic category, however, contained numerous types of mental illness which might arise. These were called insanities. They were caused either by unbridled, abnormally strong passions, or by diseases of the brain. Sometimes, both kinds of causes could be mixed.

One form of insanity Kant delineated involved hallucinations and was due to an abnormality of perception. It was a condition similar to that of dreaming or imagery occurring in normal people when they were falling asleep or waking up. Modern psychiatric terminology would refer to these as hypnogogic and hypnopompic hallucinations. The individual was deceived by his senses, he perceived phantoms or hallucinations. Images became vivid, often because they stirred up passions. They were percepts of real objects. Judgment and reason were not the affected faculties in these conditions. Other kinds of imaginary sensations attributed to the body produced a chronic hypchondriacal state.

A second form of insanity was due to the derangement of judgment. (Both Linnaeus and de Sauvages also had this category). Sensation and perception were normal. The individual, however, laboured under false beliefs as to the nature, import, and meaning of the things he perceived. Various delusional states belonged to this category. These included delusions of persecution as well as religious delusions. Reasoning was normal, so the individual derived correct conclusions from false premises. The last form of insanity was due to a disorder of reason. Here logical thinking was deranged and became incomprehensible. Various combinations of the above forms of insanity were encountered among mental patients, very often with an admixture of strong passions such as fear, anger, jealousy.

Kant's scepticism about Swedenborg's psychic abilities brought him face to face with the problem of knowledge and its limitations. He was concerned with the limitations of experience and not with those of reason. Under the influence of Leibniz, Kant became preoccupied with the inner activity of the human mind. In his habilitation dissertation he tried to find the derivation of the principles of the form of the sensible and intelligible world. These were traced to sense impressions and to the inner activity of the human mind. Swedenborg's claim of being able to communicate with the spirit world was at variance with Kant's principles of sensibility and intelligibility. Thus he attacked Swedenborg in his *Dreams of a Spiritualist* (1766). According to Kant, Swedenborg's experiences were not true representations (*Vorstellungen*). They had the character of hallucinations. Somewhat humorously Kant tried to give a rational explanation of "spiritual phenomena." These appeared to be hypnopompic hallucinations which he attributed to a resonance of spiritual fantasies with related fantasies of the external world expressed in terms of ordinary language or as human figures. Although they were fantasies, they were interpreted as true experiences (*Empfindungen*).

According to Kant, Swedenborg experienced three kinds of mental disturbance which he interpreted to be spiritual phenomena, in a religious sense, and which Kant challenged as being irrational. First, he saw spirits while in a state halfway between sleeping and waking. In modern terms these were hypnogogic hallucinations. Second, Swedenborg claimed that he had experienced a feeling of being transported out of his body and of really being present in other places. Such an experience was not uncommon in religious ecstasies as a similar one was attributed to Mohammed. Third, Swedenborg claimed to have a steady interaction with the world of spirits to which he had opened his mind. That is, he claimed to know the memories of deceased spirits. Kant argued that such psychical experiences, if not fraudulent were hallucinations which occurred in mental illness.

In his attempts to explain Swedenborg's mystical experiences in terms of mental illness, Kant operated completely within the framework of the enlightenment. He followed the reasoning of French materialists and sensationists like de La Mettrie, Helvetius, and Cabanis. He was also in agreement with Philippe Pinel, the great French psychiatrist who explained possession of spirits and mystical experiences as manifestations of the diseases of the mind. Here was the breakthrough to the modern understanding of mental illness, for the last remnants of ancient and medieval superstitions about possession were cast aside in favor of natural science theories.

Kant had, then, prepared the way for the acceptance of a modern understanding of mental disturbances. At the end of his essay, Kant remarked that he found Swedenborg's musings to be cobwebs of the mind (*Hirngespinste*). One ought to expect more of the other world than ghost stories. Certainly such another world would be more interested in receiving a pure soul from this one, rather than in entering this world and being judged by its standards, he commented.

Kant resumed the discussion of the topic of mental illness in his *Anthropologie* where he presented a more complete classification of the diseases of mind, as well as a more complex development of the ideas presented in his 1764 essay. Kant defined mental illness in terms of a fault or failure to know (*Fehler des Erkenntnisvermoegens*). These diseases could be divided into broad categories such as: (1) weaknesses of mind, or *Gemuetsschwaechen*; and (2) illnesses of mind, or *Gemuetskrankheiten*. In the first case, the weaknesses of mind included inborn mental defects as idiocy, feeble-mindedness, and "lack of wit." Kant believed that such persons had to be cared for in the same way as the aged, in hospitals and special homes. It required the reason of others to keep them neat and clean. Yet he did not think them defective enough to be put in special homes for idiots (the mentally retarded). Here Kant affirmed the pietist and humanitarian values which dominated the age of enlightenment. These aimed at providing the secure and proper welfare of all human beings, even those born with non-moral defects. In this group were persons who definitely did not belong in the same group as those suffering from disturbances of mind. The group could be compared to chronic welfare and unemployable cases in contemporary society.

In the second case, mental illnesses proper, were classified by Kant into three sub-categories of "disturbed mind." These were (1) disturbances of sensory input or cognitions (*Sinnesvorstellungen*). Here was found a group which included monomania, frenzy, and mania with delusions. In these cases affect was present in the delusions (*Wahnsinn* or *Tollheit*). Reason was beclouded and ideas were flooding uncontrollably as in frenzy or mania with delusions. Here also were included monomania or the fixation of one idea. This might involve excessive ruminations as when the patient refused to stop ruminating about the loss of a spouse. Superstition (*Aberglaube*) was also included in this group, and was compared with *Wahnsinn* or delusional mania.

The second major sub-division of mental disturbances (2) included mental illnesses proper. There were three sub-divisions here: hypochondriasis, disorders of judgment, and disorders of reason. These disorders affected the ability to judge and think consequently. They were known as *vesania* or *Wahnsinn*, sometimes also called *Aberwitz*. It could be observed in a type of patient whose mind was flooded with dream-like ideas (*Schwaermerei*). Milder cases of this nature were called "eccentricities." More severe cases showed disturbed judgment such as occurred temporarily in the delirium of a fever. The category of *vesania* included hypersensitive individuals who manifested arrogance and insulted others. They had a chip on the shoulder attitude, were *leichtbeleidigt*. Some of those who suffered from *vesania* were depressed and had a severe distortion of their inner sense. *Vesania* was thus a term applied to a broad category of disturbances which could range (a) from cases of rational and otherwise healthy persons who merely suffered from some eccentricity, or who had a peculiar hobbyhorse in which they indulged; or (b) to cases of profound insanity.

Melancholia was the most important illness among the disturbances of mind, proper. In melancholia, a depressed person created a false belief by which he tormented himself. If the individual persisted in holding his false belief, a product of his imagination, he might very well develop a full blown disturbance of mind. In melancholia, the disordered judgment preceded the disturbance of mood. Kant's theory of melancholia thus anticipated the modern cognitive theory of depression developed by Aaron Beck (1967).

Disorders of understanding (*Verstand*), and of reason (*Vernunft*), had a particular bearing on forensic psychiatry and medicine. Kant therefore believed that the philosopher, and not a physician or a jurist, ought to judge whether or not an act was committed in which a man was in full possession of a healthy reason. In consequence of his taxonomic system of mental derangements, Kant undertook what he called "a small didactic," or lesson on how to judge the consequences of these disorders from a moral perspective.

In this context, insanity was divided according to whether the type of thought disorder was (a) tumultuous, (b) methodical, or (c) systematic. Tumultuous disorders of thought occurred in *amentia* (*Unsicherheit*) or mental deficiency. Such patients suffered from an inability to relate experience in the necessary way. Frequently they were females and one encountered them in asylums. They talked incessantly about imagined things. Their discourse was tumultuous and confused.

Dementia (*Wahnsinn*), was characterized by systematized delusions produced by a disturbed mind. Such a person saw animosity and hostility in the words and deeds of those surrounding him. These patients were incurable, but they were not dangerous to others. They did not have to be hospitalized. In modern terms, such a patient would be described as suffering from a paranoid state.

Insania (*Wahnwitz*) was a disturbance of judgment. Those persons afflicted were often creative, even poetic, though incurable. They confused concepts which were similar. While Kant referred to this condition as a "fragmented methodical insanity," modern psychologists call it divergent thinking, overinclusiveness or condensation. In *vesania* (*Aberwitz*) there was a disturbance of reason (*Vernunft*). In the above condition, a sick person ignored the real word and looked for principles which could nullify his reality-testing of experience. He imagined that he was comprehending the incomprehensible, that he could square circles, that he had invented a *perpetuum mobile*, and that he had discerned the secret of the Holy Trinity. This was a systematic insanity, which according to Kant was not only a deviation from right reason, but involved also an affirmation of a positive unreason (positive *Unvernunft*). The soul was displaced so that it viewed things from an abnormal perspective. Such abnormality was defined from the view of normal common sense (*sensoris communi*). This belonged to the unity of life. Hence "crazy" (shattered) or in German, *Verrueckung*, derangement.

In his discussion of the etiology of mental illness, Kant lists the organic psychological and social causes. The organic causes included the diseases of the brain and also poisons. Those who made themselves ill by use of poisons, that is, drugs like opium, could develop an illness or weakness of mind, or even an artifical insanity which might become a real one. Kant doubted whether a healthy person could became insane from studying too hard. However, he thought that an impressionable person could become insane through watching mental patients. Their sight might stir the imagination of the onlooker to produce a similar condition in him.

According to Kant a mentally healthy person required the proper reality-testing of a free society, one in which there was no censorship of books or ideas, for the only universal characteristic of all insanities was the loss of common sense (*sensus communis*). This was defined in terms of the common agreement on things perceived which existed in any community. Thus a man could be presumed to be out of his right mind if he saw a burning light on his table in broad daylight which no one else saw, or heard voices which no one else heard. The reality-testing of the whole community was therefore indispensable for the freedom and dignity of the individual. The state of civilization could create unfavourable social conditions which would distort common sense and which would interfere with proper reality-testing. It could also make excessive social demands which were some of the causes of mental illness. Kant believed that primitive man, the "noble savage," was relatively free from mental illness. This obviously showed the influence of Jean Jacques Rousseau's hostility to an authoritarian political theory like that of Thomas Hobbes' *Leviathan*. Here man existed in the state of nature in a condition of perpetual warfare, as a fierce unbriddled savage, before he entered civil society where he submitted to despotic rule.

Kant's theory of mental illness is important because it represents the views of the enlightenment and of the rationalists on this subject. This may be contrasted with the irrational views of the nineteenth century Romantics and *Psychiker* psychiatrists such as Johann Heinroth. (Liebel-Weckowicz & Weckowicz, 1973).

More typical of the eighteenth century attitude toward mental disease than Kant's, was William Battie's *A Treatise on Madness* (1758), which attributed mental diseases to organic brain pathology. Battie was a physician at St. Luke's Hospital in London, and introduced the teaching of clinical psychiatry there. He divided insanity into two types, the first due to internal disorders, the second due to extrinsic factors. Battie debated John Monro, the chief physician at Bethlehem Hospital ("Bedlam"), on whether insanity was curable or not. Battie took a more optimistic position on the issue than Monro did, as he was a founder of the moral treatment school in England.

The eighteenth century was an age of paradoxes. It was a century of profound scepticism and materialist reductionism. The whole universe was conceived as governed by the laws of Newtonian physics. It was perceived in mechanistic terms, as a clock. David Hume (1711-

1776) declared that knowledge was all but impossible, and reduced mind to a bundle of sensations. Descartes' idea that animals were machines devoid of consciousness, inspired the French materialist philosophers: Julien Offray de La Mettrie (1709-1751), Claude Adrian Helvetius (1715-1771), and Pierre Jean George Cabanis (1757-1808), to reject Cartesian dualism and to postulate a machine theory of the human organism. They also rejected the idea of an immortal soul and relegated consciousness to the realm of epiphenomena. The most representative of the writings of this group was La Mettrie's *L'Homme Machine* (1738/1961) (Man a Machine). La Mettrie was an army doctor. During one of the campaigns he came down with a fever and became delirious. This episode convinced him that the material brain controlled the mind completely, and not vice versa. In his *Discours sur le Bonheur* (1750) or (Discourse on Happiness), La Mettrie put forward an extreme version of the hedonistic theory of ethics (La Mettrie, 1774-75, 1970).

Another member of the materialist group, Cabanis, maintained that "les sciences morales" (moral sciences), by which he meant behavioural sciences, belonged to the natural sciences together with physics and chemistry. He was interested in scientific principles which could be used to control normal and abnormal behaviour, and suggested their application to the treatment of mental diseases. The concept of moral sciences was elaborated further by Claude-Henri Comte de Saint-Simon (1760-1825), who applied the principles of these sciences to social theory, or as he called it, "social physiology." In his blueprint for an utopian communist society, he proposed that the government of people was to be based on the scientific principles borrowed from Newtonian physics. These philosophers were the ideological ancestors of the radical behaviourism of the twentieth century. The writings of British and French empiricists as well as those of associationists, particularly those of David Hartley (1705-1757) and of Etienne Bonnot de Condillac (1715-1780), pointed in the same direction as those of the French materialists. Although a dualist, Hartley explained sensations, ideas, images and their associations as due to vibrations of brain particles. Condillac used the example of a statue, and maintained that once the statue possessed one sensory organ, it became sentient and could construct all knowledge out of received sensations. The statue, thus, would not be distinguishable from man. Hartley and Condillac, did not commit themselves to metaphysical materialism. However, they proposed a psychology which was based on atomistic and mechanistic principles. Such reductionist, associationist, and materialist philosophies postulated determinism of human behaviour and denied that man possessed free will. Consequently, they did not present a dignified image of man.

Paradoxically, the eighteenth century was also an age of social philosophies which stressed liberalism and social optimism. This was a faith in man and a belief in his inalienable rights. It was also the age of the encyclopedists in France, of the Scottish school of moral philosophy, and of the American Federalist papers. "Liberty, equality, and fraternity" were the slogans of the French Revolution. Man was conceived as being free, rational, and the master of his own destiny. He was, therefore, entitled to the pursuit of happiness according to his best judgment. Enlightened legal systems were founded on the assumption that man was a free and responsible agent, capable of and entitled to making free choices. These legal systems became the foundation of Western societies. The assumptions of this philosophy were undoubtedly indeterministic and libertarian. The social philosophy of liberalism gave an impetus to political and social reforms. The old feudal system which was based on the rights of the monarchy, the authority of the Church, and the privileges of the aristocracy, had begun to crumble. The American and French Revolutions dealt the final blow to it.

The new liberal credo held that the downtrodden had to be freed and the old injustices rectified. The age of the enlightenment believed that its task was to destroy superstition, obscurantism and prejudice. Mental patients were incarcerated in prisons and madhouses, they were kept in chains, they were abused by the keepers, and they were mocked by the ignorant public. They became the focus of attention of social reformers who defended their rights along with those of other disadvantaged groups.

St. Mary of Bethlehem mental hospital in London, popularly known as "Bedlam," may serve as an example of a typical madhouse. Converted from a monastery into a mental hospital during the reign of Henry VIII, it had an evil reputation for the degrading treatment of the inmates. They were kept in chains, frequently flogged and mocked. Many of them were placed at the bottom of a pit with a spectator gallery from which members of the public could, for a small fee, watch the "lunatics." The spectators could, for an additional payment, rent long poles for prodding and stirring inmates who were too quiet (Bowen, 1780; Byrd, 1974; MacDonald, 1981).

The conditions in continental mental hospitals were not any better. Emil Kraepelin in his *One Hundred Years of Psychiatry* (1962), describes the appalling conditions and the plight of patients in many German and Austrian institutions at the end of the eighteenth century and the beginning of the nineteenth century. In the *Juliusspital* in Wuerzburg, the attendants restrained patients with chains, manacles, and shackles. They flogged patients with leather-encased bull whips for the slightest breach of hospital rules. The patients were punished for complaining, for littering their cells, or disobeying orders. Flogging was a great part of the daily routine.

Even hospital reformers such as Langermann of St.George Hospital in Bayreuth, believed that doctors could at times resort to flogging and to imprisonment. Others advocated physical punishment for stubborn, resistent, malicious and willful patients. Even as late as 1845, the superintendent of the Stralsund Hospital in Germany, advocated whipping with a birch rod as a remedy for the uncleanliness of patients. According to him that procedure was not only useful in controlling the unruly behaviour of patients, but it also invigorated their blood circulation and increased the tonus of the urinary bladder and anal sphincter muscles.

The *Narrenturm* hospital in Vienna had a particularly bad reputation. It was a forbidding, circular shaped, five-story building with 139 cells situated between the circular outside wall, and the straight inside walls. The cells were very small with scanty, filthy straw for bedding. The massive iron cell doors had little holes guarded by a heavy iron grill, through which food and water was given to the patients. A visiting physician communicated with the patients through the door holes. The patients were shackled with heavy chains and iron rings to the walls of their cells. The diet was meager, because it was believed that restricted food intake helped to control the rages and the outbursts. There was a constant wailing and raving, which expressed the despair and suffering of the patients. An unbearable stench pervaded the place. A visitor compared the patients in the *Narrenturm* to a menagerie of wild animals. In the *Juliusspital* there were huge stone posts with iron rings to which the patients were chained.

Eighteenth century English madhouses were immortalized in the paintings of Hogarth. One can see isolated rooms without air and light in which many patients spent most of their time; one can see heavily grated windows. There were massive, bolted doors. Gutters in the stone floor carried refuse.The patients can be seen wearing a motley of strange costumes expressing their delusional beliefs. At the end of the eighteenth and the beginning of the nineteenth century, chains were replaced by new restraining contrivances which represented the latest in the state of the arts. The strait jacket or MacBride camisole replaced the chains. William Cullen of Edinburgh University strongly recommended them because they were supposed to soothe the mind and induce reflection. This would prevent over-excitement. Another device recommended, was a leather girdle with straps and gloves to immobilize the madman's hands. Various types of masks were used to prevent patients from biting and screaming.

Benjamin Rush introduced a contrivance known as a "tranquilizer," which became very popular. It was a heavy oak restraining chair with devices for immobilizing the body, legs and arms. It was claimed that the "tranquilizer" would make the most irascible and recalcitrant patient gentle and submissive. Patients were known to spend several months in restraining chairs.

The attendants in mental hospitals were selected for their physical strength. They were uncouth, unsympathetic and brutal. They often relied on dogs for their protection. Semicircular catching sticks were used to pin patients against walls in order to overpower them. The brutal handling and unhygienic conditions led to an extremely high mortality rate in mental hospitals. Often statistics were altered to hide the number of deaths due to maltreatment.

The violence used against the patients and their maltreatment provoked aggression and rage which were directed against the staff of the madhouses. The atmosphere of violence and abominably filthy conditions that prevailed in the institutions at that time, gave rise to many false beliefs and superstitions about lunatics. It was believed that lunatics were endowed with superhuman strength. They could outrun normal people, they could jump from high places without harming themselves. Consequently, the work in mental hospitals was considered very dangerous. The attendants had to be on constant guard against sudden attacks. The patients had to be handled brutally and kept in a state of fear and subjugation. The job of the attendant was like the job of a wild animal trainer in a circus. Visiting doctors had very little contact with the patients and left the actual treatment of them to attendants and keepers.

The filthy conditions of the madhouses produced a permeating stench which became associated with these places. Boerhaave, of the famous Leyden school of medicine, described this stench as a symptom of insanity. The belief that mental patients exuded a peculiar odor persisted well into the nineteenth century. Another common belief entertained by both the alienists and the general public was that mental patients were less sensitive to pain, to cold, and to hunger pangs than normals. This justified the subhuman status alloted to mental patients and the brutal treatment meted out to them. They were regarded as no longer possessing human attributes, but like wild animals, they were treacherous and dangerous.

These and similar beliefs created a superstitious fear of insanity and of lunatics. The fear was mixed with a fascination and curiousity which induced the members of the public to pay admission fees or bribes to the attendants in order to be allowed to watch the lunatics. Many authorities, including Immanuel Kant, considered the fascination with lunacy as morbid. The latter cautioned nervous people against visiting asylums because the sight of lunatics might influence the imagination of a person and provoke madness. The belief that insanity was contagious through the intermediary of imagination, persisted for quite a long time and extended the stigma of insanity from the patients to the staff of the asylums: the alienists and the attendants. The common belief that insanity was considered incurable and hereditary, even if not shared by all alienists, was widespread and only served to augment the fear and the stigma associated with mental disease.

Public demands were made for the legal protection and the human rights of mental patients, for licensing private madhouses, and for the rules of commitment to mental institutions. The English novelist and journalist, Daniel Defoe (1661-1731), drew the attention of the general public to the abuses of the madhouses. In his pamphlets, he pointed out that they were frequently used to get rid of inconvenient relatives (Defoe, 1728). These criticisms led the British Parliament to pass the "Act for Regulating Madhouses" in 1774. It established clear rules for commitment to mental asylums (14 Geo. 3, Chapter 49).

In France, and in other countries, enlightened physicians in charge of institutions for the insane, became imbued with the humanitarian spirit of social reforms at the end of the eighteenth century. Psychotic patients came to be perceived as human beings who were entitled to enjoy human rights and thus had to be treated accordingly. The French physicians who belonged to the new reform movement were: Jean Columbier (1736-1789), Joseph Daquin (1733-1815), and most importantly, Philippe Pinel (1745-1826) in France. In Germany, Anton Muller (1755-1827), and Johann Gottfried Langermann (1768-1820), a follower of George Ernst Stahl, represented the new attitudes. So did Vincenzo Chiarugi (1759-1820) in Italy.

Chiarugi was an eighteenth century pioneer in developing modern psychiatric theory. As director of San Bonifacio Hospital in Florence, he had acted at the behest of Peter Leopold, Grand Duke of Tuscany in 1788, to introduce a novel approach to the treatment of mental patients. According to the new regulations, the mental patients were to be treated with respect, tact and kindness. Cruelty, physical punishment and restraints were forbidden. Even ducking , long favored in England and the United States, was rejected. Chiarugi's system seems to have influenced the French reforms of Pinel at Bicêtre a few years later. Pinel, however, thought that Chiarugi's theories had been overestimated. The reforms in Florence marked part of the enlightened reforms of the ruler, Peter Leopold, the younger brother of Joseph II, who succeeded his brother as German Emperor and ruler of Austria in 1790.

Chiarugi wrote his *Medical Treatise on Insanity* (1794) in which he discussed human personality, and reported one hundred case histories often accompanied by descriptions of the patients' brains examined at postmortem. Here he followed the technique of observation of Hippocratic medicine. Insanity or *pazzia*, was a chronic condition in which reason was suppressed. Like so many eighteenth century writers he placed great emphasis on the role of the nervous system, which mediated between body and soul through nerve juices in perpetual motion. Chiarugi also noticed that the deterioration of the condition of chronic patients was accompanied by a change in the disease symptoms. Thus he assumed that mental illness began with melancholia and progressed to mania and stupification. At the same time, each could also appear as an independent disease. Age, heredity, trauma, toxins, were factors in mental disease. There was a basic insanity, however, "pazzia," and many forms of mental illness seemed to be variants of it. Epilepsy was believed to be a vascular disorder.

Philippe Pinel had absorbed some of the enlightenment ideas on the more humane treatment of the insane. The French Revolution gave him the opportunity to implement some of the new treatment methods.

He then removed the chains from male patients at Bicêtre in 1793, where he was director, and in 1795 he did the same for female mental patients at Salpêtrière. We have already discussed this at the beginning of the chapter. However, it is the 1795 removal of chains from the women patients which Robert Fleury depicted in his famous painting (Deutsch, 1960).

Similar reforms followed on the continent, possibly under the influence of the reform spirit of the age. J.C. Langermann, the founder of St. George Hospital, Bayreuth, German followed in Pinel's footsteps. When he became its director in 1805, he abolished the use of physical restraints on patients. He emphasized the importance of psychological factors in the causes of mental illness, and the importance of the human treatment of the patients. Langermann proved to be an excellent teacher, for one of his students was Karl Ideler, a famous *Psychiker* psychiatrist. Together with Philippe Pinel, the French reformer, Langermann and Chiarugi may be regarded as the originators of the new moral treatment of the insane in continental Europe. Their work represents the burgeoning spirit of progress and a new faith in the advance of human civilization which was to become so popular during the nineteenth century.

Philippe Pinel was not only a humanitarian reformer, he was also an important theoretician of psychiatry, and perhaps one of the greatest psychiatrists who has ever lived. He established psychiatry as a separate specialty of medicine, although the name psychiatrist came into use somewhat later. For many years, psychiatrists were called "alienists," doctors who treated "mental alienations." When in 1793, he removed chains from the mental patients at the Bicêtre hospital, he initiated a series of enlightened reforms leading to the more humane treatment of the mentally ill.

Pinel's reflections on mental disease were published in his *Traite Medico-philosophique sur la Mania* (Medical-Philosophical Treatise on Mania) in 1801. (English edition, 1806). Here he differentiated functional psychoses from those caused by diseases of the brain. His focus was on the the psychological causes of functional psychosis. Functional psychoses were emotional disturbances, or as Pinel argued, disorders of the "passions." Their psychological causes were "moral." What Pinel called the "moral treatment" of the insane constituted a mixture of psychotherapy and milieu-therapy. He proposed several reforms of mental hospitals that would render "moral treatment" possible. Patients had to be treated with kindness and understanding, restraints were forbidden. Drastic physical methods of treatment such as bleeding and "ducking" of patients into cold water were opposed. The patients were to be re-educated by benevolent persuasion. Their false ideas were to be corrected. (For it had been believed since Locke, Linnaeus, de Sauvages, and Chiarugi, that the insane had lost their proper reason). The psychiatrist was, in his relation to the patients, to act not as a physician, but as a kind and understanding teacher. In his implementation of "moral treatment" at the Bicêtre and Salpêtrière hospitals, Pinel was aided by a very capable chief attendant, M. Pussin.

Pinel's ideas on moral treatment were adopted during the first half of the nineteenth century by many enlightened mental hospital superintendents in England and America. (In spite of the fact that his pioneering work was neglected in France itself, and that France fell behind England and the United States in the quality and care of patients in mental hospitals).

In England and in the American colonies, a more practical approach to the treatment of the mentally ill had appeared by the middle of the eighteenth century. The mental illness of King George III focused attention on an improved treatment of the mentally diseased. William Battie (1704-1776), a physician at St. Luke's Hospital in London, treated the king by "moral management." He had in 1753 begun clinical demonstrations at St. Luke's and begun the modern traditions of English psychiatry. Hygiene, diverse work, rest, walks, nourishing food, and some inculcation of fear were deemed appropriate as "moral management." In the colonies a similarly enlightened attitude began to appear when Pennsylvania Hospital in 1750, on the urging of Benjamin Franklin, provided some space for those with disordered senses. This hospital was approved by the Pennsylvania legislature in 1751 and specifically, to receive and cure lunatics (Franklin, 1954). Restoring such people to useful work was the main motive. Virginia Colony also established the special Williamsburg Hospital for those of 'unsound mind,' in 1769 (Deutsch, 1960).

The humanitarian impulse of the 1790s brought about reforms in England which paralleled those of Pinel in France. Such reforms had been initiated by Quakers with the establishment of York Retreat Hospital in 1796 by William Tuke, a Quaker layman. He was also the grandfather of Daniel Hack Tuke (1827-1895), an important nineteenth century psychiatrist. However, it was Samuel Tuke (1784-1857) whose famous *Description of the Retreat, an institution near York, for insane persons of the Society of Friends* (Tuke, 1813/1964), later influenced Quaker practices in Pennsylvania after 1817. The use of restraints had been abolished at York, and moral management introduced. The same policies were implemented by Robert Gardiner Hill at the Lincoln Asylum and by John Conolly at the Hanwell Asylum in the 1830s and 1840s. Moral treatment was everywhere introduced, and restraints removed (Conolly, 1856/1973). In the United States, Quakers followed the example of their English brethren, and opened a Friend's Asylum in Frankford, Pennsylvania, a suburb of Philadelphia in 1817. Samuel Tuke's book about York as well as the Reverend Thomas Scattergood's visit to York in 1797 had exerted considerable influence. The main idea was never to use chains and to separate the patients who were incurable from the curable, the violent from the meek (Conolly, 1830/1964; 1847/1968).

The American reforms became widely diffused. The Bloomingdale Asylum, then in New York City, was a state operated hospital. It followed the Quaker examples which were recommended by the Quaker reformer Thomas Eddy. Influenced by Tuke's book, he recommended abolishing the use of chains, and even the harsher aspects of Cullen's and Rush's old treatments (corporeal punishments). Tuke himself wrote to Eddy suggesting he also take in the poor. Authorized in 1791, Bloomingdale had in 1809 been converted into a state hospital to which local overseers of the poor sent their indigent mental patients. Later it was moved outside of the city to White Plains (Russell, 1921). The Pennsylvania Hospital took in only middle class patients (Bockoven, 1963; 1972).

Among American alienists, Isaac Ray (1807-1881), was the most prominent advocate of the no-restraint treatment (Ray, 1838). By the middle of the nineteenth century, many state legislatures introduced reforms in the state mental institutions. Much of this is owed to the dynamic, crusading spirit of Dorothea Lynda Dix (d.1887). Due to her efforts St. Elizabeth Hospital in Washington,D.C. had been founded, and congress had in 1854 granted ten million acres of federal land to fund the treatment of poor mental patients. Her zeal helped bring about the founding of thirty-two state mental hospitals (Felix,1967).

Nineteenth century reforms were, however, born in the eighteenth century enlightenment's zeal for education and for humanitarian treatment of the insane. The eighteenth century was also the age of enlightened educational reforms. The mechanistic methods which encouraged rote learning, were abandoned. In 1762, Jean Jacques Rousseau had published *Emile, a treatise on education*, in which he emphasized modern methods of teaching a child (Rousseau, 1964). The method of spontaneous observation and a spirit of discovery that Rousseau emphasized, inspired a Swiss eductor, Johann Heinrich Pestalozzi (1746-1827), who tried to implement Rousseau's ideas in educational practices.

Such interests could be applied only to the well-to-do middle class. Fearful of peasant revolts, absolutist rulers like Maria Therese had introduced a reform of the elementary school system in 1769, and like Frederick the Great had enforced compulsory school attendance (Melton, 1988). However, it was only when the new "moral treatment" emerged in psychiatry that there was an interest in educating and treating through special educational techniques, the sub-normal, the feeble-minded, the uneducable idiots.

Pinel was one of the first to try to work with a feeble-minded "wolf" boy, who had been found in a forest near Aveyron, France, in 1798. His animal-like behaviour was attributed to the belief that he had been kidnapped as an infant and reared by a family of wolves. The boy was brought to Paris and handed over to Jean Itard, the chief medical officer at the Institution for the Deaf and the Dumb. Pinel later examined the child at Bicêtre and diagnosed him as an idiot and uneducable. However, Itard believed that the boy's apparent mental deficiency was the result of a lack of human socialization in his upbringing. He achieved some limited success in socializing and educating him.

The educational approach to mental deficiency was further developed in the nineteenth century by Edward Seguin, a teacher and a Christian Socialist. Seguin regarded the education of idiots and mental defectives as part of the social reforms aimed at the rectification of social injustices, and the uplifting of the downtrodden. He was very optimistic about the prospects of educating the mentally retarded whom he regarded as merely arrested in their infantile childhood development because of their social conditions. He believed that a normal level of development could be achieved if the sensory-motor functions could be speeded up by stimulation and the proper educational methods. In 1848, when the revolution broke out in France, this educator went to the United States in order to propagate his ideas. Like Alexis de Tocqueville, he believed that the new democracy offered a more fertile soil for his liberal views than Europe.

By the middle of the nineteenth century, several schools for the mentally retarded had been established in America and Europe. In 1896, Lightner Witmer opened a guidance clinic at the University of Pennsylvania for educating the sub-normal. He also introduced the term "clinical psychology."

The humanitarian impulse of the enlightenment and the romantic era had helped to improve the treatment and education of the mentally ill and the sub-normal. The new technology of these two centuries during which the industrial revolution transformed society and politics, also had an effect on the treatment of mental and physical illness. Here one must go back to the paradox of the eighteenth century. It lay in the co-existence of the mechanistic-reductionist psychology of La Mettrie and Condillac with the social philosophy of individual rights and freedoms. Could the assertion of human rights live side by side with the belief that man was a virtual automaton who functioned according to the material stimuli which reached his nervous system? The second paradox of the eighteenth century was the contradiction between the great admiration for science and human progress and the belief that civilization corrupts man on the other. Rousseau's glorification of the "noble savage" and Kant's linking of mental illness with the complexity of civilization, are examples of the latter belief.

The great admiration for science led very often to a naive acceptance by the educated public of pseudo-scientific theories, based on pure speculations. Mesmer's theory of animal magnetism, and Franz Joseph Gall (1758-1828)'s phrenology provide two examples. Mesmer's theory played an extremely important role in the discovery of psychoneurosis, that no-man's land between insanity and physical illness and supernatural phenomena. True, the eighteenth century had been an age of enlightenment and rationalism in which the ghosts of demonology and witchcraft beliefs were finally laid to rest. Yet it was also confronted with such inexplicable phenomena as faith-healing, hypnotic states, and hysteria. A naturalistic, scientific explanation of these phenomena was sorely needed. That explanation was then supplied by Franz Anton Mesmer (1734-1815).

A secular physician, Mesmer had nonetheless begun studies in theology and philosophy at the Jesuit University of Dillingen, and turned to law and then medicine at the Bavarian University of Ingolstadt. His 1766 dissertation reflected the Paracelsian tradition of cosmic influences which Father Athanasius Kircher had transmitted. The title of his doctoral dissertation was *De influxu planetarum.* (On the Influence of the Planets). Like Paracelsus he saw the importance of the magnetic influence of the moon as well as the curative powers of magnets and in different kinds of stones (Leibbrand & Leibbrand-Wettley, 1964; Ellenberger, 1970).

Once he settled down in Vienna, Mesmer developed his famous methods of treatment. He probably took the theory of animal magnetism from J.B. Van Helmont. The theory assumed that a subtle physical force ("fluid") pervaded the universe and was present in human and animal bodies. It formed bonds among men and between men and the celestial bodies. This force could be concentrated and passed on to another person by use of special techniques such as the application of a magnet or of the human will. But items of clothing such as a handkerchief, or even a pillow made of the physician's hair, could exert magnetic force upon the patient. Illness was deemed to be the result of an unbalanced distribution of magnetic force in the human body. The cure could be obtained through a concentration of such a "magnetic force" by the magnetizer who passed it on to the patient in order to produce a "crisis." Once the crisis occurred, the patient often collapsed and had convulsions.

Mesmer's major work was published in 1779 as the *Treatise on the Discovery of Animal Magnetism* (Mesmer, 1971). The method of treatment based on it became very fashionable in Austria, Germany, and France. The question is very often asked whether Mesmer was a quack and an imposter. Probably not. In terms of the knowledge about physics which existed in the eighteenth century, his theory was plausible even if speculative. In his dissertation, Mesmer called the mysterious force universal gravitation (*gravitatio universalis*) and considered it similar to Newton's gravitation force. This was an age during which mysterious electrical forces were being discovered. As the mind had moved away from beliefs in demonology and witches, the mysterious influences among humans had to be explained in a new way. They then came to be attributed to semi-magical, yet natural forces like magnetism. This was also a time when such mysterious forces were being discovered by science. Luigi Galvani (1737-1798), Alexander Volta (1745-1827), and Benjamin Franklin (1706-1790) were experimenting with electricity. This "fluid," and mysterious force could be produced by rubbing a glass rod with a piece of leather. It could be accumulated in batteries, and when discharged, it could produce a painful shock. It could also make the muscles of a dead frog twitch. Electricity was seen to be as mysterious as animal magnetism. While electricity was later harnessed in a concrete way, animal magnetism was not proven to be a physical force. One eventually discovered that its putative effects were due to suggestion. Unbeknown to him, Mesmer's work initiated a tradition in psychiatry which was revived in the treatment of hysterics by hypnotism in the nineteenth century, and led, one hundred years later, to the development of psychoanalytical theory.

Mesmer's initial successes in Vienna, made him famous in Germany as well. He came to some prominence in 1775 when the Elector of Bavaria appointed him to a commission to investigate the cures of demonical possession performed by Father Joseph Gassner, a well known exorcist. The latter had been treating patients afflicted with nervous conditions which he attributed to demonical possession. He used the technique of the laying-on of hands and of reciting prayers. During these procedures some patients collapsed and had fits before they got better. Gassner called such a temporary relapse a "crisis" and claimed that it resulted from the struggle and the resistence of the devil. In his report, Mesmer attributed the cures performed by Father Gassner to animal magnetism and not to exorcisms. Father Gassner was endowed with such magnetic powers to an extraordinary degree. In recognition of his services, Mesmer was appointed to the Bavarian Academy of Sciences and went back to Vienna.

There his fame continued to grow when he treated a harpist, Maria-Theresa Paradis. A musical prodigy, she was an accomplished harp player, but was blind. Mesmer convinced Fraeulein Paradis, under the influence of animal magnetism, that she had regained her sight. However, this was only her subjective impression, because objectively, she remained blind. The case caused a scandal in Vienna because Frauelein Paradis was a protegee of the Empress Maria Theresa. To avoid the royal anger, Mesmer left Vienna and went to Paris in 1778.

Mesmer met with a tremendous initial success in Paris where the old order was crumbling and any new ideas, however implausible, were hailed by the avant-garde. He attracted a following which included aristocrats, the wealthy, and the learned. Among his followers were Dr. D'Eslon, the physician to one of the king's brothers, and Nicholas Bergasse, a prominent lawyer, as well as Kornmann a wealthy banker.

The most important of Mesmer's followerss was Armand Maurice Jacques Marquis de Puysegur (1751-1825). The latter took over the leadership of the Mesmerist movewment and gave it a new direction after Mesmer retired to Vienna. The original financial support came from D'Eslon.

At the height of his career Mesmer built up a wealthy practice in Paris. There he occupied a mansion at the Place Vendome, the most fashionable district in that city. His seances took place in a large room, in the middle of which was the *baquet*, a tub filled with magnetized iron filings and water. Iron rods protruded from the sides of the *baquet*, through holes. They could be touched by the participants of the seance. The lights were dimmed, and there was semi-darkness in the room. Soft music was played from behind a screen. The musical instruments, one of them a glass harmonica, were also magnetized. The musicians played haunting and weird tunes.

Mesmer himself appeared, wearing the robes of a magician and touched the participants with a wand. To heighten the effect of the suggestion, huge mirrors were hung upon the walls which were supposed to reflect magnetic fluids. The participants sat in silence. After a while, they began to experience strange bodily feelings, and some of them went into a crisis. During the crisis, the symptoms from which the patients suffered, got worse. They often lost consciousness, developed convulsions, and had to be carried into a "crisis room." There they were treated by attendants. When the crisis was over, the symptoms got better. According to Mesmer, diseases were caused by a deficiency or an uneven distribution of animal magnetism in the bodies of the patients. The treatment during the seances rectified these conditions and restored the balance of animal magnetic fluid. The only medicine given by Mesmer to his clients was magnetized water which had previously been placed in the vicinity of a magnet and exposed to its influence.

Following his early success in Paris, Mesmer's fortunes declined. Many of his followers, among others, Bergasse, left the movement and started out on their own. Several leading scientists and prominent physicians became critical of the claims made by the Mesmerists. In 1782, a royal commission was convened by the Academy of Science and the Sorbonne medical faculty. It included the famous astronomer Bailly, the famous chemist Lavoisier, Benjamin Franklin then the American ambassador in France, and Dr. Guillotin, the inventor of the new decapitating machine named after him. The commission had found that "animal magnetism" did not exist. The reported cures were due to suggestion, and there was a potential danger of female patients developing sexual attraction to the magnetizer. This last finding was not made public and was only privately communicated to the king.

Discouraged by his change of fortune, Mesmer left Paris in 1785 and returned to Vienna. During the revolutionary era he was accused of having Jacobin sympathies and was even arrested. Mesmer eventually settled down in Switzerland and faded into obscurity. He died in 1815 of apoplexy in the Bodensee resort town of Meersburg.

In France, after the restoration of monarchy, the Marquis de Puysegur became the acclaimed leader of the Mesmerist movement and gave it a new direction. Puysegur discovered "magnetic sleep," a sleeplike state induced in a subject by a magnetizer.

A simple peasant named Victor was the first subject in Puysegur's experiments with "magnetic sleep." During it, Victor revealed a guilty secret from his past. Such experiments then began to uncover unknown reaches of the human mind. Experiences were revealed during magnetic sleep of which the subjects were unaware when awake. The subjects also displayed unusual clearness of thought and some mysterious faculties such as clairvoyance.

Confessing a guilty secret which the subject had forgotten, had a therapeutic effect. The subject felt relieved and better. The result of these findings was to increase the emphasis on psychological factors such as the will power of the magnetizer rather than on the mysterious magnetic fluid present in the bodies of animals and men. Gradually, the term "animal magnetism" was abandoned, to be replaced by that of "mesmerism."

If we survey the eighteenth century psychiatric scene, and try to distinguish conceptual models which at that time guided thinking about mental illness, we may reach the following conclusions. The disease model had become extremely influential during the enlightenment. This led to elaborate nosological classifications, and to attempts to localize pathological lesions in the brain. At the same time, elements of the psychological, cognitive-learning model of mental illness as well as the micro-social model, may be discerned in Pinel's writings. Here he advocated the "moral" treatment of the insane. The socio-cultural model was also anticipated in the works of Cheyne at the beginning of the century, and in the writings of Kant at the end of it. Mesmer's theory represents a throw-back to the theory of Paracelsus, because of its emphasis of the balance of the magnetic fluid in the body. It may be classified as an example of the medical constitutional model. However, since this theory had to do with the manifestations of the unconscious, without Mesmer being aware of it, there is a historical link between Mesmerism and psychoanalysis.

Certainly, the use of hypnosis by Charcot in Paris in the 1880s, and the fact of young Sigmund Freud's studies with Charcot, point in the direction of a continuity between French and Viennese Mesmerist heritages. Mesmerism can be classified as an early example of the psychoanalytical model. Mesmer's conception of a "magnetic fluid" (or force) represents a misinterpretation of the unconscious psychological forces.

In the eighteenth century there also existed other models of mental illness besides those of disease, and Mesmerism. The model of demonical possession still had some adherents. Father Johann Joseph Gassner (1727-1779), an Austrian contemporary of Mesmer, was a famous exorcist. His patients included not only the peasantry, but also members of the aristocracy. He differentiated mental diseases caused by demonical possession from those due to natural causes. Mesmer had investigated his work in 1775 and had attributed Gassner's cures of putative demonical possession to exorcism to animal magnetism (Ellenberger, 1970).

Finally, it is necessary to mention the science of phrenology, which made it appearance at the end of the eighteenth century. Phrenology was the name given to it by a pupil of Franz Joseph Gall (1758-1828), the founder of "organology." Together with G. Spurzheim (1776-1823), Gall worked out a system for classifying the powers or "organs" contained within the mind. It turned out to be a system of constitutional, faculty psychology. Like Mesmer, Gall started in Vienna, and then moved to Paris in 1804. Gall's work was based on extensive anatomical studies of the brain and also the study of many different cranial types. He was to influence the subsequent development of the French positivism of Auguste Comte, and was well received in the scientific circles which had rejected Mesmer. Like Mesmer, he encountered difficulties with the government in Vienna and was accused of fostering materialism (Lesky, 1979).

Gall's system was described in his *Anatomy and Physiology of the Nervous System in General and of the Brain in Particular* (1810). He distinguished thirty-seven "powers" of the mind, a spectrum of intellectual abilities and character traits. Gall (1840) borrowed the concept of "powers" of mind from the writings of the Scottish Moral Philosophers; Thomas Reid (1710-1796), Dugald Stewart (1753-1828), and Thomas Brown (1778-1820)(1840), see Zilboorg (1941). These "powers" were localized by him in thirty-seven areas of the brain. The degrees of development of these regions, manifested themselves by protusions of the skull. By examining the skull, a diagnosis of the individual's abilities and character could be made. The phrenologists were only marginally interested in the problem of mental illness. But Gall's anatomical studies proved to be important. Broca later verified his location of the speech area of the brain. He was also the first to observe that the eight major crainial nerves did not originate in a pulpy mass, but were already highly developed in the brain stem. Gall had also included mental hospital patients in his studies. Having begun with the characteristics of artists, professionals, and gifted persons, he had proceeded to study criminals and the mentally ill in order to include examples of extreme character traits. Gall also believed that the seat of hysteria was in the cerebellum, the "organ" of carnal love. Some of his studies proved interesting to the evolutionists, since he believed that man had all the animal instincts plus human abilities.

Andrew Combe (1792-1847), a Scottish physician and a prominent phrenologist in the first half of the nineteenth century, described the application of phrenology to the study of mental illness. He was aided by his barrister brother George Combe (1788-1858), in the propagation of theories of phrenology. Both Spurzheim and George Combe came to the United States to deliver a series of lectures where they received an enthusiastic welcome. George Combe's *The Constitution of Man Considered in Relation to External Objects* was published in Boston in 1839. It was just in New England that reform ideas associated with founding new mental hospitals were most prominent in the 1820s and 1830s when phrenology, as a movement, also came to American shores (Grob, 1973). Phrenology could be considered an example of the constitutional medical model. Mental diseases represented an extreme of certain constitutionally determined personality traits. It assumed a continuity of mental diseases with the normal personality. Phrenology caught the popular imagination and had many devotees despite the fact that the science establishment later condemned it. It had many followers throughout the nineteenth century, particularly in the United States.

Phrenology was historically important because it gave impetus to research on the localization of brain functions.

Another early contribution to the constitutional approach was made in the beginning of the nineteenth century by L. Rostan who proposed a bodily typology. He distinguished four somatic types:digestive, respiratory, muscular, and cerebral. This approach had been anticipated by Hippocrates in Antiquity, and eventuated in the work of the Padua school of medical anthropology, and later in the typologies of Ernst Kretschmer and William Sheldon in the twentieth century.

The contribution of enlightenment thought was in anticipating the modern systems of disease classification and locating mental illnesses within the system of modern medicine. The new empiricism of the age also brought a changed view to the treatment of mental illness which led to bedside observations, the founding of new mental hospitals, and especially to introducing the more humane, "moral treatment" of the mentally ill. Once the humanity of the patient was restored, the possibility of a cure also now became part of the faith in progress so characteristic of the modern age.

7

Nineteenth Century: Vitalist-Mechanist and Psychic-Somatic Controversies

Early Psychodynamic Psychiatry

Mental Hospital Reforms and Moral Treatment. During the nineteenth century, psychiatry became a recognized medical specialty. Those medical doctors who worked in mental hospitals were at first known as "alienists," and not as psychiatrists. Although trained as physicians, they functioned primarily as administrators. Sometimes they continued their general practice alongside their duties as "moral management" supervisors of the insane and mentally ill. It was the Germans who began to use the expression psychiatrist, early in the nineteenth century. Yet the designation "alienist" remained prevalent until the middle of the century.

A medical doctor who specialized in mental diseases was often designated by a German word, *Psychiater*," although alienist was more common. The first use of "psychiatrist" in English, according to the *Oxford English Dictionary* (1937) was given as 1857. However "psychiatric" was in use in 1847, and "psychiatry," in 1846. But "psychology," was already current in 1693, and "psychological," in 1776.

The professional work of the nineteenth century psychiatrists was mainly to observe and describe their psychotic patients. Autopsies were done to examine the brains of deceased patients. Thus began a tradition of practical clinical work which was to culminate in the discovery of specific organic diseases of the brain.

Psychiatrists were also hospital administrators and innovators of humanitarian reforms, such as the moral and no-restraint treatment of the insane. In the United States, where the first public hospital for the treatment of mental patients was established in Williamsburg, Virginia in 1773, new hospitals were established throughout the nineteenth century. Gerald Grob's *Mental Institutions in America. Social Policy to 1875* (New York, 1973), gives a detailed analysis of the early nineteenth century movement to establish both private and state operated mental asylums. The shortcomings of the eighteenth century almshouse with its mixed population of pauper insane and welfare cases led to the establishment of a few new type hospitals like the one at Williamsburg and the Pennsylvania Hospital. The widespread philanthropic attitudes of this era led to fundraising campaigns and the creation of asylums financed partly from endowments and partly by state appropriations. Examples are the McLean Asylum in Boston which opened in 1818, the Bloomingdale Hospital in 1821 in New York City, Connecticut's Hartford Retreat in 1824, and Worcester State Hospital in Massachusetts (Grob, 1973,1966). Bloomingdale Hospital in New York, had developed from the city's general hospital founded in 1769. The first mental case had been admitted in 1792. Under the influence of the ideas of Pinel and the Tukes, the moral management policies were introduced by 1815 when a new hospital was built to house 50 patients at Harlem Heights for $50,000. It opened in 1821 and accepted the pauper insane from the towns of New York State which paid their costs. Most patients were middle class and were financed by their families. In 1868, this hospital, then considered the best in the United States and in England, was moved to White Plains, New York. Of the 13,411 cases treated there from 1821-1921, some 8,524 or 63% discharged as cured or improved (Russell, ed.,1921). Of the 666 patients at McLean's between 1818-1830, 247 were discharged as recovered. Of the 1,762 at Bloomingdale's between 1821-1844, 672 were sent home as cured. The efforts of private philanthropy were exhausted by the 1830s, even though privately operated mental hospitals were still common in 1870. Increasing urbanization, the massive immigration of Europe's poor, especially of the Irish after the hungry 40s, led to overcrowding in the asylums, a loss of faith in the curability of the inmates and even a return to the use of restraints. Moral treatment was to be forgotten by the end of the century (Grob,1973, 1983).

The growth in the numbers of mental hospitals in theUnited States was considerable. Thanks to Dorothea Dix' efforts, state operated asylums became common by the middle of the nineteenth century. The leadership for modernizing treatment of the mentally ill came from the asylum superintendents who were also the first professional psychiatrists. A group of enlightened superintendents of state and private hospitals emerged. These included such men as Isaac Ray (1807-1881), Samuel Woodward (1787-1850), Amariah Brigham (1798-1849), Pliny Earl (1809-1892), Thomas Kirkbride (1809-1883), William

Awl (1799-1876), Luther Bell (1806-1862), John Butler (1803-1890), Nehemiah Cutter (1787-1859), Charles Stedman (1805-1866), Francis Stribling (1810-1874), John Galt (1819-1862), Samuel White (1777-1845), and John P. Gray (1825-1886). Many corresponded with eachother. Woodward wrote to Pliny Earle, Thomas Kirkbride was a friend of Horace Mann the American writer and reformer, and the great English novelist Charles Dickens concluded from his 1842 visit to the United States that the Americans were more progressive than the English in the care of the pauper insane. Dickens visited the hospital on Blackwell's Island (now Welfare Island) in New York City. Isaac Ray was active in Philadelphia and John P. Gray superintended the Utica Asylum from 1825 to 1886. In spite of the English tradition, in which training of physicians at St. Luke's Hospital was begun by William Battie before 1758, little real clinical training was possible in the United States before 1840. Much was owed to the efforts of the special group of asylum superintendents. They founded the first professional association, one which was later to become the American Psychiatric Association. This group, calling itself "the original thirteen," in 1844 established the Association of Medical Superintendents of American Institutions. It changed its name in 1893 to the American Medico-psychological Association, and in 1921 to the American Psychiatric Association. As the Association of Medical Superintendents (AMSAII) it offered leadership in establishing standards for hospital care and strongly opposed encroachments on the profession by external, state intervention. Isaac Ray's 1875 resolution against supervisory intervention received an overwhelming endorsement from the members (Grob, 1973). The sometimes cruel treatment of the mentally ill led to crusades for the rights and freedoms of the patients. A notable case is that of Elizabeth Packard in Illinois, who had been maltreated in the Illinois State Hospital during a three year confinement.

Towards the end of the nineteenth century, as their early enthusiasm diminished, some of the disillusioned superintendents began to take a pessimistic view of mental disease. Isaac Ray even anticipated Freud's *Civilization and its Discontents*, when in 1852 he expressed the view that mental disease was the "price" of civilization. William Awl in 1851 attributed the high rate of insanity to the development of a refined civilization, and linked it to the demands made upon the Anglo-Saxon ethnic group (1851). Like Jean Jacques Rousseau one century earlier, he too looked at the "noble savage" and claimed that little mental illness was found among primitive tribes. Edward Jarvis blamed mental disease on the stresses of upward mobility, and also on the poor quality of American education (Grob, 1973). The descriptions of the "filthy insane" of Dr. Stephen Smith of the New York State Commission investigating lunacy in the 1880s, resemble the eighteenth century descriptions of Bedlam. Mechanical restraints were back, and a new restraints controversy erupted. Pliny Earle, one of the founders of the Association of Medical Superintendents of American Institutions in 1844, was by the 1870s and 1880s arguing that the earlier cure rates had been exaggerated. Darwinian influences led to restrictions on the immigration of convicts, the feeble-minded and the insane by 1882 (Grob,1983).

Public interest in improving conditions in mental hospitals for the indigent may be seen in the work of Dorothea Lynde Dix (1802-1887), a retired Boston school teacher. She had visited the York Retreat in England while travelling there in 1836 and become friendly with Samuel Tuke. Then she had volunteered as a Sunday School teacher at the East Cambridge Jail in Massachusetts in 1841, and evidently was so shocked at the abominable conditions, that she devoted the remainder of her life to crusading for better conditions for the impoverished who were mentally ill. She was able to send in briefs to state legislatures. She even submitted a memorial to the U.S. Congress in 1848 asking for a land grant to support hospitals (Grob,1973). She contributed directly to founding 32 mental hospitals. The U.S. Congress responded to her 1848 petition in its 1854 bill which set aside some ten million acres of Federal land to help the states provide for the pauper insane, although President Franklin Pierce vetoed it (Felix, 1967). Perhaps more than the superintendents, Dorothea Dix's efforts led to creating facilities for more custodial care and a shift away from moral treatment and towards long term confinement. While the cure rate under the old system was claimed to be 45%, it was only 4% later in the nineteenth century (Talbott, 1981). After visiting many hospitals throughout the country Dorothea Dix began a public campaign which led many state legislatures to improve treatment facilties.

In England, Daniel Hack Tuke (1827-1895), the great-grandson of William Tuke, founder of the York Retreat, typified the enlightened superintendent of a mental hospital of the nineteenth century (Tuke, 1882, 1968). He combined administrative skill and a humane attitude towards patients with an encyclopedic knowledge of contemporaneous psychiatry.

A great many textbooks were written about mental disease in which the authors propounded new psychiatric systems and theories. In fact Zilboorg (1941) characterizes the nineteenth century as an age of systems. The new and more systematic observations and classifications of psychotic patients represented one of the two mainsprings from which modern psychiatry developed. The second development may be traced to mesmerism, or as it was later called, "Braidism," and eventually, "hypnotism."

Hypnotism. Although rejected by the medical profession in the first half of the nineteenth century, mesmerism not only had a wide following in France, but also spread to Germany, England, America, and other parts of the world. The interest in mesmerism in France and Britain was mainly clinical. In Germany, however, it focused on the clairvoyant and prophetic powers of the mind revealed during "magnetic sleep." In Britain, mesmerism had a medical application in the work of John Ellioston (1791-1868), and James Esdaile (1808-1859). The German Romantic physician-poet Justinus Kerner (1786-1862) applied mesmerism to the exploration of parapsychological phenomena. In the United States, Mary Baker Eddy (1821-1910), experienced a mesmeric cure and established the Church of Christian Science as a result.

Mesmerism became associated with spiritism in the United States and reached the peak of its vogue in the 1840s. Although shamans had been communicating with the spirits of the deceased since times immemorial, modern spiritism began in New York state in 1847. John Fox, a farmer, and his family were bothered by strange noises like a knocking on the walls. His two daughters interpreted these noises as messages from a man who had been murdered some time earlier before the house was occupied by the Fox family. They began to communicate in code with the spirit of the murdered man. Stories like this one are reminiscent of the English belief in haunted houses, and hearken back to an era when belief in witchcraft was still common. Bavarian stories of the seventeenth century also feature the knocking sounds when a house was haunted. However, at the level of popular culture, the Fox affair led to a spread of seances during which people tried to communicate with the spirits of the dead. Spiritism became popular on both sides of the Atlantic, and acquired the status of a religious sect. It continued into the twentieth century. William Lyon MacKenzie King, then Canadian prime minister, attended seances even during the second World War.

At such seances, a medium in a mesmeric trance served as a channel of communication between the participants in the seance and the spirits in the other world. Thus in the United States, England, and Germany in particular, mesmerism became associated with the occult and supernatural. By the 1840s, however, the American mesmerists had abandoned the theory of "magnetic fluid" or force and came to regard mesmeric phenomena as due to psychological factors such as "will power." These were panpsychic bonds among men, or between men and nature.

The panpsychic interpretation was emphasized by the German Nature Philosophers, Romantics, and the psychiatrists influenced by them. The mesmeric treatment method was widely used during the 1820s when nobles and literati sometimes found it helpful. For example, Dorothea, the wife of the writer Frederick Schlegel, was treated by it.

The professional associations rejected mesmerism, especially in England where Dr. John Ellioston, a physician, had to resign the chair of medical practice at University College, London, because of it. He had treated his patients by the mesmeric method, and founded the journal *Zoist*, which was devoted to mesmerism. Dr. James Esdaile, a surgeon for the East India Co., operated on patients who were put into a mesmeric sleep, although this was scarcely believed. The French Academy of Sciences condemned mesmerism after investigating it. Although rejected by "official medical science" in Germany, which was becoming increasingly positivistic, mesmerism went underground. Particularly in Germany, and together with parapsychology, it became part of the stream of mystical, herbalist, popular medical lore which is sometimes referred to as "Romantic medicine."

James Braid (1795-1860), a Manchester physician, made mesmerism more acceptable to the medical profession by denying that mesmeric phenomena were the result of mysterious forces, either physical or psychological. He attributed them to suggestion and auto-suggestion. mesmeric sleep was viewed as a kind of "nervous sleep" (neuro-hypnology). It is from this that the term "hypnotism" evolved.

During the first two decades of the nineteenth century, the French mesmerist movement was led by Amand-Marie-Jacques Marquis de Puysegur. His younger brother, Antoine-Hyacinthe de Puysegur, a naval officer, introduced animal magnetism to the French colony of

Santo Domingo (now Haiti) in the Carribean. mesmerist practices became widespread among the Black slaves and were incorporated into their Voodoo cult. The followers of the Marquis de Puysegur formed a society of harmony, the *Societe Harmonique des Amis Reunis*. The purpose of this society was to train mesmerists, to propagate the teachings of mesmerism and to provide free treatment for the needy.

Soon new men appeared on the scene. One of them was Abbe Faria, a Portuguese priest. Faria spent some time in India and combined mesmerism with Hindu yogi practices. He gave public demonstrations of lucid sleep in mesmerized subjects. During such sleep, the subjects experienced visions.

Another French mesmerist who attained prominence, was J.P.F. Deleuze, who published a textbook on the subject. He gave several public lectures in which he tried to organize and systematize he existing knowledge and practices of mesmerism. Alexander Bertrand investigated mesmerism experimentally, while trying to establish the scientific foundations of the mesmerist practices. His friend, General Noizet, who also practiced mesmerism, published a monograph on the subject in 1854 (Noizet, 1854). Both Bertrand and Noizet emphasized that a large domain of the human mind was unconscious. They argued that unconscious thoughts could be recognized only indirectly. August Ambroise Liebeault (1823-1904), the founder of the Nancy School of medical hypnotism was influenced by the work of Bertrand and Noizet. He based his concept of hypnosis on their teachings (Ellenberger, 1970).

Medical hypnotism developed into an important school in Paris under the leadership of Jean Martin Charcot (1825-1893), while Ambroise Liebeault (1823-1904) and Hippolyte Bernheim (1837-1919) established an important center in Nancy. These centers of hypnotic treatment became known as the Paris and Nancy schools. Hypnotism came to be used in cases of hysteria, which were widespread at the time.

The controversy in French medical circles about the nature of hysteria had become prominent during Louis Napoleon's Second Empire. It was then seen to be a very common condition which took the form of a crippling paralysis and of dramatic seizures. Hysteria was especially prevalent among women from the lower social classes and many patients in poorhouses were diagnosed as suffering from this condition. The questions which were widely debated were, first, whether hysteria was confined only to women, or whether it occurred also in men ? Secondly, there was an argument about whether the primary site of the disease was in the brain or in the female reproductive organs. Thirdly, it was queried whether this disease was associated with frustrated sexual desires.

The detailed clinical manifestations of this disease were described in 1859 by the Parisian physician, Pierre Briquet (1796-1881), in his *Treatise on Hysteria* (1859). Briquet believed that the pathology of hysteria was located in the brain. He claimed that there was a strong family predisposition, although environmental factors were also important in the etiology of this condition. Further, he believed that although hysteria was prevalent predominantly in women, it occurred although rarely, in men. Briquet rejected the theory that frustrated sexual desires caused hysteria, because he frequently found this condition among prostitutes. Others speculated vaguely about the possible psychological causes of hysteria.

The great neurologist Charcot was in charge of the Salpetriere hospital for women in Paris. He was interested in hypnosis and applied it to the investigation and treatment of non-psychotic patients who were suffering mainly from grand hysteria or hysterical epilepsy. Charcot came to the conclusion that all hysterical patients were susceptible to hypnosis, and that both hysterical patients and those people who were susceptible to hypnosis had a hereditary organic abnormality (*diathesis*) of the brain. Normal people could not be hypnotized. Thus, Charcot came to regard hypnosis as a hysterical symptom, a "stigmatum" of hysteria. This theory of hypnosis was opposed by the Nancy school which maintained that everybody could be hypnotized and that hypnotic phenomena were manifestations of suggestion and auto-suggestion. This view also implied that everyone, if subjected to proper suggestion, could develop hysterical symptoms. There was no inherited organic abnormality of the brain associated with hysteria. In the end, the view of the Nancy school prevailed. After Charcot's sudden death in 1893, information came to light which discredited his work with hysterics. It was discovered that his assistants coached the hysterical patients so that they would give the expected performance during the clinical demonstrations of hypnosis for which Salpetriere became famous all over the world. Joseph Babinski, Charcot's successor at Salpetriere discontinued the hypnotic treatment of hysterics and resumed a purely organic orientation in neurology.

In 1885, a young neurologist from Vienna, Sigmund Freud, won a travelling grant to study with Charcot at Salpetriere. Subsequently he spent some time in Nancy with Bernheim and Liebeault. Sigmund Freud (1856-1939) was then an unknown Viennese neuropathologist. Freud was impressed by Charcot's hypnotic techniques. On his return to Vienna he began to use hypnosis in psychotherapy. This constituted the beginnings of the psychoanalytical method of treatment which brought fame to Freud.

In France, itself, however, Charcot's influence lived on in the work of his student, the philosopher-physician, Pierre Janet (1859-1947). He too used hypnosis when he investigated cases of multiple personality. Nineteenth century medical research was fascinated by the problem of multiple personality which in the past had been viewed as having occult qualities. Janet's psychodynamic theory of mental illness accounted for this condition by arguing that it was a manifestation of hysteria. Janet's theory of mental illness was based on the concept of mental energy (Janet,1889,1903,1909,1919,1926). The latter had two aspects: 1)"psychological force," conceived as potential or latent energy. 2) "psychological tension," conceived as kinetic or manifest energy. Here the essential ideas of the scientific revolution in physics and biology made themselves felt. Janet juxtaposed "psychological force," with "psychological tension." Perhaps Comte's positivism with its focus on dynamic and static institutions in history played a part in Janet's thinking. His uncle, Paul Janet was a well known philosopher, and he himself had taught philosophy at the lyceum level before studying medicine. Yet the idea of psychological tension is not static, and was conceived as kinetic or manifest energy. Psychological disorders were due, either to 1) a low level of "psychological force," or to 2) a low level of "psychological tension." Inadequate levels of force produced weakness and fatigue. Insufficient tension impeded the integration and synthesis of mental functions.

For Janet, mental functions formed a hierarchy of three levels ranging from higher to lower. The lowest level mental functions included simple motor responses, acts of perception, and rudimentary responses to social objects. At the second level were "immediate actions" and "assertive beliefs." These functions were under the control of language. The highest level of mental functions involved internalization of social values as that of work, and the achievement of individual uniqueness or self-actualization.

Janet isolated three basic forms of psycho-neurotic affliction: asthenia, hysteria, and psychosthenia. The first was caused by a low level of psychological force, while the low level of psychological tension caused the other two. In hysteria, however, the low level of psychological tension affected only a few of the mental functions, leaving most of the others unaffected. Yet consciousness narrowed because of the accompanying tendency to dissociate. Low "psychological tension" prevented the proper integration and synthesis of mental functions which led to dissociation, disintegration, and psychological automatism. Once the dissociated functions of hysteria became unconscious, their existence became autonomous and manifested itself in unconscious automatisms. Extreme dissociation resulted in multiple personality.

In psychosthenia a low "psychological tension" produced a mental automatism which invaded consciousness, and interfered with integration and synthesis of immediate experience. The manifestations of psychosthenia were obsessional thoughts, doubts, compulsions and fixed ideas. Janet's school was continued in France by Henri Ey, Henri Baruk and Jean Deley. They further elaborated Janet's theory of hierarchical organization of psychological functions.

In America a similar line of research was pursued by Morton Prince (1854-1929) who investigated cases of multiple personality by hypnosis. His most famous case is that of Miss Beauchamp (Prince, 1906). At the University of Geneva, Theodor Flournoy (1854-1920) professor of psychology and friend of William James, used hypnosis to investigate cases of multiple personality as well as phenomena like mental telepathy and automatic writing. His most famous case was a woman known under the pseudonym of "Helen Smith" (Flournoy, 1900). She was a medium and claimed to be possessed, at different times, by three personalities, that of Marie Antoinette, that of an Indian princess, and that of a Martian extra-terrestial being. She even claimed to be fluent in the Martian language. Flournoy explained these apparently supernatural phenomena by assuming natural causes such as repressed memories of stories previously read in books. Frustrated motives for adventure and recognition also played a role.

Thus we may conclude that the historical roots of the modern psycho-dynamic theories of mental illness lay in mesmerism and in its offspring, hypnotism. In the nineteenth century, mesmerism became more self-consciously psycho-dynamic. It eventually gave rise to the modern conception of the unconscious. Since Descartes' famous, *cogito ergo sum*, psychologists had given great emphasis to the conscious forces operating within the psyche. The use of mesmeric techniques, and then of hypnotism, led to a better understanding of the less conscious forces. It was here that Sigmund Freud produced one of the revolutions of the modern mind, when he argued in *The Interpretation of Dreams* (1900) that conscious forces had been "overestimated." He then reduced consciousness to the role of a perceiving sense organ (Baumer, 1977). The modern view of the unconscious emerged in two main streams of thought. The first of these, like Freud's psychoanalytic theory, regarded the unconscious as the domain of primitive, immature psychological forces, which were not under the ego's control. They caused psychoneurotic phenomena. The second conception involved a return to the idea of divine madness which had been popular in ancient times. Yet it too now took on modern dress in the theories of Carl Gustav Jung who developed an idea of a "collective unconscious." Post World War II psychedelic theory of mental illness also derived from the second conception. This second conception of the unconscious endowed it with transcendental powers and parapsychological capabilities. It viewed the unconscious as the ultimate source of creativity and enlightenment.

The use of hypnotism in unlocking the secrets of the mind appeared as central in the development of modern psychoanalysis. The mesmerism-hypnotism development had culminated in the work of Charcot in Paris, and that of the Nancy school from which modern psychoanalysis emerged. The relationship between the use of hypnotism as a medical treatment and the emergence of psychoanalysis is indeed a unique one. The hypnotists treated patients who were sane, but who suffered from baffling conditions such as hysteria, multiple personality and somnombulism. All of these conditions are now categorized as psychoneuroses. They could not be easily fitted into the medical model of disease. Consequently, they were given a psychological explanation and were treated from that perspective. Patients suffering from these conditions were usually treated in doctors' offices rather than in hospitals. Doctors who used hypnosis usually were not "alienists," but general physicians. Later they tended to be neurologists. In fact, Charcot had established neurology as a separate medical specialty, while Moritz Romberg (1795-1873), who held the chair of medicine at Berlin, wrote the first systematic textbook of neurology in 1846.

At the end of the nineteenth century, neurologists very often divided their time between organic neurological patients deemed incurable, whom they attended in general hospitals, and patients suffering from psychoneurosis who were treated in their private offices by hypnotism and other kinds of psychotherapy. Often a neurologist also became a medical psychologist. Modern psychiatry has developed from two different roots then, from the treatment of psychotics in mental hospitals, and from private neurological practice which dealt with psychoneurotics. The different antecedents explain the tension between the medical (organic) and the psychological models which are characteristic of modern psychiatry.

Yet the development of psychiatry is far more complex than recounted so far. In order to understand various psychiatric systems and theories, both organic and psychological, it is necessary to summarize briefly some developments in general medical theory. The prevailing philosophical currents were also important. Generally speaking, the nineteenth century was an era characterized by a tension among three major currents of thought. These included: first, the irrationalism of Romanticism and of the Philosophy of Nature (*Naturphilosophie*) which accompanied it. Secondly, we may see the effect of historicism and evolutionism in the influence of Hegel, Marx, Spencer, and Darwin. Thirdly, Comte's positivism and the closely related force of reductionist materialism played their role. The irrationalism of Nature Philosophy clashed with the positivism of the materialists, in turn exerting an influence on the development of psychiatry. Romanticism and Nature Philosophy dominated the first half of the nineteenth century, while positivism was dominant during the second. This distinction was particularly important for German psychiatry.

Although positivism had already become dominant in French psychiatry during the early nineteenth century, its conflict with Nature Philosophy influenced the Germans only later. Positivism advocated a scientific outlook on life based on the empirico-rational method. It actively encouraged the development of physical and biological sciences. General medicine was dominated by scientific thinking and was based on experimental physiology, chemistry and other laboratory sciences. To quote E.H. Ackerknecht: "Medicine has been scientific in intention for a long time. But only during the nineteenth century did it become to a large extent scientific in fact" (Ackerknecht, 1968, p.146). This thinking influenced the further development of the medical disease model.

The disease model of the eighteenth century had been expressed in various systems of nosology. Complex classificatory systems of disease were offered, which were modeled after the plant taxonomy of Linnaeus. These nosological systems were based on symptomatology and the natural histories of disease entities. The result was an "ontology" of diseases associated with an Aristotelian quest for the essences of the disease categories, that is, their "essential features." Characteristic of this period was Philippe Pinel's *Nosographie Philosophique* (Philosophical Nosography), of 1813. Pinel (1845-1826) had been influenced by Cabanis and other eighteenth century French materialists. His 1801 *Medico-Philosophical Treatise on Mental Alienation* became a classic in the history of psychiatry. Pinel was imbued with the reform spirit of the French revolutionary era and was highly critical of previous work in his field.

He tried to simplify the classification of mental disease by recognizing only four ailments as genuine mental illnesses. These were the delirious hallucinatory kind of mania, then the well known melancholia, and dementia and idiocy. (Ackerknecht, 1985). Among other subjects, Pinel discussed the notion of "essential fevers." Yet Pinel's theorizing was criticized by the younger generation of clinicians and medical scientists in Paris, a city which had become the center of the new scientific medicine. In part, however, he was considered suspect by the postwar generation of the Bourbon restoration because of his freer political views.

The new medical thinking was based on careful observation of mass clinical data provided by public hospitals. These were the results of physical examinations in which percussion and auscultation were used, along with the newly invented stethoscope of Rene Laennec. Much of the data came from autopsies. In addition, Pierre Charles Alexander Louis (1737-1872) introduced a simple statistical method to assess the association between clinical symptoms and autopsy findings. Experimental physiology and pathology became the foundation of medicine (Ackerknecht, 1968; Pagel, 1901).

The "Vitalist-Mechanist" Controversy

During the nineteenth century, biology and physiology were the subject of controversy between the two schools of thought: the "vitalistic" and the "mechanistic." The vitalists believed that life processes were controlled by their own, *sui generis* laws, while mechanists believed that these processes were controlled by the laws of physics and chemistry. However, both schools of thought had moved away from focusing on the whole organism and on disease entities. Instead they examined the normal and abnormal functions of various organs in detail. This led to a search for strict localization of pathological lesions. The concept of disease became also a subject of controversy. Marie Francois Xavier Bichat (1771-1802), a pupil of Pinel and a vitalist, replaced the concept of global disease entities by one of the disorders localized in specific tissues. Each bodily tissue was characterized by a specific vital force (irritability). The disturbance of these specific tissue irritabilities led to various diseases localized in different organs. The principle of strict localization was carried further by Francois Joseph Victor Broussais (1772-1838), who transformed the disease essentialism of the eighteenth century into a theory of lesions caused by irritation. The irritation lesions of the stomach and the other digestive organs were central for Broussais system. He believed that similar to other diseases, mental illness was also due to the effects of irritation. The opponents of the disease ontology and of "essentialism" were divided between the Paris clinical school, led by Broussais, and the "pathological anatomical school," led by Antoine Laurent Bayle (1774-1816) and Rene Theophile Hyacinthe Laennec (1781-1826), the inventor of the stethoscope. The clinical school put more stress on bedside observation, while the pathological anatomical school put more stress on autopsies and on laboratory medicine.

Laboratory medicine applied the concepts and methods of chemistry to medicine with increasing rapidity. It had moved away from the structural-anatomical approach of the lesion localizers to a functionalist approach. It viewed the human organism as a system of physiological functions. This development culminated in the work of Claude Bernard (1813-1878) who investigated the regulatory mechanisms of organisms by the method of experimental physiology. Thus he developed the concept of the *milieu interieur* or internal environment. This made it possible for body cells to maintain their integrity and to survive. The constancy of the internal milieu was maintained by a sensitive homeostatic mechanism. The use of the term "homeostatis" was added in the twentieth century, however, by Walter B. Cannon (1932). Bernard's theoretical conception of physiology appeared in his *Introduction to Experimental Medicine* (1865). He viewed the human organism as "merely a living machine so constructed that. .

. the outer environment is in free communion with the inner organic environment," while the organic units had "protective functions to place in reserve the materials of life," and to maintain "the humidity, warmth and other conditions for vital activity." Most importantly, he believed that "*Sickness and death are merely a dislocation of disturbance of the mechanism which regulates the contact of the vital stimulants with the organic units*" (Italics are mine-TW). (Bernard, 1865/1957, p.76, citing Gasking, 1970, p.158).

Bernard also believed that medicine would become a true science when pathology was based on physiology. Thus, according to Bernard, the difference between disease and health was quantitative and not qualitative. The organism was regarded as a homeostatic system, described by a set of mutually dependent variables. A variation beyond a certain range on a variable, unless compensated for, was not compatible with the state of health and therefore denoted illness. Bernard's was a continuity theory of disease, while the theories of the eighteenth century nosologists implied a discontinuity between the state of health and the state of disease. Rudolf Virchow (1821-1902), the great German pathologist, the creator of the theory of cellular pathology, and contemporary of Bernard, implies similar conceptualisations. In an article written in 1847 he rejected the notion of diseases as self-subsistent autonomic entities which force their way into the body, but instead regarded them as names for disordered physiological conditions. Members of the *physiologische Heilkunde* school such as Wilhelm Roser and Carl Wunderlich, also rejected the ontological conception of disease in favor of physiological dynamics (Ackerknecht, 1968). At about the same time, the ontology of disease was attacked by Friederich Oesterlen in his *Medical Logic* (1852). The latter criticized implicit metaphysical assumptions which endowed disease entities with independent being, or ontological reality, leading to a quest for their "essences," beyond their clinical manifestations and the pathophysiological mechanisms.

It seemed as if the classical disease model which implied an extrinsic entity implanted on an organismic system was on its way out. However, an important development occurred in the middle of the nineteenth century, which caused the pendulum to swing again in favor of the disease (nosological) model. The new development was associated with the conclusive proof that infectious diseases were caused by bacteria. The theory that micro-organisms were responsible for epidemic diseases was quite old, and went back to Fracastorius in the sixteenth century, possibly even to ancient times. However, this theory had never been conclusively proven or generally accepted. Even Justus von Liebig (1803-1873), the great chemist, rejected the idea that bacteria could cause fermentation. Then, in 1850, Casimir Davaine (1812-1882) and Pierre Rayer proved that anthrax bacteria were the causal agents in anthrax infection. That discovery was followed by the discovery of the cause and treatment of rabies by Louis Pasteur (1822-1895). In Germany, Robert Koch (1843-1910) discovered the bacilli which caused tuberculosis and cholera. Thus the new science of bacteriology emerged.

These great discoveries in the second half of the nineteenth century, revolutionized medical thinking and firmly entrenched the disease model. The conclusion followed, that specific bacteria caused specific diseases. The causal relation was codified by Robert Koch's famous postulates. He posited the notion that the same bacterium was always found with the disease. Yet, this bacterium was not found with any other disease. The bacterium isolated from a diseased person would produce the disease in a susceptible experimental animal.

The same bacterium could be isolated from the experimentally infected animal. This simplistic notion assumed an unifactorial and unidirectional causality which tended to play down the organism's reaction to the pathogenic agent.

During the nineteenth century, infectious diseases constituted the most serious hazard to human health. Thousands of people died in epidemics of typhoid fever, typhus, and cholera. Even greater numbers were dying of tuberculosis and puerperal fever. The fact that the causal agents of infectious diseases were discovered, led to a successful prevention and treatment, and represented the greatest practical achievement in the history of medicine. The disease model, which envisaged the pathogenic agent entering the organism, and causing the specific pathological process ending in death or recovery became very influential again. Numerous attempts were made to apply this conceptual model to pathological conditions other than those of infectious diseases. As a result, the new experimental and theoretical developments in general medicine were soon reflected in theories of mental illness.

The mainstream of science and of scientific medicine had been strongly influenced by Auguste Comte (1798-1857) during the nineteenth century. His philosophy of positivism was particularly important, since it had a tremendous influence on scientists, social reformers, and physicians in the nineteenth century, in particular on those in France and in Great Britain. It also presented a philosophical outlook which was opposite to that of subjective idealism and that of Nature Philosophy. Both of these were influential in Germany during the Romantic period, early in the nineteenth century. Positivism was associated with the scientific outlook of French utopians like St. Simon and Comte. It rejected metaphysics, except for a semi-mystical interest in propagating the religion of Humanity, and also rejected questions about the ultimate nature of the universe. It stressed objectivity versus subjectivity. Positivism was a philosophy of the industrial revolution. It glorified technical progress and practical achievements. Auguste Comte (1908) was a follower , even the secretary of Count Henri Saint-Simon (1760-1825) (1952), who believed that scientific principles could be applied to the understanding of human behaviour and to the evolution of society. Saint-Simon called the science of society, social physiology. Comte believed that the development of society occurred in three stages: the theological, the metaphysical, and the positive. These were in turn, deemed representative of fictitious, abstract, and positive forms of thought. Human understandinmg grew as society developed, from the early stage to the scientific. Humanity and not God constituted a Great Being. During the second phase, men had already substituted Nature for God. At each stage, the individual human being also matured and developed. The progress of the mind and of moral behaviour seemed to be the only kind peculiar to the human race. Only when the positivist stage was reached, could a rational human behaviour and rational interpersonal relations be achieved. The pinnacle of all the sciences was the science of sociology according to Comte.

Comte's social positivism influenced British Utilitarians, especially John Stuart Mill (1806-1873), the famous son of James Mill (1773-1832). The founder of Utilitarianism, Jeremy Bentham (1773-1836) had been a family friend of James Mill and the intellectual mentor of John. John Stuart Mill had been a child prodigy (he knew Greek at the age of three), and emerged from a depression and life crisis experienced at age 25, to challenge the beliefs of the Benthamites. He objected to Comte's degrading psychology as a science, but accepted the belief of the positivists about social progress. Social positivism gave impetus to many reforms, in which he believed.

Evolutionary positivism, another species of this form of thought, became associated with Darwin's theory of biological evolution. Its exponents were Herbert Spencer (1820-1903), Thomas Huxley (1825-1895) in England, and Ernst Haeckel (1834-1919) in Germany. It was an evolutionary theory of the universe. It traced its development from atoms and molecules to man. Men were endowed with reason and consciousness and formed complex societies.

Finally, a third form of positivism was empirico-critical positivism. This represented an extreme version of empiricist philosophy associated with the names of Richard Avenarius (1843-1896), and of Ernst Mach (1838-1916). They were precursors of logical positivism of the kind which was followed by the Vienna Circle in the twentieth century.

The importance of positivism for nineteenth century psychiatry was its association with the organic school of thought in this branch of medicine. Building on the work of Albrecht von Haller and Samuel Thomas von Soemmering (1755-1830), that generation of psychiatrists focused mainly on the anatomy and physiology of the brain. Thus introspection was downgraded, as was the psychological approach to the problems of mental illness. The *Somatiker* psychiatrists like Wilhelm Griesinger in Germany, and Jean Etienne Esquirol in France, Henry Maudsley, Thomas Laycock, and John Hughlings Jackson in England were all influenced by Comte's positivism. Esquirol attended private lectures given by Comte on his philosophy to a small audience of prominent scientists in 1825. These lectures were the basis for Comte's *Cours de Philosophie Positive* (1830-1842/1908).

The materialist version of positivism opposed vitalism and tended to consider the "vital force," a metaphysical concept which could not be established experimentally. Diverse kinds of reductionist materialism and sensationism propagated in philosophy had also played their role. These may be traced to the work of Antoine Destutt de Tracy (1754-1836), to Ludwig Feuerbach (1804-1872), and to Ludwig Buchner (1824-1899). Others who figured here, were Jacob Moleschott (1822-1893), and Karl Vogt (1817-1895). They assumed that the universe was composed of nothing but atoms, possibly shaped like billiard balls, which had accidentally formed more and more complex aggregates. James Mill conceived the human mind to be only a mosaic of sensations. Such ideas had the comforting appeal of monism for many scientists.

The vitalists who opposed this mechanistic outlook were steadily losing ground. The synthesis of urea by Wohler in 1828, the discovery of the conservation of energy and the formulation of the laws of thermodynamics by Robert Mayer in 1842, tipped the scales in favor of the mechanistic theory. This is illustrated by the "pact" made in 1845 by four distinguished physiologists to combat vitalism and to support the materialist explanation of life: Ernst Brucke, Carl Ludwig, Emil du Bois-Reymond, and Hermann von Helmholtz. All of them were students of Johannes Mueller, the famous German physiologist and zoologist (Boring, 1950).

Vitalism continued to have its adherents into the beginning of the twentieth century. Philosophers like Henri Bergson gave it a new prominence, as did the biologist Hans Driesch. William McDougall continued the tradition in psychology. Scientists like Liebig and Virchow did not want to identify with materialist philosophy. They left metaphysics to theologians and philosophers in order to pursue their scientific enterprise within a positivist framework. Mysticism, metaphysics, and speculations were shunned. Science became an honorific word. It was going to solve all of mankind's problems, and it was going to help build a better society. Following Cabanis, many other thinkers believed that moral laws could be reduced to natural laws. Belief in progress became an article of faith.

The Controversy of Psychological vs. Somatic Theory of Mental Illness

The new science was opposed by an intellectual undercurrent flowing in the opposite direction to the mainstream of Positivism and Materialism. This found expression in the irrationalism and mysticism associated with the Romantic movement in literature and with the Philosophy of Nature (*Naturphilosophie)* in science.

The conflict between these intellectual movements was particularly acute in Germany during the first half of the nineteenth century. Johann Wolfgang von Goethe (1749-1832) may be considered a precursor of the Philosophy of Nature movement. The most important philosophers of Nature were:Friedrich Wilhelm von Schelling (1775-1854), Gotthilf Heinrich von Schubert (1780-1860), Ignaz Paul Vital Troxler (1780-1866), Carl Gustav Carus (1789-1869), and Arthur Schopenhauer (1788-1860). Gustav Theodor Fechner (1801-1887) was an important epigone of this philosophical movement. In addition, two other philosophers who are not usually classified as Nature Philosophers, should be mentioned. These were Johann Gottlieb Fichte (1762-1814), and Johann Friedrich Herbart (1776-1841). Both were followers of Kant, and influential in shaping the views of German psychiatrists during the period of Romanticism. More indirectly, they were the source of some ideas found in psychoanalytical theory.

Both the Philosophy of Nature movement in science, as well as Romanticism in literature, reflected important technological and economic changes. The beginning of the Industrial Revolution in Europe, was associated with the harnessing of energy, first of hydropower and then of steam. This accomplishment led to the perception and glorification of energy as the underlying principle of the universe. All forms of energy were emanations of the same dynamic power which was behind the observed phenomena. Nature was perceived as a manifestation of striving dynamic forces, expressions of all-encompassing energy, the origin of which was in the sun. The Newtonian, eighteenth century, conception of the universe as a clock was replaced by that of a dynamic, living system.

The French Revolution and its aftermath in the Napoleonic Wars, brought out the importance of social conflict and struggle. These developments also gave birth to nationalism and to the struggle for freedom which was associated with it. There was a cult of individual heroism and of men who by the strength of their will and their determination could attain seemingly unattainable goals. This was indeed a time of *Sturm und Drang* (Storm and Stress). Much of this spirit was reflected in the thinking of the Philosophers of Nature. For them, energy was conceived in animistic terms, as a cosmic will to create as well as to destroy things. Such a cosmic force or will, was perceived as a unifying principle which seemed to be underlying both natural phenomena and those of the human mind. Arthur Schopenhauer, a widely read philosopher of the nineteenth century, presented those ideas in the most articulated form.

The notion of mental energy stemming from the unconscious regions of the mind led to a dynamic psychology which was a precursor of Freud's psychoanalytical theory. The stress on free will and on maintaining self-identity in the flux of change put a premium on personality growth, on self-actualization and on individual autonomy. It thus anticipated the Humanistic psychology of the twentieth century.

The interest of the Germans of the early nineteenth century was colored by their experience with the French Revolution and Napoleon. Since the middle class intellectuals had supported the Prussian monarchy, their search for human freedom did not find much realization in the political arena. Instead they turned to philosophizing about the nature of man's restricted sphere of activity. Here their interests coincided with that of psychiatry.

The most important philosophers were Johann Wolfgang von Goethe, the greatest poet and dramatist of his age, Friedrich Wilhelm Joseph von Schelling (1907, 1988) much admired as a modern Plato by King Maximilian II of Bavaria, and Arthur Schopenhauer (1819), a notorious anti-feminist and the greatest pessimist of his age.

The first two represented the optimistic version of the Philosophy of Nature, while Schopenhauer represented its pessimistic variant. All three were influenced by the philosophy of Gottfried Leibniz and its dynamic view of the world. Thus they influenced the mainstream of dynamic psychiatry the history of which was recounted by Ellenberger (1970). The Philosophers of Nature had all been influenced by Kantian transcendentalism and particularly by the philosophy of transcendental and moral idealism of Johann Gottlieb Fichte (1762-1814) (1969), a follower of Kant. For Fichte, (much like Hegel), reality was the pure activity of spirit. It was prior to any specific definable, substance, thing or person. By a series of acts, the transcendental ego (the spirit) first posited itself. Once it affirmed itself it could posit the non-ego which represented the external world. In a third step, the transcendental ego posited the limited phenomenal ego. Also, the limited phenomenal external world. As a result, the transcendental ego hid the springs of its motivation from itself. The aim of philosophy was to free man from these self-imposed limitations.

Fichte was mainly interested in ethics. He developed a theory of ethical idealism. This was based on Kant's conception of a categorical imperative and freedom of the will. Only the achievement of full freedom could lead to the implementation of spiritual ideals. Fichte had identified himself with the struggle of the German nation for freedom and for liberation from the Napoleonic occupation. As a quintessential Romantic philosopher, he preached and lived his philosophy.

The optimistic Philosophers of Nature were Goethe and Schelling. Goethe claimed to be in love with nature and affirmed a pantheism all his own. As a belief system, pantheism was still identified with atheism. The pre-Romantics like Goethe were also influenced by the debate about Spinozism which raged amongst such literati as Friedrich Jacobi, Moses Mendelssohn, Herder, and Goethe himself. All were influenced by Spinoza's philosophy and committed to monism and pantheism.

However, in spite of the fact that Spinoza had been accused of atheism by most commentators since the seventeenth century, Goethe found him to be a theist. In 1785, he observed to Jacobi, that Spinoza showed that existence (*Dasein*) was God (Hettner,III/3, 1909). Goethe's own ideas placed God outside of nature itself. He believed that the universe was driven by a creative force which was responsible for its evolution and its unfolding. He identified this creative force with the God of the theologians. God was not just the primary mover, the first cause. He was the spiritual force within, the essence of the world, its all-enveloping and fully embracing actuality; the plenitude of existence. According to Goethe, nature was animate. It consisted of an infinite number of unique living beings (Leibnizian monads). Each being was harmonious with all other beings. Nature was characterized by a continuous activity, creativity, and change or metamorphosis. Its beauty expressed the underlying harmony. Goethe stressed the importance of intuition and imagination for the understanding of nature and of human beings. These faculties supplemented the senses and reason.

Goethe's work on the metamorphosis of plant life dated from the 1780s and 1790s. In this inquiry Goethe was looking for the general laws of organization which lay behind the expressed form, and which linked the internal system of organization with external forms. The major idea was that the form (*Gestalt*) was already contained within the seed (*Kern*). Goethe (1790) believed that the variety of forms observed in nature stemmed from a few prototypes or the primordial forms such as the primordial plant (*Urpflanze*). They represented blueprints or designs which set a limit to the variations produced by metamorphosis.

It is not clear whether the primordial forms (*Urphaenomene*) were the ancestral archetypes, or whether they existed as Platonic ideal forms outside time. According to Goethe, the primordial archetype of man was the *Androgyne*, a hermaphrodite who was both male and female. He took this idea from Plato's *Symposium* in which Plato discussed the original of the two sexes. The *Androgyne* myth maintained that Zeus separated the primordial bisexual human being into the male and the female types. Subsequently men and women were searching for one another, longing to be reunited. The idea of Androgyne became very influential in Romantic circles and became the basis of the theory of romantic love.

Goethe distrusted Newtonian science which was based on mathematics. The new science presupposed gradual variation in nature and aimed at quantifying them. In contrast, Goethe believed that nature was characterized by fundamental opposites such as light and dark, or good and evil. It was also characterized by polarities such as contraction and expansion, as seen in the heart muscle's systole and diastole. The attraction and repulsion of elements. the uniting and parting of polarities, were underlying the cyclic processes of nature.

However, superimposed on these processes was the constant striving upward of nature, to create every higher forms. This upward drive of nature was reflected in insatiable strivings of human beings. An illustration of that point was the unquestionable love of life and the curiousity of Faust.

Yet human character seems to have been determined, even unalterable. Thus Faust's destiny was inevitable even though he made some seemingly free will choices (Ungar, 1963).

Friedrich Wilhelm Joseph von Schelling, the other optimistic philosopher of nature, started as a follower of Fichte with whom he taught at the university of Jena. At that period, he subscribed to the philosophy of subjective idealism and believed with Fichte that the beginning and end of all philosophy was freedom. Under the influence of Goethe and the theory of aesthetics of Samuel Taylor Coleridge, Schelling was able to find a more objective middle ground. He became the main spokesman of the "Philosophy of Nature" movement (Schelling, 1797/1988).

The cornerstone of Schelling's philosophy was psycho-physical or panpsychic monism. For Schelling, nature was a visible spirit, while spirit itself was an invisible nature. These were all manifestations of the world soul (*Weltseele*).

Here was a unity of subject and object. Further, there was a unity of nature and of man's knowledge of nature. The world soul was identical with God, while individual human minds were emanations of the former. Nature was conceived to be an infinite self-activity, realizing itself continually in finite matter, but never accomplishing self-realization. Nature was alive, according to Schelling, a living, breathing organism. Ultimate reality represented a universal mind thought to be underlying both the observable material phenomena of the external world, and the individual minds. Accordingly, men were linked by a "bond" of sympathy with eachother and with the whole of nature.

The universal mind represented the deepest layer of what later was called the collective unconscious, the creative source of the life force, of instinctual impulses, of the will to power and of the procreative drive (Lovejoy, 1955). Intuition and emotions were the source of knowledge which could be attained by introspection. Nature was characterized by dynamic polarities striving against one another to attain a balance. There were polarities everywhere: day and night, acids and alkalines, male and female. According to Schelling, there was no life without opposites.

In living organisms, the organizing intelligence was unconscious, and it only manifested itself in its product; the living organism. Only in artistic activity did it become self-conscious. Schelling attributed a great importance to aesthetic experience and artistic creativity. He believed that while the theoretical intelligence merely contemplated the world, and the practical intelligence merely ordered it, the aesthetic intelligence created the world. Schelling's philosophy radiated optimism. Evil existed only to fulfill its purpose of awakening in man the distinction between good and evil. It would be overcome in the process of realization of the good. Imperfection was only a stage in attaining the state of perfection. Man stood at the pinnacle of the creative processes of nature. His free creative activity represented the essence of the world. In his emphasis on becoming, and on freedom, Schelling anticipated existentialism, particularly when he asked the question, "Why is there anything at all ? Why not nothing?" The collective unconscious might be viewed as a "cultural unconscious." It was the seat of ideal primordial forms and symbols with their own *a priori* logic. These were utilized by man in his myth-making and they were the foundations of culture and religion (Jaspers, 1955; Knittermeyer, 1929).

Arthur Schopenhauer offered the pessimistic version of the Philosophy of Nature. His most important book was *Die Welt als Wille und Idee* (1818). (The World as Will and Idea). The title of its enlarged second edition was *Die Welt als Wille und Vorstellung* (1844). The position of departure for the philosophy of Schopenhauer was the Kantian doctrine of phenomena or the perceived appearance of things. These are separate from noumena, the things-in-themselves. However, the noumena also represented the real nature of things underneath their perceived appearances. According to Kant, the things-in-themselves could not be perceived by the senses. They could only be postulated *a priori*, by reason. Schopenhauer disagreed with Kant, on this point.

He believed that since man was part of the universe he could perceive intuitively his inner nature (thing-in-itself), by introspection.

Man's inner experience consisted of desires, strivings, and acts of will. This inner experience of human beings, gave them a glimpse of the real nature of the world. However, introspection gave a misleading picture of human motivation and strivings.

For those who had introspective minds, their own strivings appeared to be goal directed and rational. This was a misperception according to Schopenhauer. The cosmic will underlying the individual wills, was irrational. It was a blind power whose strivings had no ultimate purpose or design. For Schopenhauer, nature was an endless and meaningless struggle for existence. It was full of tension, under constant stress, and was torn by internal conflicts. According to Schopenhauer, intellect was not the master, rather the servant of the will. In addition to being blind and purposeless, the universal cosmic will was evil. Man was a play thing of the malign cosmic will. He was helpless in the face of blind drives emanating from his unconsciousness which completely determined his behaviour.

His conscious reasons for his actions were not the true reasons for his actions, they constituted a sham. The attempts at social reforms were futile because they served only to disguise the aggressive and antisocial urges. In addition to controlling behaviour, the will controlled human thought as well. It repressed unpleasant ideas. (Here we see an overiding of the utilitarian view that the mind responded to pleasure and pain). For Schopenhauer, insanity was caused by a breakdown of repression, a flooding of the intellect by unpleasant thoughts.

In Schopenhauer's system, the sex drive was the most important aspect of the universal will. It was the "focus of the will," and the dominant motive of human behaviour.

However, sex did not bring a lasting satisfaction. Since everything else led to disillusionment, Schopenhauer had few kind words to say about art and music. Genuine art revealed archetypal (Platonic) forms, which were only incompletely and inadquately reflected in the material world. Good music approached most closely and gave the best insight into the ultimate reality: the universal cosmic will. According to Schopenhauer, music was the universal imageless language of the heart. (One of the admirers of Schopenhauer was Richard Wagner, the composer, who felt that his artistic work was inspired by the philosophy of Schopenhauer). However, Schopenhauer had a few words of encouragement for human beings. Their moral duty lay in resisting the dominance of the universal will and also liberating themselves from it.

This could be achieved by mystical experience in which man transcended his nature. Towards the end of his life, Schopenhauer became interested in the Eastern philosophy of Upanishads and Buddhist texts as the guidance for mystical experiences.

In spite of his pessimism, Schopenhauer, like Leibniz and the contemporary Romantic philosophers, developed a dynamic concept of man. He rejected the mechanistic notions of associations, ideas, and impressions. He believed that human beings were motivated by drives which were largely unconscious. The similarity between Freud's psychoanalytical theory and the philosophy of Schopenhauer is obvious and was commented on by Max Scheler (1929), Ernst Cassirer (1946), and Thomas Mann (1936). Schopenhauer was widely read and became very influential in the second half of the nineteenth century. In addition to Richard Wagner and psychodynamic psychiatry, he also influenced Friedrich Nietzsche, another philosopher of pessimism, demystification and debunking.

Another philosopher of nature was Carl Gustav Carus. As well as being a philosopher, Carus was a physician, a biologist, and a painter. He did research in comparative anatomy, and was interested in the process of development and evolution. Carus was influenced by Aristotelian philosophy and conceived of the development of nature as an unfolding of the multiplicity and complexity within a unity which he identified with God. The deity was revealed in nature through its organization and its unifying structure. During the development, the collective unconsciousness of nature (the unknown "Divine") evolved through progressive stages into individual consciousness. The individual consciousness renewed and maintained themselves by sleep during which they periodically returned to the unconscious state. His most important book was *Psyche, Zur Entwicklungsgeschichte der Seele* (1846). (Psyche, On the Developmental History of the Soul).

For Carus, the access to the understanding of the human mind was through the unconscious. He considered the unconscious to be a biological force, directing and regulating the human organism. It regulated both the physiological and psychological functions. According to Carus, the unconscious was stratified into layers. At bottom, was the "general absolute unconscious" which was completely inaccessible to the conscious experience. The next stratum was the "partial absolute unconscious" which directed the dynamics of bodily and mental processes, and finally at the top was the "relative unconscious" which was similar to Freudian preconscious.

In the development of the human fetus, the higher strata of mind emerged gradually. The pre-embryonic stage of the "general absolute unconscious" was followed by the embryonic stage of the "formative unconscious." This directed the individual's growth, and the functioning of his body. Consciousness emerged gradually, after birth, but remained under the control of the unconscious. According to Carus, the unconscious was aware of the past and the future, but not of the present. The unconscious was indefatigable. It was a source of strength for consciousness, and had healing powers. It was governed by its own inborn wisdom. Human beings could communicate through their unconscious minds, since the individual unconscious mind was linked with the unconscious minds of all men.

The next philosopher of nature to be discussed, was Gotthilf von Schubert. He proposed a theory of dreams which anticipated both the Freudian and Jungian theories. According to him, man lived in harmony with nature in his original, primordial state. Through egoism (self-love) he became alienated from nature, and "fell from grace." However, human beings would eventually overcome the state of alienation and become reconciled with nature. This theme could be detected in the ancient religious myths of death and resurrection, such as those of Adonis and Mithra. The three constituent parts of human beings were the living body (*Leib*), the soul, and the spirit. Human life was a process of becoming, and went through a series of metamorphoses. The ego developed early in childhood. After middle age, a second center of self-consciousness (*Selbstbewusstsein*) developed in the soul.

Thus, the human being can be metaphorically compared to "double star." (This idea is similar to that of Jung, who postulated the existence of two centers in the human psyche; the ego and the self). In man, the longing for love cannot be separated from that for death. (One is reminded of Freud's postulation of a life and death instinct). The two centers of man represent the cycle of birth, death and rebirth, the theme of many myths and religious mysteries.

In his book, *The Symbolism of Dreams* (1837), von Schubert asserted that the pictorial symbolic language of dreams was different from that of waking life. It is the archaic, universal language of the whole of mankind. It represented abstract concepts pictorially. Sometimes several concepts were combined into one image. The idea of condensation, was further developed by Freud. Often the meaning of a concept was disguised and was represented by its opposite. The image of a man might be disguising that of a woman. Fire could be represented by water. Dreams were usually immoral and had a demonic character. They gave expression to aggressive and antisocial desires.

The next to be discussed, Ignaz Troxler (1812), a Swiss Philosoper of Nature, taught at the University of Basel for many years. This was about fifty years before Carl Gustav Jung was a student at that university. In contrast to von Schubert, who divided the human being into three parts, Troxler divided man into four parts that formed two sets of polarities (*Tetraktys*). The two sets of polarities were soma versus soul, and body versus spirit. Body or corpus (*Koerper*) referred to the dead body as dissected by anatomists. The soma or *Leib* represented a living body. The body was complemented by the soul and the soma by the spirit. The four were united by the *Gemuet*, which was a core feeling of the personality. There is a strong resemblance between Troxler's *Tetraktys* and Jung's typology based on four fundamental personality functions. For Jung these were thinking complemented by feeling, and sensing complemented by intuiting. The self united all four functions and constituted the core of the personality. Troxler's theories further resembled those of Jung, in that both of these authors envisaged the personality development as aiming to attain higher levels of spirituality. According to Troxler, the aim of human development was to make the spirit the organ of knowledge and to open the human mind to the divine light.

To summarize briefly, Philosophy of Nature postulated panpsychic monism.The ultimate reality was a universal mind underlying both the observed material phenomena of the external world and that of individual minds. Accordingly, men were linked by a "bond of sympathy" with each other and with the whole of nature. The universal mind was the collective unconscious, the creative source of life force, of instinctual impulses, of the will to power and of the procreative drives. (According to Schopenhauer, the universal mind was evil). It was the seat of ideal primordial forms, which were reflected in the imperfect forms of external reality, and were aslso revealed in imagery and dreams. The individual unconscious was an outgrowth of the collective unconsciousness which further evolved into individual consciousness. Intuition and emotions were the sources of knowledge. Nature was characterized by dynamic polarities, striving against one another to achieve a balance. Philosophy of Nature was a holistic philosophy which contrasted with Cartesian dualism and rationalism and encompassed the whole man in his relations to other men and the universe. The universe was not a concatenation of atoms or sensory qualia, but a dynamic, organic whole.

The Philosophers of Nature and many Romantic poets believed that there was a mystical union between man and the universe. However, they also emphasized the autonomy of the individual and the need for self-actualization. This notion was paralleled by the stress on subjectivity and on individuality. There was a glorification of the hero which was characteristic of the Romantic literature of that period. The Romantics viewed aesthetic experience as a communion with the universe in which individual ego merged with nature. They also distrusted dry reason and preferred intuition and emotion. The Philosophy of Nature school then, produced a dynamic depth psychology, a precursor to Freud's psychoanalytical theory, and even more so, to Jung's analytical psychology. By postulating the existence of an unconscious, the Nature Philosophers anticipated psychoanalysis and other psychodynamic theories.

Distinct from the Philosophy of Nature was the new associationist psychology of Johann Friedrich Herbart (1776-1841). (Herbart,1824) He was not a Nature philosopher, but probably influenced Freud more directly than Schelling, Schopenhauer, and Carus. (He studied G.A. Lindner's *Lehrbuch der empirischen Psychologie nach genetischer Methode* of 1858, based on Herbartian psychology, in Gymnasium). Herbartian psychology was the first psychological system to which Freud was exposed. Herbart was a follower of Kant, but took his idea of psychodynamics and of the unconscious from Leibniz. It was the latter who had postulated that there were degrees of consciousness from a vague and undefined variety, to a clear and articulated kind. Percepts and ideas or representations (*Vorstellungen*) strove to become clear and to actualize themselves in apperceptions.

In contrast to the Romantic Nature Philosophers, Herbart developed a dynamic-mechanistic system of psychology. According to him, ideas competed to reach the threshold of consciousness. The ideas which became conscious, inhibited (repressed) those which remained unconscious. Once inhibited or repressed, such representations or ideas turned into drives (*Triebe*). Thus the soul which was a simple unknowable substance was engaged in a struggle for survival against foreign representations. Consciousness was an intelligible space or region in which representations interacted. Herbart proposed that the dynamics of the striving and interaction of ideas had to be studied as a mathematics of the representations or ideas which were developed. The result would be a metaphysics of psychology (Windelband, 1907). Herbart's psychological system, in particular, his notion of "apperception" had a tremendous impact on the German theory of education during the nineteenth century. It could be compared to the influence of John Dewey on American education in the twentieth century. In addition, several important German psychiatrists such as Griesinger based their psychological theorizing on Herbart's philosophy. Freud's notion of repression and of psychodynamics in general, shows Herbart's influence.

Important for the history of abnormal psychology as well, was Friedrich Eduard Beneke (1798-1854), a contemporary of Hegel at the University of Berlin. Beneke (1837) was neither a Nature Philosopher nor an absolute idealist. He in fact represented a reaction to the idealism of Fichte, Schelling, and Hegel. As both a psychologist and a philosopher, he was strongly influenced by English empiricism, especially by Locke and Hume. Thus his interests lay in philosophy of mind and in moral philosophy. He rejected the idea of an absolute as well as *a priorism* which had become associated with the followers of Kant.

Using an empirical approach, Beneke's psychology focused on human motivation and individual differences. He was also interested in abnormal and criminal behaviour. His psychology represented a combination of associationism and a theory of mental faculties (powers). The human mind was perceived as a composite of internal drives activated by external stimuli. Consciousness organized the representations of these drives and stimuli. This was done by mutual attraction and blending. It was through an inner preception that human beings could obtain an immediate knowledge of their mental acts.

Although not medically qualified, Beneke was interested in abnormal behaviour. He developed a system of psychology and psychopathology that anticipated modern phenomenological psychiatry. His theory offered a subtle phenomenological analysis of consciousness described in terms of its volume, time, stimulation, and vitality dimensions. He described a range of mental distrubances using these dimensions of consciousness. Experience could thus occur too rapuidly or too slowly along the time dimension.

Beneke also extended the concept of psychopathology and considered immoral behaviour as a manifestation of mental illness. He considered crime to be a medical problem. This had to be treated and was not to be morally condemned. For him, moral laws were not different from natural laws such as those of physics. His views on morals and the human mind scandalized the contemporary idealist philosophers, and as the result of their intervention, he had to leave the University of Berlin for a time.

Beneke believed that there was a connection between man's physical constitution and mental characteristics. He attributed individual differences in normal and abnormal behaviour to the variation of human constitution. Beneke considered abnormal behaviour as quantitatively and not qualitatively different from the normal.

The Herbartian trend, supported by Beneke's work as well, helped to produce Fechner's psychophysics. Gustav Theodor Fechner (1801-1887) was an epigon of Philosophy of Nature. However, he was also an experimental psychologist who developed the method of psychophysics (Fechner, 1860). Fechner started as a physicist interested in the physiology of vision, and he eschewed mysticism. Among other phenomena, he studied visual after-images by exposing himself to the direct view of the sun. As a result, he suffered from a temporary blindness, and also at the age of 39, he developed a serious nervous breakdown. The nervous breakdown could have been severe depression or what Novalis called "sublime hypchondriasis," a creative illness (Ellenberger, 1970). More recently, Kasimir Dabrowski (1964) has referred to such a breakdown as a positive disintegration.

After his recovery, Fechner switched from physics to philosophy and developed his version of Philosophy of Nature (Fechner, 1848;1851). Many of his more esoteric works appeared under the pseudonym of Dr. Mises. He continued with his experimental psychological work with the purpose of proving his philosophical theories of monism and panpsychism. Like other Nature Philosophers, he believed in a pantheistic universe which was monistic and had two aspects, physical and mental. The first was external and was responsible for the appearance of things. Fechner called this the "night" view of nature. The other aspect was internal perception of things and constituted what he called the "day" view of nature. The gravity force uniting the universe corresponded to mental energy which was described as the pleasure principle. The amount of energy which can be potential or actual in any system was constant. In the human organism, some purely physical energy was transformed into the psychophysical, but the total amount of energy was conserved. The method of psychophysics offered a logarithmic, mathematical function (S=log R), relating physical energy (stimulus=R) to mental energy (sensation=S). There was a threshhold of consciousness for sensations.

However, the psychophysical function allowed negative sensations to be extrapolated below the threshold of consciousness. Thus, Fechner removed the notion of the unconscious from the realm of philosophical speculation, away from anecdotal clinical observations. He even took it away from naturalistic observations of hypnotic phenomena and provided a scientific basis for it.

In addition to the psychophysical law, Fechner postulated other psychological principles. One was the topography of mind. According to this principle, mind was divided into two regions: that of waking, and that of dreams. The laws governing mental phenomena in these two regions were different. Another principle was that of pleasure-pain. This one was the most important one for understanding morality, because it governed human behaviour. Pleasures were associated with lowering tension to the optimal level, while its increase was associated with pain.

Fechner's second contribution to experimental psychology was that of experimental aesthetics (Fechner, 1873). He used the principle of pleasure and pain to explain aesthetic experience as well as to explain the psychology of humor. Finally, there were principles of stability (constancy), to complement the principle of causality, and of repetition. According to these two principles, a system tended to achieve a stable state of equilibrium, and also certain events in a system, such as the activity of human organs, could repeat their actions. The principle of stability and repetition were especially important in biology at the level of the individual organism and of the species.

Freud was acquainted with Fechner's work, and, influenced by many of his ideas, he incorporated them into his metapsychology. All of Fechner's "principles" may be found in Freud's metapsychology.

Finally, there was Eduard von Hartmann (1842-1906), a follower of Schopenhauer. He was the last German speculative idealist philosopher. Von Hartmann together with Schopenhauer represented the pessimistic version of the Philosophy of Nature. He combined the Schopenhauerian notion of universal will, the metaphysical essence of the world, with the Hegelian notion of ideas and categories. While the will was a blind, driving force, the ideas and categories provided order and purposes to the world. The interaction between the will and the ideas resulted in the emergence of individual consciousness which would be annihilated in the end. Thus there were three levels of reality. 1) The metaphysical order of the unconscious, 2) the objective order of nature, and 3) the subjective ideal level of consciousness.

In 1869, von Hartmann published his *Philosophy of the Unconscious*, which was widely read in Austria and Germany. Von Hartmann divided the unconscious into (a) the absolute unconscious, which was its deepest level and which constituted the essence of nature. Then (b) the physiological unconscious which underlay the phenomena of life. And (c) the relative or psychological unconscious which was the source of conscious mental life. There was a similarity between the physiological unconscious of von Hartmann, and the partial absolute unconscious of Carus. Both were responsible for guiding life and growth processes. In his book on the philosophy of the unconscious, von Hartmann supported his speculations by many examples from the field of psychology, linguistics, and ethnology. These notions of the unconscious were widely debated and Freud seems to have been aware of them, especially of von Hartmann's theories.

Nineteenth century positivism and materialism which had emerged from the enlightenment's Condillacism, had been opposed by several streams of idealist thought. First by the idealistic German Nature Philosophers, then by the Romantic literati, and also by the Pietist tradition stemming from German Lutheran theology. The Pietist tradition stressed personal independence and responsibility. It also stressed the necessity of ethical self-improvement of service to the community and of the fulfillment of one's duty. Selfishness, self indulgence, and self-deceit were punished by the pangs of guilty conscience, which was harsh and demanding. Sin was associated with a loss of divine grace and a loss of personal freedom. The reward for pious living was the attainment of a higher level of spirituality. Pietism downgraded the importance of intellect and stressed the importance of feelings and of devotion. Consequently, it was congruous with the Romantic ethos and the Philosophy of Nature. Some psychologically minded (*Psychiker*) psychiatrists incorporated the notions associated with Pietism into their theories of mental illness and into their psychotherapeutic practices.

Both the Philosophy of Nature and Positivism had a strong impact on German psychiatry during the first half of the nineteenth century. One result was that psychiatrists were divided into two camps: the psychologists (*Psychiker*) and the Somatologists (*Somatiker*).

Psychiker Psychiatrists. In their approach to mental illness, the *Psychiker* were influenced by the Vitalistic medicine of Stahl, by the Philosophy of Nature, by the Pietist tradition, and by the Romantic *Zeitgeist* of Germany in that period. They belonged to what, perhaps in error, is called German Romantic Medicine (Harms, 1967). The important representatives of this school were Johann Christian Reil (1759-1813), the author of *Rhapsodies on the Application of the Psychic Cure Method to Mental Disorders* (1803). In addition there were Johann Christian August Heinroth (1773-1843), discussed in the same breath with Pinel by James Cowles Prichard (1835). Still immersed in theological considerations, Heinroth attributed madness to passions arising from guilty and sinful behaviour (Hirsch,1893). Others of this animist school derived from Stahl's mysticism, were Alexander Haindorf (1782-1862), Friedrich Groos (1768-1852), Karl Wilhelm Ideler (1795-1860), Heinrich Wilhelm Neumann (1814-1884), and Ernst Feuchtersleben (1806-1849). Ideler's teacher, Johann Gottfried Langermann (1768-1832), and Justinus Kerner (1786-1862), also followers of Stahl, must also be included. Langermann was a public health official in Berlin and believed in re-educating the mentally ill to a more reasonable outlook, and treating them as children while doing so. He was a humanitarian reformer and a pioneer of "moral treatment" in Germany. Although their systems had certain features in common, all of these men developed somewhat different psychodynamic systems to explain mental disease.

Reil and Langermann spanned the end of the eighteenth century and the beginning of the nineteenth. They were influenced more by the spirit of the eighteenth century enlightenment than by the nineteenth century Romanticism and Philosophy of Nature. Both Reil and Langermann represented the "moral treatment" of the insane movement which was originated by Philippe Pinel. As the reformer of the asylum at Bayreuth, Langermann's contributions have already been mentioned. His association with Romantic medicine and the *Psychiker* psychiatrists of the nineteenth century were his comittment to Stahl's vitalism and the fact that he was the teacher of Ideler, a prominent

Psychiker. It will be remembered that on the advice of Langermann, Ideler translated Stahl's *Theoria Medica Vera* from Latin into German.

Johann Christian Reil, the author of the *Rhapsodies*, was a product of the enlightenment and rationalism of the eighteeth century. He could have been discussed in the context of the hospital reformers and the "moral treatment" school. However, his approach to psychotherapy was much more systematic than the approach of the hospital reformers. He was also more committed to the psychological and psychodynamic points of view than the other reformers. Reil was a versatile man. He made important contributions to neuroanatomy as well as to clinical and theoretical psychiatry. A region of the brain, Reil island, still bears his name.

Reil was the son of a Lutheran minister and was influenced by German religious, Pietist, traditions. Although his psychological theory presented mechanistic features of enlightenment materialism, he also showed a concern for the ethical and for spiritual aspects of human nature. He dedicated his *Rhapsodies* to Wagnitz, the Lutheran preacher who apparently inspired some of his psychotherapeutic ideas. Reil stressed the role of the philosopher in the understanding and treatment of mental illness. He founded an *Archiv* or journal for philosophical questions of medicine in 1796. Together with the philosopher Kayssler he also founded the *Magazin fuer psychische Heilkunde* (Journal of psychological healing). This illustrates the interest of the *Psychiker* psychiatrists in positive mental health as well as in mental illness. This was not surprising, since life itself depended on the coherent cooperative functioning of many diverse materials for Reil.

In psychiatry, Reil manifested some psychodynamic insights when he compared cases of multiple personality with multiple characters appearing in dreams. Both multiple characters appearing in dreams, and multiple personalities in pathological cases represented dissociated parts of one's own personality. Reil also described psychopathological conditions which are nowadays called psychoneurosis.

In some respects, Reil's approach to psychotherapy was quite mechanistic and associationist. It was based on "practical empirical psychology" (Ellenberger, 1970). In his *Rhapsodies*, he advocated the method of treatment based on the principle of emotional abreactions such as provoking fear or anger. However, the means suggested by him of bringing about emotional abreactions, were rather crude and were reminiscent of the methods advocated by William Cullen and Benjamin

Rush. Reil believed in frightening and shocking patients by firing a pistol or by throwing patients into a water pool to frighten them back to their senses. He advocated such therapies as confining over-excited patients in a dark room, or infecting stuporous patients with itch (scabies). He called these methods of treatment "noninjurious torture." (Zilboorg, 1941). It is interesting to observe that William Battie had been much more cautious in his 1758 *Treatise* when he warned against using harsh purgatives, shocks, or bleedings on insane patients because one did not really know the cause of mental illnesses.

Reil used a rather unique therapy. Dramatic performances staged by hospital employees acted out plots which filled the psychological needs of patients and also aimed at strengthening their moral fiber. The themes of such plays were concerned with justice and divine order. Thus Reil was interested in the moral uplifting of his patients.

Johann Christian Heinroth (1818), a professor of medicine at the University of Leipzig, was the most typical representative of the philosophically oriented German *Psychiker* psychiatrists. Heinroth's theory of psychopathology was perhaps the most interesting and the most controversial of all the theories of the *Psychiker* psychiatrists. Heinroth was strongly influenced by Lutheran Pietist theology and by German transcendental idealist philosophy as formulated by Kant and Fichte. His interests were not limited to the problem of mental illness. He considered this problem in the wider context of general psychology. To put it more correctly, in the context of philosophical anthropology. Mental illness was equated with sin, and positive mental health with a state of grace. Sin and grace were used as metaphors. They had an existentialist connotation. Heinroth equated the state of mental health, or grace, with an unimpeded exercise of transcendental reason, and of free will. It will be remembered that in the Kantian philosophy, the metaphysical free will of the transcendental ego was guided by the categorical imperatives of pure reason. Strong emotions and carnal desires impeded the exercise of free will and consequently, debased human nature. Mental illness and sin was attributed by Heinroth to a loss of freedom of will. This state of affairs occurred when a person succumbed to egoistic self-love and passions. The result was a loss of freedom and guilt feelings. Heinroth's ideas could be interpreted in theological terms, as a state of sin and a fall from grace. They could also be interpreted in terms of existentialist philosophy as a loss of authenticity. The association of free will with reason can be found in the philosophies of Spinoza and of Kant. The association of evil and sin with laxity and disloyalty in the exercise of the free moral will, may be found in the philosophy of Fichte.

Heinroth believed that psychological processes were divided into three levels which emerged from one another. The lowest and the earliest level was that of animal instincts, impulses and feelings, which aimed at attaining pleasure. As the result of the confrontation of the stimuli of the external world there emerged a self-consciousness or an ego (*Ich*). Its motives were self-love (*Ich-Sucht*), the enjoyment of living, and a security in relation to the external world.

The highest level of psyche was conscience (*Gewissen*). It differentiated from the ego as the representation of the external world opposing the self-centered striving of the ego. This highest psychic stratum was also called by Heinroth "over-us" (*Ueber-uns*). Heinroth equated it with pure reason, which pointed the way to God. Mental illness was due to the conflict between the self-love of the ego and the duty of loving and serving others which was demanded by the "over-us" (one's conscience).

Heinroth equated the state of mental health with bridging the gap between ego and "over-us." Consequently conscience became assimilated to the ego. The similarity between Heinroth's personality theory and Freud's structural model of id-ego, superego, is obvious. Heinroth rejected the body-mind dualism and believed that man was a psychobiological entity with the body representing the external aspect and the mind the internal aspect.

In his clinical approach Heinroth believed in accordance with the Romantic stress on individuality, that each individual case was unique and required a specific treatment which depended on the sex, occupation, social class and the personality of the patient. Nevertheless, Heinroth offered some diagnostic categories. Since mental diseases originated often through the patient's voluntary pursuit of evil, the different clinical entities represented different modes of dealing with the resulting guilt feelings. According to Heinroth, *melancholia atonita*, melancholia of atonement, was caused by a profound impression on mind, one incapable of offering resistence to a temptation. Exhaustion and indecision in the face of evil produced *abulia melancholica*. Indecision coupled with madness described an *abulia anoa*. This was the result of sexual promiscuity. *Mania simplex* was a product of a sinful will occurring in moral degenerates. General madness, *eknoia catholica*, was characterized by rash, misguided thinking, and impulsive behaviour which caused intense suffering in the patient. Frantic madness (*eknoia maniaca*) caused extreme suffering from which the patient could achieve relief only by the most hideous forms of debasement. Religious melancholia was a product of worldliness, foolish conduct and dissolute life. In this condition, the patient's guilty conscience terrified his defenseless mind. This shattered mind dwelt in a shattered body. According to Heinroth, strong emotions were detrimental to mental health. Violent emotions of love and jealousy produced a state of delirium. This was a dream-like state of confusion. Melancholia was caused by grief, worry and resentment. Other emotions such as greed, pride, ambition, conceit, arrogance and avarice could also be involved in the causes of insanity. Indulging in such vices as alcoholism, gluttony, debauchery, and masturbation could produce imbecility.

Heinroth believed that the best safeguards against insanity were abiding religious faith and moral living. The restoration of religious faith was an important part of the therapy conducted by a doctor who played the role of the father, saviour, benefactor and compassionate friend of the patient. The doctor was for the patient a benevolent monarch who presented an image of God. Heinroth believed that Mesmer's animal magnetism, which he described as a wild branch of religious faith, had a place in the treatment of mental patients. According to him, a healthy, divinely inspired mind could by using the powers of animal magnetism, establish a spiritual contact with a sick mind and bring about a cure.

Heinroth played down the importance of somatic factors in the causation of mental illness. He made a distinction between the primary, idiopathic insanity caused by a deliberate choice of the patient to pursue evil ways, and a secondary insanity in which the free will was not completely obstructed, but only temporarily limited. Brain injuries and brain diseases caused by mechanical or chemical agents, produced only a temporary restriction of the patient's freedom. They did not affect his soul. A delirious state produced by a febrile illness, or by inebriation, was different in its essential features, from true insanity.

Friedrich Groos (1828), who was associated with the University of Heidelberg, had degrees both in philosophy and medicine. As a philosopher, he was influenced by Fichte and by Philosophy of Nature. He received his psychiatric training under Friedrich Nasse (1778-1851), an organically oriented psychiatrist. Consequently, Groos tried to reconcile the philosophical and the biological points of view.

Groos' concept of free will differed from that of Heinroth and was more in keeping with the views of Philosophy of Nature. He believed that the feeling of freedom was associated with the actualization of one's nature. This was prompted by vital drives stemming from one's unconsciousness. Mental health depended on a feeling of freedom. This was why the drive for freedom (*Freiheitstrieb*) was the most important one to govern human life. This drive was present even in the foetus.

In keeping with Fichte's philosophy, Groos believed that the inner springs of human motivation and the aims of man's vital drives were unconscious, hidden from his phenomenal ego. These drives directed human development and personality growth. Mental illness was due to an impediment to the fulfillment or inhibition of man's vital drives. This applied in particular to the drive for freedom. Thus Groos, viewed the human being as a continually developing psychobiological organism. An interference with personality growth and its actualization, whether external or internal, caused mental illness. For Gross, mental illness was a negation of positive mental health associated with personality actualization.

There is an obvious similarity between the theory of Groos and the theories of Carl Rogers and of other humanistic personality theories of the twentieth century. There is also a similarity between Groos and Freud in their views on the inhibition of vital drives as a cause of mental illness. The stress on freedom and on the unimpeded exercise of free will, brings Groos in line with the existentialist philosophy and psychology.

Alexander Haindorf was less prone to philosophical and metaphysical speculations than were the other *Psychiker* psychiatrists of the period. He was the author of the first systematic textbook of psychiatry written in German (Haindorf,1811). Haindorf proposed a speculative psychological system which was based on the physiology of the nervous system. He believed that there was a hierarchy of lower and higher neuropsychological functions. The seat of the lower functions was in the spinal cord. These functions were associated with reflexes and with behavioural asutomatisms (instincts). They were the foundation of animal egoism which was an important aspect of human nature. They were also a source of primitive emotions (*Gemueth*), the biological core of personality. Animal drives and wishes sought expression through the motor system. The cerebellum was the seat of self-feeling associated with the functioning of the organism. The brain was the seat of "inner sensations," which were identified with consciousness. The "inner sensations" constituted the highest level of psychological functions. The drives and impulses flowed within the nervous system from the lower centers to the higher ones and returned from the higher back to the lower ones. This condition created a possibility of conflicts. Such conflicts could cause mental illness. Thus Haindorf stressed the psychobiological unity of man and envisaged the possibility that emotional conflicts could cause mental illness.

The importance of sexual and aggressive drives was also emphasized by Karl Wilhelm Ideler (1835). It will be remembered that Ideler was a pupil of Langermann and that he translated Stahl's *Theoria Medica Vera*. He was influenced by Stahl's theory of vitalism, and believed that the constant self-destruction and self-reconstruction lay at the basis of life processes. To maintain the proper balance between self-destruction and self-construction, the organism had to incorporate the needed supplies of energy and matter from the external world at all times. This dynamic view of living organisms was responsible for Ideler's psychological theory which emphasized instinctual drives and "passions."

Ideler was for many years the director of the Charite Hospital in Berlin. He was an experienced clinical psychiatrist and a prolific writer. According to him, mental illness was caused by hypertrophy of agressive and sexual drives. He observed that many patients who developed paranoid delusions of persecution had previously displayed a marked personality trait of aggressiveness. Ideler also believed that frustrated, unfulfilled sexual desire might lead to psychological disorders. The frustration of sexual drive was according to him a major cause of mental illness. However, usually more than one cause was responsible for the onset of mental illness. The constitutional predisposition, childhood experiences, and contemporary emotional frustrations combined to produce insanity.

Ernst von Feuchtersleben, the dean of the medical faculty of the university of Vienna came closest to anticipating modern psychodynamic psychiatry. His major work, *The Principles of Medical Psychology* (1845/1897) showed the influence of Stahl, Pinel, and Kant. It was concerned with psychoneurosis and psychosomatic disorders which he thought to be psychologically determined. He believed that there was a relation between each organ and several psychic functions. Some bodily symptoms were according to him symbolic expressions of unconscious ideas. He thought that dreams should be analyzed in terms of the symbolic language of the body.

Von Feuchtersleben believed that mind and body constituted a single psychobiological unit, and that they were indivisible. He believed that psychoneurosis and psychosis were disorders of the total personality. He also believed in a continuity of psychosis, psychoneurosis, and normality. There was a similarity between dreams, the states of inebriation, and insanity. In his *The Diatetics of the Soul* (1838), von Feuchtersleben argued that every person harbored in the depth of his mind the seeds of insanity. *The Diatetics of the Soul* was concerned with mental hygiene and the prevention of mental illness. An important step in maintaining one's sanity was the understanding of one's feelings and motives. Von Feuchtersleben believed that psychotherapy was a form of "second education." During it the patient gained an insight into life experiences and into his reactions to them. These had produced his illness. The patient was also advised to engage himself in an absorbing work which would divert him from his morbid preoccupations.

Heinrich Wilhelm Neumann (1859) was the last of the German *Psychiker* psychiatrists. His life overlapped with that of Wilhelm Griesinger whose organic orientation he opposed. He also opposed the preoccupation with nosology (classificatory schemas) of the organically oriented (*Somatiker*) psychiatrists. Like all the other *Psychiker* psychiatrists, Neumann was influenced by the Vitalism of Stahl. Life for Neumann was a manifestation of a constant process of self-destruction and reconstruction. On the psychological level,the self-destruction was associated with forgetting, while self-construction had to do with remembering.

The human being was guided by external sensations and also by internal *Aestheses*. The latter represented drive impulses and indicated the way of coping with them. Fear indicated the presence of danger and the way of avoiding it. However, *Aesthese*, which represented danger, could lose its useful prupose. It could become a state of unfocused anxiety. Unsatisfied biological drives, particularly the unsatisfied sex drive, could produce a chronic state of anxiety. Frustrated sex drive was, according to Neumann, a common cause of insanity. Neumann did not believe in the usefulness of classification of mental diseases. He believed that there was only one progressive mental disease which manifested different degrees of severity depending on the stage of its development. In its early stages, mental disease manifested itself as a state of groundless anxiety, with difficulty in focusing attention. This stage was followed by that of persecutory delusions leading to further aggressive behaviour, and eventually to profound personality deterioration. All of these stages were characterized by the more or less disguised preoccupation of the patients with sex. Neumann advocated psychological methods of treatment which were appropriate for each individual patient.

Justinus Kerner, a physician-poet, was not a psychiatrist. However, he has to be grouped together with the *Psychiker* psychiatrists because he illustrates the interest in mesmerism, the occult, and para-psychology which was characteristic of the *Psychiker* and of Romantic medicine. He became famous because of his work with Friederike Hauffe (1801-1829), the seeress of Prevorst. On several occasions Kerner put Friedericke Hauffe into mesmeric sleep during which she acted as a clairvoyant and medium, in communication with the world of spirits, and able to prophecy the future. These seances were watched on several occasions by such Nature Philosophers as Schelling and von Schubert. Kerner was interested in imagination and in the process of creativity. He wrote a series of verses inspired by a series of inkblots. His verses about them were published in his *Klecksgraphien*.

Another famous hypnotic medium who caused a stir among Romantics was Katherina Emmrich, a simple peasant woman and a former nun. She had visions of Christ and developed the stigmata of the passion. Clemens Brentano, who was like Kerner, also a Romantic poet, studied her case and published an account of her dreams and visions (Ellenberger, 1970). One may see from such studies, that the Philosophers of Nature and the *Psychiker* psychiatrists took an interest in occult subjects. These included their interests in mesmerism, and the occult phenomena associated with it. Mental illness was believed to have positive as well as negative aspects. Some followers of Romantic medicine like the poet Novalis (Friedrich von Hardenberg) were interested in "creative illness." Novalis wrote about "creative hypochondriasis." Further, they were interested in consumption (tuberculosis) which was regarded as an ennobling disease that could elevate the victim to a higher spiritual level (Rene and Jean Dubos, 1952). The same feelings were sometimes expressed about madness.

The *Psychiker* psychiatrists looked upon body and mind as an organic whole, subject to vital polar forces emanating from the unconscious. These were neither completely mental, nor completely somatic.

With few exceptions, they rejected classificatory schemas and concentrated on each unique patient whom they were treating by psychotherapy. The theories of the German *Psychiker* psychiatrists provided an example of the psychological-dynamic model, and they anticipated Freud's and Jung's psychodynamic theories. The *Psychiker* theories also had many features found again in the twentieth century psychedelic model of mental illness as well as an existentialist approach. They also brought back the ancient idea of a divine madness.

Although the French psychiatrist Jacques Joseph Moreau de Tours (1804-1884) cannot be identified with the German *Psychiker*, he presented some similar conceptions of madness. The idea that madness conferred an aura of intellectual and spiritual superiority gave rise to a theory of *degenere superieur*. This was reminiscent of the ancient idea of divine madness. Moreau de Tours (1859) was less given to philosophical speculations and was more empirically oriented. He represented the French version of Romantic medicine. As a pupil of Esquirol he acknowledged the importance of organic factors but focused on the inner experiences of the patients. Interested in psychodynamic mechanisms, Moreau de Tours rejected the prevailing descriptive and classificatory trends of the Pinel school in France. He regarded mental illness as a disorder of total personality, having a hidden meaning and design. He saw in normal people secret irrational forces lurking behind the mask of sanity. True to the Romantic spirit he was interested in the irrational aspects of human nature.

Moreau de Tours perceived a similarity between madness and dreams of normal people. Hallucinations of dreams were according to him, the same as those of madness. Both dreams and madness represented a different order of experience than the experience of normal waking states. The wide awake experiences reflected the reality of the external world. The dreams of normal people and the experiences of the insane reflected the inner world of the psyche. They represented primitive, illogical, irrational desires and impulses. These were ruled by wish fulfillment rather by reality. According to Moreau de Tours, a psychotic patient was "dreaming while awake." He was alienated from the external world and lived in a private world of inner fantasy.

Moreau de Tours believed that hallucinations which occurred as a result of drug induced toxic states, were identical to those occurring in dreams and madness. He also believed that in order to understand an insane patient one had to enter the patient's inner world. He had to share the latter's experiences. Consequently, Moreau experimented on himself with the then commonly prescribed anti-maniacal drug, opium, and also with hashish. He had as a young physician accompanied a neurotic patient on a three year journey to the East. Travel and change of scenery were regarded as therapeutic in those days and considered a cure for psychoneurosis. During that journey, Moreau de Tours investigated toxic states induced by hashish and opium (Mora, 1989). In Paris he attracted a group of Bohemians which included prominent writers, poets, and painters. The group organized "Le Club de Hachichins" with the purpose of investigating the psychological effects of hashish intoxication (Grinspoon, 1971). Their particular interest was in the aesthetic aspects of hashish induced experiences. Moreau de Tour's artistic friends included some of the outstanding men of the time: Pierre Gautier, Charles Baudelaire, F. Boissard the painter. Victor Hugo, H. Balzac, and de Narval also participated in some of the sessions. In consequence, Baudelaire wrote his *Les Paradis Artificiels* (1860).

From a scientific point of view, Moreau de Tours published a monograph analyzing the hashish induced experiences in 1859: *Du Hashich et de l'alienation mentale*. Moreau put forward a hypothesis that certain types of psychosis were produced by an organismic endotoxin which had similar properties to those of hashish. Gautier appended to the monograph a description of his own experiences under the title: "Le Club de hachichins" (Solomon, 1966).

Moreau de Tours was one of the first to argue that genius and insanity were closely related. Both were caused by an overactivity of mind. In the case of genius, the overactivity of mind was channeled into socially useful activity while in the case of insanity it led to mental aberration. Moreau thus anticipated some of the interests of twentieth century psychiatrists in the psychedelic model of mental illness.

With the passing of Romantic medicine and Philosophy of Nature, the more empirical, modern psychiatry began to emerge. This in part resulted from an increasing knowledge of brain anatomy. The *Psychiker* psychiatrists vacated the stage and were replaced by the organically oriented *Somatiker* psychiatrists.

8

Positivist Reaction: The Rise of Modern Organic Psychiatry

Organic (Somatiker) Psychiatry in Germany

The *Somatiker* psychiatrists, the somatologists, were influenced by positivistic and materialistic philosophies. They believed that mental diseases were manifestations of pathology of the brain. They were represented by such men as Maximilian Jacobi (1775-1858), who had insisted that there was no need for psychology, and that insanity was only an epihenomenon (Thiele,1956, 1970). Also by Ernst Bartels (1778-1838), who stressed the importance of cerebral localizations, as well as by Johannes Friedreich (1796-1862), who believed that since the brain had two halves there was "half-sided" insanity (Zilboorg, 1941).

Friedreich (1836) was an erudite man, a director of the Wuerzburg clinic, he employed J.L. Schoenlein in 1817. He was the author of several monographs on psychiatric topics. These included a review of psychiatric literature between 1801-1836. In 1837 he edited the *Blaetter fuer Psychiatrie* (Zilboorg, 1941; Hirsch, 1898). As a materialist, he was a critic of Heinroth's psychological-philosophical theory of mental illness. He considered it "false, immoral, and wrong." According to him, Heinroth's theory was erroneous, idealistic philosophy (Zilboorg, 1941). If a physician failed to find the physical causes of mental illness it was his fault. Friedreich did not reject the possibility of the existence of an immortal soul as a metaphysical entity. However, the immortal, perfect soul could not be sick. A disease could only affect the material brain. Friedreich thus left the metaphysical soul to the theologians and believed that the study of the physical brain belonged to the domain of medicine and science. Even if there were an immortal soul it would be a sacrilege to discuss it from a scientific point of view. The result was that the *Somatiker* derided the psychologies and psychopathologies developed by their *Psychiker* colleagues as useless, confused, philosophical, theological and mystical speculations.

Another member of the *Somatiker* school, G.H. Bergmann (1781-1860), associated insanity with the changes in brain ventricles. This approach to psychiatry culminated in the work of Wilhelm Griesinger (1817-1869) who opposed the psychological psychiatry and became the leader of the somatologist school. The somatologists tended to classify mental diseases not according to their symptoms, but according to the hypothetical lesions of the brain and other organic causes. Thus, they were following the tendency, prevalent in general medicine at that time, of abandoning noslogies based on symptoms and of searching for localized pathological lesions to be found during autopsies. They distrusted psychology and philosophy, and believed that these two disciplines had nothing to offer to the understanding and treatment of mental diseases. Consequently, they rejected *Psychiker* psychologies and psychopathologies. They were deemed to be useless, confused, philosophical, theological and mystical speculations.

By the middle of the nineteenth century the somatologists (*Somatiker*) psychiatrists won the struggle and became the dominant school of German psychiatry. The psychological (*Psychiker*) psychiatrists of the first half of the nineteenth century were soon forgotten. Psychiatry became closely associated with neurology. This development coincided with the passing of Romanticism and of Philosophy of Nature. Positivism and Materialism became dominant philosophies in the realm of natural science.

The greater emphasis on clinical training and better scientific observation entered German medicine with the work of Johann Lucas Schoenlein (1793-1864). His dissertation *On Brain Metamorphosis* (1816), had been written under the influence of the Nature Philosophy. However, he had made first Wuerzburg, then Berlin, the centers of a new kind of clinical training. His nosological system considered the nervous system one of three major areas of disease. In anticipation of psychoanalytical thinking, he had considered the ego all important to human health. It had to maintain itself against tensions and contradictions stemming from external influences. His emphasis on seeking the anatomical and pathological reasons for illness, made it possible for the next generation of psychiatrists to adopt the same positivist approach (Hirsch, 1898).

Although at first a member of the still more romantic Tuebingen school, Wilhelm Griesinger (1817-1868) was a student of Schoenlein, and became the founder of modern scientific psychiatry. He too established anatomical pathology as a more rational, modern, basis for diagnosis of mental illness. As a young man, he had argued in 1845 that all psychic illnesses ought to be diagnosed as brain disease (Thiele, 1970). He announced the modern positivist position which later psychiatrists like Kraepelin were to follow too. He had been educated at the Stuttgart Gymnasium, as Hegel had too. Then he had been trained at the universities of Tuebingen and Zuerich. Something of a Hegelian at first, he was Schoenlein's student and only later broke with the latter's natural history school of medicine. He had visited the hospitals in Paris in 1838 and in 1840 worked with Dr. Zeller at the Winnenthal Asylum in Wuerttemberg. During the 1840s Griesinger turned positivist. Thiele (1970, p. 126) quotes him as saying: "Facts! Only facts! This is the cry of positivism which has no idea that one has to use negation at every stage of science in order to go to the next stage."

In 1847 Griesinger became professor of psychiatry in Kiel, but gave it up for the more interesting assignment as chief physician to the viceroy of Egypt in 1850. After a few more years as director of the medical clinic in Tuebingen (1854-60), he became director of the canton hospital and insane asylum in Zuerich, where he served until 1865. (This later became the Canton Hospital Burghoelzli in 1870). Wilhelm Griesinger assumed the leadership of German psychiatry when in 1865 he became professor of psychiatry and neurology at the University of Berlin, and simultaneously Director of the Berlin Charite Hospital, where he founded the clinic for nervous disorders in 1867, but died the following year (Kolle, I, 1970). He also founded the psychiatric journal, *Archiv fuer Psychiatrie und Nervenkrankheiten*. His major work, was published in two editions in 1845 and 1861: *Die Pathologie und Therapie der psychischen Krankheiten fuer Aerzte und Studierende*. (Pathology and therapy of the mental illnesses, for physicians and students).

Griesinger is credited with introducing the English no-restraints policy to the care of psychiatric patients in Germany. This was some two generations after the policy had been introduced abroad, but at a time when its use was already being discarded again, particularly in American asylums. In Germany too, there was much opposition, especially from Dr. Ringseis in Munich, who believed that mental illnesses were the result of a fall from grace and of human sin.

Griesinger is usually classified as a somatologist, even if he also opposed the earlier generation of *Somatiker*. He made the forceful statement that every mental illness was associated with a disorder of the brain and offered a classification of mental illness on the basis of hypothetical brain lesions and other somatic disorders.

He rejected the notion of nosology which was based on the clinical description of syndromes. He believed that clinical symptoms and syndromes were manifestations of brain pathology. Therefore, the anatomo-pathological changes in the brain provided the only basis for clinical classification. In research, the dissection of the brain was the starting point for psychiatric work. An attempt was made to relate the brain lesions to the impairment of its functions and to the clinical symptoms. This approach was adopted by the followers of Griesinger, the members of the so-called neurological school of psychiatry. Human psychologyy was conceived by him in terms of nerve reflexes. In these views, Griesinger was influenced by the work of Marshall Hall (1790-1857) on reflexes. However, he was also concerned with the total, integrated functioning of the brain and of the whole organism. He proposed an ego psychology (possibly influenced by Schoenlein's), which anticipated the one proposed by Freud. His system featured a functionalist psychology of adaptation. Its dynamic aspects included the notion of the unconscious which he took from Johann Friedrich Herbart (1776-1840), a philosopher-psychologist. Thus, Griesinger, to a great extent, tried to synthesize the *Somatiker* and the *Psychiker* points of view.

The men who came after Griesinger included Bernard von Gudden (1829-1886), the psychiatrist who treated the insane King Louis II of Bavaria and was murdered by him. Also, Theodor Meynert (1833-1892), Carl Westphal (1833-1890), Carl Wernicke (1848-1905), and Paul E. Flechsig (1847-1929). These psychiatrists were all more organically oriented than Griesinger, and mainly concerned with neuropathology. They originated the German school of neurological psychiatry. The German tradition of organic psychiatry culminated in the work of Emil Kraepelin (1856-1926), the founder of the modern psychiatric system. Kraepelin was trained under von Gudden, a professor of psychiatry at Munich. Von Gudden espoused the neurological approach to psychiatry and was one of the leading neuroanatomists of his day. He had been director of the Munich District Asylum in 1872, and had also treated the insane Prince Otto von Wittelsbach of Bavaria (Gruenthal, 1970). That was why he with several others, was consulted in the case of King Louis II. The commission of which he was a member, found the king to be insane, but could not at first remove the monarch from his throne, since he used his troops against them. Gudden was able to bring the king to Castle Berg on June 12,1886. He planned to treat the king according to principles of moral management. On June 13, the king seemed to regain his senses, so that he went for a walk with him in the morning, accompanied by two attendants. However, the evening walk proved fatal. The king, now free of the attendants, seems to have jumped into the nearby lake, the doctor seized his jacket, but the king seems to have drowned, first his physician after a struggle, and then himself (Gruenthal, 1970, p.131).

Gudden's out-and-out materialism, his insistence on finding the anatomical reasons for all changes, appeared anti-religious in the Bavaria of that age. The very idea of removing the king from his throne was also viewed with suspicion by the populace. His experimental work had been epoch making, however, and he was an opponent of the earlier brain localization theory of mental illness. Some ideas of Darwinian adaptation had been expressed in his 1874 work, (French, 1876). (*Experimental Investigations of the Growth of the Cranium*). Both the form of the brain as well as the form of the cranium determined both brain form and cranial form. One is reminded of Herder's statement (*Ideen*) of 1784, that the large capacity brain and cranium peculiar to man, is possible only because of the structure of the spinal column: man stands erect !

Amongst the members of the early neurological school, Theodor Meynert (1833-1892), Freud's professor of psychiatry and neurology, was perhaps the most extreme in his views. He rejected the term "psychiatry" and insisted that the so-called mental diseases should become a domain of neurology. According to him, the main goal of scientific research was to provide psychiatry with an anatomical foundation (Bellak, 1961). Pursuing this goal, Meynert became the leading neuroanatomist of his time. However, he complemented purely morphological studies with physiological speculations. He believed that the forebrain and the brain stem had opposing functions and that their reciprocal interactions produced psychic processes. These opposing functions derived from the differences in the microscopic anatomy of the blood vessels of the cerebrum and the brain stem. Disturbances of blood circulation in the brain could produce disorders of synergy between the higher and lower centers. These would affect perception, thought and mood. Consequently, Meynert believed that mental diseases were caused by disorders of blood circulation in the brain. They resulted from a pathology of blood vessels, or from irritations of cortical or subcortical nerve tissues. He rejected the idea of nosology based on clinically described entities. Following Griesinger, he believed clinical entities to be epiphenomena of the underlying neurological lesions. Meynert proposed a classification of mental diseases which was based on the anatomy of the central nervous system.

Carl Westphal (1833-1890) of the Charite Hospital in Berlin, was an important neuroanatomist as well as a psychiatrist. He described obsessional states which were considered by him to be an "abortive insanity." Westphal also described phobias and was interested in sexual pathology. His explanations of these conditions were neurological rather than psychological. Together with Wilhelm Erb (1840-1921) he investigated tendon reflexes and discovered that the knee jerk was absent in syphilis. Erb was particularly interested in the effects of Faradic electric currents on the peripheral nerves and muscles. On the basis of his research, he developed the electric treatment of hysteria and other nerve conditions which was widely used at the turn of the century.

Another important representative of the neurological school of psychiatry was Carl Wernicke (1848-1905). He was a student of Meynert and of Westphal. Like Westphal, he was also a follower of Griesinger. Wernicke became professor of psychiatry, first at Breslau University (Wroclaw), and then at Halle where he came into contact with the young Karl Kleist, who carried the neurological tradition into the twentieth century. Wernicke (1874) is best known for his work on aphasia. The description of the sensory aphasia is associated with his name. He linked sensory aphasia with pathology of the left transverse temporal gyrus (Hersch's convolution) of the brain. Wernicke (1883) used aphasia as a model to explain mental diseases. He believed that brain functioning can be conceived in terms of the psychosensory input, the psychomotor output, and the "intrapsychic functions" which coordinated the two. These three aspects of brain functioning can be localized. All psychological disorders could be understood as resulting from a combination of these factors: 1) insufficient or excessive psychosensory inputs, and 2) insufficient or excessive psychomotor outputs. There could also be an insufficient or excessive activity of the "intrapsychic function." Brain functions could be further subdivided into three major areas. First, those dealing with the external world or *allopsyche*. Second, those having to do with the body or *somatopsyche*. Third, those dealing with the concept of self or *autopsyche*. Some mental disorders were caused by the disturbance of coordinations of the different brain functions.

Thus, Wernicke attempted to reduce mental diseases to abnormalities of brain functions which could be precisely localized. He rejected the notion of clinical nosology which was not based on neurological signs and symptoms. Consequently, Wernicke was critical of Kraepelin's nosological system, which was based on clinical observation.

In addition to his description of sensory aphasia, Wernicke described the memory loss for recent events associated with the presence of chronic pathology of the brain. He also described an acute toxic-confusional state occurring in alcoholics, which is named for him as Wernicke's encephalopathy. Associationist psychology was still presupposed, however, and he believed that mental illnesses involved disturbances of the associative pathways. Psychoses were classified according to how much they disturbed the regions of consciousness in the brain. The added anxiety psychoses, hallucinations, even presbyophrenia and motility psychoses to the classical disturbances of mania and melancholia (Kleist, 1970).

Among nineteenth century neurological psychiatrists, two other men could be mentioned; Paul E. Flechsig and Moritz Romberg. Flechsig (1847-1929), a leading neuroantomist and neuropathologist, directed the Flechsig Clinic in Leipzig. It was famous for the meticulous postmortem dissections of the brains of psychiatric and neurological patients. Flechsig was the psychiatrist who treated Judge Schreber, whose memoirs Freud used as a basis for his theory of paranoia.

Moritz Romberg (1795-1873), who preceded Griesinger at the University of Berlin, wrote the first systematic textbook of neurology. He vies with Charcot for the title of "father of neurology." Romberg rejected psychological and philosophical explanations of mental illness. He tried to establish causal links between psychopathological phenomena and neuroanatomical changes. Among his contributions to neurology, is his description of the loss of balance associated with *tabes dorsalis*, named for him as "Romberg's sign."

The new neurological explanation of mental illness was confronted with the problem of localization of pathological lesions of the brain. Were different psychopathological symptoms caused by lesions ? Could these lesions be localized in specific areas of the brain ? Or, were they the result of general disorders of brain function,like those which might occur in toxic states ? These questions were related to broader ones of the localization of brain functions. By and large, there were two traditions in neurological research. The one emphasized strict localization. The other stressed the total function of the brain or that of its main parts. Wernicke had argued for the former.

The idea of strict localization of the brain functions can be traced to the work of phrenologists. Later on, it came to be based on more exact empirical evidence. Paul Broca (1824-1880) in 1861 described the motor center of speech at the base of the third frontal convolution of the left hemisphere. (A similar claim was made thirty years earlier by M. Dax, but did not then make much of an impression on the scientific community). During the 1870s, Eduard Hitzig (1838-1907), a student of Griesinger, and Theodor Fritsch (1838-1897) mapped motor centers in the frontal precentral gyrus by using electrical stimulation. Their work originated in Fritsch's observation, made during the Prussian-Danish War in 1864, that stimulation to one side of the brain caused twitching of body parts on the opposite side.

The work of Hitzig and Fritsch was continued by David Ferrier (1843-1928) in England, and H. Nothangel in Germany. In 1880 Herman Munk (1839-1912) localized the visual centers in the calcarine region of the occipital lobe. About the same time, C. Wernicke described the sensory speech center in the left temporal lobe of the brain (Boring, 1957).

The holistic tradition of neurological research can be traced back to the work of Pierre Flourens (1794-1967) early in the nineteenth century. On the basis of his work on the brain lesions of pigeons, Flourens postulated the existence of the *action commune* (total function) of the whole brain.

In addition, the brain had *actions propres* or specific functions too. This point of view was espoused later, by Friedrich L. Goltz (1834-1902) who opposed the idea of strict localization. He emphasized the total function of the cortex. Goltz extirpated the cortex from the brains of dogs and observed their behaviour. Early in the twentieth century, the holistic point of view was represented by Karl Spencer Lashley (1890-1958).

At the turn of the century, the clinical neurologists could also be divided into two camps. Those who stressed the strict localization of brain centers, and those who took a holistic view and stressed a dynamic organization of brain functions. Some of the names have already been mentioned in connection with the experimental work. The followers of the strict localization school were represented by such prominent men as C. Wernicke, T. Meynert, C. Westphal, E. Hitzig, J.M. Charcot, J. Babinski (Charcot's successor in Salpetriere), and J. Dejerine. The holistic point of view was represented by John Hughlings Jackson (1835-1911), Alois Alzheimer (1864-1915), and Arnold Pick (1850-1924). More recently, this group also included Henry Head, Kurt Goldstein, Otto Potzl, and C. von Monakow (Ey, 1969). Hughlings Jackson postulated the existence of phylogenetically and ontogenetically higher and lower levels of the functioning of the nervous system. The higher functional organizations, according to him, tended to suppress the lower organizations. When the higher functions dissolved, the lower functions were released. As a result, neurological symptoms could be divided into 1) those due to an absence of higher functions, and 2) those due to a release of lower functions (Hughlings Jackson, 1932).

The two traditions in neurology, the localization and the holistic, were important for understanding the influence of neurological thinking in the changing conceptualization of mental disease in organic psychiatry. The German and Austrian neurological schools of psychiatry were represented by Griesinger, Romberg, Gudden, Westphal, Meynert, Flechsig, Wernicke, and more recently, by K. Kleist. Many, though not all, believed in the strict localization of brain function. Yet many of these theories were based on pure speculation. This is seen in Meynert's theory, which linked mental diseases to specific brain blood vessel pathology. Such theories were often referred to as "brain mythology." Other organic psychiatrists of the nineteenth century thought in terms of abnormal functions of the total brain. These were brought about by such factors as toxins and metabolic disorders. The disorders of the functioning of the whole brain were regarded by them as causes of mental diseases. This point of view was represented by Karl Kahlbaum (1828-1899) who described catatonia and cyclothymia. Also by Ewald Hecker (1843-1909) who described hebephrenia, and by Paul F. Moebius (1853-1907), who differentiated exogenous from endogenous psychoses and described toxic goiter. Alois Alzheimer and Arnold Pick described presenile dementias which bear their names. Both were also inclined to this point of view. Their position was also espoused by Emil Kraepelin (1856-1926).

In addition to the different views on the brain localization, there were also different views on the research strategies. On the whole, the members of the neurological school who believed in the localization of brain functions, took as their point of departure, research into morbid anatomy founded on a histological examination of the brains of deceased patients. They tried to associate pathological changes localized in different parts of the brain with psychiatric symptoms. The classification of mental diseases was to be based on neuroanatomy and neuropathology. On the other hand, the researchers who espoused the holistic point of view, emphasized clinical observations and clinical descriptions. They attempted to group clinical symptoms in various syndromes and to observe their development in time. They favored a clinical approach to nosology. In this choice of strategy, these researchers were influenced by the following considerations. There were some mental diseases such as general paralysis of the insane or senile dementia which could easily be attributed to anatomo-pathological changes in the brain. These could be localized or diffused. In other mental diseases in which insanity appeared to be equally profound, such changes could not be easily established. However, many somatic diseases such as tuberculosis, Bright's disease, malaria, and Sydenham's chorea had been differentiated by clinical observations. Their pathological basis had been established by subsequent research. Thus it seemed reasonable to assume that the same strategy would work in the case of mental diseases. It was thought that these diseases could also be differentiated on the basis of clinical observations in the hope that future research would reveal the pathological changes in the brain or general systemic pathology. This line of thinking, and the course of research, was followed by Kahlbaum and Kraepelin.

French Psychiatry. French psychiatry played an extremely important role in early nineteenth century medicine, but was less dominated by philosophical issues than was German psychiatry. However, it was influenced by trends in contemporary general medicine. French psychiatrists were more empirical and more pragmatic in their orientation and less interested in theory than their German colleagues. Throughout the first half of the nineteenth century, the tradition of Pinel continued to dominate French psychiatry. His students became its leaders. Their approach can be described as eclectic, since it made allowance for both the organic and psychological factors involved in the causation of mental illness. They believed that many mental diseases were functional and could respond to moral treatment. Jean-Etienne Dominique Esquirol (1772-1840) succeeded Pinel as the leader of French psychiatry. He was an excellent clinician and teacher, eclectic in his orientation. He believed that mental illness can be a manifestation of emotional disorder rather than of disordered reason. He was interested in forensic psychiatry and criminology (Amadur & Messinger, 1939). In contrast, his contemporary, Guillaume Ferrus (1784-1861) who was a student of Pinel, believed that mental illness was a product of brain disease due to a localized lesion or a constitutional predisposition. He was a capable hospital administrator and was one of the early pioneers of occupational therapy in mental hospitals.

The criticism of nosology and disease "ontology" in general medicine, associated with the Paris Clinical School, also affected the concept of disease as applied to mental disorders. Classification according to symptoms was considered a futile exercise in an Aristotelian "essentialism." The etiology of mental disorders was considered as the only valid basis for classification.

However, since in a great majority of cases, the etiology was unknown, classificatory attempts were considered premature. This attitude may be illustrated by the views of Etienne J. Georget (1795-1828), another student of Pinel. Georget believed that mental illness was a manifestation of one ideopathic disease of the brain with a great variety of forms, which however, were not separate disease entities. The idea of one mental disease implied that there was a general pathological process occurring in the brain, brought about by a variety of causes, some of which were organic and some psychological. Each case was idiopathic and therefore unique. Thus, the focus of attention shifted from the disease to the patient. The disease "ontology" became the patient "ontology." Similar opinions were voiced by Fodere (1764-1835), who believed that the differences among mental patients were as great as the differences among normal people. His view seemed to imply a continuity between normality and mental illness.

The question of whether there was one mental disease or many, occupied French and German psychiatrists throughout the nineteenth century. The German *Psychiker* psychiatrist, Heinrich Neumann, was a proponent of one mental illness theory. In his textbook of psychiatry (1859) Neumann stated that there was only one mental illness, and that it was characterized by different stages. The first stage of hypersensitivity and inattention was followed by further stages of more severe symptoms. This question of whether there was only one essential mental disease, of whether there exist only a few broad nosological categories, or several narrow categories, had been debated by nosographers up to the present day. However, during the second half of that century, as a result of the discovery that specific bacteria caused specific diseases, the disease model was again firmly established in general medicine. A search went on for specific pathogenic agents, bacterial or other types, which caused specific pathological processes, manifesting themselves in typical disease histories and configurations of symptoms. These developments in general medicine were also reflected in psychiatric thinking. The disease model in psychiatry received a boost from the clinical delineation and eventual discovery of the cause of the General Paralysis of the Insane (G.P.I.) Since this discovery affected psychiatric thinking about other pathological conditions, its history will now be briefly presented (Henry, 1941).

It had been known, at least since the seventeenth century, that many cases of insanity were associated with paralysis and epileptic fits. By the end of the eighteenth century, the British physician John Haslam (1764-1844), had described insanity associated with paralysis. Haslam (1798, 1817) had been apothecary at Bethlehem Hospital (Bedlam), in London, a position created by William Battie when he was one of the governors of that hospital. During the nineteenth century, two students of Esquirol, A.L.J. Bayle (1799-1858) and J.L. Calmeil (1798-1895), described the condition more systematically. They also described pathological changes in the brain associated with the disease. These were then identified as an inflammation of the brain membranes. For quite a long time, clinicians were not clear as to whether insanity and paralysis constituted one, or two separate diseases. Battie had pointed out in 1758, that some forms of madness could be "mixed." By the nineteenth century, however, it was not certain whether paralysis was associated with a specific type of insanity or could occur as a complication in all cases of insanity. They were also uncertain whether there was one kind of paralysis or at least two kinds. They apparently were confusing G.P.I. with *tabes dorsalis* (*taboparesis*). Finally, they were uncertain as to whether pathological changes in the brain were "causes" of the disease, or whether they were secondarily produced by changes in blood circulation associated with insanity.

In accordance with the prevailing "idiopathic" causation model, the clinicians believed that G.P.I. could be produced by many causes. Bayle divided the causes of the disease into moral and physical ones. Among the physical causes he mentioned excessive drinking, suppression of hemorrhoidal flow, injuries to the head, and heredity. Amongst the moral causes, he mentioned mental shocks, disappointments in love, violent passions, profound jealousy and excessive intellectual endeavours. Subsequent investigations of J.B.M. Parchappe (1800-1866), Jules Baillarger (1809-1890) and Jean Pierre Falret (1794,1870) tended to delineate G.P.I. as a disease entity, and to localize the pathological changes in the cortical cells.

The label: *General Paralysis of the Insane* or, *Progressive Paralysis* was attached to the condition and attempts were made to find the cause. A controversy raged for many years about whether the cause of G.P.I. was a syphilitic infection or something else. Towards the end of the nineteenth century, the theory that G.P.I. was due to an old syphilitic infection became generally accepted. This was the result of an experiment carried out by Richard von Krafft-Ebing (1840-1903). This showed that a G.P.I. patient could not be infected with syphilis. However, a definite connection between G.P.I. and syphilis was established early in the twentieth century when ,in 1906, the serological test, devised by August von Wassermann (1866-1925), was applied to G.P.I. patients. In 1913, *spirocheta pallida*, the micro-organism causing syphilis was discovered in the brain of G.P.I. patients by Hideyo Noguchi (1876-1928) and Joseph W. Moore (1879-1957).

The investigation of G.P.I. provided a conceptual model for the investigation of the etiology and pathology of other mental diseases. A disease had to have a specific cause, a characteristic beginning, a typical course and a typical outcome. The causal mechanisms were to be described in organic terms, and not in psychological ones. The psychological manifestations were only "epiphenomena" caused by pathological organic processes and had no intrinsic meaning at all.

Materialism, Positivism, and Organic Psychiatry. By the middle of the nineteenth century, in all countries, academic psychiatry became organic and accepted the medical disease model. Some researchers looked for specific localized lesions of the brain, others searched for more global physiological or biochemical disorders. However, both groups came to regard psychology as completely irrelevant for their task. Parchappe insisted that only lesions in the brain could serve as a basis for a classification of mental diseases. Griesinger held a similar view. In Russia, Ivan Michalovich Sechenov (1829-1905), a physiologist, in 1863 published his *Reflexes of the Brain*, in which he laid down the foundations of reflexology.

This represented a materialist point of view and claimed to be a completely objective psychology, without any mind philosophy. A similar kind of positivism had also emerged in Great Britain. Thomas Laycock, a Scottish neurologist and positivist philosopher at the University of Edinburgh, had in 1860 published his influential *Mind and Brain*. Laycock stressed the importance of studying the anatomy and physiology of the brain for the understanding of the human mind. In Britain also, Henry Maudsley (1836-1918), had been influenced by Comtean positivism, and in 1867 published *The Physiology and Pathology of the Mind*. Here, Maudsley argued that mental diseases were brain diseases. They were caused by anatomical brain lesions or by systemic toxic states. Toxic states or infections could produce brain disorders by "sympathy."

In France, J.J. Moreau de Trous (1804-1884) maintained that hallucinatory psychosis was caused by a toxin similar to hashish. Even in cases when pathological lesions were not found, the tendency was to delineate disease entitis in the hope that eventually an organic pathology could be found. Jean Pierre Falret (1794-1870) described *la folie circulaire* (circular madness), which eventually became known as manic-depressive psychosis. Karl Ludwig Kahlbaum (1829-1899) offered a description of *catatonia*, and also proposed the term *cyclothymia* to describe morbid swings of mood.

Kahlbaum's student, Ewald Hecker (1843-1899) described *hebephrenia*. Somewhat earlier, in 1860, Benedict Morel had distinguished *dementia praecox* as a clinical entitity. It was a condition of progressive general mental deterioration which occurred in juveniles. In the United States, Edward C. Spitzka (1852-1914) described paranoia. Paul Moebius (1853-1905) divided mental diseases into "exogenous" and "endogenous." The first were reactions to some noxious organic or psychological factors. In the second, the cause was unknown, but was presumed to be hereditary and of an organic nature. As the nineteenth century was drawing towards its end, the foundation was laid, and the building blocks were provided for the nosological system of psychiatry which was built by Emil Kraepelin (1856-1926).

Developments in Forensic Psychiatry. Some important developments in forensic psychiatry took place in midcentury England. They were to provide rules for the grounds on which a plea of insanity could be made in the courts of law in English speaking countries. The English common law required that an accused had to have *mens rea*, an evil intent to commit a crime before he could be found guilty of it. He had to be capable to exercise a judgment with regard to the deeds he perpetrated. He had to be aware of its consequences and had to make a deliberate choice in order to commit the crime. An individual whose mind was affected by a severe disease and was completely unhinged, was not capable of exercising those mental functions and did not have *mens rea*. He could be excused from responsibility for his crime on the grounds of insanity. However, there were degrees of insanity ranging from mild to total. The mild kind affected only certain mental functions. A seventeenth century English jurist, Lord Hale, introduced the concept of partial insanity. More than a century later, Esquirol proposed the term "monomania" to describe conditions in which only certain ideations of the patient were abnormal, while the rest of his ideations were normal.

The question was often asked whether a partial insanity or "monomania" was a sufficient ground to absolvc thc accused from responsibility for his crime. This became an issue in 1843, at the trial of one Daniel McNaughton , a Glasgow man.

McNaughton was accused of murdering Edward Drummond who was the private secretary of Sir Robert Peel, the prime minister of Great Britain. McNaughton had suffered from a paranoid delusion of persecution which centered on Sir Robert Peel. He believed that Sir Robert was plotting against him, and tried to harm him. Eventually he decided to shoot his enemy. However, by mistake he shot and killed his private secretary. At the conclusion of the trial he was found guilty, but insane. He was then committed to a mental institution until "her Majesty's pleasure was known."

This verdict caused quite a controversy and was widely criticized. It was argued by many that althought McNaughton was labouring under a delusional belief that Sir Robert Peel was plotting against him, he was responsible for his crime and ought to be hanged. It was argued that if his belief had been true, and Sir Robert Peel had in fact been plotting against him, McNaughton would have committed a crime by taking the law into his own hands and killing his enemy.

Thus, although his belief was delusional and false, he was guilty of murder. The case was debated in the House of Lords. During this debate the "legal lords," the British equivalent of the justice of the Supreme

Court in America, were asked certain questions. On the basis of their answers, the guiding principles were formulated for deciding the validity of the insanity plea in future cases. These principles became known as the "McNaughton rules." They may be stated briefly as follows: An accused could be excused from the responsibility for his crime if at the time of his criminal act he was suffering from a defect of reason caused by a disease of the mind so that he did not know the nature and quality of his act. However, if he knew the nature and the quality of his act, he could also be excused if he did not know that what he was doing was wrong. The McNaughton rules were widely accepted in all English speaking countries (Rieber, 1981).

The onus of proof of insanity was on the defendant. Until recently, in most jurisdictions, the verdict was either "sane" or "insane." The Scottish law was an exception; it accepted a plea of diminished responsibility. More recently, many jurisdictions have followed the Scottish example. The plea of diminished responsibility was enacted in England in 1957 and it has been accepted in many states of the United States.

As years went by, the McNaughton rules have been criticized because of their stress on rational judgment and compartalization of the human mind. There have been some reformulations of the rules which have stressed the presence of mental illness rendering the individual incapable of controlling his behaviour. Another issue was that of an irresistible impulse. The latter was a hallmark of the psychopathic personality.

In 1835 James Cowles Prichard (1786-1848), a Bristol physician, introduced the concept of "moral insanity," or "moral imbecility." The individuals who suffered from this condition had an inborn defect of "moral sense." They did not suffer from delusions and hallucinations and their intellect was not impaired. However, their moral judgment was defective and perverted. They were not capable of conducting themselves with decency and propriety. They acted on impulse, without thinking about the consequences. Moreover their behaviour was incorrigible despite punishment. This concept was accepted by German psychiatrists and given a constitutional interpretation. I.L.A. Koch (1891) described it as "psychopathic inferiority" or "constitutional inferiority," and also as "psychopathic personality." Two French psychiatrists, Benedict Morel and Valentine Magnan incorporated Prichard's concept of moral insanity into their broad category of "hereditary degeneracy." Kraepelin believed that psychopathic personalities were *formes frustes* of psychoses.

Kurt Schneider (1958) believed that psychopathic personalities constitute extreme deviations from the mean personality traits characterizing the general population. Recently the term "psychopathic personality" has been abandoned and replaced first by "sociopathic personality" and then by "antisocial personality." However, the concept has remained the same. Psychopathic behaviour is impulsive. Psychopaths are thought to be incapable of resisting their impulses. Consequently, in addition to the McNaughton rules, an attempt was made in some jurisdictions, to introduce an "irresistible impulse" as ground for a plea of insanity. This innovation encountered legal opposition. It was argued that if an impulse was not resisted, it was be definition "irresistible."

Hereditary Degeneracy Theory. The disease model was not the only organic or biological model put forward in academic psychiatry in the nineteenth century. Benedict Morel (1809-1873)(1857), and Valentin Magnan (1835-1916), at midcentury, proposed a "hereditary degeneracy" model. It subsequently became known as the "neuropathic diathesis."

The term "neuropathic diathesis" (Tredgold, 1929) was used to describe a nonspecific impairment of germ plasm ("Blastophoria") which, it was believed, was the cause of all mental and nervous diseases that were not caused by infection. It was alleged to be the cause of mental deficiency, chronic alcoholism, psychopathy, and habitual crime. Neuropathic diathesis could originally be produced by external factors such as toxic or infectious agents which damaged the germ plasm. The common toxic agent was believed to be alcohol. The damage of the germ plasm led to irresistible, progressive, hereditary degeneration of the family stock (Penrose, 1949). There was continuous decline from one generation to another, with more severe forms of "degeneration" succeeding milder ones. Thus, psychopathy occurring in an earlier generation might be succeeded by insanity or idiocy in the next generation.

Morel and Magnan believed that the type of insanity which could not be attributed to localized lesions was a form of nonspecific hereditary degeneracy. It was attributed to a general degeneration of the family hereditary stock that could manifest itself in different forms of insanity, in mental deficiency, in psychopathic personality, as well as in alcoholism and habitual crime. The presence of the familial predisposition could be detected by the presence of the "stigmata of degeneracy." Morel had also observed that the frequency of degenerative diseases, even of cretinism and feeble-mindedness, was higher in certain regions of France. He was one of the first to notice that industrial pollution and chemical wastes might be implicated the emergence of more hereditary disease. However, he believed that such degeneration involved a negative variation in the human species, and that the whole species could remain healthy and reproduce.

In 1860, Morel introduced the term "dementia praecox" to describe degenerative insanity occurring in young people. In his rejection of the concept of disease and the substitution for the concept of degeneracy, Morel was influenced by his close friend Claude Bernard, a critic of the disease model.

Valentin Magnan (1874) elaborated the degeneracy concept further. This was partly the result of his studies of alcoholism, then a prevalent medical and social problem in France. He believed that alcoholism could be a possible cause of hereditary degeneracy and also one of its effects. Both Morel and Magnan in formulating their theory of degeneracy were probably influenced by the theory of evolution of Jean Baptiste Lamarck (1744-1929). According to the latter theory, the acquired characteristics were inherited. Therefore the organic impairment and bad habits caused by such noxious agents as alcohol, could also be inherited.

An earlier conception of "moral insanity," suggested in 1835 by James Cowles Prichard (1786-1848), and the subsequent work of Caesare Lombroso (1836-1909)(1876) on the hereditary criminal constitution, were easily assimilated to the heredo-degenerative model of insanity. So was Hughlings Jackson's theory of the higher and lower functions of the nervous system. The impact of Darwinism, and of the British eugenics movement also shaped the subsequent interpretation of degeneracy theory.

John Hughlings Jackson's (1835-1911) theory of higher and lower levels of the functioning of the nervous system,could also be fitted to this schema. Jackson had been trained at York Hospital and in 1859 had gone to New York to gain further experience. Later he turned to medical writing and was to publish more than 300 essays (Jackson, 1884). He searched for the relations between life processes and the conscious mind. However, as a follower of Herbert Spencer, he remained a dualist, keeping soul and body in separate realms as co-existent. Consciousness was held to have a real substrate in the nervous system. Like Spencer he believed that the simple evolved into a more complex system. This general theory could also be applied to the nervous system. He assumed that the dissolution of the higher nervous functions resulted in a release from a state of inhibition of the lower ones. Dissolution caused a reduction to a lower evolutionary stage within the nervous system. Mental illness was seen as a dissolution of higher brain functions which formed the substrate for the brain's activity. It was not a bodily illness. This theory was based on the concepts of ontogenetic and phylogenetic development (Holmes, 1956, 1970; Lassek, 1970; Dewhurst, 1982). In his thinking Hughlings Jackson was very much influenced by Darwin's theory of evolution, particularly as it was interpreted by his teacher Thomas Laycock (1812-1876) and by Herbert Spencer (1820-1903), both followers of Comte and Darwin as "evolutionary positivists."

While the new science of bacteriology was instrumental to the revival of the disease model, the theory of evolution gave boost to the "heredo-degenerative" model. About the same time, that the bacterial theory of disease scored its triumphs, Charles Darwin (1809-1881) published his *The Origin of Species* (1859). The theory of evolution made its tremendous impact on the thought of the nineteenth century.

Its revolutionary importance could be compared to that of the Copernican heliocentric theory. Evolution meant progression to higher biological forms. It also implied the possibility of regression to lower forms, a kind of degeneration, or "attavism" (the term used by Lombroso). Francis Galton (1822-1911), a half-cousin of Darwin, applied the theory of evolution to the hereditary differences of human intelligence and character. In his *Hereditary Genius* (1869) he pointed out that both superior intelligence, or genius, and inferior intelligence were inherited, that there was a superior and inferior human stock. Moreover, high intelligence correlated with desirable character traits while low intelligence correlated with undesirable ones. Francis Galton proposed a new discipline of "eugenics" concerned with improvement of the human race by encouraging the breeding of superior stock and discouraging the elimination of inferior stock.

The eugenics movement became very influential both in Great Britain and the United States. When early intelligence tests were introduced in the twentieth century, it was found that the I.Q. of members of the working class was lower than that of the middle class. At the same time it was also found that the birth rate of the middle class was lower than that of the working classes. These findings led to dire predictions about a progressive deterioration of the intelligence of the British nation. In the United States and Canada these findings led to the enactment of laws which enforced sterlization of mental defectives. During World War I intelligence tests were used to evaluate millions of soldiers in the United States Army. They were afterwards used in the school system in order to locate and identify talented children. Galton's original theory excluded nutrition as a factor in intelligence and argued solely for the hereditary elements.

At the end of the nineteenth century the United States and Canada were confronted with the problem of mass immigration. The immigrants often came from ethnic and linguistic backgrounds that were different from those of the Anglo-Saxon local population. That led to cultural conflicts and a backlash of xenophobia. One of the consequences of this situation was an innundation of mental hospitals by patients who could not speak English. (Blackwell's Island Asylum in New York even had a majority of foreign mentally ill). They were diagnosed as having "dementia praecox" and left to rot for years in chronic wards. The result was a lowering of the standards of patient care when compared with that given in the "moral treatment" of the insane, before the mid-nineteenth century.

There were two conflicting views of the problem. The first subscribed to the idea of "social man" molded by his social milieu and culture. It subscribed to the "ideology of a "melting pot" of races and nationalities, promising Europe's "huddled masses yearning to breathe free" an opportunity in the new land. The other view embraced the biological or Darwinian idea of man which viewed him as the product of natural selection and evolution. The first view advocated the assimilation and acculturation of the new comers. The second, supported selective immigration and the exclusion of "inferior races" which represented an inferior biological stock. Its supporters found scientific justification in the eugenic theories, and in the writings of some prominent geneticists such as Thomas Morgan at Columbia University.

The leading exponent of eugenics in the United States was Charles Benedict Davenport (1866-1944), the director of the Station for Experimental Evolution at Cold Spring Harbor. In 1911, Davenport published his *Heredity in Relation to Eugenics*. In that work, Davenport recounted the story of the Jukeses from upper New York state and presented their geneaology. They descended from Max, a drunken backwoodsman and a promiscuous, mentally defective woman. All the members of this family were alcoholics for several generations. They were petty criminals of low intelligence and chronically unemployed. Many of them were syphilitic or insane. They constituted a drain on the public purese. According to Davenport, the Jukeses cost New York state taxpayers over 1.25 million dollars (Richards, 1987). The story of the Jukses was contrasted with that of the descendants of Jonathan Edwards, an American philosopher, a clergyman and writer of old American Mayflower stock. The descendants of Edwards were prominent clergymen and professional people. According to Davenport, the spread of an inferior germ plasm such as that of the Jukeses presented a threat to American society. The society had the right to remove an inferior and vicious germ plasm from its midst by the same right that it had to deprive a murderer of his life.

The mass intelligence testing carried out on the draftees into the American army during the first World War, indicated that soldiers of eastern and south European extraction, as well as negroes, scored lower on the I.Q. test than the Americans of Nordic stock. Moreover, the incidence of mental illness and crime was reported to be higher in these racial groups than amongst Americans of Anglo-Saxon extraction. These findings reinforced the fears that the United States was being inundated by immigrants from eastern and southern Europe who were of an inferior biological stock. The "passing of a great race" was lamented. These fears led to the introduction of strict immigration quotas in 1924, directed against immigrants of "lower" racial stock. William McDougall, a proponent of inborn human instinct theory and Lewis Terman, a pioneer psychometrician, were supporters of the eugenic movement and of the legislation inspired by it.

The early American behaviourists, in particular J.B. Watson, were opponents of eugenics. They believed that the environment and learning were complete determinants of human behaviour. Some prominent laymen such as Clarence Darrow, the famous trial lawyer, and Walter Lippmann, the journalist, were also vociferous opponents of eugenics.

The opponents subscribed to the idea of "social man," and they believed that the "melting pot" policy was the answer to the problem of ethnic conflicts. The eugenics movement also became influential in Germany where it was supported by such prominent scientists as Ernst

Haeckel, and more recently by Konrad Lorenz. The latter was an ethnologist who studied the inborn patterns of behaviour, mainly in birds. He emphasized the importance of heredity, of natural selection, and of evolution for the understanding of the animal and of human behaviour.

Lorenz also believed that natural selection in the wild was necessary to maintain biological vigor and fitness. Domestication in animals and civilization in human beings led to a state of degenration. In the case of human beings, the protection from natural selection led to intellectual and moral degeneration of a kind that manifested itself in psychopathological behaviour and mental illness. (In addition to being a zoologist, Lorenz was a physician and worked as a psychiatrist during World War II, and so had direct experience with psychiatric diseases). Both Lorenz and Haeckel were strong supporters of Social Darwinism. Lorenz believed that the laws of nature were laws of society. It appears that Lorenz presented a modern version of Morel's theory of degeneracy, based on extreme Darwinism. In Germany, eugenics became incorporated into the race hygiene movement, an important part of Nazi ideology.

In psychiatry, the "heredo-degeneration" theory of Benedict Morel and Valentin Magnan came to be perceived as an application of the theory of biological regression to mental illness. Although originally conceived in terms of Lamarckian evolution, it could be assimilated into the Darwinian theory, particularly since the latter in its early version, was vague on the subject of the inheritance of acquired characteristics.

Only at the end of the nineteenth century, did the German ultra-Darwinist August Weismann preclude the possibility of the inheritance of acquired characteristics. He conceptually separated germ plasm from somatoplasm. The first was concerned with the reproduction of an organism, with its genotype. The second had to do with its adjustment to the environment, its phentotype. According to Weismann, the germ plasm could be affected by the environment only indirectly, through natural selection.

Mental illness was fitted into the evolutionary schema of things. Parallels were drawn between the minds of children, savages, and the insane. The "heredo-degeneracy" model represented a type of constitutional model and presupposed a continuity between the state of normality, and the state of disease, as well as continuity among various pathological states. It, however, added a strong valuational element to the traditional Hippocratic constitutional model. It attributed inferiority to certain family stocks and by an extension to certain racial stocks. Herbert Spencer and others extended this general idea to human societies, to economics and politics. In this way the theory of Social Darwinism originated, to complement the biological version of evolution, and was applied to justify social inequality.

The "heredo-degeneracy" model can also be called "the impaired" model, a term proposed by Siegler and Osmond (1974). These authors contrast the "impaired model" of mental illness with that of the "disease model." They argued that these two models are associated with very different attitudes to mental patients. While the impaired model is associated with a rejection of mental patients and with therapeutic nihilism, the disease model is associated with a positive attitude and therapeutic optimism. Moreover, since the stigmata of degenration were taken as signs of a tainted stock, the attitude of rejection associated with the impaired model, extended to the relatives of the patients who became ashamed of the occurrence of insanity in their families.

The contention of Galton that negative characteristics were highly correlated, thus postulating the general inferiority of a stock, was not accepted by everybody. Accordingly the predisposition to constitutional insanity did not necessarily imply an absolute inferiority of the stock; it could also be associated with genius. This idea can be found in the writings of Moreau de Tours (1859). The association of genius with madness had previously been mentioned by Reil. The terms *degenere superieur* (superior degenerate) and "creative psychopath" were coined. They implied a constitutional link between genius and insanity. Pursuing this line of inquiry, Paul Julius Moebius (1853-1907) played an important role in bringing psychology back into psychiatry. He wrote several pathographic studies of prominent individuals, and was working on one of Charles Darwin, when he died. Moebius also diagnosed himself as a *degenere superieur*. He may have had in mind the prominence of his grandfather, August Ferdinand Moebius, a mathematician and astronomer (Bodenheimer, 1963). The idea of an association between genius and insanity was taken up and developed further in the twentieth century by Ernst Kretschmer, the leader of the constitutional psychiatry school.

The adoption of the hereditary degeneracy ("impaired') model of mental illness, led to a therapeutic nihilism. The "moral treatment" of the insane, originally introduced by Philippe Pinel, was abandoned.

Mental patients were herded into large institutions, built on the model of prisons, and situated in remote, isolated places. The emphasis was on separating the degenerate from the healthy stock. The role of the psychiatrist was perceived as that of a protector of the society, not only from dangerous lunatics, but also from the tainted stock of insanity. Only secondarily was he regarded as a custodian of patients. This attitude, fostered by the hereditary degeneracy model, attained full expression in the twentieth century in Nazi Germany, where it led to mass "euthanasia" of hundreds of thousands of mental patients.

There were exceptions to the later nineteenth century trend of institutionalizing mental patients in prisonlike hospitals. Some hospital administrators advocated boarding out patients with normal families, believing that a family milieu would have a psychotherapeutic effect. The most famous example of this was the Gheel colony in Belgium, where patients lived in cottages and private farm homes, and could enjoy a maximum of personal liberty and family care.

The Impact of Socio-Economic Conditions. The harnessing of energy, first of hydropower and later of steam, which was mentioned earlier in the discussion of Philosophy of Nature, produced the Industrial Revolution. Although it had its roots in the agricultural reforms of the eighteenth century, especially in the enclosure of fields, it took off only in the early nineteenth century as factories and cities grew. It started in England and by the 1830s it was beginning to spread to Belgium, Germany, and France. The industrialization of the United States and of most European nations led to tremendous social dislocations. The Industrial Revolution spawned new urban centres with their "satanic mills," grimy factories, and squalid slums.

The economic changes associated with the Industrial Revolution brought in their wake the accumulation of prodigious wealth by successful entrepreneurs, but also the grinding povery of the industrial proletariat. Moreover, the Industrial Revolution produced the economic cycles of boom and bust which led to feelings of uncertainty and insecurity, particularly in those at the bottom of the social ladder. The values of the market economy now replaced those associated with kinship relations and feudalism. Labour became a commodity which was to be bought and sold in the free market like any other commodity. There was an affirmation of the Protestant work ethic in the entrepreneurial classes, but also an alienation of the masses of industrial workers. Karl Marx (1818-1883) was, like so many of the European social critics of his age, concerned with the plight of the industrial workers labouring in the factories as well as with their alienation (Marx, 1963). In contrast to the artisans of the medieval world, who saw in the products of their labour the expression of their creativity and the realization of their abilities, the factory workers suffered mental anguish from having to perform meaningless mechanical tasks (Fromm,1955; Schacht, 1970). Of course, many modern historians now argue that this presented an overdrawn picture, for the medieval artisans were by no means a contented lot, and frequently rebelled. (The Jacquerie of 1356 and the Wat Tyler Uprising of 1381 present illustrations). However, the causes of alienation in the nineteenth century were more impersonal and institutionalized than those which caused resentment in earlier periods.

According to such modern psychiatrist-critics of industrial society as Erich Fromm, the reduction of the status of the labourer to a commodity, the obstacles to his creative expression, resulted in a dehumanization. The worker felt that he was just a cog in the industrial machine, that he lacked meaningful relationships with his fellow workers, and with his employer. He was perceived by others and he perceived himself to be an object, powerless to control his own destiny or to influence the course of political events. Marx took the concept of alienation (*Entfremdung*) from Georg W. F. Hegel (1770-1831), especially the *Phenomenology of Mind* (1807/1949), *and Philosophy of Right* (1821/1942) (Lukacs, 1948). In the *Phenomenology*, Hegel referred to the spirit being alienated from itself. There could be an alienation from nature, from society and from the self. Marx offered a concrete interpretation of the Hegelian concept of alienation in the context of nineteenth century capitalist society.

The influence of Hegel and Marx on modern thought proved to be enormous, and as a result, the concept of alienation has been used widely in philosophical, theological, and sociological literature (Schacht, 1970). In the twentieth century Erich Fromm (1941, 1961, 1955) and Karen Horney (1939, 1945, 1950), two sociologically oriented neo-Freudians, introduced the concept of alienation to psychiatry. They used the expression, "alienation from oneself," to describe a robot-like conformity which led to stunted personality growth and to a "paucity of inner experience." Another type of alienation described by these authors was an alienation from society which, in its extreme form, led to an autistic withdrawal and to schizophrenia.

About fifty years after Marx discussed the alienation of industrial workers, Emil Durkheim (1858-1917), the French sociologist offered an alternative concept of "anomie" or "normlessness" to account for the phenomena of social disorganization. Anomie denoted an absence of internalized social controls or norms. Durkheim belonged to a famous generation and had been a classmate of Pierre Janet. In his famous work, *Suicide* (Durkheim, 1897/1951), he described four types of suicide: 1) altruistic, 2) egoistic, 3) anomic, 4) fatalistic. The altruistic suicide was one in which the individual sacrificed himself for the good of others. In the case of egoistic suicide, the individual lost the identification with his society. In anomic suicide, the individual lacked social norms to guide his expectations and behaviour. Finally, in fatalistic suicide, the individual found himself in a predicament from which there was no way out. The conditions which led to an anomic or an egoistic suicide were similar to those subsumed uner the concept of alienation.

An American sociologist Robert Merton (1938/1968) introduced the concept of anomie to American Sociology. This concept was assimilated to that of social disorganization. Earlier studies of social disorganization in relation to urban ecology (Park & Burgess, 1925) indicated that incidence of schizophrenia was high in socially disorganized city areas, as exemplified by the "transitional zone" (Farris & Dunham, 1939). The theory of anomie became one of the theories explaining the etiology of schizophrenia.

The psychological and environmental factors were not completely forgotten by the organic psychiatrists of the nineteenth century. However, the type of psychological explanation offered by them was quite superficial, and was influenced by popular prejudices. The social mores of the middle of the nineteenth century, particularly in Great Britain, have led to identifying mid-Victorian norms with sexual repression. The culture asserted male dominance and a double sexual standard, although some notable thinkers like John Stuart Mill did favor the improvement of women's political rights. The Victorian norms on both sides of the Atlantic were associated with the glorification of the Protestant ethic by the newly developed industrial society. Sexual indulgence was regarded not only as a sin, but also as a disease. Many forms of insanity were attributed to masturbation. Hysteria became associated in the medical and popular mind with nymphomania. Some physicians advocated clitorotomy as a cure for hysteria. Masturbation was regarded as a sign of mental degeneration and in its turn, as a cause of insanity. David Skae (1814-1873), in his classification of mental disease, attributed many neurotic and psychotic conditions, as well as suicide, to masturbation.

Kierkegaard and Nietzsche: the Harbingers of Existentialism and Psychoanalysis. In a discussion of the history of ideas in relation to psychiatry, it is necessary to present briefly, the teachings of two nineteenth century philosophers, namely, those of Soren Kierkegaard and of Friedrich Nietzsche. These two philosophers were outside the mainstream of those intellectual currents represented by materialism, positivism, German Idealism, and Philosophy of Nature. They were precursors of existentialism, and in the case of Nietzsche, of both existentialism and psychoanalysis. The impact of their philosophies came to full fruition only in the twentieth century. Their major impact was on the twentieth century psychiatry as well as on its philosophy.

Existential themes may be discerned in the writings of the fifth cenury Church father, St. Augustine (1961), and in the poetry of the medieval Persian, Omar Khayyam (Weckowicz, 1981). Also in the writings of Blaise Pascal (1967), a seventeenth century mathematician and philosopher. In the nineteenth century, the Danish theologian, Søren Kierkegaard and the German classicist, Friedrich Nietzsche turned to the existentialist themes as a form of protest against such dehumanizing philosophies as positivism and rationalism. These two philosophies had come into prominence against the background of social disintegration and psychological alienation brought about in the wake of the Industrial Revolution. Together with the Marxian materialists, rationalists and positivists tended to disregard the meaning of an unique, individual existence and to "lose" the individual in an objective world of things and in philosophical abstractions. Both Kierkegaard and Nietzsche strongly protested against this degradation of the importance of the individual.

Søren Kierkegaard.

Søren Kierkegaard (1813-1855) (1941, 1944, 1954a, 1954b, 1959) passionately attacked rationalism and objectivity, both in philosophy and theology. His attack was directed in particular against the Hegelian system. He insisted on the subjective or personal meaning of truth and saw man condemned to loneliness, guilt, "sickness unto death," and trembling in fear. This was because he was irrevocably confronted with making choices between good and evil. In his *Concluding Unscientific*

Postscript, Kierkegaard argued that truth was" subjectivity." It had meaning only in the context of the relation between the self and the object. To quote Kierkegaard:

> When the question of truth is raised subjectively, reflection is directed subjectively to the nature of the individual relationship; if only the mode of this relationship is in truth, the individual is in truth even if he should happen to be thus related to what is not true (Kierkegaard, 1941, p. 178).

Thus, Kierkegaard anticipated the existentialist notion of "being-in-the world," the inseparability of the subject and of the object. He also stressed the necessity of commitment to a particular faith, a particular philosophy, or a particular way of life. Truth is only actualized in decisions and deeds. To quote Kierkegaard again (1941, p.313):"But passion first and last; for it is impossible to think about existence in existence without passion."

The problem of choice was discussed in *Either/Or* (1941/1944) in the context of choosing between the aesthetic and the ethical values. This choice involved more than a choice between two sets of values. It involved a choice between two ways of life: the aesthetic one, motivated by the desire for pleasure, the ethical one, by a sense of duty. The ethical way of life involved the unconditional acceptance of the universal rules, and the fulfillment of one's duty. However, there was no criteria for making the choice. It was up to the individual. By making the choice, the individual constituted himself. He committed himself to one mode of existence rather than to another. All choices depended on subjective judgments and on individual points of view. When one has made a choice of the ethical way of life, the superiority of this choice might be spurious, because the transition from the ethical to the religious way, might demand a violation of universal rules in order to obey God's commands. In such an exigency, one had to make make a "leap of faith," and to accept the absurd. Kierkegaard's conception of the religious way of life set him against the established Lutheran Church in Denmark. The latter was based on an established social order and on a system of dogmas. His animosity was in part determined by his own earlier studies in which he aimed at becoming a clergyman.

Beset by fits of depression, and somewhat shocked by his father's revelations of youthful sins and shady business ventures, he reacted against the entire established order (Ostenfeld, 1972, tr.1978). The established church had nothing to do with the inner, personal character of the Christian faith. A moral choice was not based on a rational judgment nor on one's feelings. It was completely undetermined. This aspect of the choosing situation could be understood only when one was confronted by a moral choice. A confrontation with moral choices was necessary for personal growth and for becoming a real person.

The individual was confronted by choices which would allow him to actualize himself and to become true to himself. "Ethics concentrates upon the individual, and ethically, it is the task of every individual to become an entire man; just as it is the ethical presupposition that every man is born in such a condition that he can become one." (Kierkegaard, 1941, p.309). The individual was aware of the possibilities of his moral development. This could be achieved by an exercise of free choices for which the individual is entirely responsible. He could abandon pretense, drop the mask of conventionality and become the real self. The situation in which he was confronted by these choices was the human predicament. It was responsible for despair and for a state of ontological anxiety or dread (Kierkegaard, 1944). The failure to make the right choice produced a chronic state of guilt which he characterized as "sickness unto death" (Kierkegaard, 1954). Kierkegaard focused on the subjectivity of experience, and above all on what it meant to be man as a unique individual, in contrast to an actor playing conventional social roles.

Kierkegaard's philosophy rejected both the rationalism of Hegel and the sentimentality of contemporary Romantics. His central thesis "truth is subjectivity," broke with all traditions of western thought since Descartes, and as H.V. Martin argues, with all Christian theology since Melanchthon (Martin, 1950). He shared the Romantic belief in the importance of the individual and of his passions. At the same time, he rejected the notion of the "bond of sympathy" uniting all individuals with one another and with the pantheistic universe or the all embracing spirit. Each man was condemned to loneliness and faced his personal God.

The entire world of external objectivity was real only in relation to man's inner being. The human ego became important, because it alone could participate in the world. Further, man was an individual only in a community. Society was the ethico-religious world. In the tradition of Augustinian theology, he argued that only when sin (a fall from grace) became real, could man know the difference between good and evil. But what was sin ? For Kierkegaard every act of doubt, all despair was sin. Why ? Mainly, because man refused to actualize the self God had intended him to be (Martin, 1950). In his early short story, *Johannes*

Climacus of 1842-43 (Kierkegaard, tr. 1958), doubt is still external to the individual mind. However, the idea of a subjectivity becomes clearer as its introspective nature is emphasized. If Christianity is subjectivity, he argues, then it is an "inner transformation." Introspection was essential for the thinking individual, because the objective world outside of him was indifferent to him. The individual existed because he was a thinking, conscious subject interested in his own thoughts. In that way he reflected a more universal structure of existence in his personal life (Johnson, 1972). The early twentieth century psychiatry of a man like Karl Jaspers, who helped rediscover Kierkegaard, drew much of its inspiration from his conceptualization of the existential dilemma.

Friedrich Nietzsche.

Another precursor of existentialism, Friedrich Nietzsche (1844-1900) (1954, 1966), rejected the value system based on the natural order, reason, and conventional religion. Instead he insisted that the "superman," or "ideal man," will create new values which will be beyond good and evil as traditionally conceived. His aphoristic philosophy was directed against shallow enlightenment, glib rationalism, and philistine reasonableness. It penetrated into the dark abyss where the roots of reason and human existence were to be found.

In the *Birth of Tragedy* Nietzsche argued that there existed two aspects of Greek culture, the "Apollonian" and the "Dionysian." Underneath the reasonableness, moderation, serenity and emotional control of the Appollonian ethos of Greek culture, there was hidden the wild, lustful, orgiastic "Dionysian" ethos. The latter ethos surfaced during the mysteries of which the Greek tragedy was born of it. The theme that anti-social, aggressive and self destructive motives were hidden behind the facade of morality and altruism, recurred in several of Nietzsche's works. It anticipated Freud's theories of the unconscious, of the death instinct, of sublimation, and of the ego defence mechanisms.

Nietzsche was a great admirer of Schopenhauer and of his philosophy of the malign world will. According to Nietzsche, the Schopenhauerian man destroyed those whom he loved and also the institutions which had shaped him, in order to assert the truth about himself. Consequently, Nietzsche attacked current ideologies, the established religion and the social order. Influenced by the idea of physical energy and its vicissitudes, Nietzsche thought of the human mind as a seething cauldron of drives fighting one another, in the process of transformation, and eventually discharged under controlled or uncontrolled conditions. Emotions were complex representations of the state of the will.

According to Nietzsche, the mechanisms of sublimation inhibited the expression of sexual and aggressive instincts. Good intentions were really sublimated evil ones. The repression of unpleasant memories was an active purposeful process aiming at self deception and was allied with sublimation. Nietzsche believed that the task of the philosopher and also of the yet to emerge "superman", was to remove the cloak of false morality and to unmask self deception. He was to some extent also a Darwinist, since his *Uebermensch* in reality represented a new type of humanoid on the evolutionary scale. That is the import of *Thus Spake Zarathustra*. This "overman" as Walter Kaufmann has translated the old "superman," was to be superior in morality as well as intellectually, and was to make the present species look like a missing link between itself and its own ape-like ancestors. The leadership of which the present species was capable, would thus appear to behave more like a circus performer on a tightrope.

Nietzsche's views might be interpreted to mean that he believed in a philosophical and moral nihilism. They might also imply the need of a necessary preliminary step to the reconstruction of ethics and of the social order. Nietzsche sought to elucidate the irrational, unconscious sources of man's drive to power and greatness. With this, he would also shed light on the origins of madness and of self destruction. Thus he may be regarded as a precursor of both existentialism and psychoanalysis. According to this philosopher, man was motivated by a "will to power," which for him meant the actualization of man's potential (*potentia*) (Nietzsche, 1966). By affirming his potentialities the individual had the courage to become his real self. In his book *Ecce Homo* (Nietzsche, 1966), was concerned with the problem of "how one becomes what one is" ("Wie man wird, was man ist"). Man's dignity was not given to him automatically, but he had to attain it by his own choices. He had to actualize himself, and to create his own individuality by creating his own values of life. Man became his real self by his own free choice.

In *Genealogy of Morals* (Nietzsche, 1968), dealt with the problem of human motivation. He believed that the conventional morality of altruism and selflessness was a result of repressed hostility and resentment. The internalization of these two sentiments produced guilt feelings. Nietzsche believed that it was important to unmake self-deception and to reveal true motives.

According to Nietzsche there existed two types of morality. The morality of masters and that of slaves. The first contrasted good with bad, the second, good with evil. Slave morality was born of resentment and was basically negative. The present day morality was a mixture of the two types with slave morality being dominant. This was characterized by resentment and guilt feelings. Guilt feelings were at the bottom of conscience. They were the by-products of civilization. In the state of nature, primitive man was still a beast of prey who could satisfy his instincts freely. In the civilized state, man had to repress his instincts and turn them inwards. This caused guilt feelings and produced the moral conscience in man. The development of moral conscience, which did not come from God, but from the parents, paralleled the development of civilization. Nietzsche's views were similar to those of Denis Diderot, an eighteenth century French encyclopedist, who equated civilization with illness and the suffering of mankind. There was also a similarity between these views and the ideas of Sigmund Freud on this same subject as he presented them in his *Civilization and its Discontents*.

In *Thus Spake Zarathustra*, Nietzsche developed the theme of the "superman," or *Uebermensch*. The superman did not dominate other men by his own power. He "overcame himself," transcended his present moral state and attained one which was superior. He cast off conventional and false morality, gave vent to the repressed instincts and was purged of them. By doing so he achieved a superior state of morality guided by higher values and lofty ideals. Due to the principal of "eternal return," the superman would return again and again through the eons of time, bearing the names of different prophets each time.

Nietzsche had a tremendous impact on his contemporaries. There was a fascination with his life story and with the possible relationship between his philosophy and his madness. His mental illness was diagnosed as a general paralysis of the insane, a form of tertiary syphilis. There was also the possibility that it was an inherited condition, because his father became incurably insane at the age of forty-five. In the times when speculations were rife about the relation between genius and madness, Nietzsche's case caused widespread interest among scholars and psychiatrists.

Nietzsche's philosophy influenced both the psychodynamic psychiatry and existentialism. Freud's ideas of the unconscious, of defence mechanisms, and of the superego, bear a resemblance to Nietzsche's ideas about human nature. Alfred Adler's notion of the "will to power" as the main human motive, was obviously influenced by Nietzsche. At the first Wednesday evening meeting of the early followers of Freud, Adler reviewed Nietzsche's *The Genealogy of Morals*.

Many of the ideas of Carl Gustav Jung, such as the achievement of a higher moral state, the ideas of archetypes, "persona," and "shadow, could all be traced back to Nietzsche. Jung was particularly fascinated by his *Thus Spake Zarathustra*. Among the existentialists, both Martin Heidegger and Martin Buber in their youth, fell under the spell of Nietzsche.

The historical survey of the present chapter ends in the late nineteenth century. It ends on the eve of the emergence of modern psychiatry and psychology. The end of the nineteenth century saw the rise of Freudian psychodynamic psychiatry. It saw the establishment of the modern medical model by Emil Kraepelin, followed closely by its alternative, the constitutional model of Ernst Kretschmer. At about the same time, Wilhelm Wundt established the first laboratory of experimental psychology. Soon afterwards, Ivan Pavlov carried out his early experiments on conditional reflexes, thus providing a scientific alternative to a purely somatic approach. In philosophy, the beginning of the twentieth century saw the rise of the Phenomenological Movement, followed by Existentialism. These developments were going to have a great impact on psychiatry, particularly in continental Europe. In the social sciences, philosophical speculations were replaced by the empirical approach which provided a new foundation for social psychiatry.

The Twentieth Century: Modern Psychiatry is Born

If the nineteenth century has been called an era of system building (Zilboorg, 1941), then the same could be said about the first half of the twentieth century. Different systems implied different, very often incompatible conceptualizations about mental illness, different research paradigms, and entirely different methods of treatment. Followers of particular schools of psychiatry ignored and were often hostile towards members of different schools.

The main twentieth century schools of psychopathology singled out for historical appraisal in this section of the book are : 1) the Kraepelinian nosological system, which was a disease model; 2) the constitutional psychiatry of Ernst Kretschmer; 3) the dynamic psychiatry of Sigmund Freud and his followers and opponents; 4) the psychobiology and common sense psychiatry of Adolph Meyer; 5) behaviour therapy (discussed under the title of "The roots of behaviour therapy"); and 6) the phenomenological and existentialist schools (discussed under the title of "The impact of philosophy on psychiatry at the turn of the century"). These different traditions in psychopathology will be discussed in separate chapters.

Kraepelin's Nosological System: The Disease Model.

The modern disease model of psychiatry has its origins in the noslogical system developed by Emil Kraepelin at the end of the nineteenth century. Emil Kraepelin (1856-1926) had been born in Neu-Strelitz, Mecklenburg. His father was an actor and his older brother Carl, a biologist, who became the curator of the Museum of Natural History in Hamburg. Their father's stage readings of the north German writer, Fritz Reuter, earned enough to finance their university education. Kraepelin studied medicine at the University of Wuerzburg. As a medical student he became interested in the new science of experimental psychology and spent one semester at the University of

Leipzig studying with Wilhelm Wundt (1832-1920), the founder of that discipline. This interest was reflected in the title of Kraepelin's M.D. thesis, "The Place of Psychology in Psychiatry." After graduating from Wuerzburg in 1878, he spent four years in Munich studying neuroanatomy with Bernard von Gudden (1824-1886), the professor of psychiatry and one of the leading neuroanatomists of the day. After four years in Munich, he went to Leipzig again to pursue advanced studies with Paul E. Flechsig in psychiatry, with Wilhelm Erb in neurophysiology, and subsequently experimental psychology with Wilhelm Wundt. He left Flechsig's clinic to work with Wilhelm Wundt in psychology. Wilhelm Wundt (1832-1920) was the founder of experimental psychology as a discipline, and Kraepelin hoped that the new science would add to his training. Wundt had advised against his making a career of psychology, so that he returned to Munich in 1884, to work with Bernhard von Gudden, the professor of psychiatry.

Kraepelin acquired a sound knowledge of the basic sciences and these were to provide the foundations of his system of psychiatry. His study of Griesinger's works influenced his acceptance of an organic approach to mental illness. As Kurt Kolle has pointed out, he was the initiator of the Heidelberg and Munich neuropathological school (Scholz, 1961). As Kraepelin himself argued in the eighth revised edition of his *Psychiatrie. Ein Lehrbuch fuer studierende und Aerzte* (4 volumes, Leipzig, 1909-1915), "Psychiatry is the discipline of psychic illnesses and their treatment." A scientific understanding of such diseases was needed. Wundt's influence was to make this possible. Kraepelin contributed an obituary to the *Zeitschrift fuer die gesamte Neurologie und Psychiatrie* in 1921 in which he praised Wundt's significance for psychiatry. It lay primarily in his experimental work, and in creating what he called a "natural science way of thinking in psychology."

Kraepelin's main interest in relation to psychology was in Wilhelm Wundt's "physiological" psychology (Wundt, 1911). The founder of experimental psychology, Wundt divided psychological science into two major parts. One was concerned with elementary mental phenomena such as sensations, associations, and reaction times. Wundt called this "physiological" psychology. The second was concerned with such higher, synthetic mental functions as "apperceptions," judgments and reasoning. Wundt called the latter folk psychology or *Voelkerpsychologie*(Wundt, 1910-1920). (Literally, psychology of peoples, or social psychology). While "physiological" psychology could be studied by experimental laboratory methods, *Voelkerpsychologie* was a cultural science which required a hermeneutic approach. That is, an understanding of phenomena in their cultural context. Wundt's laboratory was directly concerned with the contents of consciousness as reported by introspection. However, since Wundt espoused the philosophical position of mind-body parallelism, his psychological laboratory was indirectly concerned with the underlying cerebral physiological events behind mental phenomena.

Kraepelin became one of Wundt's early students and carried on research in his laboratory on the effects of drugs and fatigue on mental phenomena. Earlier on, while still a medical student, Kraepelin wrote a paper "On the Influence of the Acute Diseases on the Origin of Mental Illness." (Zilboorg, 1941). Thus, quite early, Kraepelin became interested in the influence of organic and physical factors on the psyche. In contrast to such other organic psychiatrists of the nineteenth century, like Griesinger, Kraepelin did not reject psychology as irrelevant to psychiatry. However, he limited the relevance of psychology to the experimental-physiological version of it. The earlier organic psychiatrists used the term psychology to refer to philosophy of mind, a school of thought which they had rejected together with the teachings of the *Psychiker* school of psychiatry of the early nineteenth century. Such philosophical speculations were also rejected by Kraepelin. Consequently, his psychology was purely descriptive. It was not concerned with motivation, dynamics, and the deeper understanding of human behaviour. These aspects of psychology were investigated empirically by Kraepelin's contemporary, Sigmund Freud. Eventually, in 1885, Kraepelin was to return to clinical psychiatry on the advice of Wundt.

In 1886, after a year as the chief physician of the city asylum in Dresden, Kraepelin had accepted an academic position at the German language university of Dorpat in the Baltic province of Russia, where he was appointed to the chair of psychiatry. There he continued to work on the psychological effect of drugs which he started in Wundt's laboratory (Kraepelin, 1892). Although the encounter with a strange culture proved interesting, he felt ill at ease and after four years moved to the professorship of psychiatry in Heidelberg in 1891, and then to Munich in 1904. In 1903, between the Heidelberg and Munich professorships, Kraepelin travelled to Ceylon and to the Dutch East Indies where he did some studies in transcultural psychiatry (Kraepelin, 1983).

Earlier, in 1899, Kraepelin carried out similar studies in Africa, where, while in Egypt, he investigated hashish psychosis. He was able to make the interesting observation that melancholia and mania were rare in Java. Patients suffering from melancholia did not express guilt feelings. Alcoholic psychosis was absent (Kraepelin, 1983). On the other hand, Kraepelin found *dementia praecox* (schizophrenia) in all non-European societies he visited (Kraepelin, 1909). On the basis of these studies, he concluded that the same forms of mental disease occurred in all cultures. Their symptomatology, however, was modified by the particular cultural factors.

Finally, in 1904, Kraepelin was appointed to the chair of psychiatry at the University of Munich where he did most of his reasearch in clinical psychiatry and eventually founded the Munich Research Institute of Psychiatry of which he became director when he retired from active teaching in 1922. The Munich psychiatric clinic and the Munich institute became the most important centres of psychiatric research in Germany. There, in addition to clinical work, studies were conducted in neuro-anatomy, neuro-pathology, bio-chemistry, genetics, and experimental psychology. Among his collaborators were such famous psychiatric scientists and neuro-anatomists as Alois Alzheimer (1864-1915) and Franz Nissl (1860-1919). The sections on anatomy in the Kraepelin handbook, in fact, owe much to his association with Alzheimer. The latter is famous for the description of a form of presenile dementia named after him as Alzheimer's disease. His contemporary, Arnold Pick (1851-1924), of the University of Prague, described another type of presenile dementia (Pick, 1913), and also did important work on aphasia.

Kraepelin was a careful observer who kept meticulous and detailed records of patients and was a systematizer who wanted to bring an order into the multiplicity of mental illness classifications which existed at that time. He believed that by careful observations, very often over a period of several years, he would be able to arrive at a "true" nosology or taxonomy of mental diseases. The weakness of the earlier classificatory systems was their exclusive reliance on cross-sectional descriptions of patients. Kraepelin decided to remedy it, and to use the longitudinal method of study.

Following the tradition of Hippocrates and Sydenham, Kraepelin attached a great importance to "natural histories" of different diseases and their prognosis. He believed that mental diseases were organic in nature and were caused by a pathology of the brain. Kraepelin opens his *Lectures on Clinical Psychiatry* (Kraepelin, 1913, p.1) with the following statement:

> Gentlemen, the subject of the following lectures will be scientific psychiatry, which, as its name implies, is that of the treatment of mental diseases. It is true, in the strictest terms we cannot speak of the mind as becoming diseased, whether we regard it as a separate entity or as a sum total of subjective experience. And, indeed, from the medical point of view, it is the disturbance of the physical foundations of mental life which should occupy our attention. But, the incidence (manifestations) of such diseases are generally seen in the sphere of psychical events, a department with which the art of medicine has dealt very little as yet.

Psychopathological phenomena were regarded by him as only the symptoms, the manifestations of the diseases of the brain. In this respect, Kraepelin followed the footsteps of Griesinger and Maudsley, and also followed the whole tradition of nineteenth century organic and neurological psychiatry. He believed in the importance of brain dissections, of histological studies, and of laboratory findings. Kraepelin thought that these would provide the ultimate answer for the causes of mental illness. In some conditions, such as senile dementia, brain tumors, or general paralysis of the insane, there was an obvious brain pathology to which these diseases could be attributed. In others, in which insanity was equally profound, no obvious anatomo-pathological changees in the brain, or abnormal laboratory findings could be established. However, in the past history of medicine, many diseases such as diabetes, tuberculosis, malaria, Bright's glumero-nephritis, or typhoid fever, were described only on the basis of clinical observations. Their pathology and causes were discovered much later. An approach to nosology based purely on clinical observations was taken in general medicine by both Sydenham and Pinel. In the period immediately preceding Kraepelin's, the same approach in psychiatric research, was taken by Kahlbaum and Hecker in regard to functional psychoses.

Kraepelin decided to adopt the same strategy. He was interested in the natural history of mental diseases. In his search for nosological entities, the diseases themselves, Kraepelin did careful cross-sectional observation of symptoms and a longitudinal follow-up study.

He hoped that future research would use more refined laboratory methods and would reveal the pathological changes in the brain associated with nosological entities which were previously differentiated clinically. Growing out of the anatomical emphasis of the Griesinger school, was the firm belief of Kraepelin that mental illnesses were associated with changes in the cerebral cortex (*Hirnrinde*). As he developed his ideas from edition to edition of his *Lehrbuch*, however, his understanding changed. He came to emphasize metabolic brain disorders, rather than structural abnormalities.

Using the method of longitudinal observation on patients who did not show gross pathological changes in the brain, but were obviously psychotic, Kraepelin distinguished two separate disease entities. The first started early in life, soon after puberty. It was characterized by such bizarre symptoms as hallucinations, delusions, and gross disorders of thought. It was also characterized by profound apathy, a loss of interest in the environment and by signs of dementia. A recovery never occurred or was extremely rare. The other disease started later in life. It was characterized by severe affective disorder, manifesting itself as melancholia or mania. This disease had a recurrent course, since its attacks alternated with periods of health. It had often a cyclic course, attacks of depression would alternatre with those of mania. Kraepelin called the former *dementia praecox* (Kraepelin, 1919), and the latter, a *manic-depressive* psychosis (Kraepelin, 1921).

The term dementia praecox had been first used by Morel in 1860 when he described a juvenile mental deterioration which he attributed to an inherited familial degeneration.

For Kraepelin, dementia praecox was a disease with a typical symptomatology and history. This nosological entity encompassed the catatonic syndrome described by Kahlbaum in 1874 and the hebephrenia described by Hecker in 1871. Thus it was rather a broad category which included a variety of symptoms and was characterized by an early onset and a poor prognosis. In 1854, Falret described a manic-depressive psychosis and called it “la folie circulaire.” Kraepelin’s manic-depressive category was a rather broad one. It encompassed a classical circular psychosis, recurrent depression, and recurrent mania as well as various mixed states.

Kraepelin, who was a great systematizer, aimed at discovering the true taxonomy of real diseases as well as their specific etiology, pathology, and natural history. He wanted to know whether certain syndromes represented proper nosological categories — the true diseases, subvarieties of diseases, or artificial categories imposed by the investigators on the observed phenomena. Consequently, he often changed his classification. In his famous textbook of psychiatry, published in nine editions between 1883 and 1927, he modified his classificatory system several times. In the first to the fourth editions, *dementia praecox* figured as one of two, then three major groupings of mental disturbances. Only in the fifth, 1896 edition of this text, did he present dementia praecox as an authentic nosological entity. Here the major groups had become more generally abstract and were grouped into three categories: 1) acquired mental illnesses, 2) constitutionally determined mental illnesses, and 3) metabolic disturbances including *dementia praecox* as a sub group of this one. This marks the beginning of the modern classification system in psychiatry. Yet Kraepelin lists manic-depressive psychosis as a nosological entity only in the sixth edition of 1899. He also described paranoia as a separate entitiy here, different from dementia praecox. But he was uncertain about the nosological status of involutional melancholia and paraphrenia. The latter was a delusional psychosis with hallucinations which occurred in middle aged and elderly patients. In some editions of his textbook, he described them as separate nosological entities, in others, as sub-categories respectively, of manic-depressive psychosis and of dementia praecox.

In the eighth edition (1909-1915) of his textbook, Kraepelin offered the following classification:

1. Mental conditions resulting from brain injuries.
2. Mental conditions resulting from brain diseases.
3. Intoxications: acute and chronic (alcoholism, morphinism, cocoainism).
4. Infections (fever delirium, infection delirium, amentia, mental weakness).
5. Syphilitic mental conditions, aside from paralysis.
6. Dementia paralytica.
7. Senile and presenile psychotic conditions.
8. Thyrogenic condition.
9. Endogenous conditions with evolution toward deterioration.
   a. Dementia praecox; simplex, hebephrenia, catatonia, depressive form, circular form, periodic form, agitated form, schizophasie (*Sprachverwirrheit*).
   b. Paraphrenias.
10. Epilepsy.

11. Manic-depressive psychosis.
12. Psychogenic conditions,
13. Hysteria.
14. Paranoia.
15. Mental disorders resulting from organic conditions.
16. Psychopathic personalities.
17. Oligophrenia (mental deficiency).[1]

Kraepelin speculated about organic disease processes underlying psychoses without obvious post-mortem pathological changes in the brain. For instance, in the fifth edition of his textbook, dementia praecox and dementia paranoides were described as a sub-category of metabolic diseases, called "dementifying processes" (*Verbloedungs-process*). Later he believed that dementia praecox was caused by an endotoxin, probably by an abnormal metabolism of sex hormones occurring at the time of puberty. He placed psychopathic personality, which included many conditions nowadays regarded as psychoneuroses, in the category of constitutional disorders. In his classification of manic-depressive psychoses, Kraepelin vacillated between categorizing them as diseases or as variations of constitutional conditions. Kraepelin's system thus included both the disease model and the constitutional one.

Although Kraepelin died before he was able to complete his ninth edition, some hint of the further changes he made in his thinking, may be seen in his 1921 essay "Die Erscheinungsformen des Irreseins." Here he admitted that clinical research in psychiatry might have reached a dead point. The nineteenth century use of autopsies and the data they yielded, no longer sufficed for studying mental diseases. Nor did the use of the microscope, because its technology appeared still inadequate. He now believed that a real brain disease was not present in all cases of mental disturbances. Accordingly, he divided his diseases into three broad categories: 1) the delirious, paranoid, emotional, hysterial, drives oriented (*triebhaften*) forms, 2) the schizophenic, speech hallucinagenic forms, and 3) encephalopathic, oligophrene, spasmodic forms. The forms of the second and third group could be mixed, group one lacked brain pathology, and disturbances of the third type usually also showed

1 Menninger, 1963, pp. 462-463. See also Kraepelin, 1909-1915, Vol. 2, pp. vii-x; Vol. 3, pp. vii-x; Vol. 4, pp. v-xii.

symptoms of the first type. He did not then believe that one could genuinely distinguish between schizophrenics and manic-depressives.

Throughout his career in Munich, Kraepelin had been interested in disease categories and processes. This more than in individual patients or in their unique personalities or singular life histories. He was interested in the formal aspect of their psychopathology, rather than in the contents of their psychopathological productions. For him it was important that the patient had delusions or was subject to hallucinations. Consequently, Kraepelin was interested in formal disorders of thought rather than in their contents. Briefly, Kraepelin's attention was focused on disease entities rather than on individual patients. He attempted to relate clinical syndromes and nosological entities to pathological changes in the brain and other laboratory findings, including those obtained by the methods of experimental psychology which he learned in Wundt's laboratory. However, the methods of experimental psychology were soon abandoned because they demanded a collaboration of subjects. It was difficult to secure this when the patients were psychotic. Thus the psychological investigations were replaced by bio-chemical and other physiological tests.

The work of the Research Institute for Psychiatry founded in 1917 clarifies Kraepelin's approach. He organized the research institute into four sections so that the main areas of psychiatric research could be covered simultaneously. These were 1) the clinical division under Johannes Lange (1891-1938), 2) the brain pathology division which included Korbinian Brodmann (1868-1918) and Franz Nissl (1860-1919), and later Walther Spielmeyer (1879-1935). Neuro-anatomy was still of primary importance (Spielmeyer, 1920). Then, 3) a serology division under Felix Plaut (1877-1940) and Franz Jahnel (1885-1951), and 4) the genealogical (genetic) division under Ernst Ruedin (1874-1952), a Swiss. After the Second World War the Munich Institute for Psychiatry became one of the Federal Republic of Germany's Max Planck Institutes.

Kraepelin's approach toward mental illness went beyond pure theorizing. He was a capable hospital administrator who believed that mental hospitals should be modeled on the scheme of general ones. Mental patients were to be treated exactly the same way as patients suffering from physical illness. Like other patients, they were to be kept in bed. In his essay, *One Hundred Years of Psychiatry*, written in 1917 on the occasion of the opening of the Munich Psychiatric Research Institute, he made it clear that:

> An important step toward proper treatment was the practice of keeping patients under constant surveillance . . .and confining newly admitted patients to their beds. . .These experiences clearly proved to the doctors that the sick brain, like every other unhealthy organ, needs rest above all else. Patients became calmer and less obstructive; the atmosphere of the insane asylum became more like that of a regular hospital. (Kraepelin, 1962, p.142).

Kraepelin was intent on casting mental patients in the "sick role." The social role of a lunatic was to be changed into that of a patient suffering from a disease of the brain. Yet Kraepelin did not ignore the role of environmental factors in the causation of mental illness. He believed that consumption of alcohol was a contributing factor in the etiology of this condition. Consequently he was a total abstainer and a fervent supporter of the temperance movement. He served only a cold, non-alcoholic punch at his once a year party for his assistants on New Year's Eve. In addition, Kraepelin believed that the penal system should aim at the rehabilitation of prisoners rather than at their punishment.

His life-long interest in showing the evil effects of alcoholism and of smoking tobacco, produced some intersting statistics which he relates in the eighth edition of his *Lehrbuch*. Of the 1,907 mentally ill in the Munich Clinic in 1907, 22.4% suffered from alcohol abuse, while another 22.1% showed an influence of alcohol abuse. Of epileptic patients, 43.3% drank. Also 42.9% of traumatic neurotics, 38% of arterio-sclerotics, and 35% of paralytics. Also some 33.8% of psychopaths drank, 28.1% of dementia praecox patients, 22.1% of senile dementia patients, 21.7% of hysterics, and 12.8% of manic depressives. Women drank much less in the proportion of 1 to 6.8 males (Kraepelin,I,1909, p.87).

On the whole, Kraepelin emphasized the disease model of mental disturbance, and this was also in keeping with the prevailing *Zeitgeist*. The medical profession was at that time much impressed by the fact that specific bacteria were etiological agents responsible for many diseases. In particular, the discovery that general paralysis of the insane was a sequel of syphilitic infection had a dramatic impact on medical thinking. Moreover, the discovery of the pathogenic organisms often led to the finding of a cure as exemplified by the Salvarsan treatment of syphilis, introduced by Paul Ehrlich (1854-1915) in 1910. Another example was the malarial fever treatment of general paralysis of the insane introduced about the same time by Julius von Wagner Ritter von Jauregg (1857-1940), the professor of psychiatry at the University of Vienna. Wagner-Jauregg was to become the only psychiatrist ever to receive the Nobel Prize in 1927 because of this discovery.

Wagner-Jauregg was the most important member of the so-called Vienna school of neuropsychiatry. An organic psychiatrist and neurologist, he not only discovered the malaria treatment for G.P.I., but was also able to persuade international health authorities to adopt a preventive measure against epidemic goiter which was associated with cretinism. Under the auspices of the League of Nations, an international convention was agreed upon, which made it obligatory for manufacturers to add small quantities of iodine to table salt. The consequence of this preventive measure was an almost total elimination of endemic goiter and cretinism. His discovery of the cause and the treatment of G.P.I. became the model to be emulated in psychiatric research.

In the first decades of the twentieth century, psycho-therapists were preoccupied with hysteria while psychiatrists practising in mental hospitals came to focus their attention on “dementia praecox,” or as it was soon to be renamed by Eugene Bleuler (1857-1939) “schizophrenia.” dementia praecox posed a challenge to both clinicians and psychiatric researchers. The brain’s pathological changes in cases of organic pychoses could be perceived under the microscope. The pathology of these conditions was, therefore, to some extent understood, although many were incurable. The patients with organic psychoses who could not be cured tended to die quickly. On the other hand, patients suffering from dementia praecox tended to live a normal span of life, and thus they filled up the mental hospitals. Dementia praecox was a mystery, since it combined a profound mental derangement and social alienation with no obvious pathology of the brain. A lot of ingenuity was invested by both researchers and clinicians into properly delineating the scope and the boundaries of this condition. Also efforts were made to determine its etiology and cure. First there was the problem of nosology. The following questions were asked. Was dementia praecox a disease entity? Was it a sub-variety of a broader etiological category? Or perhaps, was it a group of diseases which included several nosological entities ?

Eugene Bleuler and the Concept of Schizophrenia

Eugene Bleuler (1857-1939) a Swiss contemporary of Kraepelin, who was the director of Burghoelzli as well as professor of psychiatry at

Zuerich University, challenged the conceptual validity of "dementia praecox" as a category. According to Bleuler, the onset of dementia praecox could take place later in life than during adolescence. Moreover, the prognosis in dementia praecox was not as hopeless as was maintained by Kraepelin. Fully one third of cases recovered spontaneously within one year. One third recovered, but then relapsed again. Only one third ran a downhill course, never left the hospital and became chronic. Further, according to Bleuler, such patients did show very profound thought disorder, yet did not manifest any signs of intellectual impairment like those with organic dementia.

Bleuler changed the name of the disease from dementia praecox to schizophrenia. In his monumental work, *Dementia Praecox or the Group of Schizophrenias* (1911), he offered a new interpretation of this condition. Instead of using the history and the prognosis as a basis for distinguishing the nosological entity of schizophrenia, Bleuler focused his attention on the clinical symptoms. He subdivided symptoms into several categories. The first division of symptoms proposed by Bleuler was into *fundamental*, and *accessory*. The *fundamental* symptoms were: 1) disorder of associations ("looseness of associations"), 2) disorder of affect and 3) ambivalence. They were present in all cases of schizophrenia and distinguished this condition from other mental diseases. The *accessory* symptoms: 1) hallucinations, 2) delusions, and 3) psychomotor disorders, could be present or absent.

By basing the concept of schizophrenia on the fundamental symptoms, Bleuler went back to the tradition on "nosological essentialism" as espoused earlier by Thomas Sydenham and Philippe Pinel. According to the essentialist view a certain combination of symptoms constituted the "essence" of a disease. However, Bleuler also offered an explanation of the etiology of schizophrenia. He believed its etiology was organic and that some symptoms were organically determined while others resulted from psychological reaction to the impairment of the brain function produced by an organic pathological process. The latter could be reversible. These etiological considerations led Bleuler to the second division of symptoms into *primary* and *secondary*. The primary symptoms which included disorder of associations (looseness of associations), affective changes, stereotypy, and vasomotor disorders were caused by an organic disease process in the brain. The secondary symptoms which included hallucinations, delusions, and catatonic disorders of motility were due to the patient's psychological reaction to the organic disease process. They were determined by the reaction of the patient's personality and by the psychodynamic factors. An anaology could be drawn between the psycho-pathological productions of patients and the dream contents of normal individuals. The fact that the dreams were illogical, out of touch with reality, and soon forgotten, could be explained by a lowered level of brain functioning. The brain cut off from the input of external stimulation, was "idling". However, the content of dreams, particular themes, could be explained by the previous individual experiences of the dreamer. These could be recent, or they might have taken place in childhood. Moreover, the contents could be determined also by desires, needs, conflicts, and motives of the subjects.

Bleuler took the ideas of psychological determinism and of the unconscious from Freud's psycho-analytical theory with which he became acquainted through Carl Gustav Jung. (Jung had been Bleuler's first assistant at Burghoelzli.) A schizophrenic patient was autistic, out of touch with reality, living in his own private world. He was dreaming while awake. His thinking was determined by primitive emotional complexes, often split from the rest of the personality and submerged in the unconscious, while the thinking of normal individuals was reality determined. The idea of fragmentation of mental life in schizophrenic patients into primitive emotional complexes, was reflected in Bleuler's term, *schizophrenia*, or split mind.

This interpretation of psycho-pathology of dementia praecox by Bleuler was anticipated by two Austrian psychiatrists associated with the University of Vienna. The first was Erwin Stransky (1877-1962), who interpreted the symptoms of dementia praecox as "intrapsychic ataxia." According to Stransky, the essential characteristic of this disease was a dissociation of *thymopsyche* (affective processes) from *noopsyche* (cognitive processes). The second was Josef Berze (1866-1958), chief physician at the Am Steinhof Hospital in Vienna. He suggested that the psycho-pathology of dementia praecox could be conceived as being due to the "hypotonia of consciousness," a fundamental disorder. The "hypotonia of consciousness" produced secondary compensatory reactions by the patient's personality. These were responsible for bizarre symptoms (Berze, 1911;Hoff & Arnold, 1961). He had a wider definition of dementia praecox than the Kraepelin school. In 1904 he included under this heading *paranoia completa* as well as fantastic madness (*Verruecktheit*). Berze believed that the basic disturbance of apperception progressed to deterioration rapidly, rather than slowly. In 1911 he associated reduced tonus of consciousness with dementia praecox and apathy, although there were explosive outbreaks when inhibitions were reduced. The psychology of schizophrenia was discussed further in greater detail by Berze and Gruehle (1929).

Bleuler as well as Berze (who did not always agree with him) had a broader conception of schizophrenia than the Kraepelin school of Munich. Bleuler did not commit himself to the theory that schizophrenia was a unitary disease. It could be a group of diseases displaying similar symptomatology. Nevertheless, Bleuler's category of "schizophrenia," which he sub-divided into "simple," "catatonic," "hebephrenic," and "paranoid," was considerably broader than Kraepelin's original category of dementia praecox.

The Neurological Psychiatry of Karl Kleist. While Bleuler widened the scope of the concept of dementia praecox, other investigators endeavoured to subdivide it into narrower nosological entities. This approach was taken most prominently by Karl Kleist (1879-1960) (1960). Kleist represented the nineteenth century tradition of the neurological school of psychiatry and was a follower of such men as Westphal, Meynert, Wernicke, and Flechsig. In Germany, the chairs of psychiatry were not separated from neurology and neuro-anatomy as in other countries. After obtaining his M.D. at Munich, he went to Halle to specialize in neurology and psychiatry under Theodor Ziehen. Later he also studied with Carl Wernicke. The neurological approach of the latter had a life-long influence on Kleist's thinking. After Halle, he spent some time in Munich working under Kraepelin and Alzheimer. Eventually he was appointed in 1920 to the professorship of psychiatry at Frankfurt. At that university, the neurological tradition had been founded by Ludwig Edinger (1855-1918), who had specialized in comparative brain anatomy and had in 1882 found Charcot's demonstrations too theatrical.

Karl Kleist tried to reconcile the neurological approach of Wernicke with the clinical-nosological approach of Kraepelin. The first emphasized the neurological localization of pathological processes, the other the etiology, history, and prognosis of various clinical conditions. Kleist believed that noslogical categories should reflect specific "allopsychic," "somatopsychic" and "autopsychic" disorders which had precise localizations. Thus he wanted to delineate psychiatric syndromes more precisely than did the Kraeplinean system. Kleist viewed psychiatric symptoms as defects similar to those occurring in aphasia and agnosia. They interefered with active, productive and plan-oriented thinking. Moreover, according to him, these defects in psychological functioning could be precisely localized. He tended to conceive neuropathology of the endogeneous psychoses in terms of heredo-degenerative processes, similar to those occurring in many neurological diseases.

Kleist's study of schizophrenia led him to conclude that there were twenty-five different varieties of this disease. These were sub-divided into typical and atypical kinds (Fish, 1962). The atypical schizophrenias had a strong familial association, the peculiarity of a particular family stock. Kleist has considered the twenty-five varieties of schizophrenia heredo-degenerative diseases. Each was associated with a putative degenerative lesion at the specific site of the brain. They were diseases of the nervous system, like Friedrich's ataxia, or Creutzfeldt-Jacob's disease. Since such putative lesions, associated with different varieties of schizophrenia could not be confirmed by other investigators, Kleist's theory was called by his critics, Kleist's "mythology of the brain." It was said of him that "Er hat das Gehirn beseelt." (He infused the brain with a soul).

This approach to the nosology of schizophrenia had been continued by Karl Leonhard (b.1904) (1948) a student and follower of Kleist. Leonhard continued the tradition of the neurological school of psychiatry but was less concerned with specific and localized lesions of the brain. Instead he tried to link them with specific pathogenic genes. He distinguished "systematic" and "non-systematic" schizophrenias, corresponding to Kleist's "typical" and "atypical" varieties of schizophrenia. Altogether he believed that there were nineteen different varieties of this disease: sixteen were systematic and three were non-systematic. Each represented a different disease (Fish, 1962). The taxonomies of Kleist and Leonhard were reminiscent of the taxonomies of the eighteenth century nosographers such as Linnaeus, Boissier de Sauvage and Pinel. They read like botanical or zoological taxonomies.

Manic-Depressive Psychosis. By the early twentieth century, the problem of taxonomy and of the discovery of the "true" nosological entities became a focal point not only in the field of schizophrenia, but also in that of manic-depressive psychosis. The latter condition occurred often in atypical forms, such as attacks of depression without mania, or attacks of mania not followed by depression. Also there was the question of how to classify involutional melancholia. Kraepelin was not certain whether it was a distinct nosological entity, or only an atypical variant of manic-depressive psychosis. Kurt Schneider (1920) followed the distinction between exogenous and endogenous psychosis made decades earlier by Moebius. He differentiated between reactive (exogenous) and endogenous depression. The first was a reaction to psychological or physiological stress. The second occurred spontaneously and could not be attributed to any precipitating factors. For Schneider (1958,1959) this distinction had an application wider than to the classification of depression. He divided all psychiatric conditions into endogenous psychoses (disease processes), abnormal reactions and psychopathic personalities. In endogenous psychosis there was a disease process going on, presumably in the brain. The disease process was responsible for psychopathological symptoms that were incomprehensible and could not be explained by the patient's personality, past history, or present circumstances. Abnormal reactions were reactions to environmental events which could be understood. However, their intensity was abnormally high and their duration abnormally long. Psychopathic personalities were described as constitutionally determined, extreme deviations of otherwise normal character traits. Thus, according to Schneider, endogenous depression was due to a disease process and reactive depression was an abnormal reaction to a life crisis. Dysthymia was a character trait predisposing to a life long mood of sadness.

More recently Leonhard (1957) distinguished between "bipolar" and "unipolar" depression, which were two different nosological entities. The first occurred in the setting of manic-depressive psychosis. The second manifested itself as recurrent attacks of depression which did not alternate with attacks of mania. Some more detailed classifications were also proposed (Lehmann, 1977; Dupue & Monroe, 1978). It is obvious that there was no agreement on the breadth of various disease categories as well as on their number.

Search for the Organic Causes of Mental Disease

The discovery of etiology and cure of various mental disorders was of a greater practical importance than their nosology. As has been mentioned earlier, the discoveries in the field of bacteriology and serology made the disease model very attractive and plausible. Bacteria were the causal agents, they caused damage to the organism and also provoked defensive reactions which sometimes could go astray, producing additional damage. The final discovery of the etiology of general paralysis of the insane, which previously was a mystery and puzzled the medical profession for more than one hundred years, had a particularly dramatic impact. The discovery that a dormant syphilitic infection was the "cause" of general paralysis of the insane and its treatment by malaria infection, introduced soon afterwards by Julius Wagner-Jauregg, provided a model to be imitated and emulated by researchers looking for the etiology and cure of schizophrenia and of manic-depressive psychosis.

If such a severe mental illness as G.P.I. could be the sequel of an infection which occurred several years earlier, so could schizophrenia represent such a sequel. The lapse of time between the original infection and its psychiatric manifestations would make it difficult to perceive the connection. But, once the connection was found, the etiology and more importantly, the cure, could be discovered. This idea produced a more optimistic outlook on the prognosis and treatment of mental diseases than prevailed in the second half of the nineteenth century.

The breakthrough in the research into the etiology of general paralysis of the insane and the discovery of its therapy came too late to affect Kraepelin's thinking. He believed that mental diseases were caused by metabolic errors which produced endotoxins. As far as therapy was concerned, Kraepelin took a nihilistic position and used only symptomatic treatment, hoping that perhaps future progress in bio-chemistry and physiology would lead to more specific methods of treatment. However, after the first World War, bacteriological speculations became popular with regard to the etiology of schizophrenia and manic-depressive psychosis. All sorts of bacteria were suspected as pathogens. Schizophrenia was linked to syphilis (Babonoix, 1921; Marie & Topokoff, 1929), to tuberculosis (Baruk, Bidermann, Albane, 1932; Lowenstein, 1944), to influenza and other acute infections (Menninger, 1926). A specific strain of streptococi was suspected to be the pathogenic agent of schizophrenia (Rosenow, 1955). A focal infection theory of schizophrenia proposed by H. Cotton (Kraepelin's American student) (1921, 1923), became very popular in the twenties. Bacteria encapsulated in the foci of infection produced toxins which affected the brain. This theory led to such heroic therapeutic measures as total extractions of teeth, removal of the uteri, disfiguring operations on sinuses and resections of portions of the bowel. V.M. Buscaino (1929) maintained that schizophrenia was caused by a toxin containing indol, which was produced by certain coli bacterias of the intestinal flora and absorbed by the body. The toxin affected the brain. These early bacteriological speculations proved to be blind alleys which did not lead to a breakthrough.

An alternative to the quest for the exogenous bacteriological factors of the causes of schizophrenia, was the search for possible endogenous physiological and bio-chemical factors. Such physiological and biochemical abnormalities could be the causes of mental symptoms. These studies were a continuation of Kraepelin's search for the possible metabolic disorders responsible for dementia praecox. Only the most important contributions can be mentioned here.

In the 1930s a group of biological psychiatrists and physiologists led by R.S. Hoskins (1946) at the Worcester Hospital in Massachuesetts, conducted an extensive study of the physiological functions of schizophrenic patients in the condition of rest and under stress. Such physiological measures as pulse rate, blood pressure, respiration rate at rest and during exercise were recorded. The oral and anal body temperature under the conditions of cold and heat were also measured. The intensity of thc occular nystagmus in response to vestibular stimulation was investigated, as well as physiologocal response to various pharmacological agents such as adrenaline, insulin and thyroid. Few differences between schizophrenics and controls were found in physiological functions in the condition of rest. However, schizphrenics showed lower efficiency of many physiological homeostatic mechanisms. Their blood circulation adapted poorly to physical effort and their vestibular reaction to rotation was weaker. Their compensation for heat loss was less efficient than that of controls. Their reaction to the pharmacological agents was less than in controls. Schizophrenics displayed a deficient adaptation of their organismic internal milieu to changing environmental conditions. Hoskins concluded that schizophrenics showed numerous defects of adaptive efficiency and that their psychological withdrawal was accompanied by a physiological one.

At the same time that the Worcester group in the United States conducted its studies into the physiological functioning of schizophrenic patients, a group of researchers at the Diekemark Hospital in Oslo, Norway, led by R. Gjessing (1938, 1947) carried out pioneering research into biochemical abnormalities in schizophrenic patients. They anticipated the present day flood of biochemical research findings and theories.

Gjessing focused on a relatively rare condition of periodic catatonia which accounted only for two to three percent of all cases of schizophrenia. In this condition short periods of excitement and confusion alternated with longer periods of apathy and withdrawal. Following Kraepelin's longitudinal method, Gjessing carefully followed psychological and biochemical changes in a small group of periodic catatonics over a period of several years. He found that periodic changes in the clinical conditions of the patients were accompanied by phasic variations in the total nitrogen balance which was associated with their mental state. Catatonic stupor as well as excitement were associated with nitrogen retention, while the periods of relative freedom from symptoms were associated with increased excretion of nitrogen. Gjessing suggested that the changes in the nitrogen balance may be indicative of the presence of a toxic substance produced by a disorder of protein metabolism. The fact that the changes in the nitrogen balance tended to precede the onset of psychological symptoms and not come as an after effect, led Gjessing to believe that the nitrogen balance caused the symptoms. Gjessing found that the nitrogen balance in periodic catatonics could be affected by the administration of the thyroid hormone. Indeed, appropriately timed administration of this drug could prevent the periodic attacks of catatonia.

The importance of Gjessing's work was in its meticulousness, thoroughness, and the degree of control. It set an example for future researches into the metabolism of schizophrenic patients. However, his work was based on a small sample of schizophrenic patients and was not followed up, or replicated.

Physical and Drug Treatment of Mental Diseases

The physical methods of treatment, which were introduced in the thirties and the forties, fared somewhat better. They were based on physiological speculations, but more importantly they appeared to produce cures. Moreover, they fitted the organic disease model very well. If mental illness was an organic disease of the brain, then a direct, very often dramatic therapeutic interference with the functioning of that organ seemed to be the most straight forward approach to therapy. Some of the physical methods had a blunderbuss character aimed at giving a "shock" to the brain and to the whole organism. It was believed that a "shock" would stop the faulty pattern of functioning and would allow the normal pattern to re-establish itself. It was like giving a bang to a radio set to remove an interference and to restore the proper reception. The physical methods of treatment undoubtedly introduced more optimistic attitudes towards treatment. These replaced the therapeutic nihilism characteristic of mental hospitals in the second half of the nineteenth century. However, they also represented a return to the drastic methods of treatment used at the end of the eighteenth century by such psychiatrists as Benjamin Rush in the United States, and advocated by Johann Christian Reil in Germany. The difference was that the procedures were couched in physiological terms, rather than psychological ones. Instead of "shocking" the patient as a person out of his madness, a shock was applied to his brain in order to rectify its abnormal functioning.

Insulin treatment was introduced by Manfred Sakel (1900-1957), a Berlin psychiatrist. In 1922, Frederick Banting, C.H. Best and J.R. Mcleod who were working in Toronto, Canada, isolated insulin, thus providing a cure for *diabetes mellitus*, previously a dreaded and incurable disease. It was the period in which the science of endocrinology came of age and experimentation with hormones was in vogue. Insulin was used not only in treatment of diabetes, but was also tried in other conditions. It was found that insulin improved appetitie in emaciated patients and produced weight gain. It was also discovered that it had a calming effect. Sakel used insulin in the treatment of withdrawal symptoms in morphia addicts. He speculated that the calming effect of insulin was due to its counter-action of an overactivity of the adrenal and thyroid glands, and also of the overactivity of the sympathetic nervous system. In 1933 he reported beneficial effects of insulin treatment in acute schizophrenias. Sakel increased its doses to produce comas. He believed that by putting temporarily higher brain centres out of action and by producing a regression to lower levels of brain activity, its normal function would be subsequently restored. Insulin shock became the standard method of treatment for acute paranoid schizophrenics, although it was associated with dangerous complications. It was abandoned only in the fifties when it was found in controlled studies that sleep produced by barbiturates produced exactly the same results as insulin coma with a lesser risk. At that time, also, phenothiazine drug therapy was introduced into mental hospitals.

Schizophrenia was also treated by inducing epileptic seizures. This form of treatment was originated by Ladislaus Joseph von Meduna (1896-1964), a Hungarian psychiatrist. However, there were some earlier, isolated reports of application of this treatment in mental patients (Alexander & Selesnick, 1966). Basing himself on his clinical observations and some statistics, Meduna observed that schizophrenic patients did not suffer from epilepsy and epileptic patients from schizophrenia. This inference could be faulted by the fact that in those days, any epileptic patient who displayed psychotic symptoms was diagnozed as suffering from the epileptic psychosis. Meduna also noticed at the postmortem microscopic examinations of the brain, that there was a thickening of the glial tissue in epileptic patients and an atrophy of it, in schizophrenics. He came to the conclusion that there was a biological antagonism between epilepsy and schizophrenia and suggested that schizophrenic patients may benefit from artificially produced epileptic seizures. He produced these seizures by injecting the patients with a convulsant drug, Metrazol (Cardiazol). It was soon noticed that only those schizophrenics who were concomitantly depressed benefitted from the treatment. Soon afterwards it became clear that Metrazol shock treatment was more useful in severe depression and manic-depressive psychosis than in schizophrenia. The Metrazol shock treatment had drawbacks. There was rather a long time gap before the injection of the drug and the seizure. This time gap was filled with a very unpleasant "aura," a feeling of impeding death. The convulsions were rather strong, causing fractures and possibly also minimal brain damage.

Ugo Cerletti (1877-1963), a distinguished Italian psychiatrist and the professor at the University of Rome, in collaboration with Lucio Bini (1908-1964), found that in animals, convulsions produced by electric currents caused much less damage (practically no damage) than those produced by convulsant drugs. These workers utilized the procedure used in the abbatoir of Rome. In this procedure pigs were stunned with electricity before being slaughtered. Cerletti and Bini modified the method used for stunning pigs and developed from it the electric convulsive shock method applied to human beings. It was first given to a schizophrenic patient in 1938. It soon becomes obvious, however, that only schizophrenic patients who were simultaneously depressed, responded to the electric shock treatment. Consequently, it was tried with remarkable success on severely depressed patients. The electro convulsive therapy (ECT) in its standard or modified form became the treatment of choice for psychotic depression for many years. Only in recent years has it been replaced gradually by anti-depressant drugs, although it is still used occasionally.

Radical surgical treatment of a disease has had a tremendous appeal both to the medical profession and to the lay public. It is like cutting the Gordian knot. Egas Moniz (1874-1955), Nobel Prize winner, and a professor of neurology at the University of Lisbon in Portugal, developed a method of psycho-surgical treatment with a neurosurgeon, Almeida Lima. Moniz believed that psychosis may be caused by reverberating circuits in the brain. Neuronal impulses underlying morbid thoughts could be repeatedly circulating in the brain. He thought that the neuronal fibres projecting from the thalamus to the frontal lobe and and back again from that lobe to the thalamus could constitute such a reverberating circuit. He proposed an operation of prefrontal lobotomy in which the cortico-thalamic and thalamo-cortical pathways would be cut. The first pre-frontal lobotomy was performed on psychotic patients resistant to other methods of treatment. Its modification, the trans-orbital lobotomy which was a relatively simple operation, allowed this method to be used on a mass scale in state hospitals. The topectomy in which certain parts of thc brain are exposed and removed under visual control, constituted a more controlled approach to psycho-surgery. Lobotomy produced an irreversible brain damage and was associated with undesirable side effects and its results were uncertain. Consequently, under the pressure of public opinion, it has been largely abandoned.

The anti-psychotic drug therapy which was introduced in the 1950s has truly revolutionaized treatment in psychiatry and given a boost to the disease model. Sedatives such as bromides were introduced in the first half of the nineteenth century; opium had been in use longer. During the 1920s, these were replaced by barbiturates. These drugs could be used only as symptomatic remedies.

By the 1950s a new category of drugs referred to as tranquilizers was introduced. The first to be marketed was Reserpine, an alkaloid obtained from an Indian plant. *Rauwolfia serpentina* (Snakeroot). This plant had been used in Indian medicine since ancient times, for the treatment of insanity. Reserpine was introduced to Western medicine during the 1940s. It was found to be an anti-hypertensive drug which had tranquilizing (ataraxic) properties. Reserpine was tried on schizophrenics with success. It had a beneficial effect. The new drug transquilized the patients and alleviated their psychotic symptoms without making them sleepy. However, Reserpine had many undesirable side effects. In some patients it produced clinical depression. For this reason, its use has been largely discontinued.

In 1952, two French psychiatrists, Jean Delay and Pierre Deniker reported beneficial results in schizophrenic patients produced by another tranquilizing drug, chloropromazine, which was a member of the phenothiazine group of compounds. Its side effects proved to be rather harmless. Chlorpromazine and other members of the phenathiazine group, as well as more recently introduced butyrophenon drugs, were found to affect specifically psychotic symptoms such as hallucinations, delusions and thought disorder. These anti-psychotic drugs completely changed the prognosis of schizophrenia and made it possible to discharge many chronic patients from hospitals.

Soon afterwards, new anti-depressant drugs were introduced. The first, iproniazid, a menoamino-oxydase inhibitor was found to have anti-depressant properties by serendipity. Iproniazid was originally used as an anti-tuberculosis drug. It was noticed that the patients given this drug became euphoric. Iproniazid was then tried by Jean Delay on depressed patients and was found to elevate their mood. Other monoaminoxydaze inhibitors were found to have a similar effect. Some drugs belonging to the tricyclic group of compounds such as imipranine, were found to be even more effective in the treatment of depression.

The Genetics of Mental Diseases

Another approach to the discovery of the etiology of mental illness, and to its prevention, was through the study of heredity. Speculations about the inheritance of mental illnesses have been abundant throughout the entire history of psychiatry. Many pre-scientific notions such as "taint of insanity," "heredo-degeneration," and "neuropathic diathesis" were offered to explain the high incidence of mental illness in some families. Such early studies as Francis Galton's *Hereditary Genius* (1869) pointed to the importance of heredity for all psychological characteristics. Only the rise of modern genetics placed studies of the inheritance of mental illness on a scientific footing.

The science of genetics was originated by Gregor Johann Mendel (1822-1884), a prior of the Augustinian monastery of Brno. Mendel studied the inheritance of the morphological characteristics of pea plants. He discovered certain lawful regularities in the transfer of these characteristics from one generation to another. His work, published in 1865, in an obscure journal, was largely disregarded and soon forgotten. At the turn of the century, three botanists discovered Mendel's work and republished it. They were Hugo de Vries (1848-1935), Karl Erich Correns (1864-1933), and Erich Tschermak van Seysenegg. The foundations of the new science of genetics were further developed by two zoologists, William Bateson (1861-1926) and Thomas Hunt Morgan (1866-1945). It was Bateson who coined the term "genetics."

The principles of the new science of heredity made it possible to introduce scientific rigor and precision to the study of inheritance of mental illness. The more rigorous studies were aimed at finding out whether the application of Mendelian laws could replace poorly conceived and largely inconclusive studies based on mass statistics. It was hoped that various nosological entities could be linked to specific genes or combination of genes. Ernst Ruedin (1874-1952) of the Munich Research Institute of Psychiatry, was a pioneer of the new approach. He founded the German school of genetic psychiatry. In contrast to earlier studies which collected extensive pedigrees of individual families, Ruedin tried to find the frequency of dementia praecox among different classes of the relatives of patients (Ruedin, 1916). On the whole, the results were disappointing. The pattern of inheritance of mental illnesses did not follow Mendel's laws. Yet some of the findings were suggestive of the possibility of the recessive or dominant type of inheritance.

Genetic studies were carried further by Ruedin's students H.Luxemburger (1894-1976), Franz J. Kallmann (1897-1965), and Bruno Schulz (1890-1958). These men introduced the a method of studying identical and fraternal twins for the concordance of pathology. Kallmann emigrated to the United States where he continued his work on twins. Johannes Lange in Germany and Aaron J. Rosanoff (1878-1943) were two other pioneers in the field of these studies. Their work indicated that a hereditary factor seemed to be involved in the incidence of schizophrenia in identical twins who were reared apart.

In the two decades after the second World War, then, the differentiation of the constitutional and disease factors in mental illnesses had become clearer. Those forms of mental illness not previously categorized as diseases, especially some forms of depression, responded to new drug therapy. The group of phenothiazine and butyrophenones antipsychotic compounds revolutionized the treatment of schizophrenic patients. In some cases a complete cure was effected and in many cases the patients were relieved of their symptoms. As a result, a great majority of such patients could be discharged from mental hospitals. Whether these illnesses were really altogether curable remained uncertain however.

10

The Constitutional Psychiatry of Ernst Kretschmer

Science of Endocrinology: The Modern Version of Humoural Medicine

It was stated earlier that the constitutional model was eclipsed in general medicine by the disease model. With the passing of Galen's system in the seventeenth century, the attention of the medical profession became focused on disease entities rather than on individual patients. The disease model received an additional boost from the discovery and the proof, in the middle of the nineteenth century, that many diseases were caused by bacteria. Bacteriology and serology were established as important medical sciences. However, although the pendulum swung in medical thinking towards the disease model, the constitutional model had never disappeared completely from the scene. The discovery of the ductless glands, and the subsequent development of the new science of endocrinology early in the twentieth century, caused the pendulum to swing in the opposite direction and revived interest in the constitutional model.

The progress of enocrinology was slower than that of bacteriology. Overshadowed by the spectacular discoveries of the latter, endocrinology had to wait for the development of sophisticated biochemical techniques before the new science was firmly established.

The science of endocrinology was adumbrated in the eighteenth century by Theophile de Bordeu (1722-1776), of the Montpellier University, a court physician to Louis XV. He believed that the organs of the body secreted substances into the blood stream which influenced the functions of the whole organism. Endocrine research began in 1849 when A. Berthold showed that an implantation of testicular tissue prevented the effects of castration in roosters. In 1855 Claude Bernard was able to state in a public lecture, that the body's internal secretions helped to maintain a constant *milieu interieur* (internal environment).

Space does not permit us to mention all the pioneers of endocrinology. We can only highlight the more important contributors to the discipline. In 1855 Thomas Addison (1783-1860) described the clinical syndrome cause by adrenal insufficiency which now bears his name. In 1896, Sir William Osler (1849-1919) used adrenal extract in the treatment of Addison's disease. Moritz Schiff (1823-1896) in 1859 produced myxedema in dogs by extirpating the thyroid gland and in 1884 successfully cured it by introducing thyroid tissue into the abdominal cavity. A few years later, in 1891, R. Murray successfully treated myxedema in human beings. Paul Moebius in 1886 suggested that another thyroid disorder, Grave's disease, described by Robert Graves (1796-1853) in 1838, was caused by a hyperfunction of the thyroid gland.

Studies of pancreas and pituitary functions also led to the isolation of other diseases. Joseph von Mering and Oscar Minkowski showed in 1889 that an extirpation of the pancreas produced diabetes in dogs. In 1886 Pierre Marie (1853-1940) described acromegly. In 1900 C. Benda associated this condition with eosinophil adenoma of the pituitary. Further definitive work on this gland was carried out by Harvey Cushing (1869-1939). Finally, in 1904, William Bayliss (1860-1924) and Ernest Starling (1866-1927) introduced the term "hormone" and the science of endocrinology was born. However, the isolation of hormones, the understanding of their complex interactions and of their delicate balance, had to wait for the development of more sophisticated biochemical and physiological methods in the twentieth century (Rothschuh, 1973).

Attempts have been made since ancient times, to establish a typology of human constitutional types. They became part of the constitutional medical model and of general folklore. Hippocrates described the *habitus appoplecticus* and the *habitus phtisicus* associated respectively with cerebral vascular accidents and with consumption. The Arab followers of Hippocrates and Galen described the choleric, melancholic, sanguinic and phlegmatic temperaments. In Shakespeare's plays the jolly, good natured Falstaff was rotund and fat, while the aloof, secretive, scheming Cassius was lean and gaunt. Paracelsus believed that some diseases arose from a natural constitution or "firmament." The idea was described among his five basic causes of all illnesses in his *Paramirum* (1926), although this idea was still attached to a planetary system of the organs where the brain resembled the moon and the heart the sun of the firmament (Paracelsus,I,p.36). The forerunners of Kretschmer emerged more clearly by the end of the eighteenth century and up to the 1870s. L. Rostan in 1828 distinguished four basic somatic types: digestive, respiratory, muscular, and cerebral. Others like C.G. Carus (1851) and A. de Giovanni (1877/1910) introduced the idea of separating athletic and non-athletic types. F.B. Beneke also associated individual characteristics of the human mind with bodily constitution. Evidently the influence of phrenology was still making itself felt. This was also true of J. Charcot, usually known for his work with hysterics and hypnosis, who collected thousands of photographs of his patients in the 28 volumes of Iconographics to record their bodily and facial characteristics.

Psychiatry, criminology, and physical anthropology also cooperated in constitutional studies. Cesare Lombroso (1836-1909) (1876) linked physical constitution and facial characteristics with criminality. Lombroso's followers were members of the Padua school of medical and physical anthropology. They included Achille De Giovanni (1837-1916), Giacinte Viola (1878-1943), and Sante Naccarati. Their work elaborated further on the relationship of constitution to pathology. De Giovanni (1910) suggested a triparte division of types into 1) phtisic, 2) athletic-thoratic, and 3) pletheoric-abdominal. G. Viola had a somewhat different threefold division: 1) microsplanic, 2) normosplanic, and 3) macrosplanic. However, the notion of constitution did not play an important role in medical thinking before the advances in the science of endocrinology made it possible to do so. The insight had developed, that physiological mechanisms might be responsible for variations in human physique and temperament.

These developments seemed to bring back the old humoral medicine in a new scientific garb. Hormones became the modern version of the humors of the ancient Hippocratic-Galenian medical theories. Attempts were made to reinterpret physical and mental diseases in constitutional terms. Thus, G. Draper (1924; Draper *et al*, 1944), inspired by the work of the Padua school of physical anthropology, and also influenced by the discoveries in endocrinology, applied the anthropometric and endocrinological approaches to clinical medicine. He was concerned with the relation of the human constitution to various somatic diseases. Draper tried to establish various indices of the physique and of the physiological functions, and to relate them to such clinical conditions as the disorders of gall bladder, pernicious anemia, asthma and tuberculosis. These conditions were found by him to be associated with certain anatomical, physiological and psychological traits. It is, of course, an exaggeration to state that in the twentieth century, the disease model was replaced by the constitutional one. However, a claim can be made that the balance between the two models which was lost in the nineteenth century, has been restored. The medical profession has increasingly been focusing both on the nosological disease entities and on the individual patients as unique organisms with singular inherited constitutions and life histories. The modern development of genetics as a special science has also inspired research into the genotypic origins of disease.

Ernst Kretschmer

In psychiatry, the constitutional model is represented by the Kretschmerian school. Ernst Kretschmer (1888-1964) studied medicine at Tuebingen University. When he entered the university he was undecided as to whether to study theology or medicine, eventually choosing the latter. However, because of his interest in theology, he had pursued humanistic studies which included philosophy, literature and history before he committed himself to the study of medicine. Kretschmer received his M.D. in 1913 and began his psychiatric training under Robert Gaupp (1870-1953) at Tuebingen University Neurological Clinic. Gaupp had been Kraepelin's chief physician (*Oberarzt*) in Munich before he became professor of psychiatry at Tuebingen. However, he tended to reject the latter's nosological approach in favour of one which emphasized the uniqueness of a human personality development which was shaped by hereditary factors and life events. He became famous for his biographical study of the paranoid school headmaster Wagner who committed several murders. Gaupp's conception of paranoia as a personality development rather than as a disease, undoubtedly influenced Kretschmer's notion of "sensitive paranoia."

During the first World War, Kretschmer became an army psychiatrist and was put in charge of a treatment unit for soldiers suffering from combat neurosis, or as it was then called "shell shock." In the course of this assignment, he treated many cases of acute hysteria. On the basis of his clinical experience he developed a theory of hysteria which he described in a monograph called *Hysteria, Reflex and Instinct* (1923/1948). Kretschmer viewed hysterical behaviour as consisting of primitive reflexes and instinctive reactions. These were ontogenetically and phylogenetically pre-formed. They became manifest as the result of a regression to more primitive and immature levels of behaviour. However, they were used by patients for certain purposes to attain definite personal aims.

His other early work was his *Ideas of Reference in Oversensitive Personalities, A Contributution to the Theory of Paranoia* (1918). In this monograph he developed the concept of *sensitiver Beziehungswahn* (sensitive delusions of reference). Kretschmer rejected the concept of paranoia as a disease. Instead he saw it as an interaction of a constitutionally oversensitive personality with a set of environmental circumstances. This interaction could have a snowballing effect.

After the first World War Kretschmer returned to Tuebingen University where he resumed his clinical work and research. His research was focused on the problems of human constitution and on how vegetative-endocrinal mechanisms determined it. In addition, he wanted to know how the former was related to character and temperament. Kretschmer was also interested in the relationship between various psychiatric syndromes on the one hand, and on constitution and character on the other. The fruit of his endeavours was his system of constitutional psychology and psychiatry. This was described in his book *Physique and Character* (1925). For Kretschmer, the human constitution was the totality of the inborn characteristics of an individual. This included his hereditary genotype which interacted with the environmental factors to produce a phenotype. The phenotype had three aspects: physique (bodily type), character, and temperament. They represented manifestations of the same underlying constitution. Physique was equated with bodily structure, character was described as the total pattern of voluntary behaviour, while temperament was described as the affective reactivity of the individual. Underlying this notion was an assumption of a psychophysical monism and a rejection of dualism.

The constitutional approach regarded the whole organism as a total system and did not concentrate on the brain in the search for the locus of the disease processes. It viewed pathologies as "dyscrasias," imbalances of the vegetative-endocrinal processes, rather than as "diseases" conceived in mechanistic terms. According to the latter conception, disease would be caused by a malfunctioning organ or a malfunctioning part of it. In contrast, in Kretschmer's constitutional theory, mental diseases were regarded as extremes of certain psychophysical types rather than nosological entities. They were intrinsic to the organism, not extrinsic entities superimposed on it. They were due to an internal imbalance of the organismic constitution, or to a disturbed balance between the organism and its environment. Thus Kretschmer assumed a continuity between mental health and mental illness instead of discontinuity as Kraepelin had. The latter followed the tradition of the neurological school in psychiatry, which had also rejected the idea of continuity between the two.

On the basis of his clinical observations and anthropometric investigations, Kretschmer devised a constitutional typology theory in which he argued that there are three main types of physique: pyknic, leptosomic (asthenic) and athletic. There was an additional minor type called by Kretchmer, "dysplastic." These types were conceived by him as ideal types rather than discrete taxonomic categories. The bulk of the population consisted of amalgams (mixtures) of types in different proportions. The ideal types were extremes of the physique variation in the entire population. They could be conceived in terms of dimensions. Certain types of character were found to be associated with certain types of physique. Thus the schizoid character was associated with the leptosomic, the athletic and especially with the dysplastic physique.

Kretschmer described the "viscose" character of athletes which he associated with epilepsy (Kretschmer & Enke, 1936). Cyclothymic character was found to be associated with the pyknic physique. According to Kretschmer, physique, character, temperament and different kinds of mental illness were the expression of the same biological constitution (*Formkreise*). The association was structural rather than causal. Kretschmer described the leptosome as long, lanky, narrow and angular. The leptosome had long arms which could be described as spidery. He also had a long neck and a receding chin. He looked like Don Quixote, the hero of Cervantes' novel. Not only his physique, but also the leptosome's character was Quixotic. He was shy, oversensitive, eccentric, and was living in a private world of fantasy. The athletic type had powerful muscles, heavy bones, broad shoulders and narrow hips. He was like the superman of the comic books. The athletic type of physique was associated with a cold, aggressive and ruthless character. The pyknic type was described as chubby and pot-bellied. He had a round head, a moon-like face, short neck, arms and legs, and had stubby fingers. He was like Sancho Panza, Don Quixote's faithful servant. The pyknic was warm, jolly, good humoured, good natured, practical, and possessed all the earthy qualities of Sancho (Weckowicz, 1984).

These were all normal types. In the rare, displastic type, however, all the bodily proportions were out of balance. This type was associated with gross endocrinal disorders and very often with severe schizophrenia. The constitutional types were associated with inborn temperamental traits described in terms of the sensitivity of the nervous system, psychic "tempo," psychomotor speed and mood colouring. These inborn temperamental traits produced under different environmental influences a variety of character types which were associated with certain clusters of personality traits. There were three such clusters associated with the schizoid character. Another three could be identified with the cyclothymic character.

The affective reaction of the schizoid character varied between the extremes of the *psychoaesthetic* scale. This ranged from excessive reaction to insufficient reaction; from excitement to apathy. In the cyclothymic character this reaction fluctuated between the extremes of the *diathetic* scale from depression (sadness) to mania (elation).

According to Kretschmer, schizophrenia and manic-depressive psychosis were the extremes respectively of the schizoid and the cyclothymic characters. These psychoses could also be the product of the reactions to stress situations in the schizoid and cyclothymic characters. They were not diseases in the sense of nosological entities. They were continuous with the normal schizoid and cyclothymic characters. Kretschmer believed that the endocrines were the most important factors responsible for the varieties of physique, temperament and endogeneous psychoses. In his *Physique and Character*, he asserted: "To back up the secretional approach comes the following empirical material from the region of the endogenous psychoses *as exaggeration of the normal types of temperament*." (Kretschmer, 1925, p.255; italics added)

Using experimental psychological methods, Kretschmer attempted to find psychological differences distinguishing the character types. He investigated such features as 1) sensitivity to colour and form, 2) the phenomena of "splitting," 3) concept formation, 4) psychomotor speed in different types. He also researched differences in the functioning of the endocrinal systems and the autonomic nervous systems of these types. Thus, while Kraepelin had based his experimental psychological research on Wundt's structuralism, Kretschmer followed the footsteps of the psychologists who investigated individual differences. These are exemplified by Francis Galton and James McKeen Cattell (1860-1944).

Kretschmer had broad interests which included among others the interest in the relation between genius and madness, a topic which fascinated many nineteenth century psychiatrists such as Reil, Moreau de Tour, and Paul Moebius. He applied his constitutional theory to the study of men of genius and believed that many of these men were suffering from borderline psychotic and neurotic illness. Kretschmer further investigated the genetic and environmental factors conducive to the production of genius (Kretschmer, 1931). Towards the end of his career, he summarized his general views in a volume entitled *Medical Psychology* (1950).

In 1926, Kretschmer left Tuebingen and moved to Marburg University where he was appointed professor of neuro- psychiatry and the director of the neurological clinic. Many of the students he trained during that time became leading German psychiatrists. In 1946 he returned to Tuebingen as a professor, and finally retired in 1959.

The Constitutional Psychology of William Sheldon

Kretschmer's influence spread abroad. In the United States, William H. Sheldon (1940, 1942), demonstrated Kretschmer's influence by proposing a constitutional theory of physique and temperament in terms of dimensions, rather than in terms of discrete categories. Sheldon's theory outlined three basic dimensions of human physique: 1) endomorphy, 2) mesomorphy, and 3) ectomorphy. These were named for the three original embryonic layers, the endoderm, mesoderm, and ectoderm from which all the tissue of a vertebrate organism were derived. He believed that the constitutional type reflected the strength of development of any one of these layers. Endomorphy was associated with the development of the digestive system. This was derived from the endoderm. Mesomorphy expressed the degree of development of the muscle and bone structures which had derived from the mesoderm. Ectomorphy indicated the degree of development of the skin, of the sensory organs and of the nervous system.

There were similarities between the predominantly endomorphic somatotype and Kretschmer's pyknic types. Sheldon's mesomorphic type and Kretschmer's athletic type also had affinities. Then, Kretschmer's leptosome corresponded to Sheldon's ectomorphic type. Each individual was rated independently on a scale of one to seven, in regard to the three basic somatotypes. Individuals were also assessed according to the degree of dysplasia they showed. That is, disproprotion of bodily parts. Also as to the degree of gynandromorphy or degree of bi-sexual characteristics.

The three basic dimensions of physique were associated with three basic personality dimensions. Endomorphy was associated with viscerotonia, which was characterized by the love of comfort, relaxation, and sociability. Mesomorphy was associated with somatotonia. This was characterized by a penchant for vigorous exercise and athletics, and also by aggressiveness. Finally, ectomorphy was associated with cerebrotonia. The chief characteristic of this, was an excessive sensitivity to the environment, general inhibition and withdrawal.

Sheldon was mainly concerned with personality theory and regarded psychopathological syndromes as due to the imbalance of somatic components. He and his followers carried out somatotyping of mental patients. Sheldon found that hebephrenic and catatonic schizophrenics showed a high degree of dysplasia and gynandromorphy. They also scored high on ectomorphy and low on mesomorphy. Paranoid schizophrenics and aggressive psychopaths were high on mesomorphy. Manic-depressives were high on endomorphy and on mesomorphy. This latest version of constitutional psychiatry with its assumption of a continuity between normal and abnormal personality stirred some interest, particularly in Great Britain in the forties and fifties. However, the subsequent research on the relation of physique to personality and to mental illness proved to be disappointing. The high correlation reported by Kretschmer and Sheldon among the factors of physique, personality, and mental illness may have been the result of confounding the data. The persons who rated the physique often also rated the personality. Better controlled studies did not confirm the original claims.

11

Sigmund Freud: The New Dynamic Psychiatry

History of the Psychoanalytical Movement

Sigmund Freud. Sigmund Freud's discoveries and theories have been called the second psychiatric revolution (Zilboorg, 1941). If the first psychiatric revolution occurred in the sixteenth century, then the second one might be more properly dated at the end of the eighteenth and the beginning of the nineteenth century. If the first involved the rennaissance of humanistic values and the scientific revolution, then the second has as its most dramatic event, the removal of chains from mental patients by Philippe Pinel at Bicetre in 1793. This dramatic event coincided with and was followed by the reforms of mental hospitals in France and other countries. The concept of the raving lunatic changed rapidly. The lunatic was now a mental patient, a sick person. Mental disease became like any other disease, and was to be treated in hospitals by medical doctors.

However, although madness had been perceived as a disease at least since William Battie, there was no agreement about its etiology. Here two view were dominant. According to one, the causes of mental illness were psychological, according to the other, the causes were physical and mental illness was a disease of the brain. William Battie had considered them to be mixed, with one as an original type related to constitutional factors, and a secondary (consequential) type arising from physical injury, disease, and toxins. By the end of the nineteenth century the neuro-pathological school was prevalent, and Kraepelin could definitely assert that mental illnesses were diseases of the brain. Sigmund Freud's dynamic psychiatry and psychoanalytical therapy should be called the third psychiatric revolution. Henri Ellenberger's *The Discovery of the Unconscious* (1970), was concerned with tracing the emergence of a modern dynamic psychiatry. Here he could trace the roots of Freudian psychiatry to the discovery of "animal magnetism" by Franz Anton Mesmer. The mesmerists and later the hypnotists of the Paris school of Charcot, the Nancy school of Liebeault and Bernheim helped to found the tradition of dynamic psychiatry. The role of the Philosophy of Nature, of Romantic medicine, and of the *Psychiker* psychiatrists of the early nineteenth century, must not be overlooked. The distinguishing features of these approaches were attributing of mental illness to psychological causes, conceiving mind in dynamic terms as an energy system, and finally believing that alongside the conscious mind there was also the unconscious mind.

In opposition to the Romantic ideas of mental illness, the organic psychiatrists argued for the presence of damage or pathology in the brain. In keeping with the rising tide of materialist philosophy and Darwinism, these views were dominant by 1900. Freud himself began his work firmly rooted in organic psychiatry. Ellenberger refers to Freud's discoveries as the "new dynamic psychiatry." Freud as well as his followers and dissenters, ultimately came to revolt against organic and neurological psychiatry. Instead, they returned to some of the psychological ideas of the *Psychiker* psychiatrists of the early nineteenth century and attributed mental illness to psychological causes. They also developed the technique of "uncovering" psychotherapy and stressed the importance of insight resulting from it.

Sigmund Freud (1856-1939) was born at Freiburg in Moravia, a son of a woolens merchant, but spent most of his life in Vienna. He was closely associated with its university as a student, researcher, and teacher. While studying medicine, he also did research in zoology and comparative neuroanatomy. During that period he also attended lectures of the philosopher-psychologist, Franz Brentano (1838-1917), famous for his "act psychology." The "act psychology" had an Aristotelian bent. It introduced the concept of intentionality. This served as an alternative to the then prevalent mechanistic concept of associationism in psychology. Brentano's psychology "from the empirical point of view" was very different from the then dominant "associationist" psychology which Wundt was teaching. The latter followed the traditions of David Hartley (1705-1757), Herbart and Locke. However, Brentano like Robert Zimmermann (1824-1898) returned the traditions of Leibniz. He is best known for his *Psychologie vom empirischen Standpunkt* (1874).

Brentano had a threefold division of the process of perception. In part this drew on Kantian traditions as well as those of German historicism. Accordingly, mental phenomena were perceived as 1) representations (*Vorstellungen*) which involved the activity of the mind's intentionality. The famous phrase which influenced Freud was that "the mind intends an object." Even imaginary objects were real while in the mind. Then 2) judgments of objects occurred which affirmed them or denied their external reality. Finally, 3) human emotions involved the mind, brought will and feeling together, and focused on love and hate. Any object evoked a sensate reaction of love or hate. Here one may be reminded of the Freudian focus on the love-hate relationships. Certainly there is a dim echo of Hobbes, Bentham and the pleasure-pain cycle of utilitarian thinking (Johnston, 1972).

"Intentionality" implied a goal directed relation of reference between the subject and object as the hallmark of mental acts and of consciousness. Although Frued had, in his writings, not referred specifically to Brentano, a similarity can be discerned between Freud's concept of *cathexis* and that of intentionality. Also, Freud's notion of mental apparatus that performed certain functions, bears a similarity to Brentano's concept of mental acts.

Freud had like Brentano's generation, first been reared on Herbart. While at gymnasium (high school), he had been exposed to a course in elementary psychology using Lindener's (1958) texbook which was based on the theory of Johann Friedrich Herbart. The latter's theories also stemmed from Leibniz' philosophy. Herbart had postulated the existence of an unconscious filled with ideas which were striving to become conscious and which competed with each other. Still a Romantic, Herbart had in his *Allgemeine Praktische Philosophie* of 1808 identified Nature with thought and the World Soul. Here too he referred to an "act of thought" to define the relationship between the individual's will and the effects of a foreign or external one. Ideas sought to meet with the approval of the external will. Kant had defined this as common sense. Later in life, Herbart tried to turn psychology into a mathematical science, and this may be the reason that the generation of Brentano turned to Leibniz. The young Freud remained more committed to biological science than to philosophy.

Before he graduated in Vienna, Freud had begun to work in the physiological laboratory of Ernst Bruecke (1819-1892). He also continued on as Bruecke's assistant after graduation, and for a time aimed at a scientific career in neurophysiology. Altogether Freud spent six years in Bruecke's laboratory and only reluctantly gave up his career in physiology for economic reasons. Instead he turned to clinical neurology. Bruecke was at that time one of the world's leading physiologists. Together with three other giants of nineteenth century physiology, Carl Ludwig, Emil Du Bois-Reymond, and Hermann von Helmholtz, Bruecke made a commitment in 1845, to combat the prevailing school of vitalism (Zilboorg, 1941). They swore to promote materialistic explanations of life phenomena. In Bruecke's laboratory, Freud met two young and gifted physiologists, Sigmund Exner and Ernst Fleischl von Marxow. The subsequent history of Fleischl von Marxow was tragic. He became Freud's patient in 1885, and was treated with cocaine for his addiction to morphine. Eventually he was to die of drug addiction.

Both Bruecke and Exner, as well as Theodor Meynert the professor of neurology and psychiatry, proposed conceptual neuronal models of brain functioning. These influenced Freud, and proabably inspired him to develop his own *Project for a Scientific Psychology* (1957) which was never published during Freud's lifetime. In Bruecke's laboratory he also met Josef Breuer (1842-1925), a distinguished Viennese physician who specialized in the treatment of nervous diseases. Later, in the beginning of his clinical career, Freud collaborated with Breuer. However, after a few years, their paths separated. By 1882, Freud left Bruecke's laboratory and joined Theodor Meynert's Department of Neurology and Psychiatry at the University of Vienna.

During his years with Meynert, Freud combined clinical work in neurology with research in neuropathology. He published several papers on clinical neurology, neuroanatomy, and neuropathology. His crowning achievement in this neurological period, was a monograph on aphasia (*Aphasia*, 1891) which gained him international recognition. However, his early advocacy of cocaine for the treatment of depression, received a mixed reception. In due course, Freud was appointed a *Privatdozent* (assistant professor), and a few years later, professor extraordinary (associate professor) in neurology, at the University of Vienna.

In 1885, Freud won a travelling scholarship and spent a few months with Charcot at Salpetriere in Paris. He watched Charcot's demonstrations of hysterical patients, became interested in the subject of hysteria, and in the treatment of this disease by hypnosis. In 1889 he went to France for the second time, to visit Bernheim and Liebeault in Nancy. This visit enabled him to compare the Paris and Nancy schools' approach to hysteria. Back in Vienna, he introduced his Viennese colleagues to the work of Charcot and Bernheim by translating their work into German.

After his return from France, Freud collaborated with Josef Breuer whom he had met at Bruecke's laboratory. Breuer had been treating cases of hysteria with hypnosis, while Freud had visited Charcot in France, to observe the same techniques. Another Viennese disciple of Charcot was Moritz Benedict (1835-1920), a psychotherapist associated with the Viennese Poliklinik. He had given Freud a letter of introduction to Charcot. Benedikt was a pioneer in the use of the uncovering technique in psychotherapy. He believed that a hidden secret was always behind psychopathological symptoms. This pathogenic secret had to be uncovered. The access to it was through exploration of fantasies and daydreams of the patient.

In the same period in which he worked with Breuer and treated hysteria, Freud became friendly with Wilhelm Fliess (1858-1928), a nose and throat surgeon from Berlin. Fliess became Freud's alter-ego and a confidant. Their relationship bore a resemblance to the one between the analyst and the analysand. Fliess played the analyst, Freud the analysand. Fliess had a speculative turn of mind, and believed in the importance of bio-rhythmic cycles. He even used complex numerological methods to untangle them. He also believed in the constitutional bi-sexuality of human beings. While rejecting the numerology of Fliess, Freud accepted the concept of bi-sexuality. This idea became even more prominent in the Adlerian and Jungian systems. In the end, Freud and Fliess quarrelled, and their friendship terminated.

Peter Gay (1988), one of Freud's most recent biographers, found Freud to be singularly uncritical of his relationship with Fliess. He has analyzed their relationship in terms of the "I and Thou" theories of Martin Buber, and views Fliess as Freud's "Other," the product of an early transference relationship, and emotionally necessary for Freud's subsequent understanding of this phenomenon.

In November of 1882, during the period when Freud collaborated with Breuer, the latter told him about the case of a hysterical patient whom he had begun to treat a few years earlier, in 1880. This was the famous case of "Anna O" or Bertha Pappenheim. (She later became a friend of Freud's wife, Martha). During her father's last illness, she had developed gross conversion and dissociative hysterical symptoms. Breuer brought about a temporary cure by inducing the patient under hypnosis to recall sexual feelings and memories associated with her father.

The case of "Anna O" became the paradigm case on which Freud's future treatment of hysteria was to be based. The idea of talking out a problem also provided the basic model for the kind of treatment used in psychoanalysis. Less well known is the subsequent history of Miss Pappenheim, whom Breuer sent to Kreuzlingen sanatorium in Switzerland, where she was then again treated. She began to speak only in English and continued to be neurotic until 1883 (Gay, 1988).

During her treatment by Breuer, however, she was placed under hypnosis. The memories of the traumatic experiences which were recalled by such patients were then abreacted emotionally. This method was called by Freud, *catharsis*, a term borrowed from Aristotle's theory of the effect of tragedy on its spectators as presented in his *Poetics*. Freud claimed that the traumatic experiences were of a sexual nature. Very often they resulted from seduction by an adult, or even the parent of an opposite sex. Breuer did not agree with Freud's interpretation of the case when they wrote it up, much later, in 1895. The resulting disagreement caused Freud and Breuer to dissolve their partnership and to go their separate ways. The results of their work was summarized in *Studies on Hysteria* (Breuer & Freud, 1895/1957). Later on, Freud changed his opinion about the frequency of childhood seduction and attributed hysterical symptoms to repressed sexual fantasies involving the parent of the opposite sex.

The Oedipus complex was one of Freud's most seminal theories, and one which has been widely popularized by twentieth century novelists and film-makers. The idea for it arose from the work he did at the turn of the century, when his sex etiology theory of neurosis was formed, and becoming known in medical circles. The Oedipus complex theory maintained that sexual desire was directed toward the parent of the opposite sex, but that fear and hatred of the parent of the same sex accompanied it. This became the cornerstone of Freud's theory of hysteria. He further elaborated his theory of infantile sexuality and of libido in his *Three Essays on the Sexual Theory* (1905). Freud's theories were possible in this peculiar Viennese milieu because nineteenth century prudery had been relaxed. Sex as a topic of discussion became less of a taboo. An interest developed in sexual pathology. Pioneering work in the field had been carried out by Richard von Krafft-Ebbing (1840-1902), a professor of psychiatry at Vienna and a prominent forensic psychiatrist. His

Psychopathia Sexualis (1886/ 1965), exerted an enormous influence. Havelock Ellis (1859-1939) continued the Kraft-Ebbing work in England.

The original Freudian theory of sexual etiology, however, gave a new definition to human desire and sex drives than had been traditional in Western culture. Perhaps this was because he viewed the culture as an outsider. The amorphous, pleasure-seeking, sexual drive had a much wider connotation than its narrow, biological meaning as an adult procreative sexuality. Freud defined some definite stages in childhood sexual development. It was this aspect of his theory which has gained so much recognition and is widely diffused in popular culture. During the first six years of life, the child went through oral, anal, urethral and phallic stages. The earlier stages were auto-erotic, the phallic stage was associated with the Oedipal choice object which was the parent of the opposite sex. In the case of the boy, this was associated with hostility to the father, and a fear of castration, but with love for the mother. The Oedipal conflict was resolved by an identification with the parent of the same sex. In females, the complex, directed by love for the father and hostility to the mother, became known as the Electra complex.

In Freudian theory, the Oedipal phase was followed by a period of latency which lasted until puberty. Adult genital sexuality was then awakened. A fixation or regression to the Oedipal phase led to incestuous fantasies which became repressed. However, if repression failed, there was a return of the repressed in the guise of hysterical symptoms such as somatic conversions, dissociations and phobias (anxiety hysteria). This was Freud's theory of hysteria. The case of little Hans (Freud, 1909), a five year old boy suffering from a horse phobia, allowed Freud to see anxiety hysteria in the nascent state. He could easily see the fear of horses in the boy as the displaced fear and hostility towards the father.

The psychotherapeutic technique used by Freud with his hysterical patients underwent considerable modification during this early period. Since many patients were resistent to hypnosis, the classical hypnotic method of Charcot and Breuer was abandoned. Instead, the patient was told to close his eyes and to concentrate while the therapist with a hand pressed the patient's forehead. He made the suggestion that the forgotten memories would be recalled. In a further modification of the method, the patient was told to lie down on a couch. He was then to free associate and to tell everything which entered his awareness. The therapist would then sit out of the patient's line of vision. The anecdote is told, that in his later years, Freud would actually place a bust of himself on the desk and try to sit behind that. Thus the psychoanalytic technique was born.

In addition to hysteria, Freud had a general interest in psychological processes, and in the nature of the human mind. In 1895, early in his career, he attempted to construct a neurophysiological model of mind with three types of neurons forming complex reflex arcs and feedback systems. He described it as a "project for a scientific psychology," in a letter to Fliess (1957), but never published during Freud's lifetime. Peter Gay (1988) refers to it as a 'psychology for neurologists,' and dates it from September and October of 1895. Freud's ideas crystallized in his first epoch-making book, *The Interpretation of Dreams* (1900). With this work, Freud opened the twentieth century in a very personal way.

Freud's new understanding of the role of dreams in human psychology was supported by a major theory of the human mind. Here he proposed a topographical model. According to it, there were three areas of mind: the conscious, the preconscious and the unconscious. A repressive barrier separated the preconscious from the unconscious. The barrier acted as a censor, it kept the contents of the unconscious from entering the preconscious and prevented this material from becoming conscious. Only when vigilence of the "censor" lapsed during sleep, which was a period of inattention to the external world, could the unconscious material become conscious. However, even then it appeared in disguised form. The disguise was a product of a compromise between the unconscious impulses and wishes, recent memories (day residues) and the distortions produced by the preconscious (dream work). The phenomena of disguise during dreaming, was referred to as condensation, and displacement. In the first case, two objects or two persons could be combined into one. In the second, an important element was relegated to an inconspicuous position, while an unimportant element was brought to the center of attention.

Freud called the psychological processes in the unconscious primary, they were not bound by the realities of space or time or by logic. The unconscious was governed by the "pleasure principle." The wishes emanating from it demanded immediate gratification. The unconscious impulses required immediate discharge. The conscious mind was ruled by the "principle of reality," a secondary process. This situation was a source of conflict between the conscious and the unconscious. Dreams, psychopathological symptoms, as well as jokes and humour were psychodynamic attempts to solve these conflicts. Freud also believed that every day minor mistakes and slips of the tongue were not due to accidental lapses of attention and memory but were attempts at the solution of these conflicts. These further contributions to depth psychology outside the clinical field were published in book form as *Psychopathology of Everyday Life* (1904) and *Jokes and Their Relation to the Unconscious* (1905).

In addition to hysteria, Freud discussed psychopathology of paranoid schizophrenia in his comments on the autobiography of Judge Schreber (Freud,1911). He attributed paranoid persecutory delusions to the mechanisms of denial and of projection as the defence measures against homosexual love. As a result of the operation of these defensive mechanisms "I love him" became "I hate him," and "I hate him" became "he hates me."

In 1917 Freud published an important paper "Mourning and Melancholia" (1917/1957) in which he compared melancholia with mourning. In the latter state, an external object was lost. This caused pain and anguish. In melancholia, an internal object, previously incorporated in an ego, was lost. The impoverishment of the ego produced a profound feeling of worthlessness which was expressed as ideas of guilt and self-deprecation. The internal object was viewed as being cruel and sadistic because of the ambivalence feelings directed to it. It was perceived in the patient's fantasy as attacking the ego. This resulted in aggression being turned against onself with accompanying self-hate, acute guilt feelings and sucidal tendencies.

The "Mourning and Melancholia" article heralded a new phase in the development of psychoanalysis. Melancholia replaced hysteria as the paradigmatic illnesses around which new theoretical concepts were developed. The topographical model was set aside in favour of the structural, or "tripartite" model. It resulted in the division of the psyche into Superego, Ego, and Id, the main components of this model, which become widely diffused in Western thought. The main elements of this theory appeared in a monograph published in 1923, and entitled: *The Ego and the Id* (1923/1961). The three structural elements were relatively independent components of the mental apparatus and performed different functions. These were called the Id, Ego, and Superego. All three were unconscious. Their existence could only be inferred from their effect on conscious experience and behaviour. The Id was the source of libidinal and aggressive drives. Freud had borrowed the term "Id" from Georg Groddeck's work, *The Book of the Id* (1923/1928). Groddeck believed that the Id was a panpsychic force, like the one envisaged by the Nature Philosophers. This force was viewed as the principle underlying all vital, normal, and abnormal phenomena. Groddeck became marginally associated with the psychoanalytic movement, and was considered to be quite a wildman. He had introduced some psychoanalytical ideas into the treatment of patients at the Baden-Baden Asylum where he was the director. He and Freud became friendly, although Freud always distinguished his ideas in which the ego and id remained separate, from the Groddeckian "Id."

Freud's view of human drives (*Triebe*) aimed at categorizing them specifically. They had a characteristic source, impetus, aim, and object. The source referred to the erotogenic zone from which the drives originated. A kind of libidinal physics and economics emerged here. The impetus was the amount of energy possessed by the drive. It was measured as *cathexis*. The aim was the type of consumatory activity associated with discharge of the drive.

The object was the target of the drive. Libidinal and aggressive drives emanated from the Id. They demanded an immediate discharge and gratification. The drives were checked by the Ego which was the source of the secondary process, and was controlled by the reality principle and prevented or delayed the gratification of the drives. The third component of the mind apparatus was the Superego which was the introjected image of the parent of the same sex. The Superego was the source of moral standards of behaviour and could be identified with the Christian concept of conscience. The Ego, which was the executive component of the mental apparatus, was under constant pressure by demands emanating from the Id, the Superego, and the environment. It was continually trying to reconcile their very often conflicting demands.

In *Beyond the Pleasure Principle* (1920), Freud suggested that there were two basic human instincts: the life instinct, called by him "Eros," and the death instinct, subsequently called "Thanatos." Earlier, Freud had claimed that the basic drive was *libido*. This was a sexual drive which emanated from the Id. This drive was opposed and complemented by the self-preservation, aggressive drives anchored in the ego. The death instinct theory was rather speculative and was not accepted by all followers of Freud.

One may ask what was the import of Freud's theory at this particular juncture of time, Freud did not discover the unconscious and he did not invent depth psychology. His predecessors were the Philosophers of Nature, the *Psychiker* psychiatrists of the early nineteenth century, the mesmerists and later the hypnotists who were treating hysteria. The contribution by his genius was to construct the scientific foundations for depth psychology and psychodynamic psychiatry. Freud presented an alternative to the then dominant neurological and noslogical schools of psychiatry. He insisted that psychiatric symptoms were psychologically determined and had an intrinsic meaning which had to be uncovered. This view contradicted those of the neurological psychiatrists who believed that the mental symptoms displayed by psychiatric patients were epiphenomena, meaningless by-products of organic brain pathology.

The concept of the unconscious was crucial for depth psychology. It was postulated by several philosophers and clinicians, who interpreted it differently. At the end of the nineteenth century and the beginning of the twentieth,at least four different conceptions of the unconscious could be distinguished.

First, the co-consciousness concept which was used to explain multiple personality cases and dissociative states occurring in hysteria. They were induced by hypnosis. In these cases subjects possessed, as it were, two or more separate consciousnesses. Hence the designation, co-consciousness. The two coexistent consciousnesses could be unaware of one another. Or, they could be aware after all. Awareness could be one-sided. One consciousness could be aware of the other which was not simultaneously aware of the first. Co-consciousness could represent different personalities in the same individuals. They could differ in maturity. However, there were no radical qualitative differences between them. This concept of the unconscious was espoused by Charcot, Janet, and Morton Prince who were interested in cases of multiple personality.

The second concept of the unconscious was associated with the field of awareness which was outside the focus of attention. The total psyche could be compared to a dark room. Consciousness was like a light spot produced by a light beam. The objects in the focus of the beam could be sharply discerned. The objects in the periphery only dimly discerned and those in the darkness could not be discerned at all. The dark area outside the illuminated one, was the domain of the unconscious. This was the concept of the unconscious held by William James (1890) and corresponded to Freud's notion of the preconscious.

Thirdly, there was the Freudian conception of the unconscious. Here the unconscious was qualitatively different from consciousness and was subject to different laws. It could only indirectly manifest itself in dreams, in slips of the tongue and in neurotic symptoms. There was a barrier between the unconscious and the preconscious. The unconscious was the seat of primitive fantasies and impulses. It followed the principles of pleasure, not of logic. Principles of reality did not apply here. Freud had thus assumed some of the elements of the traditional utilitarian pleasure and pain principles, but had discovered an entire realm in which the simpler mechanisms of the Bentham era did not work. The Freudian unconscious was regarded as the source of pathological, disruptive forces. At the same time it could be the fountain of creative life forces. These possessed rejuvenating and healing properties. The latter view of the unconscious was stressed by Carl Gustav Jung (1964) who had been influenced by the Nature Philosophers, Carus, and Schopenhauer. Jung postulated the existence of the *collective unconscious* underlying the individual unconscious. The collective unconscious contained primordial symbols or images. These were archetypes which appeared as dreams, myths, and in psychotic production. They could be destructive, but they were also sources of the creativity and of the spiritual renewal of man.

The fourth conception of the unconscious which existed during this era, equated the unconscious with a semi-intentional denial of reality. It was a make-believe that certain phenomena which were unpleasant to the individual, did not exist. According to this view of the unconscious, the subject intentionally deceived himself that he was unconscious of certain things and happenings. However, deep down inside himself, he was really aware of them, although he would not admit it to himself. The subject wanted to deceive himself. This was the view of hysterical patients held by many contemporaries of Freud who regarded these patients as malingerers. It was also held by the early followers of Freud like Wilhelm Stekel (1927). An argument could be offered that this view was also held by Alfred Adler (1963), although his position on this score was rather ambiguous.

At the end of the discussion of Freud's contributions, it is appropriate to say a few words on the position of Freud within the context of the history of ideas. In his intellectual development, Freud was influenced by two different and conflicting philosophical traditions (Rapaport, 1960). On the one hand, he was under the spell of the idea of pure, positivistic science as represented by the so-called "Helmholtzian school of medicine." As was mentioned before, one of Freud's teachers who had a great influence on him, was Ernst Bruecke, the professor of physiology at Vienna. Freud had spent six years in his laboratory and only reluctantly gave up the career of physiology for that of clinical neurology. It will be remembered that Bruecke together with Carl Ludwig, Emil du Bois-Reymond, and Hermann von Helmholtz in 1845 had agreed to combat vitalism and to argue in favour of the materialistic explanation of life. Their view of biology and medicine was representative of the reductionist-materialist, empiricist and positivistic conceptions of science. This conceived of the whole of reality as a space-time-matter-energy system. Their materialistic ideas had been reinforced by the formulation of the law of the conservation of energy and other laws of thermodynamics by Robert Mayer in 1842. These laws which envisaged the transformation and equalization of energy distribution with the resulting final state of positive entrophy, had a great influence on many biological and physiological theories at the end of the last century.

The ideas of a run-down universe with the pre-ordained directionality of change and the pre-determined final outcome was conducive to a view of science based on the Laplacian type of absolute determinism. Classical mechanics and thermodynamics were the ideals and paradigms to be emulated by all sciences. Epiphenomenalism offered the explanation of mind-body relationship. Mental phenomena were regarded as insignificant by-products of physiological processes in the brain, devoid of any intrinsic meaning and outside of the chain of causality. Although caused by physical events these epiphenomena were incapable of causing anything. According to the view espoused by Bruecke, Exner and Meynert, the mentors of the young Freud, the human mind could be reduced to a network of neuroses. Freud's idea of complete psychological determinism, associationism, the principle of maximization of positive entrophy, and generally the economic point of view on his meta-psychology stemmed from this intellectual tradition.

At the same time, Freud was influenced by the German philosophical tradition of Leibniz, Kant, Spinoza and Herbart. He was influenced by the whole German Romantic tradition, and by the literary works of Goethe. These influences counteracted those of positivism, materialism, and determinism common to nineteenth century science. He might have been indirectly influenced by the vitalistic and voluntarist philosophies of Schopenhauer and Nietzsche. Certainly Eduard von Hartmann (1842-1906), whose work on the unconscious, *Philosophie des Unbewussten* (1869) proved to be an important influence, derived his ideas of development in part from Hegel, and his early pessimism from Schopenhauer. For Hartmann, the unconscious represented a region higher than consciousness in which the representation functions and the action of the will could take place. Freud was to accept the idea of an unconscious as a basic metaphysical principle, the ground of individual life, but did not give it a higher place than the conscious ego.

It is not known whether Freud was acquainted with the works of such Philosophers of Nature as Carus, Troxler, and von Schubert, or whether he had read the works of the early nineteenth century *Psychiker* psychiatrists like Reil, Heinroth, Ideler, and Neumann. However, Fechner's influence was obvious and is well known. Fechner was the epigone of the Philosophy of Nature movement. Freud often referred to him as the "great" Fechner. Many concepts such as mental energy, the threshhold of consciousness, pleasure principle, the topography of mind, the principles of stability (constancy) and of repetition, were borrowed from Fechner and incorporated into Freud's metapsychology (Ellenberger, 1956). The notion that ideas are striving to become conscious, that they compete and repress one another, probably came from Herbart and indirectly from Leibniz. As mentioned above, Freud's teacher of philosophy had been Franz Brentano of "act psychology" fame. This orientation was somewhat Aristotelian but offered the concept of intentionality as an alternative to the then prevalent concept of mechanistic association in psychology.

To the influences of German idealist philosophy and literature on Freud, may be added that of the Jewish mystical tradition (Bakan, 1965). This tradition might have been passed on to Freud by his parents who originally came from the eastern Galician province of the Austro-Hungarian Empire, where there was a strong Hassidic tradition among the Jewish population. Peter Gay (1988), however, claims that Jacob Freud, Sigmund's father, had broken away from the family's Hassidic traditions. He was fluent in Hebrew, but seemed to want to assimilate without giving up his Jewishness. Also some of the ideas of Wilhelm Fliess, such as the mystical meaning of numbers, the bi-sexual nature of human beings, the mystical significance of the left and the right side of the body could have originated in the *Kabbala*. This second influence of Romanticism, of German Idealism, of Philosophy of Nature, and of Jewish mysticism may be called the vitalistic-voluntaristic view of the world.

The two intellectual traditions, the positivist-mechanist and the vitalist-voluntarist, presented very different views of man and nature. The first tradition viewed man as basically a passive robot who reacted to external and internal stimuli. It regarded human experiences and human behaviour as something that happened to man as a result of causes external to him. Man was a victim of circumstances, being buffetted by and submitting passively to external forces (some emanating from his body). Allport (1955) called this view of man the "Lockean" one. It assumed that the human mind was a *tabula rasa*, on which the impressions coming from the physical and social milieu were imprinted. According to this view, man was molded by the external environment to which he became adapted by social learning. The deterministic and associationist elements of Freud's theory may be traced to this tradition.

The second tradition, the vitalist-voluntarist, was called by Allport the "Leibnizian" view of man. It regarded man as a free agent, spontaneously initiating mental and physical acts, and striving towards certain goals. This dynamic, voluntarist, striving conception of man and nature was especially prominent in the Nature Philosophers and in Romantic literature. Many of Freud's ideas could be traced to the Leibnizian conception of man. These were vitalistic and voluntarist. They included Freud's theory of instinct or drive (*Triebe*) as a psychological force, the concept of libido, the importance of the psychological and symbolic meaning of symptoms, and his later belief in life and death instincts.

Freud used two metaphors in connection with his theories. The first was the view of the human mind as an energy system. It seemed to be working in accordance with the laws of thermodynamics. This was a "hydraulic" model of mind, and it could be traced to the influence of the positivist and mechanist intellectual tradition stemming from Locke and also from Descartes. The second metaphor was the view of the human mind as a theatrical stage on which *dramatis personae* - Superego, Ego, and Id - were performing a play. The second metaphor arose from the vitalist, voluntarist Leibnizian heritage. It represented the humanistic aspect of psycho-analysis and was concerned with the elucidation of meanings, with hermeneutics, rather than with causal explanations. The first metaphor was used by Freud in his metapsychological theorizing when he tried to provide a scientific underpinning for psychoanalysis. The second metaphor was used in more informal discussion of actual cases and of the clinical aspects of psychoanalysis.

The incongruity of the notions of the human mind as a free agent, an initiator of spontaneous acts, and of the human mind as a passive target of extrinsic forces which completely determined its workings, was responsible for the many ambiguities of Freudian theory. It is ambiguities like this, which make it difficult to define Freud's conception of man. While contemporary humanistic psychologists and existentialist psychiatrists espouse a Leibnizian view, the behaviourists subscribe to a Lockean one. The Freudian position was somewhere in the middle.

According to Freud, human behaviour was shaped by internal biological forces which produced certain primitive urges and drives in the Id. It was also shaped by external social forces which checked and modified these primitive drives. The higher regions of the mind, the ego and the consciousness, tended to be passive. They reacted only to the organismic forces emanating from the Id and the external forces of the social environment. Behaviour was a product of the compromise between these two types of forces. Freud's model of mind had both Lockean and Leibnizian features. The Id and the unconscious, the source of mental energy, were Leibnizian, while the consciousness and the Ego were Lockean. At the same time, it is necessary to draw attention to the essential complementarity of these two aspects; the active and the passive elements of mind. These could be compared with the complementarity of the particle and wave theory of light and matter.

To the two major influences of positivism and vitalism, should be added the third force provided by Darwinism. This had a great influence on the intellectual world of the late nineteenth century. In German-speaking countries, the leading exponent of the evolutionary theory was Ernst Haeckel (1834-1919), a professor of zoology at Jena. He had elaborated the Darwinian theory into an all-embracing philosophical system called "Monism," and suggested that it should replace the traditional theistic religion. Haeckel's important contribution was the formulation of the "biogenetic law", which stated that the ontogenetic development recapitulated the phylogenetic one. Freud was influenced by evolutionary theory, and adopted many of its features. This included his conception of psycho-sexual development in stages. Also his ideas of fixation, regression, and Haeckel's biogenetic law were absorbed by psychoanalytical theory. He was also influenced by the neurological theorizing of Hughlings Jackson (1884) and Meynert. Both distinguished two kinds of centers in the nervous system which were phylogenetically and ontogenetically higher or lower. They were functionally antagonistic to each other. This idea was reflected in Freud's theory of the levels of mental functioning and became the basis of the developmental model of psychoanalysis.

At the conclusion of the discussion of Freud's significance for the history of ideas, it is appropriate to present Freud's views on society and the place of the individual in it. Throughout history there have been two basic conceptions of man's social nature. The first was represented by Thomas Hobbes (1588-1679) and may be called the "Hobbesian" view. Here man was perceived as essentially evil, immoral, and anti-social. he was perpetually at war with his fellows in the state of nature. Only a strong one-man rule by a hereditary monarch could maintain order. Here the society is controlled from the center as the brain directs a body, and the anti-social impulses are subject less to societal control than to an absolutist governmental one. During the enlightenment, and especially after Locke, social control and suppression of antisocial instincts was to be located in the balance of interests among the dominant classes in the society. The second view was typically represented by Jean-Jacques Rousseau (1712-1778), and earlier by John Locke. According to the new and more modern conception, man was deemed to be essentially good and moral, but often corrupted by society. Rousseau believed in the positive orientation of the general will and trusted in the sound judgment of civil society, not merely in the decisions of its elites. His ideas were popularized by the French and American revolutions. A fear of mass uprisings and a conservative attitude towards the common man had continued in those nations aligned against Napoleon. The Industrial Revolution in Western Europe, and the Austro-Hungarian Empire's relative backwardness, had produced social pressures which made the fear of revolt a real one. In 1848,the rebellions in Vienna, Prague, and Budapest had been crushed by armed force. The nationalist aspirations of the many nationalities of the Austrian monarchy, produced a constant political turmoil.

It is perhaps less because he gauged the future of Europe correctly, than Freud's own experiences with the politics of the Habsburg Monarchy, his personal fear of anti-Semitism which increased by 1900, especially in Vienna, and because of the carnage in the following first World War that he intensified his studies of group behaviour. Like Max Weber in Germany, like so many European thinkers who experienced the disintegration of values which occurred after 1918, Freud tried to interpret the psychology of events. In his *Group psychology and the analysis of the ego* (1921/1961), and in his *Civilization and its discontents* (1930/1961), he took a "Hobbesian" position on the nature of man and his relation to society. Freud maintained that culture frustrated man's biological drives. The socialization of children led to neurotic conflicts. Civilized man was condemned to leading a neurotic existence. He could only adjust to society by using neurotic defenses. Civilization should be regarded as a collective neurosis. Consequently, Freud had a pessimistic view of man's future. He foresaw a mass discontent which would lead to bloody revolutions and wars. But he hoped that the death drives would be overcome by the normal drives for survival and reproduction (Freud, 1930).

Freud had wide ranging interests in sociology, religion, anthropology, cultural history, art and literature. He applied psychoanalytical theory to all of these fields. His historical interests led him to speculate about the historical origins of religious beliefs, myths, and practices. In *Totem and Taboo* (1912), he traced the origin of monotheistic religion to a hypothetical revolt of sons against their father which occurred in prehistorical times in the primeval horde (the Cyclopian family). In a primeval horde, there was no incest taboo. The father, the patriarch, appropriated all the females and drove away the younger males who were his sons. At a certain point, the jealous sons banded together to kill the patriarch. They devoured his body in order to acquire his strength and virility. Once the controlling influence of the patriarch was gone, the leaderless group was torn by fraternal strife. It began to disintegrate. The state of affairs produced guilt feelings in the sons and a desire to restore the authority of the patriarch. The dead patriarch was reincarnated in the form of a totem animal, the ancestor of the tribe and the sons imposed on themselves incest taboo barriers. This was to prevent the males from fighting about sexual rights for females who were their mothers and sisters, within the family and clan. Freud believed that the abhorence of incest, cannibalism, animal sacrifice, and the ritual of holy communion could all be traced back to the primeval patricide which was assumed to have existed in the past. He based his speculations on the research into totemic religions, and primitive clans societies by contemporrary anthropologists like Tylor, Lang, and Fraser.

During the nineteenth century the Nietzschean cry of anguish, "God is dead!" had produced an entirely new atheism. Darwin's evolutionary theory had also reinforced this trend which began earlier with a turn to materialism on the part of European theologians. Yet a more modern kind of religiousity had also begun to emerge out of the faith in human progress. Historical analyses of Bible history had been met with some disbelief, but men like David Strauss and Ernst Renan, who both published books on the life of Jesus, had made a forceful impact. Karl Marx had represented the materialist rejection of naive religion when he proclaimed that religion was the opiate of the masses. It is not surprising to find Freud returning to religious themes after the first World War which had disillusioned so many. In 1927 he published *The Future of an Illusion* in which he interpreted religious beliefs and rituals as a collective obsessional compulsive neurosis. According to Freud, religion was an expression of infantile fantasies about an omnipotent parental figure, and of the belief in the magical efficacy of obsessional rituals to influence these figures. Religion was a manifestation of immaturity which mankind was going to outgrow.

Shortly before he died in 1939, Freud published a still more controversial work which followed the ideas of *Totem and Taboo*. Written between 1934 and 1937, *Moses and Monotheism* appeared in English in May, 1939. Although his interest in Moses might have been stirred by Ernst Sellin's researches in 1922, the fact of National Socialist anti-Semitism and persecution, affected him personally. He left Vienna for London in 1938. He was afraid to publish the work because he feared losing the protection and support of many psychoanalysts. Although he had some serious historical interests in presenting Moses as a historical figure, his concern for the meaning of Moses and monotheism also includes some soul searching about the causes of the anti-Semitism which had disrupted his life.

The *Moses* offers some speculations on the origins of Judaic monotheism. Freud identified the age of Moses with the thirteenth or fourteenth century B.C. and the times of the maverick Pharoah Akhenaten who tried to introduce a monotheistic worship of Aton, the sun, into Egypt. Akhenaten was opposed by the conservative priests of the traditional polytheistic religion whose central god was Amon-ra. In the end the priests won, Akhenaten's temple was destroyed, and the old worship restored. According to Freud, Moses absorbed the high minded religious principles of Akhenaton's monotheism. Knowing that his ideas would arose opposition, he depicted Moses as an Egyptian nobleman. Moses then led the rebel followers of Aton into the desert and joined forces with an independent tribe of Hebrews who had worshipped Yahweh for eight hundred years before. They formed one nation, and they worshipped the one god Yahweh. Freud followed the interpretation of Sellin, and argued that Moses may have been killed by rebels, the primitive act of the murder of the patriarch. However, he realized that there were two accounts of the Moses story which differed in the Pentateuch. He also argued that the accusation that the Jews killed God the father (as Jesus Christ in the trinity), had been a Christian one and had accompanied many persecutions. Then he concluded that hatred of the Jews was really a hatred of Christianity. The Jews were God's chosen, first born, and the siblings developed jealousy. He also expressed a belief in a kind of collective unconscious which was not as full of symbols as Jung's, but which carried along some of the archaic traditions orally. Although modern scholars do not really believe that Moses was an Egyptian, the idea that monotheism was conveyed by Moses from the Akhenaten monotheism is widely accepted. This was not the worship of what he called an original tribal deity, a "volcano god," but of the Eternal, one God, who was filled with truth, justice and a love of humanity.

Freud's anthropological speculations have to be considered in the context of the beginning of the twentieth century. They influenced several scholars and also helped to create an anthropologically oriented group of psychoanalysts such as Otto Rank, Geza Roheim, and Theodor Reik.

The Psychoanalytical Movement - Early Followers and Dissidents:

Sigmund Freud himself wrote an essay on the" On the History of the Psychoanalytic Movement" in January, 1914. He is not specific about the date of his dissociation from Breuer. It seems clear that Breuer's devotion to a large clinical practice and Freud's own discovery that deep analysis produced better results than hypnosis, led to a gradual dissolution of their working partnership. Freud concentrated on the clinical practice of psychoanalysis and started formulating his combined theory of defence and repression in several papers and monographs. His *The Interpretation of Dreams* (1900) received a mixed reaction. It drew criticism, but also was hailed as an important contribution to psychology and psychiatry. It is considered his first major work.

A small group of Viennese physicians interested in psychotherapy soon became followers of Freud. In 1902 they started having meetings with him on Wednesday evenings to discuss clinical cases and theory. Freud (1914/1963), attributes the inspiration for this to Wilhelm Stekel, and acknowledges that it may have been the result of Stekel's recent analysis. From this modest beginning originated the Vienna Psychoanalytical Society, and the psychoanalytical movement, which eventually became not only one of the leading schools of psychiatry, but also one of the most important intellectual currents of the twentieth century.

Among Freud's early disciples were two future dissenters, Alfred Adler (1870-1937) and Wilhelm Stekel (1868-1940). Adler's contributions will be discussed later on. Presently, a few remarks will be made about Stekel. A colourful personality with a literary gift, Stekel was a prolific writer. Although he remained faithful to the tenets of psychoanalysis, he disagreed with Freud on certain important points. Stekel, also a dream interpreter, believed in a short psychoanalytic therapy during which the psychoanalyst played a more active part than in orthodox psychoanalysis (Stekel, 1950). More than any theoretical disagreement, Stekel's erratic personality led to Freud's disapproval of him and the eventual break between the two in 1912. Stekel afterward introduced some new elements to psychoanalytical theory. He suggested that the unconscious of certain events was a make-believe, a semi-intentional denial of an unpleasant truth by the patient. It was a willful suppression of awareness rather than a repression (Stekel, 1927). Stekel also believed that some neuroses resulted from suppression of guilt feelings about morally reprehensible deeds. He attached a great importance to aggressive drives and considered anxiety to be a reaction of the life instinct against the death instinct (Ellenberger, 1970). However, in Stekel's case, death instinct apparently won; he committed suicide in London in 1940.

Freud's followers increased rapidly in number. By 1907 and 1908 foreign doctors were coming to Freud in order to learn the new therapy. Only the most important names will be mentioned here. Paul Federn (1872-1950) introduced the concept of ego-boundary and that of depersonalisation. He was also instrumental, together with Helen Deutsch and Hermann Nunberg, in organizing the Vienna Institute of Psychoanalysis.

In Switzerland at Burghoelzli, a group of young psychiatrists led by Carl Gustav Jung (1875-1961) were quite interested in psychoanalysis and became active members of the movement. In 1907 Jung met Freud and officially joined the psychoanalytical association. Freud was impressed by Jung's erudition and supported his candidacy for the presidency of the International Psychoanalytical Association in 1910. Jung also organized the first international psychoanalytical congress in Salzburg in 1908. However, important theoretical differences led to a break between Jung and Freud in 1913. Apart from Jung, whose contributions will be discussed in greater detail, the Burghoelzli group included Karl Abraham (1877-1925), Max Eitingon (1881-1943), Ludwig Binswanger (1881-1966), and Abraham Brill (1874-1928), who was a visitor from the United States. Eugene Bleuler, the director of Burghoelzli and professor of psychiatry at Zurich University also became interested in psychoanalysis. Although he did not identify with the movement, the influence of psychoanalytical theory may be discerned in Bleuler's book on schizophrenia (1911). Binswanger subsequently became the director of the private sanatorium at Kreuzlingen where Bertha Pappenheim had been treated. He became the leading existentialist psychiatrist without breaking with the psychoanalytical movement. Other members of the Swiss group were Alphons Meader, Franz Rilkin, an ethnologist, and Oskar Pfister (1873-1956), a clergyman, both non-medical. Also Swiss, was Hermann Rorschach (1884-1922), a student of Bleuler. Officially, he was not a member of the psychoanalytical group, though interested in and influenced by it. Rorschach is best remembered for having designed an inkblot test which is named after him. The idea was not new. Apparently Leonardo da Vinci used paint blotches to stimulate fantasy. Julius Kerner, a poet-physician, and representative of German Romantic medicine, published a series of inkblots in conjunction with the verses inspired by them. In 1900, George Whipple made some early attempts to develop an inkblot test. Rorschach published his version of the test in 1921 (Alexander & Selesnick, 1966). Freud himself regarded the Swiss group in Zuerich as the most important in fighting for the international acceptance of the new therapy (Freud, 1914/ 1963).

In Germany itself, the Berlin Psychoanalytical Institute was established by Abraham and Eitingon, who were trained at the Zuerich

Clinic, It grew out of their psychoanalytical group. Abraham made important contributions to the psychoanalytical theory of character formation. It is he who described anal and oral personalities in detail. He also wrote several papers on melancholia.

Other important early members of the psychoanalytical movement were Otto Rank (1884-1939), a sociologist and anthropologist from Vienna, and Sandor Ferenczi (1873-1933), a physician from Budapest; also Ernest Jones (1879-1958) a neurologist from Great Britain who became the biographer of Freud. The contribution of Rank will be discussed later. He had separated from Freud in 1929 and struck out on his own. Ferenczi was mainly interested in psychotherapeutic techniques. He believed in a more "active therapy" than was offered by orthodox psychoanalysis. He believed in a greater degree of emotional involvement between doctor and patient than Freud envisaged. In the course of this involvement, emotions of the patient were "intensified." In spite of the difference of views on the technique of psychoanalysis, Ferenczi, who never broke away from Freud was regarded by him, as a friend. Finally, Hanns Sachs (1881-1947), a lawyer, should be mentioned. He and Rank were two non-medical followers of Freud. Sachs joined the Berlin psychoanalytical group. Abraham, Sachs, Rank, Eitingon, Ferenczi, and Jones became members of the so-called "inner circle" of Freud's disciples. These were all particularly close to him.

The United States provided a fertile soil for psychoanalytical theories. The Darwinian theory of evolution, Dewey's pragmatism, and functionalism in academic psychology, stressed the importance of adjustment and of the psychological mechanisms responsible for it. Psycho-analytical theory cast important light on these topics. Abraham Brill of New York, who became acquainted with psychoanalysis in Zurich, and James Putnam (1846-1918), a Boston neurologist, became pioneers of psychoanalysis on the American continent. They were soon joined by Smith Ely Jelliffe (1866-1945), a New York neuropsychiatrist who was a pioneer of psychosomatic medicine, and William Alanson White (1870-1937), a psychiatrist at St. Elizabeth Hospital in Washington, D.C., Granville Stanley Hall (1844-1924), a prominent developmental psychologist and educator, played an important role in propagating psychoanalytical theory in non-medical circles. Hall, who became president of Clark University, invited Freud and Jung to its vigentennial celebration in 1909. On the same occasion, Adolph Meyer received an honorary degree from Clark.

On the European continent, the psychoanalytical movement existed outside the mainstream of academic psychiatry. Yet there were important points of contact between the two. The academic psychiatrists in German-speaking counties were oriented towards clinical practice in mental hospitals or university clinics. Their main interest was in psychotic patients. Their theory was primarily organic. Yet an important encounter between psychoanalysis and the mainstream of psychiatry took place at Burghoelzli. Its director, Eugene Bleuler, was at the time one of the leading psychiatrists in Europe. He became interested in psychoanalysis and tried to reconcile an organic theory of schizophrenia with a psychodynamic explanation of its symptoms. Thus, psychoanalytical theory was found to be useful in dealing with psychotic patients in mental hospitals. The significance of this development went beyond the Burghoelzli circles and the psychoanalytical movement. It ended the split between the psychiatry of the mental hospital, which was concerned with psychotic patients, and that of the consulting office where psychotherapists treated psychoneurotics. During the previous century psychotics had been treated in mental hospitals by alienists, while psychoneurotics had been treated in private practice by neurologists or "nerve doctors." The latter had also treated organic-neurological patients in general hospitals. The new realignment left the organic neurological cases in the hands of neurologists, while psychiatrists began treating both psychotics and neurotics. Thus psychiatry left the confines of mental hospitals and ceased to be a specialty concerned with the insane.

Another important contact of psychoanalysis with academic psychiatry, was through Otto Poetzl (1877-1962), who was the chief assistant of Julius Wagner-Jauregg and eventually succeeded him in the chair of neurology and psychiatry at the University of Vienna. He had graduated in medicine from Vienna in 1901 and became a psychiatric specialist in 1911, after working from 1903 to 1908 at the Lower Austrian Asylum of Kiellzg-Gegging. Only in 1919 did be become an associate professor at Vienna. Poetzl was a brilliant neurologist who tried to synthesize the organic and the psychological points of view. In his work on aphasia and neurologically caused perceptual disorders, Poetzl found that he could not separate the organic from the functional or psychological determinants of speech and perceptual defects. Therefore he rejected the brain localization theories of many neurologists. Instead, he emphasized the holistic point of view, conceiving brain activity in terms of a field theory. Poetzl believed that there was an isomorphism between the organization of brain activity and psychological phenomena.

In his studies of word-blindness and of word-deafness, published in the *Zur Klinik und Anatomie der reinen Worttaubheit* (Berlin, 1919), Poetzl praised the new "Freudian psychology." It "bridged" the boundaries between cerebral pathological studies and observation using psychological methods. He did not think there was any loss in "exactness" if one introduced a "psychology of the unconscious" to "brain pathology." In spite of this, he maintained that real brain lesions, caused word-blindness. He developed a more anatomical idea of causation in his work on aphasia: *Die Aphasielehre vom Standpunkte der klinischen Psychiatrie* (Leipzig, Vienna, 1928). However, the work dealt with more than aphasia and included optical disorders and memory disturbances. Agnosia, a perceptual disorder which occurred in the grouping and selection of percepts, occurred in only three of the five senses. These were vision, hearing, and feeling. Such ideas were continued in his collaboration with Paul Schilder (1886-1940), as both men did work on body image and its disorders.

Both Poetzl and Schilder became interested in psychoanalysis. Only Schilder became a member of Freud's circle and a practicing analyst. In 1928, however, Schilder was invited by Adolph Meyer to the Phipps Clinic as a visiting professor at Johns Hopkins. He stayed permanently in the United States, first at Phipps and then at Bellevue Hospital in New York City until his tragic death in 1940. Since Schilder went beyond the Freudian theory and tried to synthesize neurology, psychoanalysis and phenomenology, his contributions will be discussed further in the section dealing with the impact of phenomenological philosophy on psychiatry.

In 1917 Poetzl confirmed psychoanalytical theory in his experiments on dreaming. He exposed subjects to a tachistoscopic display of pictures, which the subjects had to describe and to draw afterwards. He found that during the night, the subjects dreamed about the details of the pictures which they failed to report or to record in their drawings. This finding became known as the "Poetzl phenomenon." It was interpreted as a return of the repressed material during the dream.

Although Freud inspired loyalty in the members of the original psychoanalytical movement, three of his early disciples became dissidents: Alfred Adler, Carl Gustav Jung, and Otto Rank. All of them formulated theories considerably different from Freud's. Each established his own school and each had his own following. There was also considerable affect involved in their "break" with Freud. All of them also emphasized the role of society and cultural factors in shaping the psychodynamics of the individual to a much greater extent than Freud. Although these theories sought to explain human behaviour by forces emanating from the unconscious mind, they made a clear break away from Freudian reductionism. Carl Gustav Jung and Otto Rank especially emphasized the principles of personality growth, of self-actualization, and the spirituality of man. Their theories anticipated the Humanistic or "Third Force" psychology, and existentialist psychiatry which became prominent after the second World War.

Alfred Adler. Alfred Adler (1870-1937) was born in Vienna where he spent the early part of his life. His father was a merchant of quite modest means, yet the family lived in a suburban and semi-rural environment. Adler graduated in medicine from the University of Vienna in 1895 and went on to practice general medicine with a special interest in ophthalmology and neurology. For a period of time he was associated with the Viennese Poliklinik where he probably met Moritz Benedikt. Adler was far more politically involved than Freud, and had joined the Austrian Social Democratic Party. He identified with the underdog and became interested in social problems. His early interest was in social medicine and his first publication dealt with health problems of the tailoring trade (Adler, 1898).

Adler met Freud in 1902. Even as a member of Freud's original group he tended to be rather independent and to develop his own theories. His early theory was that of organ inferiority (Adler, 1907/1917). Adler believed that each individual suffers from a biological inferiority of an organ or system of organs for which he tries to compensate. This was the early version of the inferiority feeling or "inferiority complex" which played such an important role in Adler's future theorizing. Freud accepted the theory of organ inferiority as an important complement to psychoanalytical theory. However, Freud's and Adler's views clashed when the latter put forward the theory of "Masculine Protest" as the main motive which explained human behaviour. According to this theory, human beings were constitutionally bi-sexual with the masculine component expressed in aggressive drives. These produced a quest for dominance over other people and the world. Adler believed that the "will to power," the concept which he took from Nietzsche, was the dominant drive instead of the libido. (At the first Wednesday evening meeting of Freud's circle, Adler discussed Nietzsche's *The Genealogy of Morals*.) This theory was unacceptable to Freud and resulted in Adler's resignation from the Psychoanalytical Society. He and a small group of followers formed their own group which eventually became known as the Society of Individual Psychology. As time went by, Adler put less stress on biological factors and emphasized the social ones instead. He also focused on the uniqueness and moral autonomy of each individual. This brought him close to the point of view espoused subsequently by the humanists and existentialists. His other two important publications were *The Neurotic Constitution* (1912/1917), and *Understanding Human Nature* (1927). The last was reprinted in paperback in the United States and had a mass circulation, especially after the second World War.

Adler had been in the Austrian army during the first World War, and as an ardent Social Democrat found a new freedom in the fledgling Austrian Republic which emerged from the collapse of the Austro-Hungarian Monarchy. Encouraged by many associates, he became involved in applying his individual psychology to pedagogy, child guidance, and in training child psychiatrists. In 1932 Adler moved to the United States, where he taught briefly and lectured widely. He died suddenly in Aberdeen, Scotland, in 1937, while on a lecture tour of Great Britain. He has had an enormous influence on educational psychology which became common in American general education. His followers, including Rudolf Dreikurs (1897-1972), continued his psychoanalytical work in the Chicago Adlerian Institute (Dreikurs,1950). Dreikurs was especially interested in child guidance, educational psychology, and the effect of early childhood memories on life styles.

In contrast to Freud, Adler stressed the holistic aspect of human personality. According to him, man was an organic, purposeful, system with the goal of self-realization and of social survival. Consequently, he rejected Freud's tripartite model of Id, Superego, and Ego. Adler argued that the foremost need of man was to perceive himself as an integrated whole, purposefully striving to achieve individually determined goals. Man was striving for superiority in order to overcome the feelings of inferiority which he had once experienced as a small and helpless child. The early feelings of inferiority of the child became a "complex of inferiority," which persisted to adulthood. Every individual formulated his subjective goals to be attained in the future. He was oriented towards these goals and organized his experiences and motives into his "life style." His goals were fictitious ideals, which nevertheless had a subjective reality for man. Adler's theory of "life styles" and of fictitious ideals were influenced by the philosophy of Idealistic Positivism of Hans Vaihinger (1852-1933) as presented in his book, *The Philosophy of the As If* (1911). According to this German philosopher, absolute truths and ideal norms did not exist. However, man created them as fictions that were important for individual and social survival. Adler believed that an individual's "life style" was his unique adaptation to his social milieu, which contributed to his social integration, but at the same time allowed for individual autonomy. The development of the individual was neither biologically nor socially determined, but was to a great extent self-determined. As he progressed along his life path, the individual made free choices of his goals which he wanted to attain. This aspect of Adler's theory anticipated the views of the humanistic and existentialist psychologists. There is a similarity between Adler's concept of "life style" and that of the "project" developed by existentialists.

According to Adler, the regnant human motive was not libido, but the "will to power," which was a drive to dominate others. He took this concept from Nietzsche. However, this motive implied, as in Nietzsche, not only dominance, but also the need to attain the meaningfulness and significance of life. The "will to power" was tempered by "social feeling" (*Gemeinschaftsgefuehl*) which represented a need to belong, to be integrated into society and to serve a useful social purpose. An unbridled "will to power" produced a conflict between man and society that produced isolation and neurotic maladjustment.

Psychoneurosis was the product of childhood experiences, mostly of neglect or overprotection by the parents. These experiences created in the child a negative self-image of weakness and helplessness. They also made society appear hostile and rejecting. The complex of inferiority and the negative self-image produced attempts at compensation which resulted in neurotic symptoms. There was a warping of the total personality and the tendency to adopt a maladaptive "life style." An inability to cope with the feelings of inferiority may lead to depression (Adler, 1964).

Adler attached a much greater importance to the family constellation and the child's ordinal position in it, than to the Oedipus complex. The early experiences of organ inferiority, early memories, determined life style. Later, Adler de-emphasized the importance of early experiences as the determining factors of human fate. He came to believe that ultimately the inner psychological world was each individual's own creation, rather than a product of external causes (Adler, 1938).

Adler stressed the uniqueness of each individual. Therefore he rejected the nosological categories of psychoneurosis and psychosis. He considered each clinical case as a unique attempts at adjustment by an individual. Individual patients, in their attempts to develop their consistent "life style" and to enhance their self-concepts, were using such mechanisms as "conquest through weakness." The last manifested itself as a flight into simulated physical illness. The purpose of it was to control other people, usually members of the family. Adler also described certain misguided life styles such as "the getting," "the ruling," and "the avoiding" as maladjustice. However, each individual patient created a unique constellation of symptoms, a unique *Gestalt*, which could be understood only in the context of individual development as this was subjectively perceived by each patient (Adler, 1964). A historian of psychoanalysis like Clara Thompson, has praised Adler for his emphasis on the total personality (Thompson, 1950).

Carl Gustav Jung. Carl Gustav Jung (1875-1961) was born in the little village of Kesswil in Switzerland. However, he grew up, and received his education and his medical degree at Basel University. Basel was the city in which the great Renaissance physician Paracelsus had practiced and taught. It was the city in which Ignaz Troxler, a Nature Philosopher, had taught philosophy early in the nineteenth century. Nietzsche had been a Classics professor there. The teachings of these three men, although greatly separated in time, anticipated Jung's own theories (Haenel, 1982). Quite early in his career, Jung became interested in psychology, philosophy, religion and occult phenomena. He became familiar with the writings of the Nature Philosophers, with the work of hypnotists and with the tradition of Romantic medicine. He was influenced by Theodore Flournoy, a professor of psychology at Geneva who explored cases of multiple personality. Jung's own doctoral thesis was about the case of a young woman who was a subject of mediumistic trances. He researched this by placing her under hypnosis. He found that she displayed similar features as one of Flournoy's patients, Helene Smith. Her case also had some similarity with that of the "seeress of Prevorst" described by Justinus Kerner. Motivated by these interests, Jung decided to become a psychiatrist. At the end of 1900 he joined the staff of Buerghoelzli Hospital in Zuerich. There he trained under the famous Eugene Bleuler and became his chief assistant, then also a *Privatdozent* at Zuerich University. As part of his training, Jung had also gone to Paris to spend some time with Pierre Janet.

It was during the early years that he spent at Burghoelzli that Jung did word association experiments with both patients and normal subjects. He eventually developed a word association test (Jung, 1906/1919). The experimentation on word association was originated by Francis Galton and was continued by several psychiatrists and psychologists, including Kraepelin. Theodor Ziehen (1862-1950), a philosopher, psychologist, and psychiatrist, carried out pioneering work in experimental psychology and the psychophysiology of emotion. He also did some work on word associations, with juvenile and forensic patients. Ziehen claimed that by word associations it was possible to uncover emotional complexes or "emotionally charged complexes of representation" (Ellenberger, 1970, p.692). Ziehen was concerned with defining the "I" or ego, what William James called the "permanent self." It represented a constant entity and a unity. As such, it was not substantial, nor was the so called soul of the people (*Volksseele*). Ziehen was also concerned with the conceptions of consciousness and the unconscious in psychology and did not think that consciousness represented a "substantial" psychic unity. Psychology had to be grounded in autochthonous methods which were (1) subjective or introspective, and (2) objective. The introspective was considered more reliable than an objective one (Ziehen, 2 vols., 1915).

Jung borrowed the conception of "complex" from Ziehen and eventually it was appropriated by all psychodynamic schools. In 1907, Jung published a book on the psychology of dementia praecox. In that book he attributed this condition to psychogenic causes such as an emotional conflict. If a conflict persisted, however, it could lead to physiological disorder and the secretion of a "toxin X" which affected the functioning of the brain.

Together with other members of the Burghoelzli group, Jung became interested in Freud's theories and began a correspondence with him. After meeting Freud in 1907, Jung became an active member of the psychoanalytical movement. As the leader of the Swiss psychoanalytical group he was the editor of the *Jahrbuch fuer psychoanalytische und psychopathologische Forschungen*. However, about 1911, important differences surfaced between the views of Jung and Freud. In *The Psychology of the Unconscious* (1911/1916), an English translation for the original title, which meant "metamorphosis and the symbols of the libido," Jung rejected Freud's theory of libido which equated such drives with sexual instinct. The Freudian conception of sexual drive was broadened into a theory of general psychic energy by Jung. He distinguished this kind of force or energy from sheer physical energy because it had both cause and purpose, while physical energy had only a cause. In 1913, Jung broke with Freud and resigned from the Vienna Psychoanalytical Association. About the same time he left Burghoelzli and also had resigned as a *Privatdozent* at Zuerich University (1909) in order to enter private practice. He eventually created his own institute for analytic psychology in Switzerland. Not until 1933-42 did he resume his academic ties by becoming a titular professor at the Technical University in Zuerich. In 1944 he became a full professor for medical psychology at Basel University.

Over the years, Jung developed both a theory of personality and a system of psychotherapy. This became his unique kind of "Analytical Psychology." Unfortunately only a brief outline of his extremely complex theory, rich in ramifications, may be presented here (Jung, 1923, 1928, 1933, 1938, 1939a, 1939b, 1953, 1957, 1964; also Wilhelm & Jung, 1931, Jacobi,1962). Jung offered a model of mind structure which was more complex than the one presented by Freud. According to him, the human mind was divided into three broad areas: consciousness, the individual unconscious, and the collective unconscious. Consciousness was the domain of the rational. It represented the "Apollonian" aspect of human nature. The center of consciousness was the ego which was the point of reference for subjective experiences and was the initiator of voluntary acts. It was presented to the external world as the *persona* or mask. The individual was an actor here, playing social roles, and conforming socially while his ego remained inauthentic.

The individual unconscious was the domain of personal, repressed, memories and impulses. These were socially unacceptable. Beyond the individual unconscious lay the collective unconscious. The enormous reservoir of creative fantasy which was in the collective unconscious made the formation of much of the content of the conscious possible. Here the unconscious obtained the same positive creative meaning which it seemed to imply in Eduard von Hartmann's theory, which distinguished it from the negative connotations of primitive instinctual elements that characterized Freud's theory. Consciousness moved between the two poles of instinct and spirit, while the forces of the will tried to free themselves from the instinctual world of determinacy.

The individual unconscious contained the "shadow" of the individual, the dark side of his nature. This incorporated evil, animal-like "Dionysian" aspects of his nature. In dreams these were represented by a devil or a demon. Rather than sex, they reflected internal conflicts. The other structure of the individual unconscious was the *anima* in man, and the *animus* in women. These entities represented the repressed characteristics of the opposite sex. They were present in every male and female, and appeared in their dreams as respectively female and male figures. Further, the individual unconscious was filled with autonomous complexes. These consisted of ideas and their related emotions. There they had become dissociated from the rest of the personality.

Beyond the individual unconscious, there was the collective unconscious. Here the ancestral memories reposed. One reason that Jung's theories aroused criticism during the 1930s, was that he described the memories in the unconscious as having been acquired characteristics inherited in a Lamarckian fashion. Many of these memories were common to all members of an individual family, sometimes to all members of a tribe, or even to an entire nation. Sometimes these memories were even common to all members of the human species, or they were memories of man's animal ancestors.

The idea of a collective unconscious was one that Jung had borrowed from nineteenth century Romantics and Nature Philosophers. At times, Jung called the collective unconscious the "objective mind," and believed that at its deepest level it merged with the world soul from which sprang the individual's psyche. These ideas showed a definite trace of the idealism of both Schelling and Hegel. While the ego dominated consciousness, the real center of the psyche was the self. It faced both the conscious and the unconscious. It integrated all the personality functions and controlled personality growth. In the process of individuation, the gap between the ego and the self was bridged. The full potential of the personality was realized. A state of maturity or "wisdom" was attained.

Jung had a structuralist view of the collective unconscious. It was characterized by certain tendencies or polarities, precipitated from collective memories. These tendencies determined a set of inborn categories of individual experience. They were innate ideas with the help of which the world was perceived, sensed or felt, then reflected or thought about. As constants, they were *archetypes.* They were represented by standard symbols which designated broad categories of intellectual and emotional experience. The archetypal symbols appeared in dreams, in cultural myths and in psychotic delusions. They were common to all of humanity and existed in different historical periods.They constituted a universal language of symbols which had been postulated originally, by von Schubert, a Nature Philosopher. The archetype of the human soul was symbolized by female soul and male spirit (*anima* and *animus*). These terms actually referred to "soul." The archetype of the spirit was represented by the symbol of the "wise old man." Jung had been very much influenced by Nietzsche and considered the figure of the prophet Zarathustra as an example of this archetype.

Other archetypal symbols were *Magna Mater* or "mother earth," the mother goddess, a symbol of fertility and abundance. In addition, there were archetypes of the "hero" and the "beast." However, the most important archetype was the *mandala* which was symbolized by a circle, and was taken from Hindu mythology. It stood for the principle of personal fullness, "individuation," and integration. The archetypes were responsible not only for the structure of experience of the external world, but also for guiding personality growth in order to attain higher levels of development. According to Freud, symbols stood for and disguised certain aspects of experience. Jung attributed a more vital and positive role to symbols. They not only disguised, but also sublimated and transmuted the lower forms of mental life to the higher ones by acting as catalysts to mobilize mental energy. For him, sublimation was not a defence mechanism. It was revelatory and was a mechanism by which lower motives were replaced by higher ones. As a result, the psyche progressed to a higher level of development.

In the development of his ideas, Jung was influenced by Oriental mysticism. He studied Zen-Buddhism, Tibetan philosophy, Taoism, as well as the Gnostics. He was also influenced by concepts borrowed from medieval alchemists. Their alchemic concepts had a hidden meaning, originally known only to the initiates into the art of alchemy. They really referred to unconscious mental processes rather than to chemical reactions. These represented hostility to the Church, survivals of pre-Christian culture, mostly disguised against charges of heresy in allegories. Here Jung was definitely influenced by Paracelsus to whom he also refers as having used the plural, "gods" (Jung, 1953). Jung tried to work through the pagan materials of his own heritage, perhaps as Freud did in his *Moses.* The relationship of Christianity to alchemy was discussed including such hidden meanings as the alchemist's "four in one" which became the symbol of the cross and for Christ. As historical philosophy, it is interesting to contrast Jung's theory of civilization with Freud's here. While Freud sees decline tied to the dominance of the death instinct, Jung too believed that the collective unconscious threw out more symbols whenever decay set in, in the conscious social realm in times of crisis. Here the "numinous" (prophetic) individuals who could display more archetypal content, emerged so that they could form "new dominants." Many neurotics had such activated archetypes which appeared because there was a crisis. They were melancholy because they no longer believed in the socially established "dominants" and wanted a direct experience with the everlasting roots. One might observe, that they wanted to escape from the Nietzschean 'God is dead!' notion which had appeared in the educated culture of the twentieth century. It was the alchemical mystique which tended to make these explanations less than credible. In a more traditional form, they also find expression in Arnold Toynbee's philosophy of history, again, written in response to the sense of decline common in the 1930s. Here the minority elite of the decaying culture, as the Christians in the case of the declining Roman one, open the way to the new civilization in which they become dominant. These elites would be the "numinous" types in the Jungian realm.

The human pscyhe was more than the self. The self was more than the conscious ego since it included the whole person including his unconscious as well. The psyche was characterized by two instrinsic attitudes which were basic to its functioning. These were *extraversion* and *introversion*. Jung had borrowed these designations from Otto Gross (1902) who had described them as basic characteristics of brain functions. Gross was a psychiatrist in Graz, Austria and an early follower of Freud. Unfortunately, he developed schizophrenia and was then treated by Bleuler and Jung. It is also possible that Jung may have been influenced by the concept of introversion and extraversion described by Alfred Binet in his work on intelligence (Binet, 1903;Ellenberger, 1970). The latter had described two types of intelligence: the extraversive and the introversive.

For Jung, extraversion implied an involvement with the external world, while introversion referred to an interest in internal mental processes. In addition, there were four fundamental psychological functions: thinking, feeling, sensing, and intuiting. The first function was concerned with intellectual processes. The second referred to value judgments. These were both the rational functions. The third and fourth ones were irrational functions. They were concerned with the sensory and extrasensory immediate experience of reality. These two basic attitudes and four fundamental psychological functions were responsible for the existence of eight psychological types into which people could be classified (Jung, 1923). The development of the psychological attitudes and functions in one person was usually unbalanced. Any one attitude or any one function tended to be dominant. The others might remain underdeveloped, repressed, and relegated to the unconscious where they led a subterranean existence. In addition, modern Western man was cut off from those spiritual roots which originated in the collective unconscious. He was alienated from his tribal past and the archetypal symbols. The result was spiritual disorientation. This was characterized by a feeling of meaninglessness and a one-sided development. Life had become de-humanized. The world was perceived in mechanistic terms according to the dictates of modern scince. The awe-inspiring "numinous" or sacred character of reality experienced by primitive man had been lost by modern Western man. He was "out of touch" with the archetypes of his collective unconscious. There was a type of psychoneurosis, particularly common in middle aged people, which was not the result of conflict or frustration of instinctual drives. It emerged from a one-sided development and spiritual sterility. Such persons experienced a sense of meaninglessness and existential anxiety because their natural personality growth had been thwarted. The goal of personality was its maturing or growth, its self-individuation, and its self-realization. These concepts were similar to those of self-actualization in contemporary humanistic psychology. The underdeveloped personality functions have to be fully differentiated and integrated into the self. Jung here conceptualized the self as having a separate identity from the ego. It occupied the center of the personality and balanced consciousness with the unconscious. The *mandala* was the symbolic content representing unity, cast up by the unconscious during therapy. This process could eventually cure the patient. It was one of individuation which helped the patient to get in touch with his spiritual roots, through understanding the archetypes in his unconscious. This involved a temporary regression, a journey to the nether world, which was like the Nekyia episode of Homer's *Odyssey*. In this episode Ulysses travelled to the country of the dead. Similar as well, was the descent of Christ into Hell before he rose again on the third day after crucifixion to sit at the right hand of the God the Father.

In his explanation of mental processes Jung tended to de-emphasize causality and the past determinants of behaviour. His explanations were teleological. They stressed purpose and an orientation towards the future. He did not conside dreams to be recapitulations of repressed memories. They were creative endeavours of the unconscious aimed at solving current problems. They were to anticipate future events. According to Jung, personality growth was propagated by a tension created by forces which opposed each other. Thus we find consciousness juxtaposed to the unconscious, and thinking contrasted with feeling. Ultimately the opposites flowed into one another. Here Jung resurrected the principle of *enantiodormia* postulated by Heraclitus. A similar principle of *coincidentia oppositorum* (the coincidence of opposites) was proposed by Nicholas Cusa, the fifteenth century humanist thinker.

In its growth, the human personality tried to reach an equilibrium or balance. However, this was always transcended again so that it could attain a higher level of development. Jung stressed the spiritual needs of man against the purely biological ones. Neurosis was due to a thwarted personality development and a failure of self-realization or self-individuation. This caused suffering but it could also have a positive effect when it resulted in a regression and a mobilization of unconscious forces. The final result could be an integration of personality on a broader basis and a higher level of development. This applied also in cases of schizophrenia in which the alienated consciousness was flooded by unconscious archetypal material that threatened its disintegration. With proper therapy, the unconscious archetypes could be integrated as religious symbols and brought under the control of the ego. Disruptive psychotic experiences were replaced by socially sanctioned and religious ones.

Jung distinguished two kinds of psychotherapy. First, the reductive-analytic, and secondly, the synthetic-hermeneutic. The first referred to therapy along Freudian and Adlerian lines. It was applicable to younger patients whose conflicts were the result of their biological drives. The second, was more specifically Jungian. It could be applied to middle-aged patients concerned about their spiritual and existential problems. It was oriented towards the future rather than towards the past. In any psychotherapy, the main task of the therapist was to bring the patient back to reality. It was aiming at making him aware of his present situation. Once he was engaged in a relationship with the social world he would be able to experience inner peace.

Here Jung used the search for archetypes and unconscious materials as a way of leading the patient back to reality on a higher plane. Once the deeper understanding was achieved, there could be fulfillment for men and women who could then find their spirit (the man) and their soul (the woman).

Otto Rank. Among the three important disciples of Freud, Otto Rank (1884-1939) was, like Adler and Jung, one of the earlier followers of the great master. Like them, he also broke away from Freud and formulated his own theory. Rank's psychoanalytical theory eventually became quite different from Freud's. For a long time Rank was a "*Wunderkind*" of the psychoanalytical movement. A protegé of Freud, he impressed everyone with his brilliance and erudition. Rank became Freud's secretary and associate editor of the psychoanalytical journals. Rank was not medically qualified, but had a doctorate in philosophy-sociology-ethnology, from the University of Vienna. He tried to use psychoanalytic ideas in order to interpret literature, as he did in his first book, *Der Kuenstler* (1907). Here he tried to explain artistic creativity by Freud's theories. Rank also worked on applying psychoanalytical theory to mythology and comparative religion. In 1914 he published *Myth of the Birth of the Hero*. In that book he analyzed the common theme of many legends about a national or religious hero who was described as immaculately conceived and coming out of water, the sea, or a river. Freud was himself, influenced by this idea when he wrote his work on *Moses.* Rank applied psychoanalytical theory to explain symbols that appeared in mythology. He drew a parallel to the symbols in dreams.

Eventually, a conflict developed between Rank and Freud because of Rank's criticism of Freudian treatment which appeared in the book by Ferenczi and Rank, *Development and Goals of Psychoanalysis* (1923). They advocated a shortening of psychoanalytical treatment, seting a termination date for treatment, and placing more emphasis on the emotional experiences of the patient. Freud disapproved of this work, although the final breach between Rank and Freud was caused by Rank's *Trauma of Birth* (1924). Here Rank completely reformulated Freud's theory. He argued that the memory of birth trauma was the underlying experience of all subsequent anxiety feelings. Man was torn by the conflicting desire to return to the womb and his fears of the womb. This essential mechanism was the basis of all psychopathological disorders. Feeble attempts at reconciliation failed, and Rank separated from Freud in 1929 to establish his own psychoanalytical school.

Rank rejected Freud's theories and methods of treatment, especially in their reductionist, mechanistic, and determinist aspects. Instead he emphasized voluntarism and the relativity of human nature. The patient's will, his self determinism, and his freedom became essential. Rank adopted a more humanistic orientation in his later works and completely rejected biological and social determinism (Rank, 1932, 1950, 1952, 1958, 1964).

It was mentioned earlier, that Freud was influenced by two different and conflicting philosophical traditions: the first was the positivistic-mechanistic, or Lockean; the second was the vitalistic-voluntaristic, or Leibnizian one. Following this distinction, Rank can definitely be classified as belonging to the vitalist-voluntarist tradition. He embodied the Romantic version of Humanism (Weckowicz, 1984). In the spectrum of various psychological systems stemming from the Freudian psychoanalytical movement, perhaps Rank may be placed on the opposite theoretical pole to Freud. Sigmund Freud was, of course, influenced by the Romantic tradition, but remained faithful to the end of his life, to the tenets of the Helmholtzian school of medicine. He always insisted that psychoanalysis was a science.

Rank, in contrast, rejected the scientific approach to psychology and psychotherapy completely in his later years. He was influenced by the philosophies of Schopenhauer and Nietzsche, and in his writings he singled out irrationalism and voluntarism as the key concepts to understanding human behaviour. Rank saw man as being torn between three sets of polarizing forces. These were (1) will versus impulse, (2) individuality versus conformity, and finally (3) spirituality versus biological instincts. However, the most important polarity was between the fear of life and the fear of death. These fears stemmed from the primordial experience of the birth trauma (Rank, 1952). The latter induced a fear of the novel extrauterine life and produced a desire to go back to the womb. The fear of life was counteracted by the fear of death, a fear of being annihilated as an autonomous individual. These two basic fears were the ones underlying the conflict between a desire for individuation and autonomy, as against a desire for social conformity and anonymity. These fears also lurked behind yet another conflict. This was the one between the sexual impulse to procreate biologically, and the desire to attain cultural immortality as a hero or an artist. Man attempted to transcend his biological nature and to assert his spirituality. The fear of death and the desire for immortality was the driving force behind cultural progress. At the core of Rank's psychological theory was the concept of will. This was not a desire for power, but a positive, guiding, and creative force controlled by the ego. It was an organizing and integrating agent that brought about self-individuation and autonomy. In contrast to Freud, Rank stressed the freedom of will and the self-determination of the ego. He quoted the Kantian motto: "determine thyself from thyself" (Rank, 1964, p.293). Rank rejected the biological and social determinism as illustrated by the following quotation:

> Freud being psychologically as deterministic as Darwin was biologically and Marx economically, made the less excusable error. By applying Darwin's biological and Marx's social determinism to the personality itself, he deprived it of the very qualities which make man's life human: autonomy, responsibility and conscience." (Rank, 1958, p.34).

In the Rankian system, the "self-ideal" played the role of the Freudian superego. However, the "self-ideal" did not consist of an internalized parental figure and of extrinsic social mores. It embodied the intrinsic values created by the self and those which were original to it. Rank stressed individuality, uniqueness, and creative self-actualization as the goals of personality development. He also attributed an intrinsic value to anxiety and guilt. Both of them resulted from the perception of the human condition and were driving forces motivating individual growth. The similarity between the ideas of Rank and those of Kierkegaard and other existentialists has recently been pointed out by Becker (1973). In many ways, Rank was closer to existentialism than to the American "Third Force" humanistic psychology. He did not share the optimistic outlook on man and life which is characteristic of contemporary American humanistic psychologists. Rank viewed the human predicament as intrinsically tragic, and the revelation of its truth as not conducive to happiness, but to the "courage to be." Most people tended to deceive themselves by lies as did Ibsen's hero, Peer Gynt (Rank, 1950). On the other hand, some schizophrenic patients had insight into life's truths.

Rank (1958) was hostile to the science of psychology. He did not believe that generally valid principles of such a science could be established. The psychologies of men and women were different, as were the psychologies of men living in different epochs and having a different *Weltanschauung*. Also, values were relative and individually created. Rank's idea of values in this respect, resembled that of Nietzsche. Here Rank expressed the essential hermeneutical relationship of the "horizon" of the contemporary observer versus that of humans alive at the time of an event. Rank rejected any notion of the constancy of human psychology for the formation of values. These varied throughout history.

In *Art and Artist* (1932) Rank compared the well-adjusted, conforming, "normal" man with the psychoneurotic and the artist. The conforming man suppressed his fear of death and was motivated by his fear of life. He played safe by conforming to collective norms. As a result, he was alienated from himself, failed to be himself or to self-actualize. The "normal" man, however stable and well adjusted, represented the lowest level of personality development. Both the artist and the hero represented the highest level of personality development. The artist self-actualized himself by creating a work of art incorporating new aesthetic values. The hero self-actualized by creating the new ethical values which provided the edge of advancing cultural evolution. The artist and the hero fulfilled themselves creatively and obtained spiritual immortality. The neurotic was a failed artist or a failed hero (*artiste manque*). He detached himself from the collectivity in an attempt to become an autonomous individual. In the process, he became alienated from the society and was no longer duty-bound to it. However, his fear of life prevented him from achieving full self-actualization. Torn by the conflict between the fear of life and the fear of death, he became immobilized in his progress and frustrated in his creative strivings. As a result, he was overcome by a feeling of existential guilt, because he did not fulfill his potential. His level of development was higher than that of the "normal" conforming man, but lower than that of the artist or the hero. He had left the safety of social conformity, but had not realized his individuality. Thus, Rank perceived a positive aspect of psychoneurosis, as a potential stepping stone to a higher level of personality development.

After his arrival in the United States, Otto Rank joined the staff of the University of Pennsylvania School of Social Work and became leader of the Philadelphia "functional" school of social work. His main influence was on social workers who preferred his brand of short dynamic psychotherapy to the orthodox psychoanalysis. Rank's theories also influenced Carl Rogers in the development of his psychological system and his technique of non-directive, client-centered counselling.

The Psychoanalytical Movement After the Death of Freud

After the death of Freud in 1939, the emigration of psychoanalysts from Germany and Austria to the United States and Great Britain caused by the political exigencies of National Socialism, led to the the transplantation of the psychoanalytical movement to new soil. As a result, psychoanalytical theory developed in two different directions. One was that of the psychoanalytical theory of the total personality and the ego. The other was a shift away from the biological towards the sociological orientation. This was associated with the ideas of the neo-Freudians like Karen Horney, Harry Stack Sullivan, Erich Fromm and Erik Erikson. These developments of the period between the two world wars and of the decades following the second World War are perhaps too recent to be evaluated from a historical perspective, nevertheless they are important.

In psychoanalytical theory and therapy there was a gradual shift away from the preoccupation with the repressed infantile memories and instinctual drives originating in the id, towards a greater interest in the ego defenses responsible for the current adjustment of the patient. Freud's topographical model was replaced by the structural model. The current balance between the id, the ego, and the superego came to be considered more important than the historical roots of the patient's symptoms. The analysis of the actual transference neurosis became more important than the recovery of forgotten memories of traumatic events in the past. Consequently, the focus of attention shifted to the functioning of the ego and away from the libidinal drives emanating from the id. In a psychotherapeutic situation, the analyst ceased to be a blank screen on which the image of the parental figure was projected. He became an actual person in his own right.

Some of these changes in psychoanalytical technique may be traced to Sandor Ferenczi (1926), who in the 1920s introduced changes in therapy. He attempted to intensify the patient's emotions during psychotherapy. He also encouraged a more relaxed and permissive atmosphere which would encourage the patient to perceive the therapist as a real person with whom the patient formed a relation which was in important ways different from the one which the patient had formed with the real parent. This new relation was a therapeutic corrective of the old one. For a therapeutic success it was important for the analyst to genuinely accept and like the patient. Ferenczi described these changes in his *Further Contribution to the Theory and Technique of Psychoanalysis* (1926).

Early contributions to ego psychology were made by Paul Federn and Paul Schilder. The former introduced the concept of ego boundary which could change, making the ego more or less inclusive. The latter studied the bodily image (Schilder, 1935) which provided the physical anchor for the ego. Anna Freud (1895-1982), the daughter of Sigmund, was a lay analyst who developed the concept of ego defenses. She described these in her *The Ego and the Mechanisms of Defense* (1937). Here she listed such defense mechanisms as repression, overcompensation, rationalization, projection, turning impulses against the self, isolation and identification with the aggressor as the mechanisms used by the ego to ward off unacceptable and anti-social impulses. Psychoanalytical therapy became an analysis of ego defense mechanisms used by the patient rather than as before, an attempt to recover forgotten traumatic memories. Anna Freud accompanied her father in his exile and became a member of the London Institute of Psychoanalysis.

The new insights into the defense mechanisms and the way of coping with conflicts led to a new interest in the analysis of the total personality and character. Wilhelm Reich (1897-1957) the maverick of the psychoanalytical movement developed a method of character analysis which he published in *Character Analysis* (1945).

Reich was associated with the Vienna Institute of Psychoanalysis before emigrating to the United States. In his theory he went back to the early distinction made by Freud between an "actual" neurosis and psychoneurosis which Freud subsequently abandoned. The "actual" neurosis was not caused by repressed psychological conflicts. It was, instead, to be explained by a blocking of the discharge of sexual impulse which resulted from sexual abstinence or *coitus interruptus*. Undischarged and damned up sexual energy interefered with the normal physiological functioning of the bodily organs. The human orgasm produced a discharge of physical energy. Mental and physical health depended on unimpeded discharge of sexual energy through frequent full orgasms (full orgiastic potency).

The characteristics of an individual's sexuality determined his personality and character. The character defenses developed as a result of past experiences and interfered with the normal exercise of sexuality. Another important aspect of psychoanalysis was the analysis of character defenses and resistences. Character defenses were responsible for neurotic symptoms, inhibitions, anxieties, and thought distortions. They also manifested themselves in daily habits, mannerisms, muscular tension and physical posture. As physical manifestations they constituted an armour which had to be broken down by therapy. This included progressive muscular relaxation in addition to free association.

The goal of therapy was the the achievement of sexual freedom. Children and adolescents were to be liberated from enslavement by their authoritarian families. Reich was a representative of the Freudian left. He tried to reconcile psychoanalytical theory with Marxist ideology. The achievement of sexual freedom was for Reich an integral part of the liberation of man from the serfdom of capitalism.

As time went by, Reich's theories became progressively more eccentric and grandiose. He asserted that sexual energy pervaded the entire universe, and radiated from healthy bodies. Individuals who were mentally or physically ill were deficient in this energy. Reich apparently followed some of the nineteenth century mesmerist approaches. He went so far as to construct an apparatus, the so called "Orgone" box which captured and concentrated sexual energy. This reminds one of the magnetic container (*baquet*) filled with iron filings which the Mesmerists used during some of their seances.

Reich applied his Orgone therapy by putting patients inside the Orgone box and subjecting them to concentrated radiation of sexual energy. Reich attempted to treat cancer patients with his Orgone therapy as well. His treatments were suspect and he was eventually charged with fraud, sent to prison, and then declared insane. There was a similarity between Reich's cosmic sexual energy and the idea of a vital life force of nineteenth century thinkers. Uncanny too, was the similarity between the Orgone box and Anton Mesmer's animal magnetic fluid, and his *baquet.* The stage for Reich's activity was twentieth century America, while the setting for mesmerism was eighteenth century Paris.

Ego Psychology

Important contributions to psychoanalytical theory were made by Franz Alexander (1891-1964). Alexander received his medical degree from the University of Budapest. He was trained in psychoanalysis at the Berlin Psychoanalytic Institute. In 1930, he came to the United States and was appointed professor for psychoanalysis at the University of Chicago. He then founded the Chicago Institute for Psychoanalysis and became its director. Alexander made important contributions to psychoanalytical theory, to psychosomatic medicine and to criminology. His major work, *The Psychoanalysis of the Total Personality* (1930) compared psychopathological mechanisms of hysteria, of the obsessional-compulsive states, and of manic-depressive psychosis. In hysteria, symptoms simultaneously symbolized the gratification of sexual impulses and self-punishment. In obsessional-compulsive states, some symptoms symbolized the gratification of aggressive anti-social impulses. Still others symbolized the undoing of their gratification, also expiation and self-punishment. In manic-depressive psychosis, the maniacal phase was one of self-gratification and the depressive phase was that of self-punishment. Alexander made a distinction between the psychological mechanisms of shame and guilt. The latter was characterized by turning aggression against oneself, while the psychological mechanism of shame was characterized by rage and turning aggression against others. This distinction was further elaborated by Gerhart Piers and M.B. Singer (1953) who extended it to cultural phenomena and distinguished between guilt and shame cultures. Alexander tried to develop a functionalist theory of personality which combined the Freudian structuralist concept of Id, Ego, and Superego with the notion of psychological functions. These were perception, cognition, thinking, integration and motor control. He was against a reification of abstract concepts such as Id, Ego and Superego. According to Alexander, personality represented an adaptive system which was characterized by a hierarchy of functions. The ego represented the highest coordinating and integrating function. The novel ideas about the ego were further elaborated by Heinz Hartmann (1894-1970) in his *Ego Psychology and the Problem of Adaptation* (1958).

According to classical psychoanalytical theory, the role of the ego was that of a mediator among the instinctual urges of the id, external reality, and the moral strictures of the superego. The ego was involved in the resolutions of their conflicting demands. Hartmann focused on the domain of ego activity which was conflict-free. This was also the domain of the ego which was concerned with the reception and analysis of information input from the external world and the body. The ego was as well interested in the control of motor behaviour and with solving problems of adaptation. Briefly, it was the domain of perception, thinking, linguistic competence and productivity. These ego functions were autonomous, not primarily motivated by libido, but often exercised for their own sake. They were responsible for the solution of adaptation problems and for artistic creativity. Ernst Kris (1952) developed further the idea of the autonomy of creative activity by introducing the concept of "regression in the service of the ego."

Reintegration of the personality became an important focus of psychoanalysis in the work of Thomas French (1958). He endeavoured to integrate psychoanalytical theory with experimental cognitive psychology by introducing the conception of goal structures. He emphasized the problem solving functions of the ego and postulated both an end goal and a subsidiary set of goals. His schema much resembled that of a computer flow chart.

These new ideas about the ego and the unconscious cast some doubt on the original distinction made by Freud between the primary psychic processes ruled by the pleasure principle, and the secondary processes ruled by the reality principle. The unconscious processes could not be entirely irrational and unconstrained. They had to be ruled by the principles of logic in the same way that the computers were so governed. According to French, the primary and secondary processes were continuous with each other. The secondary processes were better organized and integrated than the primary ones. Here again, there was a greater similarity to some of the assumptions made about the unconscious by von Hartmann a century earlier, than to Freud's conception of a less than rational region of the mind.

The British School and the Object Relation Theory

This is the appropriate place to discuss the contribution of the British school of psychoanalysis to ego psychology and the psychoanalytical theory in general. As will be remembered, Freud believed that the Oedipal conflict was resolved by a renunciation of the parent of the opposite sex as a sex object. This was followed by identification with the parent of the same sex. The image of the same sex parent was introjected and formed the nucleaus of the superego. Thus only in the post Oedipal phase, did the superego become an integral part of the psyche. This assumption was questioned by Melanie Klein (1882-1960) and Ronald Fairbairn (1889-1964), both members of the London Institute of Psychoanalysis. Moreover, Fairbairn and his followers questioned the instinct theory of classical psychoanalysis. One of the leaders of the British School was Melanie Klein who had been born in Vienna and was not medically qualified. She had received a training analysis with Sandor Ferenczi in Budapest and then trained further with Karl Abraham in Berlin. There she became a member of the Berlin Psychoanalytic Institute and specialized in child psychology and play therapy with children. In 1926 she was invited by Ernest Jones to join the London Institute where she developed her theories of object relation and became a leader of the British School. Her major contribution was presented in her work, *The Psycho-analysis of Children* (1949). In that work she developed a theory of the early infant-mother relationship. In the first months of life, the infant was not capable of integrating various experiences of the mother and to perceive the mother as a whole object. Instead, the infant perceived only partial objects such as a breast or part of the face. Moreover, since some of these experiences were associated with pleasure and others with frustration and pain, the partial objects perceived were divided into good and bad ones. The boundary between the self and the external world was poorly defined. It led to attributing inner experiences to the external objects. In addition, the characteristics of external objects could be attributed to oneself. Thus there was a constant introjection and projection of bad and good partial objects. Klein described this stage of development as the paranoid-schizoid position. During the next developmental stage, the depressive one, the good partial objects were integrated into a whole object representing the mother. However, the integration was incomplete. There were still strong ambivalent feelings attached to the introjected object. In later life, the early introjected objects, with the associated feelings and conflicts became part of the inner world of fantasy. They served as models for the future world of interpersonal relationships with spouses and children.

In brief, Klein maintained that the parental object was already introjected at the infantile pre-Oedipal phase, and had become the nucleus of the superego. She became interested in the psychoanalysis of young children and utilized the method of play therapy during which children were playing with toys and enacting their autistic fantasies. In the course of therapy, Klein made direct interpretations of the child-patient's play. She assumed that the child was unconsciously aware of sexual facts. Klein borrowed the idea of using play therapy as a technique from Harmione von Hug-Hellmuth, a Viennese psychoanalyst. The latter had taken her lead from Freud's analysis of little Hans and developed her technique in 1919.

Anna Freud had become a member of the British School when she accompanied her father into exile in 1938. As a member of the London Institute, her main interest was in the psychoanalytical therapy of children. During this time her technique was more didactic than Melanie Klein's. Anna Freud believed that a child required more direct guidance because of its weak ego and its lack of superego. This was more important than interpreting its fantasies.

The further revision of the structural, tripartite psychoanalytical model was suggested by Ronald Fairbairn (1889-1964). Fairbairn was himself a graduate of Edinburgh University where he received degrees in both psychology and medicine. He was trained as a psychoanalyst in the London Institute and became its member. In his book, *An Object-Relations Theory of Personality* (1954) Fairbairn went further than Melanie Klein in his attack on the structural, tripartite model. He rejected Freud's instinct theory completely.

The theory proposed by Fairbairn presented a radical departure from the orthodox psychoanalysis. Fairbairn rejected the Freudian and Kleinian assumption that gratification of instinctual bodily needs is the most basic motive of life in human beings. To him the essential motive was a need for a satisfactory relationship with other people, or as he called it, an object relationship. According to Barnard and Corrales (1979) the Fairbairnian formulation provided a bridge between intrapsychic dynamics and the interpersonal relations observed at the level of social systems such as a family or a small group. Fairbairn believed that satisfactory interactions with the significant other, constituted a basic need of human nature. Such interactions gave rise to a mixture of satisfying and frustrating experiences. This led to an introjection of bad and good objects associated with ambivalent feelings of love and hate. The internal objects became parts of the personality structure. Not only the objects, but also the relations between the self and the significant other were internalized. Each bad object was divided further into a libidinal component and an anti-libidinal one. The libidinal component represented unsatisfied emotional longing for the love object. The opposite one represented the hateful and destructive aspects of the relationship. The introjection of objects and their ambivalent relationships into the self led to internal conflicts between various parts of the ego. These objects and conflicts were later externalized. Then they were tested in real situations. Thus they could be projected to current interpersonal relationships. The result was that these interpersonal relationships became warped. If current relationships were emotionally satisfying, their distorted images could be corrected. Real persons could be recognized for what they were and a basic sense of trust in oneself and others developed.

In Fairbairn's reformulation, the psychoanalytical theory of personality ceased to rely on instinct and drive. It shifted towards cognitive concepts which were concerned with representing the objects associated with present and past emotional experiences. There was a similarity between the revision of Freudian theory by Fairbairn and those neo-Freudians to which we now turn.

The Ethnological and Sociological Vistas

Freud's classical psychoanalytical theory was biological in its orientation. Although Freud was aware of the social context in which an individual developed, he viewed man as a biological organism whose behaviour was determined by biological instincts and drives. Consequently, Freud believed that the family structure and parent-child relations were biologically determined. These were general properties of the whole human species. The early dissidents, Alfred Adler, Carl Gustav Jung and Otto Rank tended to emphasize to a greater extent than Freud did, the role of society and of cultural factors in shaping the psychodynamics of the individual. Freud opposed this trend and believed that sex drive (libido) and aggression were paramount biological motors of the individual and social behaviour.

Freud's theory inspired Geza Roheim (1891-1953), a Hungarian ethnologist who applied it to the understanding of cultural phenomena. Roheim became interested in psychoanalytical theory by reading Freud's *Totem and Taboo*. He received psychoanalytical training from Sandor Ferenczi and became an early exponent of the psychoanalytical point of view in cultural anthropology. In his field work with Australian and Papuan aborigines, he tried to find evidence for Freud's speculations about the primeval horde or the Cyclopean family, also for the origins of the incest taboo and for totemic religion. Roheim (1943) saw a similarity between the myths in primitive tribes and the dreams reported during psychoanalytical sessions. For him culture and neurosis were the products of the same psychodynamic mechanisms. The culture reflected the individual human mind with all its infantile conflicts. Culture was a neurotic defense mechanism against the fear of a loss of love objects and against separation anxiety. The idea that the fear of separation from the mother and the desire for a reunion with her was the dominant motive, was borrowed from Rank's theory of birth trauma. Roheim believed that the dependence on the mother was a biological characteristic of the human species because of the prolonged infancy and immaturity (*neoteny*) of its members. He claimed that the separation anxiety and the aggressive reaction to it were enacted in many rituals of primitive tribes.

Roheim believed that conscious and unconscious fantasies, psychodynamic mechanisms and conflicts of the individual mind determined cultural phenomena. This belief was in contrast to the beliefs of more recent American anthropologists belonging to the "personality and culture" school. Its members maintained that cultural patterns and social conditions determined personality. A great diversity existed among the basic personality types found in many different cultures. In contrast to this school, Roheim emphasized individual psychodynamics. He asserted in his major work on the subject, *The Origin and Function of Culture* (1943), that technical inventions were the products of autistic, unconscious fantasies rather than of environmentally determined economic needs.

Roheim's line of theorizing was continued by Theodor Reik (1888-1970) who investigated religious rituals in different cultures and searched for their unconscious dynamics. Reik had a wide popular audience in the United States. His work was intended to sensitize the individual to understand the underlying meaning of different levels of interactions.

Sigmund Freud had also been interested in anthropological speculations. His own were based on the work of nineteenth century authors such as James Frazer and Edward Tylor. These armchair anthropologists subscribed to the evolutionary theory of society. They believed that all societies followed the same course of development and passed through the same stages. Such theories had developed from the enlightenment philosophies of history such as those of Giambattista Vico and the Marquis de Condorcet. The positivism of Auguste Comte had also assumed a fundamental, three stage model of historical evolution. For these anthropologists, primitive societies represented earlier stages of social evolution. Subsequent generations of anthropologists, who carried out field work in various parts of the globe, became aware of the astonishing diversity of primitive cultures. This carried over to diversity in religious beliefs and family constellations as well as customs and mores.

Freud believed that the nuclear family structure which was typical for the upper and middle class Viennese was biologically determined. Consequently, according to him, the Oedipus complex was a characteristic feature of the whole of mankind.

Even in Freud's Vienna, the interactions among members of *Lumpenproletariat* (pauper) families were different from those in the upper middle class. The subsequent work of the twentieth century anthropologists stressed the notion of cultural relativism which undermined the belief in biological determination of social behaviour. It threw new light on the Freudian theory by drawing attention to the fact that family patterns varied a great deal in different cultures. For example, Bronislaw Malinowski (1884-1942) found in his *Sex and Repression in Savage Society* (1953), that the Freudian theory of the Oedipus complex did not apply to the matrilineal and matrilocal Trobriand Island family where the authority figure for a boy was not the father, but the maternal uncle who was a member of the mother's and the boy's clan. The incest taboo was directed against sister and brother, rather than against the mother-son relationship.

In the United States, a group of Franz Boas' (1858-1942) students, became interested in the relation between culture and personality, as well as between culture and mental illness. They specialized in psychoethnology or "personality and culture." Although they were influenced by psychoanalytical theory, these anthropologists believed in the social determination of cultural patterns and personality types. In contrast to Roheim, they tried to explain myths, social institutions, rituals and typical personalities as the products of culture. These were solutions to problems with which the group was confronted rather than products of the unconscious. They followed in the tradition of the functionalist school of Malinowski and Radcliffe Brown rather than the evolutionary tradition of the nineteenth century anthropologists.

In this group, Ruth Benedict (1887-1948) in her *Patterns of Culture* (1959) was perhaps the most extreme proponent of cultural relativism.

She believed that each culture had its own *ethos* and that it specifically influenced the social values, child-rearing practices and character traits of its members.

The American anthropologist, Margaret Mead (1901-1978) was also strongly influenced by psychoanalytical theory. She studied child rearing practices and child development in different cultures. Her best known work was *Coming of Age in Samoa* (1928a) in which she described Samoan adolescence and the permissive sexual practices of the group. Adolescence in Samoa, she argued, was not a period of "storm and stress" as it was in Western culture (Mead, 1928a). Sex play in children was not regarded as evil and was not punished in all cultures. She reached this conclusion in her second study of South Pacific culture in her *Growing Up in New Guinea* (1928b). By 1953, she reflected on the general meaning of the male and female sex roles, particularly in modern American culture. Conceptions of typically male and female characters differed from culture to culture, she argued in *Male and Female* (1953). However, she believed that American marriages were adversely affected by the frustrating petting cutoms of the courtship period. Margaret Mead's essential attitude was neo-Freudian as she represented the "liberated" generation which grew to maturity after the first World War. Still influenced by the Victorian past, she tried to overcome it by advocating a more permissive way of child rearing. A better attitude towards sex would produce healthier men and women was what she implied. The malfunctioning of modern American culture could be traced to its frustrating courtship patterns (Mead, 1953). However, her earlier work on Samoa was attacked more recently, by another generation of anthropologists.

The social determinants of mental illness were emphasized by the American Ralph Linton (1893-1953). In collaboration with Abram Kardiner (*The Individual and his Society*) (1939) he offered a theoretical analysis of the relation of the individual to his culture. In his *Culture and Mental Disorders* (1956), he developed the concepts of "basic personality" and of "projective systems" of fantasies which were characteristic of each culture. According to the personality and culture school of anthropology, the Freudian psychodynamic mechanisms were drastically modified by cultural and social factors.

In sociology, Charles Horton Cooley (1864-1929) (1929), George Herbert Mead (1863-1953) (1934), and Talcott Parsons (1902-1979) (1951, 1967) developed a theory of interacting interpersonal systems which focused on the fact that a human being could not be viewed in isolation from the interaction with other human beings. G.H. Mead in particular derived much of his thinking from Darwinism, and tried to add a contextual dimension to straight-forward behaviourism. Stimulus and reponse mechanisms had to be placed into a social context in order to have meaning. The social environment was thus more important than the physical alone, and Mead moved away from the Social Darwinist traditions of nineteenth century American Sociology. He taught at the University of Chicago from the 1890s on, at a time when the faculty there played a crucial role in shaping the course of modern American thought. G. H. Mead developed the theory of symbolic interactionism. According to G. H. Mead symbolic behaviour was the product of interpersonal interaction. The communicative interaction created shared meanings and reciprocal perspectives in the participants, each of whom took the other's role and monitored his own role; playing through the eyes of the other.

Parsons became the father of modern American sociology and also appears to have been influenced by European models. His focus was on the actions of the individual in society. He owed much to Emile Durkheim and Max Weber, and believed that basic phenomena existed in the world of social interaction which could be discovered as hard facts had been in the natural sciences. Thus Durkheim, Freud, Cooley, and G.H. Mead all discovered "internalization and interpenetration" in their work on human personality (Parsons, 1967). This in fact, established the foundations of a modern type of social science. All patterns of social action showed a normative pattern of behaviour which was defined for each situation. This had to be internalized and to become part of the conscience of the individual, as Durkheim, Freud, and G.H. Mead had showned, he argued (Parsons, 1967).

The Neo-Freudians

The American emphasis on the social environment soon influenced the thinking of the members of the psychoanalytical movement who had been transplanted to American soil. There was more consciousness of the influence of social and cultural factors. These were to be emphasized more than the biological factors. This development became particularly manifest among the neo-Freudian dissidents like Harry Stack Sullivan (1892-1949), Karen Horney (1885-1952), Erich Fromm (1900-1980) and Erik Erikson (b.1902). Sullivan was a native of the

United States. Horney, Fromm, and Erikson were emigres from Europe.

Harry Stack Sullivan received his psychiatric and psychoanalytical training at St. Elizabeth Hospital in Washington, D.C. His teachers were William Alanson White and Smith Ely Jellife. He was later a member of the staff of the Sheppard and Enoch Pratt Hospital near Baltimore and had contacts with the Phipps Clinic where he came under the influence of Adolf Meyer.

For some time he collaborated with Edward Sapir (1884-1939) an anthropologist with whom he taught a "culture and personality" seminar at Yale. He was instrumental in setting up the Alanson White Foundation for the study of mental health problems. He was also associated with Chestnut Lodge Sanitarium which specialized in psychotherapy with young schizophrenics. Towards the end of his life, Sullivan became a mental health consultant with the UNESCO. He died suddenly in Paris while attending one of the UNESCO meetings. In contrast to other psychoanalyts, Sullivan was interested in the problems of psychosis rather than neurosis. His particular interest was psychotherapy with young schizophrenic patients and he possessed an extraordinary ability to communicate with them.

Sullivan (1953) defined psychiatry as the study of interpersonal relations conducted by the psychiatrist as a participant observer. The unit of study was an interpersonal relation. Since man was by nature social, he had needs that went beyond his basic biological ones. These were for social recognition and acceptance. If the social needs were not satisfied, man felt insecure, had a low self-esteem and experienced anxiety. The latter was an important force that could cause personality disintegration, but it also motivated man to achieve. In order to cope with anxiety, the individual developed in his childhood, a system of dynamisms. The early relation between the child and his mother, or the "mothering one," played an important role in this process. If the relationship was satisfactory, the individual developed feelings of security and trust in the external world and in people. These were the prerequisites for a high self-esteem and self-respect. On the other hand, an unhappy relationship induced anxiety and resulted in low self-esteem and self-respect. The attitudes of the "mothering one" were reflected in the child's self-perception as "good me," "bad me," or "not me." The "bad me" and "not me" self perception tended to be repressed by the dynamisms of the self-system, and to become dissociated from consciousness. However, in the process, the growth of the self-system might be warped and could result in psycho-neurosis or psychosis.

Sullivan distinguished three stages in the emotional and cognitive development of personality: the *protaxic*, *parataxic* and *syntaxic*. The protaxic stage was characterized by the lack of distinction between the self and the external world, by the absence of a time perspective, and by magical thinking. Schizophrenia was a regression to this stage. The parataxic stage was characterized by a lack of real understanding of causality and by seeking to explain the external events by apparent temporal connections. The perception of interpersonal relations was distorted by "fantastic personifications." Finally, the syntaxic stage of the mature personality was characterized by logical, consensually validated thinking and a realistic perception of interpersonal relations. It was a product of maturity and successful socialization. Emotional security and self-esteem were needed by a child for successful navigation through the stages of cognitive emotional development. Unsatisfactory interpersonal relationships could arrest the development at the protaxic and parataxic stages or cause a regression to them. The periods of infancy, childhood, preadolescence, and adolescence, involved different types of interpersonal relationships. According to Sullivan, these were more important than infantile sex drives in the shaping of human personality.

Neuroses and psychoses were not regarded by Sullivan as diseases, but rather as personality developments which were warped by unsatisfactory interpersonal relations. In schizophrenia, the subject of particular interest for Sullivan, the dissociated attitudes became conscious and caused a state of overwhelming anxiety threatening self-disintegration (Sullivan, 1953).

Karen Horney (1937, 1939) was trained in the Berlin Institute of Psychoanalysis. Her training analysis was with Karl Abraham. In 1932 she emigrated to the United States and became a member of the Chicago Institute. There she collaborated on many projects with Franz Alexander and Erik Fromm. Although her training was in Freudian psychoanalysis, she was strongly influenced by Adler. It is a moot point whether she should be regarded as a neo-Freudian or a neo-Adlerian. The Adlerian "will to power" was regarded by her as an important motive. She played down the importance of biological factors and emphasized the importance of interpersonal relations and the present situation of the individual.

Horney rejected the biological theory of the libido, of the Oedipus complex, and of psychosexual stages. Instead, she stressed the importance of cultural factors and of interpersonal relations for the dynamics of personal development. The individual was seen by her as constantly interacting with his social milieu. Although Horney regarded the self as a unity, she distinguished three aspects of it. (1) The actual self as the sum total of the individual's experiences. (2) The real self which was the integrative agent,bringing about a state of harmonious wholeness, and (3) the idealized self, incorporating unrealistic neurotic goals. She borrowed the idea of fictitious neurotic goals from Adler. Although these goals served as defense mechanisms, they could lead to secondary conflicts and anxieties. Moreover, the individual was under a compulsion to repeat the involvement in situations which in the past led to conflicts. Thus a vicious circle was produced in which neurotic defenses led to further conflicts and anxieties.

A person could become alienated from his actual self, or from the real self. In the first type of alienation, there is a denial of personal feelings and a failure of self perception. In the second, there was a failure to actualize the personality potential for growth and creativity. According to Horney, the sources of neuroses were: (1) distorted parent-child relationships, (2) distorted relations between the self and others, and (3) a discrepancy between the potential for achievement and the actual, neurotically stunted growth of the individual. Early childhood experiences were considered to play an important role in the genesis of psychoneurosis, although the experience of the present situation was not less important.

In *The Neurotic Personality of our Time* (1937), Horney, in fact put great emphasis on the present life of the patient. Both the normal and the neurotic person were affected by the same cultural factors which undermined self-esteem and made for hostility and tension.

The conflicts resulting from inconsistent parental attitudes, from parental overstrictness, rejection, or overprotectiveness, produced general neurotic reactions in children. These were characterized as (1) moving toward a clinging dependence, (2) moving away or withdrawal to solitude and privacy. Finally (3) moving against or an attitude of general hostility.

Neurotic conflicts manifested themselves as feelings of anxiety, and certain pathological character traits developed to cope with it. However, the central inner conflict was that of self-hatred. This led to an alienation from the self and creation of a pseudo self. The sense of genuine identity was lost and was replaced by a false identity. This could lead to a depersonalization and a distortion of bodily image. More often, it led to an adoption of contrived roles in social interactions. Therapy aimed at removal of distorting and stifling influences of the past so as to allow for individual growth and self actualization. Here especially, a "paucity of inner experience" had to be overcome (Horney, 1937, 1939).

Horney (1945) was concerned with striving for "wholeheartedness" in therapy. She warned against the danger of creating new, over-idealized self images to replace those which were being criticized by the analyst. In the tradition of the Romantics, and of eighteenth century eudaemonism, she hoped to approximate ideals, but doubted that any could really be achieved. In *Self-Analysis* (1942), Horney argued for a developmental goal and for attaining a knowledge of unconscious motives. She was able to define ten neurotic needs which required attention. These were also normal human needs, of course, but when they became neurotic, they presented major problems. As such they also identified ten personality types who might overemphasize one or more of these neurotic needs for: (1) affection, (2) a partner, (3) restricting one's life, (4) power (including a need for control and a faith in one's will), (5) exploiting others, (6) social recognition, (7) personal admiration, (8) personal achievement, (9) self-sufficiency, (10) for perfection. These were all in a sense neurotic goals, much as in Adlerian theory. On the whole Horney (1950) believed that less emphasis should be placed on fulfillment of individual gifts, than on the realization of genuinely human potentialities. This also paralleled the goals of post World War II existentialists whose goal was the achievement of authentic personality.

Erich Fromm was with Horney and Sullivan, one of a group of psychoanalysts interested in the science of human culture. He had been born in Frankfurt a.M.,Germany, and had studied psychology as well as sociology at Heidelberg University, and also in Frankfurt M. and Munich. Fromm was much influenced by the Frankfurt school of social philosophy. After receiving his Ph.D. from Heidelberg, he trained as a psychoanalyst, primarily at the Berlin Psychoanalytic Institute. Fromm combined clinical practice with theoretical studies in which he applied psychoanalytical theory to the problems of society and culture. He emigrated to the United States in 1933 and joined the Chicago Institute of Psychoanalysis. He was also connected with the Washington School of Psychiatry and the William Alanson White Institute of Psychiatry. His private practice was in New York. His interests went beyond empirical sociology. He might be described as a social philosopher who was concerned with the nature of man and the nature of society. He was the author of several books. The most important ones are: *Escape from Freedom* (1941), *Man for Himself* (1947), *The Sane Society* (1955), and *Marx's Concept of Man* (1961).

Fromm was influenced both by Freud's psychoanalytic theory and by Marxist social philosophy. He rejected the Hobbesian view of human nature held by Freud. Man was not intrinsically antisocial and there was no dichotomy between man and society. According to Fromm, man could not be separated from his social and cultural context. Man was shaped in a dialectical interaction by his society and was shaping it. Fromm rejected Freud's biological theory of instincts and believed that man was motivated by social values. His conflicts and neurotic difficulties were of cultural origin. The key problem of man, underlying all other problems, was that of alienation. The predicament of the human beings was caused by men and women being endowed with consciousness of their rationality. Thus they became alienated from nature. Man tried either to enslave nature or to become disengaged from it. A new unity, with nature could be achieved through productive work, creativity and the actualization of man's potential. However, the desire to be reunited with nature could misfire and could lead to attempts to become submerged in the environment and to regress to a prehuman form of existence. Within the social context, this led to a desire to merge with the society. It could manifest itself as a compulsive conformity and as self-alienation. Man was torn between two kinds of alienation. The first kind was the alienation from himself. This meant loss of identity and a complete merging with the society. The second kind, was the alienation from the society. This resulted in complete social isolation and withdrawal. Both kinds of alienation were associated with psychological difficulties. Extreme social withdrawal led to Schizophrenia. Milder forms of social isolation led to irrational methods of relating back to the group such as sado-masochism, destructiveness and a search for a magic helper. The alienation from the self and the desire to merge with the society led to "automaton conformity," to the stunting of personality growth and of creativity. This kind of alienation also led to a fear of freedom, and a blind submission to authority, which characterized the totalitarian states. Fromm saw security as a basic human need and argued that it might be obtained either in a totalitarian state or by a more humanistic socialism (Schultz, 1960). His own preference was for the humanistic solution, and here he followed the sociology of Pitrim Sorokin at Harvard, who posited an altruism as a social goal.

In *The Sane Society*, Fromm speculated whether a whole society rather than the individuals in it, could be sick. His answer was affirmative. In his opinion, American capitalist society was sick. It generated alienation feelings, it encouraged conformity, it prevented the actualization of the human potential, and it stunted creativity. As a result, it shaped its members into two character types: (1) the "receptive" character who was oriented towards consumerism, and (2) the "marketing" character who attempted to sell himself to the highest bidder. According to Fromm, a society was sane when it was a commuterian or humanistic society. A humanistic society encouraged man to develop his human potential, it stressed the dignity and equality of men. Such a society would encourage the participation of workers in the decision-making process. It would emphasize spontaneity and the creative aspects of work. According to Fromm, none of the existing socialist societies was commuterian in the sense in which he meant to use that word. The democratic, egalitarian society he hoped for in order to actualize the human potential, seemed to elude the present and hovered in an unattainable future.

More interested in applying psychoanalytical theory to history, than the other culturally oriented analysts, was Erik Erikson who studied fine arts and education. He received professional training in the Vienna Psycho-analytical Institute where he was analyzed by Anna Freud. There he specialized in child psychology. Erikson was a professor of human development and a lecturer in psychiatry at Harvard University. He was interested in child development in a variety of social environments. His clinical practice included psychotherapy with children and adolescents. Erikson was primarily an ego-psychologist interested in psychological development within the cultural setting (Erikson, 1963).

Erikson's particular concern was the problem of "ego identity." The interest in this problem stemmed from the influence of Kierkegaard's philosophy. The individual experienced his existence as being always the identical person. This was in spite of physical and mental changes, accompanied by a shifting social context. The solution to this ego problem, had both a psychoanalytical and existentialist connotations. At the core of human inner experience was the awareness of one's identity as a distinct person who existed in a continuum of past, present, and future. There was also a sense of the ability to make free choices and of self-determination. The awareness of personal identity resulted from continually progressive, and integrative processes.

Erikson (1963) proposed an epigenetic theory of ego development. He believed that there were eight stages of ego development. Each was characterized by a typical conflict or crisis that confronted the individual. Different cultures phrased the expression of these conflicts in different ways. They also required different solutions. A progress from one stage of ego development to the next, depended on a successful solution to the conflict typical for each stage.

Although Freud had originally assumed a three stage model, in which the child's sexuality developed through and oral, an anal, and a phallic stage, Erikson postulated eight stages. The first was characterized by the conflict of "basic trust versus mistrust." This was between cravings for sameness and desires for novelty. It was concerned with a sense of continuity of the key persons involved in ministering to the needs of the infant. The second stage of ego development was that of "autonomy versus shame and doubt." During this stage, the infant strove to attain bowel control, but these attempts could lead to shame and doubt. The third stage was of "initiative versus guilt." Fantasies of aggression against the parent of the same sex led to feelings of guilt. The fourth stage of industry versus inferiority coincided with the commencement of schooling. Here also a beginning to performance chores led to an experience of feelings of inferiority. The fifth stage was associated with puberty and was characterized by a conflict of "identity versus role confusion". The change in status from childhood to adulthood produced doubts about the sex role and about individual identity. The sixth stage was characterized by the conflict of "intimacy versus isolation." It centered around the problem of establishing permanent relations with a partner of the opposite sex without losing personal autonomy. The seventh stage was characterized by the conflict of "generativity versus stagnation" and centered around the problems of procreation and creativity. The last, the eighth stage was associated with middle age. It was characterized by the conflict of "ego integrity versus despair." It was concerned with the existential problem of life's meaning, with developing a life style that expressed the values of one's culture. Erikson applied his theory of epigenetic development to the years beyond childhood and adolescence in order to cover the entire life span. This found expression in his psychoanalytical biography of Martin Luther under the title: *Young Man Luther* (1958).

12

The Psychobiology and Commonsense Psychiatry of Adolf Meyer

The internationalization of American psychiatry had begun in the age of Benjamin Rush, in the eighteenth century. A new phase of European influence commenced with the development of professional psychiatry as a specialized university discipline at the end of the nineteenth century. As psychiatry focused more on neurophysiological and neuroanatomical studies, those with such training found a greater demand for their services in the United States. It is partly for such reasons that Adolf Meyer (1866-1950), a Swiss, became one of the founders of modern American psychiatry (Lewis, 1959).

Adolf Meyer was born and educated in Switzerland, yet spent most of his professional life in America. There he had a tremendous impact on the theory and practice of psychiatry. He was a graduate of the University of Zuerich and was introduced to psychiatry at Burghoelzli by Auguste Forel (1848-1931). Forel preceded Bleuler as the professor of psychiatry at Zuerich and director of Buerghoelzli. Swiss psychiatry had not been much developed before the 1850s, and Buerghoelzli itself opened only in 1869. Zuerich soon became a major center of psychiatric medicine. Wilhelm Griesinger had lectured there, and Bernard von Gudden had been Buerghoelzli's first director. Forel was at that time, one of the leading neuroanatomists in Europe. Later he became interested in the hypnotic method and spent some time with Bernheim in Nancy. He was also responsible for establishing psychiatry as a professional examination subject in Switzerland in 1887 (Ackerknecht, 1970). In addition to being a psychiatrist, Forel was also an entymologist who published important studies of the social life of ants. His two most important students were to be Eugen Paul Bleuler (1857-1939) and Adolf Meyer.

Meyer had been born in a Swiss village (Niederwenigen) near Zuerich, the son of a Zwinglian pastor and nephew of a country doctor. He was educated at Zuerich University, except for a year spent at the University of Geneva. Two further years were spent abroad in Paris,

London, and Edinburgh. Meyer was greatly influenced by Hughlings Jackson while in London, especially with Jackson's ideas of the hierarchy of nervous system functions. His interests were very broad and included besides medicine, biology and philosophy. He came under the influence of positivist philosophy and was particularly impressed by the idea of Thomas Huxley that science was "organized common sense." At Edinburgh, the common sense philosophy of Thomas Reid still exerted an influence. Adolf Meyer's own interests were in neuroanatomy and neuropathology at this time, but he was to broaden his perspective. He came to consider neurology as a distinct field for research, and to conceive of psychiatry as concerned more with personality disorders which were perceived from a psychological perspective (Harrington, 1987). Later his interest was in the whole man as a biological and social entity who lived in and developed in a unique environment which encompassed the social milieu. However, after his return from England, he completed his dissertation under Auguste Forel in Zuerich on the forebrain of reptiles (Diethelm,1970).

In 1892 Adolf Meyer emigrated to America. For a time he worked as a neuropathologist at the Illinois Eastern State Hospital for the Insane at Kanakee. Subsequently, in 1895, he became the chief pathologist at Worcester State Hospital in Massachusetts. Here he had become an academic teacher as well, and lectured at nearby Clark University in psychology. By 1902 he moved again, this time to the New York State Psychiatric Institute as a director of pathology. From 1904 to 1909 he also taught at Cornell University Medical College as a professor of psychopathology. In 1910 he was appointed professor of psychiatry at Johns Hopkins University in Baltimore, and also chief of psychiatry in the university's hospital. Supported by a generous benefactor, Henry Phipps, he was in 1913 able to found the Baltimore Henry Phipps Clinic for Psychiatry. He resided in Baltimore then, until his death in 1950.

Adolf Meyer undoubtedly was responsible for establishing the American psychiatric profession in its modern, contemporary form. He was instrumental in setting up the American Board of Psychiatry and Neurology in 1934, after suggesting this step to the American Psychiatric Association when he was its president in 1927-28. The new board was to supervise the training of future psychiatrists and to administer the specialist examination.

Meyer's wife, Mary Potter Brooks, whom he married in 1902, was also a leading influence in the establishment of psychiatric social work as a profession. Her husband much encouraged this endeavour. This was partly because Adolf Meyer attached a great importance to the family environment of patients as well as to the care of patients after they left the hospital. This approach stressed the importance of the social milieu and of social work. It was further developed by Elmer E. Southard (1876-1920). Southard may be regarded as a pioneer of community psychiatry. He was concerned with social factors which could be responsible for mental illness. In 1907 Meyer met Clifford Beers, a former mental patient whom he encouraged to write autobiographical account of his stay in an asylum, *The Mind that Found Itself* (1908). Beers and Meyer were responsible for starting and promoting the "mental hygiene" movement. Its goal was the prevention of mental illness, the moral support of former patients and the promotion of positive mental health. The term mental hygiene appeared in the psychiatric literature in the middle of the nineteenth century. It was first introduced in 1843 by W. C. Sweetser, a Vermont physician. In 1853, Isaac Ray had published a work using the title *Mental Hygiene*. However, Meyer was responsible for the initiation of the movement. In 1908, Meyer convened the National Committee for Mental Hygiene. August Hoch, Friderick Peterson, Lewellys Barker, and the leading American philosopher-psychologist William James were also members of the committee. Thomas W. Salmon, a noted psychiatric teacher and a remarkable administrator, was appointed its director in 1912.

Adolf Meyer used a broad and integrative approach to psychiatry in the theories which he proposed. His view was holistic (Meyer, 1957; 1950-1952; Muncie, 1939; Lief, 1948). The subject of his psychobiology was the whole human being, a biological organism who was also a person with a unique history, living and developing in a particular environment to which he attempted to adjust. Each individual tried to come to an equilibrium in his mind, about the experiences of his present situation and sought to integrate them with the experiences of the past. It was this process which produced steady personality growth. During such changes, the individual nevertheless maintained a degree of stability and remained linked to his past. Meyer believed in using the case history approach, especially for what it could tell the physician about the predisposing personality of the patient. It was possible to find meaningful connections between the successive episodes of an individual life and to make predictions with regard to his future behaviour. It was the environmental situation which produced an adaptive psychobiological reaction of the individual. Such reactions could also outlive their usefulness and become maladaptive. As a student of philosophy, Meyer rejected Cartesian dualism, and from a monist point of view, considered each human being as a psychobiological whole. Therefore he was equally critical of purely organic psychiatry based on neuropathology, and of psychodynamic psychiatry which sought to explain human behaviour in terms of the mechanisms of the unconscious. He considered these two approaches as too narrow and too one-sided.

Meyer postulated a continuity between normality and abnormality, between mental health and mental disease. He rejected the disease model of functional psychoses and psychoneuroses. To put it in his own words: "We do not think of disease entities but of processes, that is miscarriage and deviation of function" (Meyer, 1957, p.118). His theorizing about mental illness was in terms of personality development with emphasis on both the constitution and the life experiences of the individual. According to Meyer, constitution did not indicate simply physique or a body type, correlated with temperament. For him the term constitution implied the totality of the individual psychobiological make-up.

Meyer's approach was holistic. It aimed at encompassing those biological and psychological factors which interacted with one another to create the unique *Gestalt* of an individual person. These factors were responsible for the uniqueness of personality development, for its particular integration, and for its adjustment. For Meyer, the constitution of an individual implied also a potential for growth and development. Consequently he emphasized taking a very detailed life history of each patient in all clinical work. This procedure was called by him "distributive analysis." It could help to elucidate all the possible factors that had any bearing on the pathology of the patient. The "distributive analysis" was followed by a "distributive synthesis." The latter aimed at understanding the past maladaptation of the patient and at designing a strategy for the improvement of his adjustment.

For Meyer psychopathological symptoms both in psychoses and neuroses were meaningfully connected with the past history of the patient, and could be understood from the point of view of his total adjustment to have a purpose. Mental illness for Meyer was a purposeful psychobiological reaction which misfired. In his dealings with the patients, Meyer tried to understand their behaviour and motivation from the point of view of common sense rather than from that of depth psychology. Meyer at times talked about "objective psychobiology" and "observation of objective facts." In his common sense approach he applied *Verstehen* (understanding) psychology as a method in diagnosing his patients.

Meyer rejected nosology. He considered each patient unique. However, he accepted broad categories of psychiatric clinical syndromes. He conceived them, not in terms of diseases, but in terms of general psychobiological reactions which he called "ergasias." The concept of ergasia involved both body and mind. It was close to that of dyscrasia, which was developed by the constitutional tradition of medicine. However, it went beyond the latter by implying a purposeful attempt at adjustment. Divergencies in personality development were responsible for different types of ergasias that made up the habitual ways of reacting to stress situations. Every psychopathological condition had to be considered against the background of environmental factors that provoked it. Meyer distinguished the following "ergasias": (1) "anergasia" was a brain functional reaction to a damage caused by organic factors; (2)"dysergasia," was a brain functional reaction to a toxic state; (3)"thymergasia" was a predominantly affective reaction to stress; (4)"parergasia," was a schizophrenic reaction; (5)"merergasia," was a psychoneurotic reaction interfering with the ability to work: (6)"kakergasia" was an antisocial personality reaction; (7)"oligergasia" was a reaction to an inborn mental defect.

Meyer became particularly interested in "parergasia" (schizophrenia). He regarded this type of "ergasia" as a personality development resulting from a non-resiliant constitution and an accumulation of maladjustive habits. The resulting psychobiological reaction was characterized by withdrawal from reality accompanied by absorption in daydreams and fantasies. Briefly, Meyer explained both psychoses and neuroses in terms of a personality development that led to broad maladaptive psychobiological reactions. He stressed the importance of the patient's life experience, in contrast to his heredity. In this respect, he differed from the German constitutional psychiatrists such as Ernst Kretschmer or Kurt Schneider who emphasized heredity.

Meyer trained and influenced many psychiatrists in English speaking countries. His leading follower in America was Wendell Muncie (1897-1985), who wrote an influential book on psychobiological psychiatry (Muncie, 1939). In Great Britain, the leading follower of Meyer was David K. Henderson (1889-1965). Henderson, together with Robert D. Gillespie (1897-1945), a psychodynamically oriented psychiatrist, wrote a textbook of psychiatry (1927/1963) used by several generations of medical students.

At this juncture a mention should be made of August Hoch (1868-1919), another Swiss psychiatrist who emigrated to America. Hoch became associated with the New York State Psychiatric Institute. He described a psychiatric syndrome which he called "benign stupor." This syndrome was associated with manic-depressive psychosis and was distinguished from catatonic or "malignant" stupor associated with schizophrenia.

Attempts to Synthesize the Disease and the Personality Development Models of Mental Illness

As has been emphasized before, the German historian of medicine Henry Sigerist (1951) made a distinction between two fundamentally different ways of looking at medical problems. These two approaches were that of (1) the disease model, and (2) the constitutional model of illness. The first stressed the "ontology of disease;" the second, the "ontology of the patient." The intellectual tensions between these two orientations persisted throughout Antiquity, the Middle Ages, and into Modern times. In twentieth century psychiatry, the Kraepelinian nosological system had emphasized the disease entities. However, in the constitutional psychiatry of Kretschmer, in the psychobiology of Meyer, and in the psychoanalytical theory of Sigmund Freud, the focus was on the unique life history of the individual. All these authors agreed that the observed characteristics of an individual were a product of both the inherited constitution and the unique environmental events. These had interacted throughout the life history of the person. The evolving constitutional and experiential factors were called personality development by Meyer.

The contradictions between the disease model and the constitutional created a need for reconciling them. There was a need to bring together the "ontology of disease" and the "ontology of the patient." Eugen Bleuler made one such attempt. In his major work on schizophrenia (1911), Bleuler put forward the hypothesis that in schizophrenia, the formal aspects of the psychopathological symptoms are determined by the disease process. Their contents were psychodynamically determined, however. To put it differently, the formal aspects of psychopathological productions were caused by a disease, while the contents of it, were caused by the unique personality development. This idea was further developed by Karl Birbaum (1923) who in his work on the structure of psychosis, distinguished the "pathogenic" disease process at work in its causation. This was modified by the "pathoplastic" personality factors.

Another attempt was made by Karl Jaspers (1885-1969) in a monumental work in 1913, on general psychopathology. In that text, Jaspers distinguished three approaches to psychopathological phenomena. These were (1) the objective, (2) the phenomenological, (3) one based on *Verstehen Psychologie* (psychology of understanding). The last approach was based on the understanding of the "meaningful connections" of the pathological symptoms to past events of the patient's life history. The contents of pathological productions could be understood in the sense of the German psychology of understanding. (*Verstehende Psychologie*). That is, in terms of the patient's total personality, his motivational system, his values, and in particular in terms of his past life experience. Jaspers distinguished between the symptoms which could be so understood and those which could not. The latter denoted a clear break with the psychological past of the patient. They were meaningless in the context of past experience. They were also totally alien to his personality. The symptoms belonging to the first category were manifestations of the personality development. Those beloning to the second, were manifestations of the disease process. The latter symptoms were not meaningfully connected with past experience and the personality development of the patient. They were a product of the disease process in the brain.

Karl Jaspers was a philosopher as well as a psychiatrist. He was a member of the group of psychiatrists associated with Heidelberg University, who are sometimes referred to as the "old Heidelberg School." The other members of the group included such prominent psychiatrists as Hans W. Gruehle (1880-1958), Willy Mayer-Gross (1889-1961), Victor von Weizsaecker (1886-1957), and Kurt Schneider (1887-1963). Of course, Schneider had spent most of his professional life in Munich and only moved to Heidelberg after the second World War. But in his theoretical orientation he was a member of the Heidelberg School. After Jaspers left psychiatry for philosophy, Kurt Schneider (1958, 1959) elaborated further Jaspers' distinction between disease process and personality development. Disease processes were produced either by manifest brain pathology, or by putative brain pathology. The first was associated with organic, the second with functional or endogenous psychoses. The second domain, that of personality development, was subdivided further into "abnormal reactions" and "psychopathic personalities." "Abnornmal reactions" were excessive reactions to stressful situations, brought about by such events as threats to life, disappointments and bereavements. The reactive depression and battle exhaustion were examples of abnormal reactions. Psychopathic personalities were determined mainly by the hereditary constitutional factors, and only to a lesser degree by personal experiences. Such constitutional factors produced personality traits which deviated to an extreme degree from the population norm.

Schneider, like other German psychiatrists, wanted to make the concept of psychopathic personality, a value-free one. Its purpose was to designate individuals who deviated considerably from the mean magnitudes of normally distributed personality traits. Some deviations had more social and moral importance than others. However, from the biostatistical point of view, all of them constituted excessive deviations from the norms of the population. There was a continuous variation in the magnitudes of individual reactions to stress situations. The degree of deviations from the population mean, of the constant personality traits, varied as well. Thus normality merged by imperceptible steps with abnormality. There was a continuity between the healthy and the pathological. In contrast, the disease developments were discontinuous with the state of health. Moreover, the pathological symptoms caused by disease processes could not be understood in terms of personality development. Nor, could they be comprehended in the context of the situation with which the individual was confronted. They did not have a contextual meaning.

This distinction could be illustrated by the difference between "primary delusions" and "overvalued ideas." The first came completely "out of the blue" they could not be explained by the individual's motives, previous experiences, and personality dynamics. The second could be understood as exaggerations of normal thought processes, or as a product of adjustive personality mechanisms. One might expect a spy who found himself in enemy territory, to imagine that he was being watched and followed. Such a reaction was quite understandable. According to Schneider, primary delusions occurred in disease process. "Overvalued ideas" occurred in personality developments.

Another example was the difference between the reactive and the endogenous depression. The first was a reaction to a bereavement or a loss. The second had no relation to environmental happenings. A remarkable feature of the Schneiderian system was the absence of the category of psychoneurosis. Psychoneurosis came under the categories of abnormal reactions or of psychopathic personalities. To conclude, Schneider found room in his system for both the disease (nosological) model and the constitutional-personality developmental model.

13

The Roots of Behaviour Therapy

Our historical survey has, until now, dealt with theories of mental illness which originated in a medical setting. The theory of demoniacal possession had remained an exception; it originated in folk beliefs and in theological doctrines. Modern behaviour therapy came into its own only after the second World War. It began in the psychological laboratory and it constituted a genuine contribution to psychiatry by experimental psychology. It is based on the application to therapy of learning theory, which in its turn is based on animal laboratory research (Weckowicz, 1984). In this section, I shall present the historical background of behaviour therapy and the behaviourist model of mental illness which is closely linked to it. The origins of behaviour therapy may be traced to the moral treatment of the insane in the nineteenth century, Russian reflexology or objective psychology, and the American behaviourist movement.

The Moral Treatment Movement

The moral treatment of the insane (Bockoven, 1963), and its German counterpart, "psychological means of help" (*Psychologische Hilfsmittel*), aimed at helping patients through a humane approach and by re-education. Pinel in his proposal of moral treatment stressed that it was important to control the behaviour of patients through a system of consistently administered punishments and rewards (Kraepelin, 1962; Bockoven, 1963). Johann Christian Reil argued in his *Rhapsodies about the Application of Psychotherapy to Mental Disturbances* (1803) that the insane had to be influenced from the external environment since they were devoid of inner motivation. He even discussed the techniques of "non-injurious torture," such as frightening the patients and shocking them out of their insane thoughts.

Somewhat later, Francois Leuret (1798-1851), a French physician at the Bicetre Hospital in Paris used contingent aversive stimuli to influence the behaviour and thinking of his patients (Wolpe & Theriault, 1971; Kazdin, 1978). Outside the field of psychiatry, early applications of the principles of behaviour modification were: the monitorial system of Joseph Lancaster (1778-1838) in education, and the mark system introduced by Alexander Maconochie (1787-1860) into the penal system of Australia. Both these systems relied on the consistent application of positive and negative reinforcements to alter the behaviour of pupils and prisoners (Kazdin, 1978).

It was a common belief of the times, that mental patients were like unruly, ill-behaved children. They had to be treated with kindness, but firmly, and to be disciplined when necessary. Such notions naturally led to attempts at the control of the patient behaviour through a system of rewards and punishments. The similarity between these ideas and the "token economy" as practiced in modern mental hospitals is obvious. The doctrine of hedonism which explained human behaviour as motivated by a pursuit fo pleasure and the avoidance of pain, provided a philosophical justification for these practices.

The doctrine of hedonism goes back to the philosophy of Aristippus (435-356 B.C.), a student of Socrates, and the philosophy of Epicurus (341-270 B.C.) in ancient Greece. Aristippus and the Cyrenaics maintained that human action was governed by pleasure, which was the *summum bonum* of the ethical system they endorsed. In the eighteenth century, hedonism played an important role in the philosophies of La Mettrie and of Jean Cabanis, as an explanation of human motivation. These were the precursors of behaviourism. However, it was Jeremy Bentham (1748-1828) who made hedonism the cornerstone of his social philosophy by introducing the idea of the "felicific calculus," namely that the goal of society was the achievement of the greatest pleasure for the greatest number of people. In its more refined form, it found its way into American political thought and was expressed by Thomas Jefferson in the Declaration of Independence as the "pursuit of happiness." The self-interest doctrine of hedonism became the cornerstone of modern ethical and economic theory expressed in Adam Smith's *Wealth of Nations* (1776) as essential to free enterprise. It also became the key idea of the utilitarian philosophers, mainly of Jeremy Bentham and his friend James Mill (1773-1836). The son of James Mill, the better known John Stuart Mill (1806-1873) had some reservations about these ideas, but continued to use them in his economic and political theories. Herbert Spencer (1820-1903) too, whose ideas of general development influenced Darwin's theory of evolution, remained true to the idea of utilitarian hedonism. Yet Spencer also tried to reconcile the utilitarian philosophy with Darwin's theory of evolution. In the English-speaking countries, utilitarianism had a strong influence, particularly on social policy and education. It undoubtedly also influenced the thinking of those alienists in mental institutions who practiced the moral treatment of the insane.

The doctrine of hedonism was an important element in the philosophical climate in which both American behaviourism and Freudian theory of psychoanalysis developed. It is significant that Freud, on the recommendation of Brentano, translated from English into German a section of the collected works of John Stuart Mill, which were being published in German under the editorship of Theodor Gomperz in 1880 (Jones, 1953).

Another philosophical tradition which provided the justification for behaviourism and behavioural therapy was that of associationism. Associationism maintained that temporal contiguity produced permanent bonds between ideas. This doctrine may be traced to the psychological writings of Aristotle. It was developed and elaborated further by the British empiricists: John Locke, George Berkeley (1658-1753), David Hume (1711-1776), and David Hartley (1705-1757). In France, Etienne de Condillac (1715-1780) espoused these beliefs. In the nineteenth century, associationism became the cornerstone of psychology. Its chief proponents were the utilitarian philosophers: James Mill, John Stuart Mill, and Herbert Spencer, as well as Alexander Bain (1818-1903), an early psychologist. The doctrine of associationism had a great influence not only on behaviourism, but also on Freud's theory of psychoanalysis. Although in the case of psychoanalysis, the principle of associationism by temporal contiguity was modified by the concept of *cathexis*, which could be construed in terms of intentionality directed towards certain objects.

The Russian School of Reflexology

The Russian school of reflexology, or objective psychology, was another source to which the origins of behaviour therapy can be traced. As was mentioned earlier, the pendulum of psychiatry swung away from psychological theories and towards organic explanations after 1850. This was largely owing to the influence of Comtean Positivism and because of the influence of science and of philosophical materialism. Even earlier Philippe Pinel had argued that mental disorders might be caused by pathological changes originating in the brain. Jean E.D.

Esquirol (1772-1840) had helped to diffuse these ideas. Subsequently, the French school had swung over towards Charcot's and Bernheim's belief in hypnotism. The Germans and Russians proved to be more directly devoted to a materialist point of view after 1850. Attempts were made to explain psychology in terms of brain physiology.

One of the exponents of this approach was a Russian physiologist, Ivan Michailovich Sechenov (1829-1905). Sechenov spent some time in Germany and France where he met some leading exponents of the scientific approach to physiology and medicine. They included Johannes Miller, Carl Ludwig, Hermann von Helmholtz and Claude Bernard. On his return to Russia he taught first at the Military Medical Academy at St. Petersburg. He later transferred to Moscow, and then to Odessa. In 1863, Sechenov published *Reflexes of the Brain*. In that work he argued that all thinking and voluntary activity can be reduced to reflexes of the brain in response to external stimulation. The book caused a controversy. Sechenov was accused of spreading materialist, anti-religious philosophy and his book was banned in Russia. In other publications, Sechenov insisted that psychology should be studied by physiologists who used physiological methods to investigate reflexes. As a young man, Ivan Petrovich Pavlov (1849-1936), was very much impressed by Sechenov's *Reflexes of the Brain*. In the West, similar views were being put forward by Wilhelm Griesinger in Germany, and by Maudsley and Laycock in England.

Ivan Petrovich Pavlov was the son of an Russian Orthodox clergyman who turned from study at a seminary to study science at St. Petersburg University. Most of his early work was in the physiology of digestion. He was able to study abroad and spent some time, first in Carl Ludwig's laboratory in Leipzig. In 1884 he joined Rudolf Heidenhain in Breslau (Wroclaw) and stayed there for two years. Heidenhain was a neurologist interested in hypnosis, although Pavlov's interests were in the physiology of the pancreas. On his return to Russia he was appointed to the chair of pharmacology at the Military Medical Academy in St. Petersburg in 1890. This was ten years after Sechenov had left. Later, he became a professor of physiology and devoted his energies to research on the physiology of the digestive system. He developed a surgical technique by which part of the gastric mucosa was exposed and gastric secretion could be directly observed. This procedure became known as "Pavlov's pouch." For this work Pavlov won a Nobel Prize in 1904. His interest in reflex actions dates from about this time as well.

During his work on gastric secretions, Pavlov had noticed that some secretions could be produced by the sight of food. He called this a "psychological reflex." His observation suggested to him a method which could be used to investigate the physiology of the brain. The method was used to establish the existence of conditioned reflexes. In his experiments with these, Pavlov (1927) operated on a dog to open its salivary gland duct and to insert a canule. This procedure allowed him to measure the amount of salivation. A morsel of food was put into the dog's mouth in order to produce salivation. If the food was preceded by a neutral stimulus such as an onset of light or metronome sound, these neutral stimuli could also produce the flow of food without food. This reaction became known as the conditioned (sometimes also called conditional) reflex. The method became known in the United States as "classical" or "Pavlovian conditioning." Edwin Twitmyer (1873-1943)of the University of Pennsylvania had discovered the conditioned knee-jerk reflex in 1902, a few years before Pavlov, by associating the sound of a bell with a tap on the tendon. However, his work did not attract much attention (Kazdin, 1978).

Pavlov's neutral stimulus became known as "conditioned stimulus" and the food as "unconditioned stimulus." When, after conditioning, the animal was exposed to the "conditioned stimulus" without being reinforced by the administration of food, the conditioned reflex disappeared or was "extinguished." The animal could also be conditioned to avoid painful (noxious) stimuli. By exploring the parameters of conditioned reflexes, Pavlov inferred the existence of a hypothetical neurophysiological procees in the cerebral cortex. Here he borrowed the ideas of central excitiation and inhibition, also that of reciprocal inhibition, from Charles Sherrington (1906), who used them in connection with spinal reflexes. Pavlov's neurophysiological processes in the cortex were "central excitation," and "central inhibition." These could be external, internal, or supramarginal. An excitation in one part of the cortext could induce inhibition in another part of it and vice versa. Thus physiological processes in the brain were described by Pavlov, which underlined the mental processes postulated by associationists and hedonists. Extending the work of Pavlov from animals to human beings, a student of Pavlov, Nicolai Krasnogorski (1882-1960), studied classical conditioning in children (Krasnogorski, 1925).

In later years, Pavlov (1941) became interested in the problems of human personality and of mental illness. He tried to explain individual differences and such pathological conditions as hysteria and schizophrenia in terms of hypothetical physiological processes in the cortex. He based his theories on the observation of experimental neurosis produced in dogs which were forced to discriminate between reinforced and non-reinforced stimuli. When the discrimination became too difficult, as for instance between a circle and an ellipse that approached the shape of a circle, the conditioned reflexes broke down. The animals became very excited or inhibited and showed general signs of neurosis. An experimental neurosis could also be produced by delaying the reinforcement of conditioned reflexes. Two American followers of Pavlov, Howard Liddell (1895-1962) (1956) and Horsely Gantt (1944) investigated experimental neurosis on this continent. Somewhat later, Jules Masserman (1943), a psychiatrist at the University of Chicago, conducted research on experimental neurosis in cats and dogs which he interpreted in psychodynamic terms.

The 1924 flood in Leningrad almost drowned Pavlov's experimental dogs. The calamity afforded an opportunity to observe neurosis in dogs produced by natural causes. As an aftermath of their traumatic experience many dogs developed similar symptoms to those occurring in experimental neurosis. Some became very excited , others, in contrast, became very inhibited. Pavlov explained the phenomena of neurosis in dogs by his hypothetical constructs of central excitation and inhibition. The latter could be external and was due to intense or novel stimuli. It could also be internal. The internal inhibition was caused by extinction or delay of reinforcement. Both the states of excitation and inhibition could spread over the cortext or induce its opposite at a distance. Normal functioning of the cortex depended on a proper balance between excitation and inhibition. Pavlov proposed that there were constitutional differences among dogs. Probably this was also true of human beings. These constitutional factors were responsible for a variety of temperaments, and for the susceptibility to a neurotic breakdown. The constitutional differences in the properties of the central nervous system could be described by two orthogonal, bipolar dimensions: the "strong vs. weak," and the "stable vs. unstable." In the "strong" nervous system, the excitatory processes predominated over the inhibitory. In the weak one, the inhibitory processes predominated over the excitatory. In the "stable" nervous system there was a proper balance between the reciprocal inhibitory and excitatory processes. In the "unstable" nervous system this balance was lacking. Therefore there were four types of nervous system: strong-stable, strong-unstable, weak-stable, weak-unstable. Pavlov thought that these four types of nervous systems corresponded to the four temperaments: sanguine, choleric, phlegmatic, and melancholic, originally described by the Arab followers of Hippocrates and Galen.

During a stress situation, whenever there was a threat or a conflict, the individual with a strong and unstable nervous system reacted by disinhibition of conditioned reflexes, and by excitement, anger, and aggression. An individual with a weak and unstable nervous system reacted to stress with a generalized inhibition of conditioned reflexes, with anxiety, and withdrawal. In a more severe stress situation, withdrawal could lead to a state of catalepsy. An overexcitation of the cortex could as a physiological defense mechanism produce the "supremarginal" (protective) inhibition leading to the "paradoxical" and "ultraparadoxical" states. In the "paradoxical" state, strong stimuli produced weak responses and vice versa. In the "ultraparadoxical" state, inhibition was produced by excitatory stimuli and excitation by inhibitory stimuli. According to Pavlov, schizophrenia was a result of an ultraparadoxical state, which caused such symptoms as inappropriate response, apathy, negativism, stereotypy and catatonic stupor.

In the contemporary behaviour therapy, the Pavlovian classical conditioning provides the basis for aversion therapy and for counter-conditioning known as reciprocal inhibition therapy (Wolpe, 1958). It also provides the basis for the desensitization procedure.

Another member of the Russian school of reflexology was Vladimir Michalovich Bechterev (1857-1927), who coined the terms "reflexology" and "objective psychology." Bechterev was a practicing clinical psychiatrist in addition to being an experimental physiologist. After obtaining his M.D. from the University of St. Petersburg, he went abroad and visited several centers of learning. He spent some time with Wundt to learn the new experimental psychology, and then with Flechsig in Leipzig. He also went to Berlin to study with du Bois Reymond. In Paris, he worked with Charcot and studied the hypnotic treatment of hysterical patients. On his return to Russia, Bechterev became a professor of psychiatry at the University of Kazan. Subsequently, he became the professor of psychiatry and neurology at the Military Academy in St. Petersburg. Bechterev was a man of very broad interests and a prolific writer. His interests were broad, and ranged from hypnosis to clinical psychiatry and neurophysiological research. In his laboratory,

Bechterev devised a conditioned reflex procedure which was an alternative to that of Pavlov. Instead of using the salivary response to food, he used the defensive reaction of paw flexing in dogs to an electric shock. As in Pavlov's experiments, a conditioned stimulus, such as a light or a bell, was followed by an electric shock, a noxious stimulus. After a few trials, the dog acquired the conditioned reflex of withdrawing the paw when the conditioned stimulus was displayed. This procedure became the paradigm for avoidance learning.

Bechterev had a more speculative turn of mind than Pavlov. He was interested in philosophy and became a metaphysical materialist. He explained mental phenomena in materialist terms. In 1910 he published a major wortk, *Objective Psychology*, and in 1917, *General Principles of Reflexology*. Bechterev tried to extend the idea of conditioned reflexes to an analysis of social life on the whole. He clashed with Pavlov on the question of how the stimuli affected the cerebral cortex (Minkowski,1970). Bechterev was also enthusiastic about Watson's behaviourism in the United States and propagated these ideas in Russia, where he endeavoured to combine behaviourism and reflexology with the dialectical-materialist doctrine of Marxism.

The American Behaviourist Movement

The nineteenth century moral treatment of the insane and the school of Russian reflexology may be regarded as antecedents of behaviour therapy. However, the connection is not a direct one. These were parallel developments on the whole. In the case of the American behaviourist movement, the connection is direct. Behaviour therapy is an offshoot of behaviourism and of its philosophy. Many practitioners of this form of therapy were originally trained as behaviourist psychologists. The next section will present a brief outline of the history and of the theoretical tenets of behaviourism. A review of contemporary behaviour therapy is beyond the scope of this book and is summarized in Weckowicz (1984).

Behaviourism is far from being a monolithic theory. It consists of several independent complexes of ideas which logically do not entail one another. Their association in the body of behaviourist theory, or movement, may be due to historical accidents.

One has to distinguish three types of behaviourism (Mace, 1948). There is (1) the radical or metaphysical type of behaviourism. It has its roots in philosophical materialism and in its theories of mind. Then (2) the methodological type of behaviourism. This has its foundation in animal psychology and in positivist schools of philosophy. It is closely related to operationalism. Finally (3) the analytical or logical type of behaviourism is a kind advocated by some analytical and by some common language philosophers. A further distinction can be drawn between the molecular or atomist kind of behaviourism, and the molar or purposive type.

Radical behaviourism tended to stress a form of mechanistic-reductionist-materialism (materialistic monism). However, this was not always done explicitly or unambiguously. Its doctrine implied that psychological phenomena could be reduced to reflexes of the central nervous system. That meant that psychology could be reduced to physical events. To a radical behaviourist, matter and energy (electrons, protons or their constituents, gravity, electric-magnetic, weak and strong forces), represent the ultimate reality. Consciousness is at best an epiphenomenon, and cannot be studied objectively. It is outside the mass-space-time framework, the ultimate reality, and the only concern of science.

Ideas such as these may be traced far back to the philosophy of Democritus and Lucretius in ancient times. In the modern age, this point of view was emphatically argued by the French Materialists of the eighteenth century. These included, Julien Offray de la Mettrie (1709-1751), the author of *L'Homme Machine* (1748), Claude Adrian Helvetius (1715-1771), Pierre Jean George Cabanis (1775-1808), the originator of "moral science,"and Henri de Saint Simon, the inventor of the term, "social physiology." Cabanis applied the principles of physical science to human behaviour and society. Cartesian dualism with its separation of mind (*res cogitans*) from matter (*res extensa*), and its conception of human bodies as reflex machines, prepared the ground for the views of the French Materialists. They rejected Descartes' *res cogitans*, but kept his *res extensa* which they used to explain the workings of both the human body and the human mind. The idea of a reflex which originated with Descartes, was elaborated further by Robert Whytt (1714-1766) (1763), and Marshall Hall (1790-1857) (1833). It became the key explanation of mental phenomena. Materialist views of the human mind were propagated more intensively during the nineteenth century by such social philosophers as Antoine Destutt de Tracy, Ludwig Feuerbach and Karl Vogt. In psychiatry, they were subscribed to by such organic psychiatrists as Griesinger, Meynert, Maudsley, and Bechterev.

Methodological behaviourism arose from the attempts to make psychology an objective and rigorous science on the model of physics. The extension of psychological experimentation to include animal subjects played an important role in this development. Charles Darwin's theory of evolution as presented in his *The Origin of Species* (1859), closed the gap between the animal and human mind. A continuity between the two was assumed. Darwin elaborated these views further in his *Expression of the Emotions in Man and Animals* (1872). The Darwinian theories stimulated an interest in animal psychology, or as it became known, comparative psychology. Several researchers started investigating animal behaviour in the laboratory and natural surroundings. Researchers tried to recontruct the putative mental processes going on in the animal consciousness by analogy with those going on in the human consciousness. However, the validity and the reliability of this procedure was questioned by many. A British psychologist Lloyd Morgan (1852-1936) (1894) applied the law of parsimony to speculations about mental processes in animals, known as "Lloyd Morgan's canon." He suggested that only the simplest mental processes which could explain an animal's behaviour, should be postulated. This would provide an Occam's razor against the tendency to anthropomorphize animal behaviour. A German zoologist, Jacques Loeb (1859-1924) (1900), who emigrated to America, developed a theory of tropism. This theory explained the behaviour of lower animals in purely mechanistic terms. In 1899 three prominent German zoologists Th. Beer, A. Bethe and J. von Uexkull published an article in which they pleaded for the substitution of mechanical terms for mentalistic ones when describing animal behaviour.

The Darwinian theory of evolution had a broader and a more profound effect on contemporary thought than the rising interest in animal psychology. This influence was particularly strong in North America, a country bound less by tradition than inspired by a vision of the future. The idea that species, and generally biological forms, change under the selective pressure of the environment, had wide appeal in the United States. Evolutionary ideas became diffused in American social thought. It meant that natural selection produced adjustment to the environment, and that the purpose of psychological functions and of social institutions was to ensure the survival of individuals and groups.

These ideas gave rise in America to the philosophical school of pragmatism and its offshoot in psychology, functionalism. According to pragmatism, the criterion of truth lay in desirable personal and social consequences. Social salvation lay in the education of the masses, the purpose of which was to inculcate the values of good citizenship. John Dewey (1859-1952) (1916,1922) became the prophet of pragmatism. He wielded a great influence, first from the University of Chicago, and later from Columbia University, where he held professorships. Dewey's ideas affected educationists and psychologists as well as philosophers and historians. In psychology, the response to the challenge of the philosophy of pragmatism was the development of the school of functionalism at Chicago and Columbia. The main emphasis of this school of psychology was on the workings of processes of adjustment, such as learning rather than on the study of the structure and contents of mind, as revealed in introspection. Studies of animals, children and mental patients became important. Among the functionalist psychologists, the most important was Edward Lee Thorndike (1874-1949) (1911). He studied learning in animals, and concluded that animals learn by "trial and error," and that rewarded responses were consolidated, while non-rewarded ones were eliminated. A reward "stamped in" a connection between stimulus and response whicvh produced the reward. This constituted the "law of effect" which in addition to the law of repetition or "exercise" provided the basis for learning. The law of effect was an experimental confirmation of the hedonistic pleasure principle. The "trial and error" learning became known as instrumental learning, and offered an alternative paradigm to Pavlovian conditioning.

Behaviourism was an offshoot of functionalism. Before we continuc with its story, two important sources of influence on the methodological behaviourism: positivism, already disacussed in Chapter 7, and the closely related operationism have to be mentioned. Positivism, inaugurated by Auguste Comte (1798-1857), represented one of the main streams of nineteenth century thought. It reflected the tremendous progress in science and technology which made the industrial revolution possible. Positivism rejected all metaphysical speculations, and eschewed making any metaphysical assumptions with regard to ultimate reality. Instead, it stressed objective and public observations, replicable experimentation and measurement. In the search for truth, it relied on scientific method. Positivists believed that science was value-free. Comte denied the epistemological validity of introspection. After all, introspection was private and personal, while all knowledge was public. It also implied that the introspecting individual tried to be both the object of observation as well as the observing subject. According to Comte, such a combination was not possible (Comte, 1908). The tradition of positivism influenced the physicist-philosopher Ernst Mach, and from him, was taken over in the twentieth century by the Vienna Circle. These Viennese philosophers of science were concerned with the experimental verification of knowledge claims. It is for this reason that they called themselves "logical positivists." The group of prominent philosophers and scientists included among others, Moritz Schlick, Otto Neurath, Rudolph Carnap, and Herbert Feigl. According to logical positivists, the meaning of a proposition was derived from the method of its empirical verification. Unverifiable propositions were meaningless. Moreover, the language of theory served only as an instrument for deriving propositions which could be verified. They were verified by observation and experiments. Consequently, there were two languages, that of theory and that of observation. For a while, there was a disagreement among the members of the circle about the nature of the language of observation. They argued whether it was a "mentalistic" language about sensory experiences, or a "physicalistic" language about material objects in the external world. The second view prevailed and the physicalistic language was designated by the logical positivists as the common language of scientific observations. Thus science was concerned with physical events. In the twenties, thirties, and forties of the present century, logical positivism was the dominant current in philosophy of science. Some of its claims, such as the separation of the language theory from that of observation, were extreme. In recent years, logical positivism has been replaced by its more liberalized version, logical empiricism. The latter has become the generally accepted philosophical framework of scientific thinking (the "received view"). In the United States there was a parallel development.

In the same year in which the Vienna Circle was officially established, a Harvard physicist Percy Bridgman (1882-1962) published *The Logic of Modern Physics* (1927). In that book, Bridgman argued that the meaning of scientific concepts was derived from the operations carried out to produce and to measure the exemplars of these concepts. This approach became known as operationism and was quickly assimilated to the tenets of logical positivism. Psychologists were very impressed by the idea of operationism. Gustav Bergman, a positivist philosopher of science, worked closely with Kenneth Spence, one of the leading behaviourists, to formulate an operationist-positivist framework of behaviourism (Bergman & Spence, 1941). It absolved psychologists from the necessity of explaining the meaning of such murky concepts as intelligence. Intelligence was "what intelligence tests measured." The methodological behaviourism was inspired by the theories of positivism and operationism. In contrast to the radical behaviourism, the methodological behaviourism eschewed making any metaphysical commitments with regard to ultimate reality. It was anti-metaphysical in its intent, in the positivist tradition of Comte and of the Vienna Circle. According to the methodological behaviourists, science *qua* science, and this included psychology, was concerned with events that could be objectively established, publically observed, measured, and replicated. Like Comte's positivism, methodological behaviourism denied the epistemological validity of introspection.

Finally, a few words should be said about analytical or logical behaviourism. This philosophical theory asserted that all propositions describing mentalistic events which appeared to refer to "mind," were really propositions about behaviour. They argued that propositions about mental events could be translated without loss of meaning, into propositions about behaviour. Logical behaviourism developed in the context of logical positivism. Two members of the Vienna Circle, Rudolf Carnap, a physical scientist, and Otto Neurath, a social scientist, put forward a thesis that all scientific propositions about the observations carried out in the context of the social, psychological, biological or physical sciences could be stated in physicalistic language, and therefore were about physical objects. Consequently, all empirical sciences could be reduced to one fundamental science. This thesis became known as the "principle of the unity of science." It argued against the traditional division between natural sciences and the humanities (*Geisteswissenschaften*). The divisions into different disciplines were, according to this view, quite accidental. They were the result of a unique historical development, and could be justified only for purely practical purposes. The proponents of the unity of science principle believed that the same scientific method was applicable to the physical, biological, psychological and social sciences. According to Carnap (1959) psychology could be reduced to the description of phsyical behaviour without any loss of meaning. This contention became the foundation of logical behaviourism. After arriving in the United States, Carnap and Neurath were joined by Charles Morris, a semioticist. They propagated the idea of the unity of science in the *International Encyclopedia of Unified Science* (Neurath, Carnap, & Morris, 1955, 1970).

Some other analytical philosophers, who were not in the logical positivist tradition, also maintained that psychological propositions were not about private happenings inside the mind, but were about publically observable behaviour. At Oxford, Gilbert Ryle (1949) used ordinary language analysis to elucidate the nature of mentalistic concepts. He reached the conclusion that propositions of ordinary language never referred to private mental events. They referred to publically observed behaviour or dispositions to such a behaviour. However, there was no agreement about the nature of the public behaviour. Questions were asked whether behaviour was best described in "molecular" terms as movement of phsyical objects using the language of classical mechanics, or whether it was to be described in "molar" terms, as intentional purposive acts. According to Ryle, there were two kinds of description in psychology. The first referred to physiological events, and the second to behavioural events. The second type of description was not in the physicalistic language, and was not about physical objects. However, it was not in a mentalistic language either. It did not refer to private events inside the mind. It referred to publically observed purposive acts and intentions or dispositions to perform such acts. While the first type of description was appropriate at the physiological level, the second was appropriate at the psychological one. This distinction corresponded also to the one drawn between "molecular" and "molar" or purposive behaviourism.

After this digresion into philosophy, we can return to the story of behaviourism. The behaviourist movement was initiated by John Broadus (J.B.) Watson (1878-1958). Watson was a Chicago functionalist interested in animal psychology. In 1908, he was appointed a professor at Hopkins. However, in 1920, he had to resign his professorship because he was involved in a divorce scandal. Eventually, Watson left academia and became an advertising executive. Earlier on, in the course of his work with rats at Chicago, he came to the conclusion that it was futile to speculate about the mental experiences of animal subjects. In 1913, Watson published a paper, *Psychology as the Behaviourist Views It*. The paper became a manifesto of the behaviourist movement.

Watson claimed that psychology, like any other science, was concerned with publically observable events, the behaviour of organisms. Although Watson was unaware of Pavlov's work when he published his behaviourist manifesto in 1913, he soon became acquainted with it and incorporated the concept of conditioned reflex into behaviourist theory (Cohen, 1979).

In subsequent publications Watson stressed other features of behaviourism: elementarism ("atomism"), associationism, peripheralism and environmentalism. Behaviour was analyzed into elementary units: reflexes or S-R connections. The S-R units and their concatenations were established by associations through contiguity, repetition, or presence of rewarding state of affairs, a reinforcement. Complex behaviour such as running mazes was explained by Watson as a chain of reflexes, with each consecutive response acting as a stimulus for the next response. He and other early behaviourists tended to be peripheralists. They tended to play down the importance of central processes and to explain behaviour in terms of peripheral processes which were observable or potentially observable. Thus, thought process was conceived as subvocal speech, hunger as stomach contractions, and expectancies as incipient tonic muscular contractions inducing certain postures. The tendency to seek the peripheralistic type of explanation eventually gave rise to an empty organism, or the "black box," theory. That theory tried to explain all psychological phenomena in terms of stimuli and responses, often hypothetical ones. It eschewed making suppositions about central mental or even neurophysiological processes in the brain, leaving the latter to neurophysiologists.

The "black box" theory found its full expression in the behaviourism of Burrhus Frederick (B.F.) Skinner (b.1904), who continued the Watsonian tradition. Apart from espousing the "black box" theory Skinner stressed the idea of contingent reinforcement as the determinant of behaviour. He distinguished two types of conditioning: (1) the respondent, and (2) the operant. The first was the classical Pavlovian conditioning. The second was a form of instrumental learning originally described by Thorndike. Skinner was particularly interested in the latter. Watson (1930) and the early behaviourists, perhaps under the influence of the American social ideology, tended to stress the importance of the environmental factors. They played down the role of heredity, of constitutional factors, and of instincts. This was entirely within the tradition of Lockean empiricism which had had such a shaping influence during the past two centuries in the English-speaking world. In addition to mind, Locke's *tabula rasa*, the total personality, the entire physical and mental constitution of the individual was regarded as being malleable. Watson made a radical assertion of total malleability of behaviour in 1930, when he said:

> Give me a dozen healthy infants, well-fed, and my own specified world to bring them up in and I'll guarantee to take any one at random and train him to become any type of specialist I might select—doctor, lawyer, artist, merchant, chief and, yes, even beggar-man and thief, regardless of his talents, penchants, tendencies, abilities, vocations and race of his ancestors. (J.B.Watson, *Behaviourism*, 1930, p.104).

Since they downplayed the importance of instincts, the behaviourists considered learning to be of paramount importance for the survival of men and animals.

Another feature of early behaviourism was the attitude of social pragmatism, a preoccupation with practical problems of human behavioiur and society, and turning away from purely academic issues. Behaviourism was also characterized by optimism with regard to personal and social betterment. This attitude may be discerned in the writings of some behaviourists, e.g., J.B. Watson and B.F. Skinner (1948). It is typical for the attitudes of contemporary behavioural therapists.

The final feature of behaviourism was the belief that basic laws of behaviour are the same for all species of animals. This applied all along the scale from fish to man. Consequently it was assumed that the study of white rats in the laboratory was the key to the understanding of human behaviour. This assumption has been called the assumption of the generality of the laws of behaviour. It continues the traditions of the naive belief in Newtonian science.

To summarize, there are nine sets of ideas which characterize behaviourism. Three of these were primary and six were secondary. These have been given different prominence at different times by the proponents of behaviourism. The three major ideas were:(1) reductionistic materialism, (2) scientific objectivism,(3) elementarism or atomism. Linked to these was a subset of six further ideas: (i) associationism, (ii) hedonism, (iii) pragmatism, (iv) environmentalism, (v) peripheralism and (vi) the generality of laws of behaviour.

Not all behaviourists accepted this schema. These sets of ideas had diverse historical antecedents, although the distinct paths they followed crossed one another more than once. Many behaviourists emphasized different aspects of the theory. Some, like Watson, were radical behaviourists, although he did not also commit himself to philosophical materialism. His contemporary, Albert P. Weiss (1879-1931) (1925), a behaviourist who taught at the University of Ohio, was a committed materialist. Weiss believed that phenomena of psychology could be reduced to physical-chemical events. More recent behaviourists such as B.F. Skinner (1938, 1953) tended to embrace the methodological brand of behaviourism and to eschew metaphysical speculations. Another division was between the "molecular" and "molar" varieties of behaviourism. The size and the nature of the S-R unit was a subject of debate. The question was asked: whether "S" was a discrete event at a sensory organ. Was it to be described in purely physical and physiological terms ? Was it an indefinite set of events signifying an external object? Also, they queried whether "R" was a discrete response to be described as a definite set of muscular contractions, or whether it was an indefinite set of movements which produced a common final change in the environment., such as depressing a lever. Erwin R. Guthrie (1952) represented the most extreme "molecular" position. For him, the response (R) was a contraction of a specific group of muscles, producing a specific movement. Most other behaviourists, including B.F. Skinner, have espoused the "molar" position. The most extreme molar view was that of the purposive behaviourists. A Harvard contemporary of Watson, Edwin B. Holt (1873-1946) (1915) was a purposive behaviourist. He argued that units of behaviour were not molecular, discrete reflexes, but were purposive acts, like going to a store to buy groceries. Edward C. Tolman (1886-1959), a student of Holt, was another purposive behaviourist who brought behaviourism close to cognitive psychology. For him behaviour was the utilization of the knowledge of the environment in order to solve certain problems (Tolman, 1932). Thus Tolman was a precursor of cognitive psychology.

Another issue which divided the behaviourists into camps, was the notion of reinforcement. Some, like Skinner, stressed the role of reinforcement in learning. He therefore emphasized the hedonistic aspect of behaviourism. Other, such as Watson, and in particular Guthrie, stressed the association by contiguity, and the importance of repetition in learning. Consequently, they emphasized the associationist features of behaviourism. Finally, those like Watson and Skinner, were also strict peripheralists. They believed then, in the "empty organism" theory.

Others, like Clark Hull (1884-1954) (1943) and Tolman, introduced "intervening variables" and "hypothetical constructs" connecting stimuli with responses.

Behaviourism has produced two different paradigms of learning: the classical or Pavlovian conditioning, and instrumental learning. There have been attempts to reduce the two paradigms to one, but they have been largely unsuccessful.

Behaviour therapy has been influenced in an unsystematic way by the ideas and theories of behaviourism. The result has been a conceptual confusion that has become characteristic of the field. Three basic models have emerged in behaviour therapy. They depend on the particular paradigm of learning used, and also on whether the stress is placed on the peripheral or central processes. They are: (1) The Pavlovian or classical conditioning model, (2) the S-R Hullian model, and (3) the operant conditioning, or Skinnerian model. In addition, some recent therapeutic practices which pass under the name of behaviour therapy have overstepped the framework of strict behaviourism (Locke, 1971). These practices utilize concepts that belong to cognitive psychology and also invoke such mentalistic notions like imagery.

The Emergence of Behaviour Therapy

In order to outline the early history of behaviour therapy, we have to go back to J.B. Watson, who may be regarded as its founder. Having possible practical applications in mind, Watson was eager to try the methods developed in the animal laboratory on humans. Basing himself on animal research, Watson came to the conclusion that mammalian infants had an inborn fear of only three types of situations: painful stimuli, loss of support, and loud noise. Other fears were produced by conditioning, by associating a neutral stimulus with a stimulus which activated an inborn fear. In 1920, J.B. Watson and his student, Rosalind Reyner, in the famous study of Little Albert, produced an experimental phobia of white rats in an eleven month old boy by pairing the sight of a white rat with a sudden loud sound, a bang on a metal bar. The fear of white rats generalized to rabbits and white fur (Watson & Reyner, 1920). Watson and Reyner speculated that the experimental rat phobia might be cured by producing an eating response which was not compatible with a fear reaction. This suggestion was taken up by Mary Cover Jones (1924), another student of Watson, who cured experimentally produced rat phobia in a little boy named Peter by pairing the feared object with the administration of food (feeding). These two experiments were the direct antecedents of the desensitization and reciprocal inhibition method of modern behaviour therapy.

In 1924, the same year in which Mary Jones' experiment was published, William Burnham published his important work, *The Normal Mind* (1924). Burnham discussed the problems of mental hygiene and child rearing within the framework of the Pavlovian conditioned reflex theory. He suggested that fears in children should be treated by exposing them to feared situations and producing an incompatible reaction to fear with soothing words and reassurance. Burnham called this method "inhibiting the inhibition." It corresponded to the modern behaviour therapy method of desensitization and reciprocal inhibition. One of Burnham's students, Florence Mateer, replicated and extended Krasnogorski's studies of classical conditioning in children (Kazdin, 1978).

During the 1930s, educational philosophy aimed at the optimum development of the individual child. Social adaptation, being "well adjusted" seemed the main goal in educational assessments of child rearing. The mid-Victorian idea that habits could be evil, also still prevailed so that the perfection of social behaviour in the school environment involved practical therapy for all forms of maladaptive behaviour. Immediate adjustments, results, were the goal, not a study of the ultimate causes of the behaviour. Thus we find Hollingsworth (1930), taking Berham's idea of "inhibiting inhibition"and suggesting a method of desensitization and reciprocal inhibition of fears within the framework of his theory of reintegration. Dunlap (1932) introduced the method of negative practice in the treatment of tics, stuttering, and nail biting. In 1938, E.R. Guthrie published *The Psychology of Human Conflict*, in which he presented the applications of his theory of contiguous S-R conditioning. This had relevance in the field of abnormal psychology. It was mainly an application of Guthrie's own theory of S-R conditioning to abnormal behaviour. According to him, in the treatment of faulty habits, a maladjustive response associated with a stimulus could be abolished by producing a different response in the presence of the stimulus. In the same year, Mowrer & Mowrer (1938) described a conditioning method of treatment for enuresis. Another early application of classical conditioning was in aversion therapy for alcoholics. In Russia, N.V. Kantorovich used electric shocks which were associated with the smell and taste of alcohol to produce an aversion to drinking.

Other Russian investigators created an aversion to alcohol by associating its consumption with nausea and vomiting. This was deone with an injection of apomorphine (Kazdin, 1978). In America, Walter Voegtlin (1940) and Frederick Lemere in 1935 started aversion therapy for alcoholics at the Shadel Sanitorium. They used injections of emetine to induce vomiting in association with the consumption of alcohol (Kazdin, 1978).

Modern behaviour therapy was inaugurated by Joseph Wolpe (1952) in his work on experimental neurosis in South Africa. Wolpe showed that experimental neurosis was produced by learning. It could be reversed by using the method of reciprocal inhibition (Wolpe, 1954, 1958). Phobias, which according to Wolpe were conditioned fear reactions, could be inhibited by inducing an incompatible reaction of relaxation. To induce relaxation, Wolpe used the method of progressive relaxation described by Edmund Jacobson (1938). Wolpe was assisted in his early work in South Africa, by two collaborators, Stanley Rachman and Arnold Lazarus.

Further work on behavioural therapy emerged in England. Eysenck had in 1952 published an article in which he had questioned the effectiveness of psychoanalysis. On the basis of statistics, he argued that the recovery rate of patients treated by psychoanalysis was not higher than that of untreated cases, or of those treated by supportive therapy only. He further argued that the treatment of psychoneurosis should be based on principles of learning theory (Eysenck, 1959, 1960). He called his method, "behaviour therapy." Inspired by Eysenck, a group of clinical psychologists was formed at Maudsley Hospital. This included Maurice Shapiro, Aubrey Yetes, H.G. Jones, and V. Meyer. These men carried out pioneering research on the clinical applications of behaviour therapy (Kazdin, 1978). Another pioneer of conditioned reflex therapy was Andrew Salter (1949). Salter based his approach to therapy on the work of Pavlov and Bechterev. Originally interested in hypnotherapy, Salter explained hypnosis in terms of conditioned reflexes. Subsequently, he relegated hypnosis to a minor role in terapy and focused on the role of conditioning in bringing about an improvement in adjustment. He believed that maladjustment was due to excessive inhibition and that conditioned reflex therapy should restore the proper balance between excitation and inhibition (Kazdin, 1978).

Behavioural therapy was soon tried on patients in mental hospitals as well. Teodoro Ayllon and his associates did the pioneering work on applications of operant conditioning to behaviour modification of chronic schizophrenic patients in the mental hospital setting (Ayllon, 1965; Ayllon & Haughton, 1962; Ayllon & Michael, 1959). The contemporary systems of behaviour therapy are reviewed elsewhere (Weckowicz, 1984). It is sufficient to state here that behaviour therapy reflects the main tenets of behaviourism. Similar to behaviourism, it subscribes to the "black box" theory of organism. It rejects the disease entities and the psychodynamic mechanisms because they are not directly observable. They are only inferred (Skinner, 1956). Instead it focuses on the symptoms which cause trouble. Behaviour therapy emphasized concrete behaviour rather than symbolic expressions by patients. Behaviour therapy techniques rely on conditioning rather than on cognitive learning.

However, in recent years, there have been some relaxations of the strictures of behaviourism as these applied to behaviour therapy. Private experiences such as thoughts and imagery have been recognized and treated as self-produced stimuli or as responses. This relaxation of the strictures was due to the fact that in many cases problems requiring therapeutic intervention were concerned with private experiences, such as morbid thoughts and obsessions, rather than with overt responses. Also, there was a recognition of the importance of self-control with respect to behaviour. Consequently certain forms of behaviour therapy have merged with cognitive therapy. False beliefs about oneself and the world have been implicated recently in the cognitive theory of depression (Beck, 1961).

These recent developments were anticipated by early pioneers who advocated various techniques of correcting one's thoughts through reasoning, persuasion, self-instruction, and self-control. A French psychotherapist, Emil Coue (1857-1926) instructed his patients to repeat "Day by day, in every way, I am getting better and better." This statement was supposed to influence the patient by autosuggestion, to improve his beliefs about himself and about his health. Such a belief in its turn was supposed to affect the patient's behaviour (Coue,1922). J.A. Bain (1928) and Dale Carnegie (1948) proposed similar techniques for control of one's thoughts.

14

The Impact of Philosophy on Psychiatry at the Turn of the Century

The Humanistic Challenge to the Scientific Point of View

The previous chapter discussed the history of the American behaviourist movement and the origins of behaviour therapy. The theory and applications of behaviourism eventually presented a challenge to both organic and psychodynamic psychiatry. As a challenge it came from the positivist views of science, included an assertion of the objectivity of science, and generally of the objectivist view of the world. Behaviorism challenged dynamic psychiatry because its critics found that its mentalistic speculations were experimentally unverifiable. At the same time, it also challenged organic psychiatry which had more claim to being an objective science.

It may seem strange that the credentials to objectivity of organic psychiatry could be questioned. However, one has to remember that in the beginning of the twentieth century, little was known about the neurochemistry of the brain. There was, it is true, a scanty knowledge of brain pathology associated with organic psychoses. In contrast, in functional psychoses, the claims about the occurrence of neuropathological changes were based mainly on speculations. Consequently, organic explanations of functional psychoses were very often dubbed as "brain mythology." Behaviorism offered the possibility of alternative explanations based on conditioned reflexes and learned habits. These could be experimentally checked.

Contemporary with the rise of American behaviourism, there were also challenges to both organic and psychodynamic psychiatry in German speaking countries. The challenges were from the subjectivist position. This was essentially a humanist criticism which asserted the primacy of subjective experience. It occurred in the wider context of a challenge posed to the philosophies of positivism, materialism, and scientism by humanist scholarship. The development of phenomenology in philosophy, and later of existentialism, continued this humanist challenge.

Positivism asserted the importance of a scientific outlook for the progress of society. Applied to scientific psychology, this meant that the world was predictable and that objective observations could be replicated. Positivism was founded on a belief in induction. It assumed the general validity of scientific laws. It was concerned with the classes of things and of events, not with unique occurrences. This outlook put an emphasis on objectivity and on freedom from subjective idiosyncrasies. The metaphysics underlying the scientific point of view assumed absolute or, at least, probabilistic determinism. It presupposed the possibility of achieving a value-free science. This classical scientific philosophy, together with the scientific methodology created by the Scientific Revolution, had been highly successful in the physical sciences and in physical medicine. There had been some difficulties with the acceptance of the mechanistic view in the biological sciences. The nineteenth century controversies between vitalist and mechanist theories demonstrated the difficulties encountered by the mechanistic and deterministic explanations in biology. In the end, the mechanistic-deterministic point of view prevailed also in that discipline. However, the validity of the scientific outlook and method when applied to the human mind, to human behaviour, and to social phenomena encountered even more severe criticism. The belief that the same kind of results might be achieved for the "human sciences" as already accomplished in physics, arose during the eighteenth century enlightenment. It had gained ground with the spread of positivist philosophy in the nineteenth century. However, this belief had not been generally accepted.

A strong opposition to mechanistic-determinism continued to exist among humanistic scholars, theologians, and jurists. The critics of scientific psychology and sociology pointed out that mental phenomena were characterized by subjective experiences which had unique meanings. These phenomena also implied the freedom of choice which was intrinsically associated with valuation. Human beings were believed to be able to exercise "free will," and to be morally responsible and accountable for their behavior. Moreover, they possessed the divine gift of creativity. Human beings produced novel ideas, novel values, and works of art. Finally human beings, to a great extent determined their own fate.

It was pointed out by the critics of scientism and naturalism that man is more than an *homo naturae*, that the legal and political systems of European society were based on the concept of the individual as a self-conscious, free, and morally responsible person. The social order could not operate without the assumption of a degree of individual freedom, of moral responsibility, and of the presence of mutual obligations.

Human consciousness, and the moral order associated with it, was permeated with meanings, as well as with ethical and esthetic values. The latter were seen to be a product of purposeful strivings rather than a product of the accidental interplay of blind causes. The critics of the positivist philosophy and of scientism also pointed out that in addition to being a member of the natural order, man was also a member of the moral and spiritual one. In short, human nature had a spiritual as well as an animal aspect to it.

The new humanist critics conceived of the spirituality of man in terms of either theistic philosophy, or in terms of a humanist one. According to the theist view, the spiritual nature of man stemmed from his possession of an immortal, divine soul. According to the humanist view, man represented the highest ultimate value, the *Summum Bonum*, in the scheme of things. He created and controlled his own destiny and the destiny of society. He could also alter and shape the physical world. According to both the theist and humanist points of view, man could not be looked upon as a member of the natural order of inanimate objects, of plants and of animals. Consequently the critics of positivism and metaphysical materialism rejected reductionist explanations of the human psyche. Many thinkers assumed that man belonged both to the moral as well as to the natural order. This produced a conflict between the humanities (*Geisteswissenschaften*) and the natural sciences (*Naturwissenschaften*) whenever one tried to apply the science to man. The question, often asked, was whether psychology, and by extension, psychiatry, belonged to the humanities or to the natural sciences ? Or, did they belong to both ? The humanist approach to psychology focused on subjective experiences, and was concerned with ethical and esthetic values. It was also concerned with the expression and creativity of the human spirit. In contrast, the natural science approach to psychology believed in an objectively observed (from the "outside") view of behaviour and social events. The data obtained by observation could ultimately be reduced to movements of matter and energy.

Quite early in the history of modern science, the question was asked whether the human mind could be investigated by scientific method. Immanuel Kant (1785/1944) did not believe that the method of the natural sciences, was applicable to psychology. This was the domain of philosophy (Kant,1785/1873). One hundred years later, Wilhelm Wundt, the founder of experimental psychology believed that the method of natural science was applicable to a narrow scope of mental phenomena. These were sensations and their associations. Higher mental processes could only be investigated by a philosophical method. By the middle of the nineteenth century, the controversy became even more acute. Some believed that human experience and behaviour, and consequently the understanding of the social order, should be approached through philosophy and from the perspective of the humanities. Others were convinced that this approach should be through the natural sciences. Since psychiatry dealt with abnormal mental phenomena, the adequacy of a purely biological approach was questioned. It was felt that a biological approach should be supplemented with one that stemmed from philosophy and the humanities.

In Germany, traditional scholarship was divided into the natural sciences (*Naturwissenschaften*) and the humanities (*Geisteswissenschaften*). These two branches of human knowledge were believed to encompass two different worlds of experience. These appeared to be irreconcilable with each other. At the end of the nineteenth century, the great speculative system of German Transcendental Idealism was gone. It had been undermined by the progress of science, and the philosophies of positivism and materialism which were associated with it. However, the world picture presented by these two latter philosophies was rather narrow and provided no room for the total richness of human experience. There was an atmosphere of crisis in philosophy.

Some philosophers, such as the neo-Kantians and neo-Thomists, retreated to the old positions, trying to develop and to elaborate the old philosophical theories. Marx and his followers rejected idealism and accepted metaphysical materialism. However, they borrowed the dialectical method of Hegelian transcendental idealism to formulate the "laws" governing the physical and social world. As a result they came up with the philosophy of dialectical materialism. Others struck in new directions trying to develop philosophical methods of a broader scope than that of traditional empiricism. They sought to come up with new philosophical solutions.

Four new currents of philosophy had an important impact on psychiatry and psychology. These were the humanist philosophies of culture: *Geisteswissenschaften*, *Kulturwissenschaften*. Important in this context, was the *Philosophie des Lebens* of Wilhelm Dilthey. The other three were the phenomenological movement, existentialism, and the philosophy of symbolic forms of Ernst Cassirer who was a neo-Kantian. Before each new development is discussed, a brief comment is needed to describe the relation between psychiatry and philosophy existing early in this century, in German speaking countries. Popular interest in philosophy in these countries had always been great. This may have been part of the heritage of Romanticism and of the culture of the universities as institutions. The interaction between philosophy and psychiatry became particularly lively at the end of the nineteenth and the beginning of the twentieth century. Many medical doctors specialized in psychiatry because of their interest in philosophy. Quite a few of them, in addition to having a degree in medicine, acquired a doctorate in philosophy and psychology. This may be exemplified by Theodor Ziehen, a professor of psychiatry in Berlin. Also by Viktor Gebsattel, a phenomenological psychiatrist, and by Paul Schilder of the Vienna University. Karl Jaspers (1958) and Theodor Ziehen left psychiatry for philosophy. Ziehen was both a psychiatrist and a philosopher, and also became an experimental psychologist. Karl Buhler, an important experimental psychologist, was also trained in medicine and psychiatry. Ludwig Binswanger made important contributions to both psychiatry and philosophy. It was common for medical students to attend philosophy lectures and seminars as exemplified by Freud who took several courses from Brentano.

We shall begin our brief survey of those philosophical currents which had an important impact on psychiatry with an account of the search for a method appropriate to the humanities (*Geisteswissenschaften*). A method was sought which would have the same validity as the experimental one for the natural sciences. The two varieties of method found appropriate for the humanities were hermeneutics and the *Verstehen* method.

The Controversy about the Method of Social Science, and the Rise of Hermeneutics

In the last part of the nineteenth century, German universities became a forum for a debate called the methods controversy (*Methodenstreit*). It began in the context of economics and was originally concerned with the question of whether economics should be treated as a historical discipline or a non-historical science (Schumpeter, 1954). Later on, this debate extended to other social sciences and focused on the relation of value to science. The question of the applicability of the natural science methods to the study of man, of society, and of history, was extensively debated. By the 1860s, German historians belonging to the prevailing school of historicism (*Historismus*) still believed that their discipline was just as scientific as the natural sciences. The word for discipline used in German academia was *Wissenschaft*, and means science. Science was less a matter of measurement or predictability then, than one of finding the correct explanatory principles according to the methods of sufficient reason. The progress of technology had changed the understanding of science, however, and shifted it towards the more mathematical side of the spectrum. By the 1890s, those historians who believed in studying economic history and in using a statistical approach, found themselves in conflict with the traditional political historians. This debate was known as the *Lamprechtstreit*, named for the economic historian Karl Lamprecht who advocated the new methods (Liebel, 1964).

Those who favored a suitable method for the humanities drew on a strong philosophical tradition. The problem of finding a methodology for the humanities and moral sciences was not new. It had been discussed earlier, by Giambattista Vico (1668-1744) and by other philosophers at the beginning of the nineteenth century. German Idealist philosophy was inspired by Romantic ideas to produce early in that century the school of *Naturphilosophie*. The mystic philosophers of Nature had as their leading figure, Friedrich Schelling (1775-1843), a friend of Hegel. He was so much revered that the historian Leopold von Ranke was even able to compare him with Plato. Schelling believed that all knowledge, including the knowledge of the material world, was acquired by self-reflection. This was the turning of consciousness upon itself. Since both individual minds and the material world were expressions of the same underlying spirit (*Der Geist*), the nature, the meaning, and the purpose of the world could be grasped and understood by imagination and by contemplation of one's mental processes. Similar ideas were expressed by some Romantic poets such as Novalis (Friedrich Freiherr von Hardenberg, 1772-1801), and Samuel Coleridge (1772-1834). These poets claimed that a profound esthetic experience of nature would lead to a mystical union of man and the universe. In this way man could grasp the ultimate meaning of the external world. The philosophy of Georg Wilhelm Friedrich Hegel (1770-1831) presented a rationalist version of these ideas. The spirit (*Der Geist*), he believed, could be revealed by dialectical reason. Later in the nineteenth century, under the impact of positivism, this belief was abandoned in the sciences, and was replaced by the modern conception of an objective scientific method. Some schools of psychology, psychoanalysis, and the humanities did not find this suitable for their studies, and continued to draw on the older philosophical traditions.

According to the transcendental idealist view, works of art, and even the histories of nations, were regarded as the creative expression of a collective spirit (*Geist*), representing a different order of reality from that of the material world. As a result, scholarship could be strictly divided between humanities (*Geisteswissenschaften*) which were concerned with the realm of spirit, and natural sciences (*Naturwissenschaften*), which were concerned with the knowledge and control of the material world. The processes of knowledge (*episteme*) involved in the two domains were different.

In the domain of *Geisteswissenschaften*, mental processes, judgments and valuations could be grasped in their totality by intuition, which provided a certainty of knowledge. On the other hand, in the domain of *Naturwissenschaften*, the external material world and its regularity was inferred from sensory experiences. The observed relations were contingent, non-necessary. Its ultimate meaning and purpose could not be known. According to the argument of the *Geisteswissenschaften*, individual minds were parts of the collective spirit (*Der Geist*), therefore, the meaning of the cultural phenomena could be grasped intuitively, through sympathy, empathy, and reflection.

In contrast to science, where phenomena observed have to be analyzed into elementary basic units and variables from which a theoretical model can be constructed, the method used by the humanities was synthetic. The object of study could not be removed from its context. It had to be grasped in its totality and its context, as a *Gestalt*. By this process, its meaning, its purpose, its value, and the intentions of its creators were revealed to the scholar. Insight and unique experience (*Erlebnis*), rather than inductive reasoning provided understanding of the expressions of individual minds, and of the collective spirit. Based on these premises, an attempt was made to find a humanistic (*geisteswissenschaftliche*) method, which would formalize and standardize the procedures of the humanistic and social sciences. It would parallel the empirical-inductive, experimental method of the natural sciences. Such a method was found in hermeneutics. The word derived from the Greek, *hermeneutikos*, which means "explaining" or "clarifying" (Bauman, 1978). Originally, hermeneutics was a method connected with biblical scholarship and the interpretation of ancient texts. It had philological connotations, its purpose was to infer the meaning of particular words from their context. A preliminary interpretation of a word was established by its context. Then, a possibly slightly altered meaning of the context by the suggested meaning of the word, was considered, and so forth. This procedure was known as the "hermeneutic circle." Early in the nineteenth century, the new method was extended to literary and art criticism. With the advent of the Romantic period, the criteria for judging literary and artistic works by the impersonal esthetic conventions of the classical period were replaced by the interest in personal meaning which a poet, a novelist, or an artist tried to convey. This could be done by empathically identifying oneself with the author, stepping into his shoes, as it were, and trying to see the world through his eyes (Dilthey,1977). Also the whole cultural context in which the literary or artistic work occurred was important. It had to be considered in its totality (Bauman, 1978). Eventually, it was suggested that the same method should be used for the study of historical events, and generally in the cultural and moral universe of discourse. Bauman (1978), who followed Joachim Wach (1926), attributes the original application of hermeneutics in humanistic studies to Friedrich Ast (1778-1841). However, Friedrich Schleiermacher (1768-1834) and Wilhelm Dilthey (1833-1911) (1954, 1961) were the two important nineteenth century philosophers who developed and established hermeneutics as the method of the humanities.

Although one may still observe the influence of Hegelian thought, both Schleiermacher and Dilthey rejected the Hegelian idea of Spirit as absolute reason. They replaced it with an idea of the totality of mental life that manifested itself in different cultural forms. Dilthey, a philosopher-historian, called his system "philosophy of life."

(*Philosophie des Lebens*). He considered man as a bio-psychological organism, a totality of body and mind, existing in a concrete historical-cultural context, and possessing a particular *Weltanschauung* (World View) (Dilthey, 1957-1960). The laws governing human conduct were relative to the historical and cultural contexts. To understand the behaviour of a historical character living in a different epoch or in a different culture, one had to bridge the gap between the two historical contexts. (Each had its independent milieu). The one context was that of the writer of the document or work of literature who reflected his times. The other was that the historian who studied the work for its meaning to him, and for its meaning in the age in which it had arisen. Thiselton (1980) refers to these as the "two horizons" of hermeneutics. The object of such hermeneutical studies was to achieve a higher level of understanding of what was assumed to be the objective structure of a given literary or historical work (Makkreel, 1975).

Both Schleiermacher and in his youth, Dilthey, suggested that the understanding (*Das Verstehen*) of another person could be achieved by emphatically identifying oneself with that person. This was done by finding the other person inside of oneself, or by putting oneself in somebody else's place. Also by copying and reliving the other's mental experience. The mature Dilthey believed that the immediate, intuitive understanding of social acts and empathic understanding of the contents of other minds has limited application in the humanities. It has to be supplemented by the contemplation of the wider cultural contexts and meanings of particular events.

The important point for the concerns of the present book was the assumption of the humanists that in addition to the knowledge of the material world, a direct understanding of the activities of the human mind was possible and important. This was as valid as the method of the sciences with their dependence on laws which described classes of events and their regularities. Such a direct insight into the activity of the human mind was based on an understanding (*Verstehen*) of the unique circumstances in which this activity took place. The meaningful connections between social acts, between an intentional act and its purpose, and between one symbolic expression and another could be immediately cognized. They were perceived as being "apodictic" or necessary. This was in contrast to the contingent associations between events studied by natural sciences. Thus, in addition to experimental psychology, which studied the human mind by the natural science methods, and in addition to other philosophical psychologies as the Kantian rationalist *a priori* psychology, there arose a *Verstehen Psychologie* (psychology of understanding). It was an empirical psychology which used a method different from that of natural science. In passing, it could be mentioned that the founder of experimental psychology, Wilhelm Wundt, believed that its method was applicable to a rather narrow range of mental phenomena, namely, to the associations between physical stimuli and sensations, and to the associations among the latter. He called it physiological psychology (*physiologische Psychologie*). The higher mental processes, the subject of *Voelkerpsychologie* (ethnopsychology), could not be studied by the experimental method, but would have to be approached through hermeneutics and by *Verstehen*. These higher processes were concerned with the apperception of meanings, of relations, and with valuations in their cultural context.

Two neo-Kantian philosophers, Wilhelm Windelband (1848-1918) (1901) and Heinrich Rickert (1863-1936) (1962) opposed Dilthey's notion that there were two different realms of discourse, one concerned with the human spirit and the other with the material world. In 1894, in his inaugural lecture at the University of Strasbourg on "History and Natural Science" Windelband (1924) argued that there were two methods of scientific inquiry which could be applied to any field concerned with physical, mental or cultural phenomena. The validity of the application of each of these two methods did not depend on the subject of inquiry, but on the purpose of the investigator. The two methods were then appropriately named by him (1) the "nomothetic", and (2) the "idiographic". The nomothetic method was concerned with classes of phenomena and events and with the discovery of generally valid scientific laws. It was concerned with explanation (*Erklaerung*), subsuming a class of phenomena under a general law. The idiographic method was concerned with understanding (*Verstehen*) of unique, individual subjects and events. It was qualitative rather than quantitative, and was concerned with unique subjects and events in their particular context. For instance, meteorology, concerned with forecasting of weather at a particular spot at a particular time, provided an example of an ideographic physical science. Climatology, on the other hand, was concerned with general laws which described the phenomena of climate. It was an example of a nomothetic physical science. Thus there could also be two psychologies. (1) The nomothetic psychology of explanation concerned with the general laws of behavior. (2) The idiographic psychology of understanding, concerned with the behavior and experiences of unique personalities. History and humanities mainly relied on the idiographic method, while the physical sciences relied mainly on the nomothetic method.

Dilthey replied to Windelband in 1895 in his work on descriptive psychology (Dilthey, 1977), where he once more defended the division of the disciplines into the human and natural sciences. Dilthey believed that his descriptive psychology could achieve the goals of a natural science by using the hermeneutical method. Contemporaries like Ebbinghaus (1896) disputed that view and believed that modern psychology as a natural science, had already achieved these ends (Makkreel, 1975). He further criticized Dilthey for not abolishing the hypothetical conception of the unique form of psychic existence (Dilthey, 1977).

Heinrich Rickert (1962), another contemporary, developed further the argument concerning the two types of knowledge further. He rejected Dilthey's subjectivist approach to humanities because it was based on empathic understanding. Rickert believed that hermeneutics was concerned with an objective examination of the circumstances and the value system surrounding the occurrence of historical and social events. Consequently, he substituted the term *Kulturwissenschaft* (cultural science) for Dilthey's *Geisteswissenschaft* (science of the mind or spirit). However, Dilthey's intention was always to focus on the individual and the unique event or person and the intrinsic value of introspection. The idea of a cultural science then, tended to lose sight of the uniqueness of the individual, which he tried to delineate.

The debate of the relevance to social and cultural sciences of the *Verstehen* and the experimental psychologies, and of the idiographic and nomothetic method, became part of the methods controversy mentioned earlier. For the social scientist, it became a question of what constituted social and behavioural facts, and how they were to be interpreted. The place and meaning of measurement was discussed, as well as the question of whether these sciences were concerned with objective facts or with subjective experiences. Above all, the place and the meaning of value in social and cultural sciences came to occupy the main focus of attention.

Max Weber (1864-1920), a German sociologist-philosopher, discussed further the topics of understanding (*Verstehen*), of scientific explanation and of methodology as applied to social sciences. He proposed two types of explanation, and therefore two types of sociology. These were (1) the *Verstehen* sociology, and (2) objective sociology (Weber, 1949). These complemented one another. The *Verstehen* sociology was concerned with the subjective intentions and the values of social actors. It included grasping the means-end relation of social acts. Understanding could be further divided into "direct understanding" and "explanatory understanding." The first was an everyday, commonsense understanding of the meaning of the utterances and of the emotional expressions of other people.

It also involved a grasp of the relation between overt behaviour and its end result or goal. It was empathic and non-reflective. The second, an "explanatory understanding," went beyond the immediately given understanding of the current mental state and the activity of another person. It was concerned not with "what," but with the "why" of the behaviour. By grasping the meaningful connections between past and present acts, it tried to uncover the motives of behaviour (Bauman, 1978). The method of understanding was "idiographic." It dealt with a particular instance of behaviour or with a particular person.

Objective sociology was concerned with scientific, causal explanation and with the establishment of general laws. Its method was "nomothetic." Starting with *Verstehen* sociology, the sociologist's task was to objectify the phenomena studied, to make them part of objective sociology (Bauman, 1978). However, there would always remain some subjectivity in the description of social phenomena. Explanation which used the category of "ideal types" lay somewhere in between *Verstehen* and objective sociology. The ideal types constructed by the researcher helped him to classify the observed phenomena. An example of this were the social acts in which the actor chose the ultimate end values (*Wertrational*). This differed from those acts in which only certain instrumental means (*Zweckrational*) were freely chosen. Another example of Weber's approach may be seen in his classification of three basic types of authority: the traditional, the rational (bureaucratic), and the charismatic.

The various types of hermeneutic understanding and the application of the ideal type concept, played an important role in German psychology and psychiatry. An example is the work of Eduard Spranger (1882-1963). Spranger, a philosopher, psychologist, and educationist, was a student of Dilthey. He applied the method of understanding and hermeneutics to psycholgical and educational problems. According to him, psychology belonged to humanities rather than to natural science.

His most important work was the *Types of Men* (Spranger, 1928). Using the method of *Verstehen* he divided human personalities into six types: the theoretical, the economic, the aesthetic, the social, the political and the religious. This classification was based on the six corresponding forms of value, which he assumed, existed objectively in their historical and cultural realms. Men chose these particular values as dominant and oriented their lives towards them. Spranger stressed the importance of the dominant value commitment as well as the life plan for the growth and development of personality. Another important contribution to the *Verstehen* psychology was the work of Hans W. Gruehle (1880-1958), a psychiatrist, who was a member of the Heidelberg School. Gruehle was quite influenced by *Gestalt* psychology. He followed *Verstehen* method and also that of descriptive phenomenology. In 1948 he published an important book, *Verstehende Psychologie*, which was concerned primarily with normal psychology.

Karl Jaspers (1883-1969) was a German psychiatrist-philosopher who tried to synthesize the naturalistic and humanistic points of view as applied to psychiatry. In 1913 Jaspers published his monumental *General Psychopathology* (1913/1963) which had a tremendous influence on German and continental psychiatry. Soon after the appearance of this work, Jaspers abandoned psychiatry for philosophy. In his early days at Heidelberg, Jaspers was greatly influenced by Dilthey's descriptive psychology, *Verstehende Psychologie*,as well as by the latter's *Typologie der Weltanschauungen* (Typology of World Views) (Dilthey, 1957-1960). He was also influenced by Max Weber who was publishing from Heidelberg at that time. This led to Jaspers' own interpretation of world views and his 1919 work, *Psychologie der Weltanschauungen* (Psychology of World Views).

Eventually Jaspers became one of the leading existentialist philosophers of the twentieth century. However, his contributions to psychiatry were not in the area of existentialism, rather in that of methodology. He introduced the method of *Verstehen* , or elucidation of meaningful connections. In this section, we shall deal briefly with *Verstehen*, or the method of meaningful connections. We shall discuss the descriptive phenomenology of Jaspers in the section devoted to phenomenology. In his *General Psychopathology*, he described three approaches to psychopathology: (1) the descriptive phenomenology of the patient's conscious experiences, (2) the psychology of "meaningful connections," and (3) the objective description of the patient's behaviour according to the principles of nomothetic science ("objective psychology" or *Leistungspsychologie*). The "psychology of meaningful connections" attempted to reconstruct by the method of understanding the meaningful connections between present and past events of the patient's life. It was an idiographic method, which took full advantage of Dilthey's suggestion to "relive" (*Nacherleben*) past events. A hermeneutic method was applied to revealing the meaning of the patient's motives, purposes and intentions, similarly to the unfolding of characters in a literary work. The *Verstehen* psychology took its inspiration from the work of such great authors as Shakespeare, Goethe, Dostoyevski and Balzac, masters of understanding and portrayal of human characters. In this method, literary intuition was used for understanding the personality of the patient on the basis of his unique biography. The psychiatrist empathized with the patient in the way a reader empathized with the hero of a novel. The themes in the history of the patient were discerned by an intuitive grasping of meaningful connections between the latter's life events, rather than by an application of the scientific laws of psychology. The method was idiographic, dealing with patients as unique individuals, rather than as members of a class. It was par excellence a contribution from humanities (*Geisteswissenschaften*) to psychiatry.

The Phenomenological Movement

Of even greater importance for psychiatry than the "*Verstehende Psychologie*" was the phenomenological movement in philosophy, and also then, existentialism. The roots of both are in German subjective idealism. Therefore a brief philosophical introduction is needed.

Phenomenology, particularly Edmund Husserl's philosophical phenomenology, should not be identified with existentialism. The intents and purposes of the two philosophies are different. Spiegelberg (1960) has discussed the history of the relationship between the phenomenological and existentialist movements. In Germany, there was a tension and an antagonism between the Husserlian phenomenologists and the Heideggerian existentialists. In France, however, phenomenology has been closely associated with existentialism. Some of the tension between the two contemporary movements has resulted from differences in appeal. Husserlian phenomenology has had a rationalist appeal, while existentialism has appealed to the irrational voluntarism in men.

Both phenomenology and existentialism stem from the tradition of German transcendental, subjective idealism. Immanuel Kant (1724-1804) posed two basic problems with which these schools had to cope. It must be remembered that Kant had assumed the existence of two spheres of knowledge: that of 1) the perceived or phenomenal world, and that of 2) the world beyond, which was not immediately knowable, the noumenal one. Kant's first basic problem was epistemological, namely that human reason was limited. As a result, human knowledge was also limited (Kant, 1966). While the phenomenal world was given in immediate sensory experience, the noumenal world had to be postulated by reason, *a priori*. The second problem was ontological, that there was an apparent contradiction between the essence of man in the phenomenal and noumenal realms. The noumenal or metaphysical self of man was endowed with freedom of will. In the phenomenal world, however, the phenomenal self was limited by causal determinacy (Kant, 1949).

The human mind could only know the appearance of things, the *phenomena*. Things-in-themselves or *noumena*, could not be known to the mind. Thus Kantian epistemology assumed a deep division in the objective world, although he did not restrict the knowable to the merely material phenomena. Kant had borrowed the term "phenomena" and "phenomenology" from his contemporary Johann Heinrich Lambert. The latter had named the theory of the illusory knowledge of the external world, "phenomenology." (Spiegelberg, 1960). The two problems posed by Kant gave rise to many attempts at their solution. Both Fichte and Hegel attempted a rationalist solution. In contrast, the precursors of existentialism, Kierkegaard and Nietzsche appealed to the irrational voluntaristic aspects of human experience. Johann Gottlieb Fichte (1762-1814) (1969) tried to solve Kantian dualism. To bridge the gap between the Kantian things-in-themselves (noumena), and the contents of experience (phenomena), Fichte attributed a unique role to the transcendental ego. By an act of creation, the human ego posited the objective world. Thus, the ultimate basis of human knowledge was an act of the *transcendental* ego of the subject "positing" (really creating or constituting) the object. The dynamic acts of the human mind were more important than its contents. Georg Wilhelm Hegel (1770-1831) maintained in his *Phenomenology of Mind* (1949) that knowledge of the external world is a form of self-knowledge. Here is the essential idea enunciated by Vico (1730) early in the eighteenth century, namely, that knowledge of nature was beyond man's reconstructive capabilities,and the sole truth or certainty available to him was by reconstructing what other men had done before him. To know what lay outside of himself, involved this kind of reconstruction. However, in contrast to Vico, Hegel believed that not only the knowledge of human mind and of society, but also the knowledge of physical nature may also be reconstructed from self-knowledge. Therefore, self-knowledge became essential to knowing. That too, derives from Descarte's famous *cogito ergo sum* since it is the conscious individual who provides the basis for knowing. As Hegel argued, the Spirit lay behind the appearance of things. His word for spirit was *Geist*, which is often translated as collective mind. Historically, mind is in the process of constant becoming. It transcends one phase of development after another through a dialectic process. Spirit had its subjective and objective aspects which stood in a dialectical relationship with one another. By attaining self-understanding, mind achieved freedom of will, or the stage of "absolute mind." More than a discussion of the pros and cons of an argument have to be involved here. Psychology played its role for Hegel too, since the giveness of the world was one of its laws. But the individual, whom Hegel tried to study, did not fall under law or necessity. Psychology could not provide a law for self-consciousness and how it related to reality. The individual constituted a self existing for and of itself (*an und fuer sich*). Mind gave form to the self, and as the spirit realized its principle (conception), it achieved absolute knowledge. Such was a comprehending knowledge, what Dilthey was to refer to as *Verstehen*. Here then truth and certainty achieved identity, as they did not in eighteenth century thought. As mind then became phenomenally manifest to consciousness, it became knowledge (science). Here mind became the existence for-itself of self-consciousness in pure form (Hegel,1949).

Hegel had a great influence on Kierkegaard, who used the Hegelian system as a target for his attacks. It was also a foil against which he developed his own philosophical ideas. Some contemporary existential and phenomenological philosophers like Sartre and Ricoeur, were also influenced by Hegel's philosophy.

German transcendental idealism, of the nineteenth century, followed the "Leibnitzian" model of the human mind (Allport, 1955; May, 1958). This was in contradistinction to the "Lockean" model, which provided the foundation of empiricism and of experimental psychology.

The first conceived the human mind as an active agent, initiating cognitive and conative acts, by which it was molding and creating reality. The second looked at the human mind as a passive object, a "tabula rasa," which reacted to, and reflected the impressions and stimuli coming from the outside world. Phenomenology and existentialism followed the "Leibnitzian" tradition of transcendental idealism. The mental act was of basic importance for both phenomenology and existentialism. However, there was a simulataneous rejection by these two movements of the metaphysical assumptions associated with German transcendental and absolute idealisms, including the concept of "mental." To make a gross generalization, which is only approximately true, phenomenology has been mainly concerned with the first problem of Kant and has tried to lay the foundation of human knowledge which is absolutely certain and, therefore, to transcend the limits of Kantian "pure reason." It has concerned itself with epistemology. Existentialism, on the other hand, has applied itself to the second problem of Kant, namely how to reconcile the freedom of choice and moral responsibility with the causal determinism of the experienced world without postulating the Kantian *Deus ex machina* in the form of the categorical imperative and of *a priori* moral laws. To put it differently, it applied itself to the problem of the ultimate meaning of human life, and has been concerned with the question of ontology; the meaning and nature of being. Also with the question of ethics; the moral predicament of man.

At the outset we may pose the question: "What does the concept of phenomenology mean?" There is more than one meaning of the term. The first meaning of phenomenology is an approach to science which stresses a pure observation and description without any preconceived ideas or attempts at causal and theoretical explanations. Any preconceived conceptual categorization is eschewed. The observer registers naturally-occurring types and groupings of phenomena. Thus, phenomenology is propaedeutic to any explanatory science. There has been a long tradition of this approach to science in Germany, as exemplified by the writings of Goethe on philosophy of nature, and in particular his theory of color (Vietor, 1950). Carl Stumpf, a student of Franz Brentano, proposed, at the turn of the century, the discipline of descriptive phenomenology as a propadeutic science both for psychology and physics. Its role was to describe pure phenomena, before they are categorized as physical or psychological events (Boring, 1950).

The second meaning of phenomenology refers to the description of conscious states in all their fullness and richness. That is, without their being reduced to some presupposed basic elements such as sensations and their associations. William James (1842-1910) described the ever changing stream of consciousness in his *Principles of Psychology* (1890). He did not use the term phenomenology. James Joyce's *Ulysses* illustrates the stream of consciousness literature. In a more technical sense, descriptive phenomenology referred to a standardized technique of exploring one's own consciousness by the method of "inner perception." This also applied to exploring the conscious state of another person by empathy and inner perception. It did not aim at a description of a unique consciousness founded on artistic intuition. It endeavoured to extract common features and the general categories of phenomena.

These were composed of the infinitely and constantly changing constituents of experience, always in movement, as in a kaleidoscope (Jaspers, 1968). Descriptive phenomenology rejected such preconceived basic elements of consciousness as sensations and their associations which made up the traditional currency of empiricist philosophy and of the structuralist psychology of Wundt. It attempted to remove the blinkers of and to counter the narrowness of empiricism as well as of the schools of psychology inspired by it.

Jaspers introduced the method of descriptive phenomenology to psychiatry (Jaspers, 1963, 1968). The purpose of the method was to disclose the variety of normal and abnormal contents in the forms of consciousness. Then to discover their distinguishing features and to arrive at a classification. Some abnormal phenomena and forms of consciousness were continuous with the normal ones, some were discontinuous. The phenomenological method was concerned with the momentary states of the patient's consciousness in the specious present. It aimed at the "static understanding" of the patient's consciousness, while the method of *Verstehen* aimed to achieve a "genetic understanding" of the meaningful connections between successive episodes in the patient's life history. This included an intuitive understanding of his motives and purposes.

Edmund Husserl. The third meaning of phenomenology refers to Husserl's phenomenological philosophy and to the so-called Phenomenological Movement in the first two decades of the century. Edmund Husserl (1859-1938) was an influential German philosopher who was a student of Franz Brentano (1838-1917) at Vienna. Brentano

(1874) in his philosophical inquiries was concerned with descriptive psychology and founded the school of Act Psychology. He maintained that mental phenomena were characterized by intentionalities or "acts," by which the individual related himself meaningfully to the contents of his consciousness. The main concern of psychology was not with contents of consciousness, but with mental acts and "intentionalities".

Brentano was a charismatic teacher and had a great following in Vienna. Apart from Husserl, his students included Carl Stumpf (1848-1920), and Alexis Meinong (1853-1920), philosopher-psychologist. Another student was Kasimir Twardowski (1866-1938) (1894) the founder of the Polish school of analytical philosophy. The latter's work on the content and object of representations influenced Husserl. As a medical student, Freud also attended Brentano's lectures and seminars. However, because Brentano identified the mental with the conscious, Freud never referred to Brentano's philosophical teachings in his writings.

Brentano presented a new version of psychology which was concerned with "mental acts" or "intentionalities" rather than with the contents of consciousness. This version contrasted with the then prevalent version of psychology, as for instance that of Wundt, which was concerned with "mental contents" and their structure. The two views of psychology led to controversy. Oswald Kuelpe (1862-1915), the leader of the Wuerzburg school which studied imageless thought processes, suggested a solution to the controversy. He suggested that psychology should be "bipartite," one part concerned with "palpable" contents, and the other with "impalpable" acts or functions (Boring, 1950).

Brentano's act psychology gave an impetus to two schools of phenomenology. The first was represented by Carl Stumpf, who eventually became professor of psychology in Berlin. Stumpf suggested that the contents of experience belong to descriptive phenomenology which was a propadeutic science for psychology and physics. The proper subject matter of psychology were "mental acts," or as he preferred to call them "functions." When he was a professor in Prague, Stumpf met William James in 1882. The two formed a life-long friendship and corresponded with each other for many years. There was some similarity between Stumpf's version of phenomenology and James' "radical empiricism."

The founders of *Gestalt Psychology* were students of Stumpf and were influenced by his version of phenomenology. These were Max Wertheimer (1880-1943), Kurt Koffka (1886-1941), and Wolfgang Koehler (1887-1968). The *Gestalt* theory influenced Gruehle, a member of the Heidelberg school of psychiatry and also Kurt Goldstein, an important neurologist. Since the three founders of the *Gestalt* school emigrated to the United States, they came to represent the phenomenological tradition there for a considerable number of years. Stumpf's phenomenology also influenced Kurt Lewin (1890-1947) who wrote his doctoral dissertation under Stumpf's supervision in Berlin at the outbreak of World War I.Lewin applied the *Gestalt* concepts to the field of motivation.The influence of phenomenology can be discerned in Lewin's concept of "life-space."

The second school of phenomenology was represented by Husserl. It was of much greater importance for both philosophy and psychiatry than the first school. Edmund Husserl was originally trained in mathematics and later switched to philosophy. After studying with Brentano in Vienna, he went to the University of Halle as an instructor (*Dozent*) and collaborated with Stumpf. Afterwards he was for many years an extraordinary professor of philosophy at Goettingen and then an ordinary professor at Freiburg. Husserl was concerned with establishing philosophy as a "rigorous science," and with the discovery of its "presuppositionless," absolutely true, premises.

Such a philosophy would provide the foundation or grounding for natural sciences, humanities, logic, and mathematics. It would remedy the fragmentation, nihilism, irrationalism, and mysticism which according to Husserl characterized the scene of contemporary European philosophy (Husserl, 1965). Husserl was concerned with epistemology, with finding the ultimate foundations of knowledge. To attain this goal, he developed the phenomenological method of philosophical inquiry. This method discarded the blinkers of empiricism which had reduced the immediately given data of experience to sensations and to their contingent associations. The empiricist tradition which started with Locke and Hume had been very influential during the scientific revolution. It had been taken over by the positivist philosophers and by early structural experimental psychologists. It had assumed an extreme form in Ernst Mach's phenomenalism.

Phenomenalism represented an epistemological position which claimed that sensory data, conceived as mind events, or as the neutral "stuff" of experience, constitutes the ultimate experiential reality. Phenomenalism should not be confused with Husserlian phenomenology. Husserl had maintained that consciousness is open to the world. The world of real objects and not a motley of sensory data was given in the immediate experience. Ernst Mach (1838-1916) (1906) a physicist-philosopher of Prague and Vienna propagated the phenomenalist version of positivism. According to this version, sensations were immediate data of scientific observation. The Vienna Circle of Logical Positivists, which called itself the Ernst Mach Society (*Verein Ernst Mach*) originally adopted the phenomenalist position. However, it subsequently substituted the physicalist language of observation for the mentalist or phenomenalist one.

Phenomenology was a reaction against (Mach's) phenomenalism. In addition, the phenomenological method discarded the method of Cartesian meditation which led to the metaphysics of mind-body dualism with its consequence of solipsism. Finally, the method also discarded the assumption of the Kantian synthetic *a priori*. Instead, it went back to the immediate experience, to the matter at hand, *Zu den Sachen*.

The phenomenological method concerned itself with the study of pure consciousness, and of its intentionalities. These were pure acts of knowing. In order to accomplish this, the natural, common sense, and everyday attitudes towards the external world had to be suspended. One had to assume a reflective attitude. The latter entailed a transcendental phenomenological reduction or *Epoche*. Judgment as to either the physical or mental nature of objects and of the external world was thus suspended or, "bracketed" (Spiegelberg, 1960). In this way the facticity of external objects was transcended and the source of their meaning in pure consciousness was revealed. Husserl took the concept of intentionality from Brentano, but he discarded the notion that intentionality was a mental act. Such a notion presupposed the existence of mind, a metaphysical entity. Consequently, for Husserl, the concept of a mental act was a psychologism and was loaded with a metaphysical meaning which he found burdensome. All the more so, because he believed in eradicating the psychological presuppositions from philosophy and science. Intentionalities, according to Husserl, constituted the structure of pure consciousness, and were to be studied by his phenomenological method. He attempted to analyze in depth the essential structure of pure acts of knowing (*noesis*) in their relation to the contents of experience (*noema*). The *noema* were the objects of pure knowing. The action of knowing, the perception of objects, was an activity of the transcendental ego. Husserl tried to analyze the structure of these elements as well as of other intentionalities of the ego towards these experienced contents. The immediately perceived, that is, experienced intuitions (*Anschauungen*) of intentionalities, and acts of knowing, revealed the nature of things in their relation to the ego. They replaced the sensory data of experience on which the empiricst-positivist epistemology was based. In phenomenological psychology "inner perception" replaced introspection which was the method of Wundtian psychology.

In discussing Husserl's phenomenology, it is important to remember that his philosophical position had shifted considerably from one period of his philosophical career to another. There was the pre-phenomenological period, followed by the period of descriptive phenomenology initiated by *Logische Untersuchungen* (Logical Investigations). (Husserl, 1900 1901). Here Husserl tried to take the psychologisms out of the assumptions made about immediate experience. However, a few years later, his interests shifted radically. The second phase of transcendental phenomenology is described in his *Ideen zu einer reinen Phaenomenologie und Phaenomenologischen Philosophie* (3 vols., 1913/1962). (Ideas Towards a Pure Phenomenology and Phenomenological Philosophy).

The final period was one of the radicalization of transcendental phenomenology. It was in the third phase of his development, that Husserl emphasized inter-subjectivity and the Life-World (*Lebenswelt*). This conception was presented in his *Cartesian Meditations* (Husserl, 1931/1960), and *Der krisis der europaeischen Wissenschaften und die transcendentale Phenomenologie* (1936/1954). (The Crisis of the European Sciences and the Transcendental Phenomenology). In the period of transcendental phenomenology, Husserl has come very close to embracing the position of transcendental absolute idealism with its notion of the acts of the transcendental ego. These acts constituted the world. In his last phase, that of the *Lebenswelt*, Husserl shifted towards philosophical realism. Other early phenomenologists like Alexander Pfaender (1870-1941) of Munich, tended to reject Husserl's idealism and to subscribe to a more realist point of view (Spiegelberg, 1960).

From the point of view of the history of psychiatry and psychology, the phases of Husserl's development concerned with descriptive and *transcendental phenomenology* are most important. In the early phase, under the influence of Stumpf, Husserl was concerned with only descriptive phenomenology. He used the method of transcedental-phenomenological reduction to grasp the meaning of concrete objects and situations as they appeared in consciousness. During the period of his *Ideen* (Husserl, 1913), he developed another phenomenological method, that of *eidetic* reduction. This aimed at comprehending the general essences of things, abstract concepts, and ideas. According to Husserl, the intuition of essences (*Wesensschauen*) by the *eidetic* method, would lead to an absolute, non-contingent knowledge. Husserl did not believe that the generality of existing things fell under the generality of natural law. He accepted Windelband's double ordering (*Regelung*) of the natural and human sciences. Yet he emphatically denied that there was a translatable underlying unity between these groups of disciplines. He argued for the absolute necessity for "rational psychology." As more modern than its metaphysical predecessors, it had to reject the vague concepts used in the past and concern itself with phenomena. This new phenomenological psychology was very much like Dilthey's, a descriptive psychology, an inquiry into life's experiences rather than an experimental psychology (Husserl, 1913; Husserl, 1925). By 1925, Husserl had become more articulate about the importance of psychology for the human sciences. These sciences tended to be regarded as an "annex" to the natural sciences which absolutized nature as the human sciences absolutized the spirit in the world. The pure psychological method was based on observation and reflection, especially of the inner life of man (Husserl, 1925). Still, many phenomenologists, including phenomenological psychiatrists, did not follow Husserl in his quest for a *Wesensschau*, but limited themselves to the study of the descriptive phenomenology of concrete intentionalities (Spiegelberg, 1960).

Husserl had many followers among young philosophers, psychiatrists and psychologists. Soon after 1900, two groups of phenomenologists came into existence. These were the Goettingen and Munich circles. The Goettingen group consisted of students and followers of Husserl. The Munich group included students of Theodor Lipps (1851-1914), a philosopher-psychologist. He was at the time, the incumbent of the chair of philosophy at Munich.

Lipps made important contributions to psychology and aesthetics. He developed the theory of empathy (*Einfuehlung*) and applied it to the explanation of aesthetic experiences. Lipps also postulated the existence of an unconscious as a source of mental energy. Freud referred to Lipps on several occasions in his early writings. Lipps did not identify with the phenomenological movement, probably because he had a predilection for psychological explanations. However, many of his students and associates did.

Alexander Pfaender (1870-1941), Lipps's successor in the chair of philosophy at Munich, was committed to phenomenology. He carried out phenomenological studies of will and motivation (Pfaender, 1900/1967). Apart from Pfaender, the important members of the movement were Moritz Geiger, Oskar Becker, Adolf Reinach, Hedwig Conrad-Martius, and Max Scheler.

Of these, Scheler was of the most importance to psychiatry. An influential social philosopher in Germany, Max Scheler (1874-1928) was a student of Rudolf Eucken (1846-1926), an *Lebensphilosoph* (philosopher of life). Eucken's thought was concerned with the totality of life experiences and the emergent spiritual values. Scheler joined the staff at Munich University as a *Dozent*. There he came under the influence of phenomenology and joined the Munich Circle. Later he moved to Cologne as a professor of philosophy and sociology. In his philosophical writings, Scheler (1954) was less concerned than Husserl, with the foundations of knowledge, but more concerned with the problems of personality, of interpersonal relations, and of values. He used the phenomenological method to study sympathy, love, and the problems of ethics. He assumed the existence of objective values which formed a hierarchy that progressed from the values of pleasure to the values of vitality up to the values of spirit and finally, to those of holiness.

In his inquiries, Scheler used the phenomenological hermeneutic method. Scheler's main contribution lay in the field of phenomenology of emotions, both normal and abnormal. He even published an essay on pension neurosis (Spiegelberg, 1972). His theories were concerned with the understanding of human personality and of interpersonal relations. Therefore, these theories helped to understand psychotherapeutic processes. Consequently, Scheler's philosophical writings influenced such phenomenological psychiatrists as Kurt Schneider, H.C. Ruemke, Paul Schilder, and V.E. von Gebsattel. At this juncture, a more recent phenomenologically oriented social philosopher Alfred Schuetz (1899-1959) should be mentioned. The latter was particularly interested in the phenomenological analysis of inter-subjectivity (Schuetz, 1932). He was concerned with a "mundane" (descriptive), non-transcendental phenomenology of the social world. Schuetz made some important contributions to its structural analysis (Spiegelberg, 1960).

The Impact of Phenomenological Philosophy on Psychiatry

Philosophical phenomenology had a great impact on Continental psychiatry and psychology. In Munich, a group of psychiatrists led by Wilhelm Specht (1874-1945), established contacts with the phenomenological circle. Specht had studied the phenomenology of emotional expression and held degrees in both law and medicine. In 1907 he transferred from the medical to the law faculty and became professor of theoretical criminology. The Munich group of psychiatrists perceived the importance of descriptive phenomenology (descriptive psychology) for psychopathology. It could provide a key which would open the inner worlds of mental patients. In this context, the views of the French psychiatrist, Blondel (1914) were influential. The latter argued that mental patients lived in their subjective worlds and that normal persons could neither understand nor enter these. Phenomenology provided a method and a framework for describing and making sense of the subjective experiences of mental patients. Psychiatrists were in a position to reconstruct the subjective worlds of their patients. This approach appeared particularly attractive to those psychiatrists who were critical of both the "brain mythology" of the neurological psychiatrists and the "mythology" of the unconscious as propagated by psychoanalysts. In addition, the Munich group believed that the study of abnormal experiences could cast additional light on normal inner experiences.

Specht had distinguished between pathopsychology and psychopathology. Pathopsychology could use abnormal phenomena to extend the understanding of normal mental phenomena. Psychopathology, however, was concerned with abnormal phenomena in their own right. Wilhelm Specht and his group started a journal in 1912, called the *Zeitschrift fuer Pathopsychologie*.Many important psychiatrists and philosophers, including Karl Jaspers and Max Scheler, became important contributors to this journal.

Karl Jaspers too, became an adherent of the phenomenology movement. In 1912, he published an important paper on the applications of the phenomenological method to psychopathology. This was followed in 1913 by his work on *General Psychopathology*. As mentioned above,

Jaspers described three approaches to psychopathology:(1) descriptive phenomenology, (2) the *Verstehen* method of meaningful connections, and (3) that of objective psychology. The important features of descriptive phenomenology have been outlined before. Jaspers followed Husserl's phenomenology of the earliest phase, of the *Logical Investigations*. He did not remain an adherent of these views as they developed through Husserl's later phases.

At the same time, Jaspers' contemporaries went further and applied the phenomenological method more boldly to reconstruct the structure of the subjective worlds of their patients. Willy Mayer-Gross (1889-1961) (1914), a member of the Heidelberg group, carried out a phenomenological analysis of abnormal feelings of happiness. In a later study, Mayer-Gross (1924) offered a phenomenological description of mental confusion and of dreamy states. Kurt Schneider (1921a), who had been influenced by the phenomenological anthropology of Max Scheler, engaged in a phenomenological study of depression. In his description of personality, Scheler distinguished four levels: the sensuous, the vital, the psychic, and the spiritual. Kurt Schneider described two types of depression: endogenous and reactive. In the first type, the emotional disturbance was at the vital level. In the second, it was at the psychic level. In another publication, Schneider (1921b) discussed the phenomenology of love and sympathy in the light of Max Scheler's theory of emotions. H.C. Ruemke, a Dutch psychiatrist in 1924, published a monograph on the phenomenology of feelings of happiness. he distinguished the autochtonous feelings of happiness, the responsive ones, and those due to intoxication. More recently, Jakob Wyrsch (b.1892), a Swiss psychiatrist, offered a phenomenological analysis of the inner worlds of acute and of chronic schizophrenics (Wyrsch, 1937).

Another important member of the Munich circle was Victor von Gebsattel (1883-1976) who had degrees in both philosophy and medicine. A student of Lipps, he was also influenced by Dilthey, Husserl, and particularly by Scheler. His important contribution was a phenomenological study of obsessional-compulsive states (von Gebsattel, 1958). Von Gebsattel went beyond phenomenology and was concerned with existentialist themes. However, his most important contributions were in the field of philosophical anthropology as applied to medicine (von Gebsattel, 1954). Philosophical anthropology attempted to synthesize the insights of Dilthey's *Lebensphilosophie*, of phenomenology and existentialism, as well as those of Marx, Nietzsche, Freud.

This type of anthropology was interdisciplinary and had some unique features. It attempted to provide a philosophical framework for the study of man in his biological, psychological, social, cultural and spiritual aspects. Besides von Gebsattel, Max Scheler and Helmut Plessner (1892-1985) were important philosophical anthropologists. Von Gebsattel was influenced in particular by the anthropological writings of Scheler and by Heidegger's *Sein und Zeit* (Being and Time). For Gebsattel, neurosis was a disturbanced which blocked human development or becoming. In this way he anticipated such American humanist psychologists as Carl Rogers.

Another important phenomenological psychiatrist was Eugene Minkowski (1885-1973), a Pole, who studied in Warsaw, Munich, and Paris. He also spent some time at Burghoelzli with Bleuler. While in Munich, he became interested in phenomenology and there attended lectures by Pfaender and Geiger. Eventually Minkowski settled down in France where he became the leader of the phenomenological school of psychiatry. In Paris he came under the influence of Henri Bergson (1859-1941), a famous French philosopher. Bergson's vitalistic philosophy was based on the notion of the Heraclitean flux of experience, the "flowing time" (*duree reelle*). The latter was an expression of the vital impetus (*elan vital*). Bergson rejected the mathematical conception of time assumed by classical physics as an illusion. A "real time" was experienced emotionally as a flow which continued on. Since men had memory, the past lived on in the present. Evolution was a creative process, and this also implied that the past continued into the present. Bergson also accepted the existence of a rather formless unconscious against which the ego functioned with a lively sense of duration (Bergson, 1907/1911).

Bergson's theory of time stimulated Minkowski's interest in the phenomenology of time experience. In his book, *Lived Time* (1933/1970), Minkowski distinguished "lived time" from the objective, abstract, time of the physical sciences and of the clock. "Lived time" was characterized by subjective feelings of flow, of duration, and of becoming. It was characterized by the subjectively felt speed, by a feeling of relatedness to the past and of an openess to the future. In depressed patients "lived time" moved very slowly or was even at a standstill. The access to the future was blocked. The future did not exist.

In mania, on the other hand, "lived time" speeded up. The experience of certain schizophrenics and mystics appeared to be "timeless," and to be "outside of time." (Minkowski, 1953). Some schizophrenics experienced a feeling of disconnectedness between the past, the present and the future. In schizophrenics there appeared to be an absence of synchrony between the "lived time," the time of the clock and social time which caused a loss of contact with the external world. Minkowski also investigated the subjective, "lived," space. The latter was characterized by an orientation to the self, and by subjectively felt vastness or constriction. It could be "clear" and open to movement, or be "dark" and impenetrable.

The last among important early phenomenological psychiatrists was Erwin Straus (1891-1975). Straus (1963,1966) was concerned with phenomenology of the meaningful world of sensory experiences, in all its richness. He maintained that in the world of the immediately given sensory experience events were always meaningfully connected. The individual was in direct communication with the world. This state of affairs contrasted with the Pavlovian notion of conditioning, which assumed that the connections between events were contingent, arbitrary, and meaningless. In the states of depersonalization, the relation with the world of immediate experience was severed. In the schizophrenic auditory hallucinations or "voices" were autonomous and were dissociated from the speakers. Straus was teaching psychiatry at the Berlin University prior to his emigration to the United States. There he held a research position at the Veterans' Hospital in Lexington.

Finally, there was Paul Schilder, who was already mentioned in the context of the history of the psychoanalytic movement. Schilder was trained in philosophy as well as in medicine. As a philosopher, he was influenced by the descriptive psychology of Brentano, by Husserl's phenomenology and by Scheler's anthropology. His ambition was to synthesize the neurological, the psychoanalytical, the experimental psychological, and the phenomenological approaches. He started his career in the department of psychiatry at the University of Vienna under Julius Wagner von Jauregg. Another important member of that department was Otto Poetzl, with whom Schilder collaborated. During that period, Schilder made important contributions to organic psychiatry and neurology. He described *encephalitis periaxialis diffusa*, which was named for him as "Schilder's disease." At the same time, he carried out tachistoscopic experiments on perception in neurological patients and normal subjects. He also came under the influence of Freud and became associated with the psychoanalytical movement.

Schilder did not accept psychoanalysis uncritically. He rejected Freud's theory of the death instinct and his theory of regression as well as Freudian reductionism. Instead, he proposed a holistic theory of organism, and a theory of "constructive" psychology which stressed the growth of the organism and its orientation towards the future. In this respect he anticipated Heinz Hartmann's ego psychology. His holistic orientation led him to emphasize the ego and self-consciousness rather than the id and its instincts. Schilder also rejected Freud's notion of the unconscious and identified it with the fringes of consciousness. Following Brentano and Husserl he believed that the mental or psychological was synonymous with the conscious. The concept of "sphere" which he borrowed from Karl Buehler (1878-1963) helped to explain the apparent unconscious phenomena. Buehler, who was at one time a member of the Wurzburg school, became after the first World War the professor of experimental psychology at Vienna. In his experiments on imageless thinking processes, Buehler introduced the concept of the "sphere" of consciousness, with clearly perceived contents of consciousness in the center, and vaguely discriminated contents on the periphery. The vague peripheral contents were influencing the clearly perceived central contents.

Schilder rejected the mind-body dualism and believed that all organismic manifestations, normal and abnormal, could be approached both from the psychological and the somatic perspective. His main interests were in self-consciousness and in the consciousness of body image. He attached a great importance to the latter. In formulating his concept of "body image," Schilder was influenced by Wernicke's concept of "somatopsyche" and by the English neurologist Sir Henry Head's notion of "bodily schema." He also assigned an important role in the formation of body image to the Freudian libido, which was invested in various parts of the body. According to Schilder, the body image determined the individual's relation to himself, to other persons, and to the external world. In his studies of perception, of body image, of motor functions, and of self-consciousness, Schilder combined the method of descriptive phenomenology with the principles of *Gestalt* psychology. His two most important works were *Medical Psychology* (Schilder,

1924/1953) and *The Image and Appearance of the Human Body* (Schilder, 1935).

Existentialism

The phenomenological psychologists and psychiatrists were historically identified with, and influenced by the second major philosophical movement of the twentieth century: existentialism. Its interests and intents were different from Husserl's phenomenology. However, the paths of both movements were often intertwined. Existentialism is a philosophy of the "predicament of man," or to put it differently, a philosophy which examines the question, "What does it mean to be man?" While Husserl was mainly concerned with epistemology, existentialists were interested in ontology. This referred to the grounds of existence, the meaning and nature of being. Modern existentialists have adopted Husserl's phenomenological method of the analysis of pure consciousness and have applied it to the analysis of being. Heidegger's version of phenomenological method, the hermeneutic phenomenology, did not have to do only with the "here and now" of actual consciousness, or with the essence of pure consciousness. It also examined the totality of man's life. It stressed the historicity of man, the existential time span from birth to death (Heidegger, 1927/1962).

Martin Heidegger (1889-1976) was originally a follower of Husserl who greatly influenced his work. He later became critical of the latter's philosophy and turned his attention to the problem of human existence. Spiegelberg (1960) points out that Heidegger adopted Husserl's method, but took it a step further. Instead of descriptive phenomenology of the Husserlian kind, the Heideggerian was called "hermeneutic phenomenology." It was intended to provide insight not only into pure consciousness, but also to a wider panorama of the totality of human life. Heidegger applied his method to such existential themes as the meaning of life, the meaning of death, existential anxiety, and generally to the problems of being. These were very like Karl Jaspers' designated boundary situations (*Grenzsituationen*). Heidegger was very concerned with defining the historicity of life situations, and these went beyond those encountered in everyday occurrences.

Not all versions of existentialism accepted the Husserlian phenomenological method. For instance, Karl Jaspers' version of existentialism was critical of the Husserlian phenomenology. Jaspers (1955) rejected Husserl's idea of scientific philosophy as a contradiction in terms. In place of the phenomenological method Jaspers proposed one of elucidating or enlightening existence (*Existenzerhellung*). The descriptive phenomenology he had used earlier in the context of psychopathology was abandoned (Jaspers, 1963, 1968). Jaspers made much of the boundary situations, those questions of life and death, of the ultimate meaning of life, which troubled the mind, and which had to be overcome in order to restore the normal functioning of the individual. This method appealed to the idea of a Kierkegaardian "leap of faith" made in an attempt to realize the full potential of existence.

Existential themes have tended to occupy philosophers since time immemorial. This preoccupation became intense whenever there was a cultural crisis, when old values were questioned, when the existing social order was disintegrating and when the hitherto prevailing *Weltanschauung* was no longer meaningful or valid. At such times, questions were asked about the meaning of human life and death, and the meaning of individual existence.

Existentialism had its strongest appeal in Europe, in Germany and France. Defeated and economically ruined after the first World War, and all the more so after the second, Germany provided a setting for the rise and the popularity of existentialism. So did France, which had also suffered a great deal from both wars, but because of its defeat in 1940, existentialism was more popular there after World War II. Existential themes could be discerned in the writings of St. Augustine (1961) and in the poetry of Omar Khayyam (Weckowicz, 1981). Jean Paul Sartre had begun to write before the second World War, because he felt a need to try to come to grips with Heideggerian philosophy which was then becoming popular in Germany. Existentialism might be traced to Pascal (1967) who tried to resolve his religious doubts, and also in the novels of Dostoyevski, filled with the Russian despair of the crumbling tsarist regime. During the nineteenth century both Soren Kierkegaard and Friedrich Nietzsche, who were outside the main stream of philosophy, turned to existentialist themes as a form of protest against the philosophies of rationalism and positivism. Theirs was a protest against the dehumanizing influences of these two currents of thought. Their philosophies emerged against the background of sociological disintegration and psychological alienation brought about in the wake of the industrial revolution. The materialist and positivist world views tended to disregard the meaning of unique individual existence and to lose sight of the individual, as it were, in the objective world of things, or in philosophical abstractions. Both Kierkegaard and Nietzsche strongly protested against the devaluation of the importance of the individual.

The philosophies of Kierkegaard and Nietzsche have already been discussed in the context of the history of nineteenth century psychiatry. Their influence extends to twentieth century pioneers of existentialist philosophy. These included Karl Jaspers (1955), Martin Buber (1878-1955), Gabriel Marcel (1889-1973), and Martin Heidegger. Karl Jaspers rediscovered Kierkegaard and developed the method of the elucidation of existence based on the Kierkegaardian "leap of faith." Gabriel Marcel, a French philosopher, developed the theistic version of existentialism. Buber and Heidegger were two existential philosophers important for psychiatry. Martin Buber (1878-1965) (1958), a liberal Jewish theologian, and a "philosopher of dialogue" developed a theory of relationships between individuals. He divided these relationships into the "I-it" and the "I-thou" types. The "I-it" relationship was impersonal, manipulative, and devoid of reciprocity. It was that between the subject and an object. The "I-thou" relationship was inter-subjective, a reciprocal. It was a relationship between two subjects conscious of the reciprocity of their mutual experience. The very use of the familar, "thou" assumes a highly empathetic and close interaction. The idea of "encounter," which is the backbone of existential psychotherapy, is based on the "I-thou" relationship which Buber first described.

Martin Heidegger. Jaspers, Marcel, and Buber developed their versions of existentialist philosophy independently of Heidegger. However, the mainstream of twentieth century existentialism was considerably influenced by the systematic philosophy of Martin Heidegger. His version of existentialism had a particularly profound impact on Swiss and German psychiatry. Heidegger had originally studied for the priesthood. Under the supervision of Heinrich Rickert, he received a degree in philosophy from Freiburg. Rickert had been a neo-Kantian cultural philosopher. Heidegger at first stayed on at Freiburg as a *Privatdozent.*

There he came under Husserl's influence when the latter replaced Rickert in 1916. Later Heidegger moved to Marburg as an extraordinary professor and returned to Freiburg only in 1928 to replace Husserl when the latter retired. Heidegger used a variant of phenomenological method, that of hermeneutic phenomenology, to elucidate the meaning of existence and the themes associated with it.

In his most important book, *Sein und Zeit* (1927/1962) Heidegger was concerned with ontology, the problem of being in general. According to him, the human being was a special kind of being because man was conscious of his own being. Heidegger searched for a theory of how man exists in his world. Consequently, an analysis using the hermeneutic phenomenological method could provide an insight into the general categories of being. These were the *existentia*.

The predicament of the human being conscious of his existence, was his finitude and temporality. "Thrown into the world" without the ability to exercise any choice in the matter, he faced the certainty of death, total dissolution, and nothingness. Heidegger referred to the being conscious of being, as *Dasein* ("there is"). *Dasein* was always "being in the world." It was embedded in the network of meaningful involvements with the world. It sought self-understanding, searched for the meaning of its existence and of the world it encountered. *Dasein* oriented itself in time, relating to the past, and at the same time projecting itself towards the future. It related to his world, was rational, had the ability to explain and to understand. Dasein could be human consciousness and in that sense it related to the individual human being, to daily life, to the consciousness of those humans existing around one. The existing self maintained the attitude that it was "there" or *da*. As such, the existing human constituted understanding (*Verstehen*) and gave structure to the consciousness of being alive (Heidegger, 1927/1962).

The method which analyzed the meaning of *Dasein* in relation to the general problems of being, was called by Heidegger, *Daseinsanalytik*. It was an ontological or *existential* analysis of *Dasein* or conscious existence. Heidegger went so far as to give this a special name, *Eksistenz*, defined as an individuality which stood out in what might be called a 'clearing of being.' Heidegger argued that such existence was there as independent of experience, of knowledge of it, and of any understanding of it. While Husserl tried to eradicate psychologisms in his earlier work, Heidegger kept them as the foundation of *Dasein*. Hence it is filled with both anxiety and concern (*Sorge*) (Heidegger, 1927/1962).

The Heideggerian *Dasein* must not be confused with Binswanger's *existentiell* (individual) kind of *Daseinsanalyse*. This took place on the ontic level for the concrete individual. Its purpose was to establish philosophical anthropology. For Heidegger, however, each *Dasein* was characterized by an individuality or *Jemeinigkeit*. Each individual world was also a *Mitwelt*. It was shared with others with whom he communicated. The *Dasein* was confronted by the facticity of its world which to some extent limited its freedom. Yet, it also had the possibility of making free choices and of facing its existence and death. The more important choice to be made was that between an authentic and inauthentic life. *Dasein* had concerns about its destiny, but at the same time it tended to escape into the facticity of the world. It tended to be occupied with social conventions and trivia in order to escape from anxiety (*Angst*) which was an undifferentiated emotion. Anxiety was not a fear of any particular object or situation. It was a fear of nothingness, of non-being, and these were the consequences of the temporality of human existence. However, death gave meaning to human life, and human life gave meaning to death. Authentic existence had to face this predicament squarely.

Ludwig Binswanger and Existentialist Psychiatry

Ludwig Binswanger (1881-1966) inaugurated existentialist psychiatry and was its most important proponent. He was both a phenomenologist and an existential psychiatrist. His approach (*Daseinsanalyse*) has been called "phenomenological anthropology" (Spiegelberg, 1972). Binswanger was a life-long student of philosophy although he did not have a formal training in it. His contributions were original. He came from a well-to-do family which owned a private hospital, the Bellevue Sanatorium in Kreuzlingen, Switzerland. In due course, he became its director. This position gave him the independence and the leisure to pursue his philosophical studies in addition to his clinical work. After studying medicine at Lausanne, Jena, and Heidelberg, he specialized in psychiatry under Eugene Bleuler at Burghoelzli, the Zuerich cantonal mental hospital. While in that institution he collaborated closely with Carl Gustav Jung. Like everyone else at Burghoelzli, at that time, Binswanger fell under the spell of Freud's psychoanalytical theory. In 1907 he accompanied Jung on a visit to Vienna, where they met Freud. For a period of time, Binswanger became the president of the Zuerich Psychoanalytical Society. Although later he became critical of psychoanalysis and recognized its limitations, he never abandoned it completely. Despite Binswanger's subsequent involvement with the phenomenological and existentialist movements, he and Freud remained on friendly terms as he himself related in his *Sigmund Freud:Reminiscences of a Friendship* (1957a).

Binswanger objected to the reductionism of psychoanalysis. The latter was concerned with only the *homo naturae* (natural man), with man as a biological organism. It was not concerned with the spiritual aspects of man and presented only a one sided view of him. Binswanger always believed, that within its limits, psychoanalysis was a useful therapeutic technique. Binswanger believed that Freud's theory needed to be placed in the proper framework of the philosophy of man. His introduction to philosophy came from reading Kant's *Critique of Pure Reason*.

He was impressed with the idea of transcendentalism. Binswanger later studied the works of Paul Natorp (1854-1924), a neo-Kantian idealist who was a philosophy professor at Marburg. After he completed his psychiatric training at Burghoelzli, Binswanger assumed the directorship of the Bellevue Sanatorium. As a result of his interests in philosophy and psychology, he established at the Bellevue an interdisciplinary studies center and invited many prominent philosophers and psychiatrists to visit it. His distinguished visitors included Sigmund Freud, Alexander Pfaender, Edmund Husserl, Max Scheler, Martin Heidegger (visited twice), Martin Buber, Ernst Cassirer, and Wilhelm Szilisi. The visitors gave lectures and seminars and were engaged in philosophical discussions with the staff. These visits were supplemented by a voluminous correspondence. On the basis of these studies and encounters Binswanger tried to formulate a philosophical anthropology as the foundation of psychiatry. He summarized his philosophical concerns by the motto: "Above all, let us hold fast unto what it means to be a man," taken from Kierkegaard's *Concluding Unscientific Postscript* (Binswanger, 1930/1963). Spiegelberg (1972) divides Binswanger's philosophical development into four phases:

(1) The pre-phenomonological phase of Kant and Natorp.

(2) Early Husserlianian phase of descriptive phenomenology.

(3) Heideggerian, existentialist phase.

(4) Late Husserlian phase of transcendental phenomenology.

In our discussion, we shall focus on the existentialist phase. This resulted from the impact of Heideggger's *Sein und Zeit* (1927/1962) on Binswanger and his contemporaries. The Heideggerian phase of Binswanger's philosophical development resulted in his *Grundformen und Erkenntnis menschlichen Daseins* (Basic Forms and Knowledge of Human Consciousness), published in 1942. This work presented the foundations of Binswanger's "phenomenological anthropology" and his existential psychiatry. The central theme of his anthropology was that of *Daseinsanalyse.*

Binswanger did not stress the concept of being as an abstract category, but emphasized a concrete "being-in-the world," as a particular "individual-in-the world." Thus, Binswanger's concerns were ontic (*existentiell*) rather than ontological (*existential*). He was concerned with real individuals rather than with general categories of "being." The accent of *Daseinsanalyse* was placed on the *Mitwelt*, or the relationship with, and the relatedness to other human beings. This was in contrast to the relationship to the environment, or *Umwelt*, and to the world of self-reflection or *Eigenwelt*. In existentialist terminology the *Umwelt* was the world of man as a biological organism without his ability of self-reflection taken into account. The *Mitwelt* was the world of interpersonal relationships. It was here that encounters with others took place. These were also conscious persons, and hence this was a human and social realm. Then there was the inner world of the individual conscious human being, or the *Eigenwelt*. It was here that self-reflection took place and self-identity developed. It was the world in which man transcended his biological and his social determinism. Similar to Heideggerian analysis, this was the realm that opened developmental possibilities. Yet Binswanger tended to give more prominence to the *Mitwelt* in his *Daseinsanalyse* than Heidegger did in his *Daseinsanalytik*.

While Heidegger focused on the individual and his *Eigenwelt*, and singled out anxiety and care (*Sorge*) as important feelings pervading it. Binswanger substituted the concept of love for Heidegger's concept of care. For Binswanger the idea of love had some special connotations. These were spiritual and transcended the biological limits of Freud's conception of the libido. Love referred to an encounter between two unique individuals, it was to be conceived as an "I-thou" relationship which created the situation of a "we-ness." In its spirituality, love transcended human temporality. The purpose of the Binswangerian existential therapy was to make use of the concepts of *Mitwelt* and of love. According to Binswanger, the unfolding *Dasein* of a particular person presented a unique structure of meanings. It could not be reduced to causal psychological mechanisms as was postulated by psychoanalytical theory. Uniqueness was the important idea here. The meaning of events in the course of the history of an individual and the meaning of his acts was decidedly unique. The same principles applied also to dreams since these were not conceived to be the symbolic productions of complexes, conflicts, and archetypes that could be traced to the unconscious. Dreams were individual expressions of a *Dasein* and had to be taken as phenomena in their own right. This particular aspect was developed by Medard Boss, a disciple of Binswanger.

In his late Husserlian phase of transcendental phenomenology, during which he was also influenced by Wilhelm Szilasi, Heidegger's successor at Freiburg, Binswanger was concerned with the schizophrenic and manic-depressive forms of *Dasein*. His views on these subjects were presented in *Schizophrenie* (1957b) and *Melancholie und Manie* (1960). Binswanger tried to discover the ways in which the worlds of schizophrenics, depressives and manics were constituted. One important new feature of *Daseinsanalyse* was the claim that a schizophrenic's subjective world and behaviour could be understood in the same way as the subjective world and behaviour of a psychoneurotic. This was in contrast to Karl Jaspers' view expressed in his *General Psychopathology* (1963). According to the latter, only the "personality development" of a psychoneurotic could be understood by Dilthey's method of *Verstehenspsychologie,* thepsychology of understanding. The schizophrenic symptoms produced by a "disease process" were believed to be incomprehensible. The *Daseinsanalyse* claimed to be able to understand the schizophrenic "world." A schizophrenic condition, similar to a psychoneurotic one, was a manifestation of a unique personality. It represented the development of a particular *Dasein*.

The existentialist philosophy of Heidegger influenced other psychiatrists than Binswanger and von Gebsattel. In Switzerland, two other significant existentialists were: Medard Boss and Roland Kuhn. Both were disciples of Binswanger and developed his ideas after he died. In Germany, the group of young psychiatrists who formed the new Heidelberg school of psychiatry included: Walter von Baeyer, Heinz Haefner, Karl Peter Kisker, and Hubert Tellenbach (Spiegelberg, 1972). While the old Heidelberg school followed the lead of Karl Jaspers which limited itself to descriptive phenomenology, the new one had an existentialist orientation. Victor Frankl's logotherapy (1963) provides another example of existentialist psychiatry, although it was not, in his case, influenced by Heidegger. The post World War II developments in European existential psychiatry are covered in detail by Spiegelberg (1960, 1972), and by Weckowicz (1984).

American Humanistic Psychology and its Relation to Existentialism

After the second World War, the development of American humanistic psychology movement came to be known as the "third force." The very use of this term conveyed the fact that humanistic psychology provided an alternative to both psychoanalysis and behaviourism. It was akin to European existentialism and opened a new perspective on the problem of mental health and mental disease.

The leading representatives of this movement were Gordon Allport, Carl Rogers, Abraham Maslow, Charlotte Buehler, Rollo May, James Bugental, B.M. Moustakas, Sidney Jourard, and Erich Fromm. On the European continent, humanistic psychology was represented by Casimir Dabrowski (1902-1980) (1964) and by Roberto Assagioli (1971), the creator of the psychosynthesis method of psychotherapy. Carl Gustav Jung and Otto Rank may be regarded as precursors of the humanistic approach, although they are usually classified as representatives of the psychodynamic school. Erich Fromm has already been mentioned as a neo-Freudian. However, his theory considered humanistic values to be important, and this places him into the "Third Force" group of humanistic psychologists.

The humanistic psychologists were not mere theoreticians. All of them were praticing psychotherapists. They tried to apply their theories in a clinical setting. Thus they formulated their theories of personality as well as their methods of psychotherapy, independently of European phenomenological and existentialist traditions. However, in subsequent years the theories of humanistic psychologists and those of existentialists have tended to converge.

The theories of the individual humanistic psychologists shared many similarities, despite important differences. All of them were holistic and organismic. They emphasized the integration of the whole person. Thus they were opposed to the traditions of Cartesian dualism, and critical of the Freudian division of the human psyche into ego, id, and superego. They disliked the behaviourist focus on the elementary, atomistic units of behaviour such as reflexes and habits. All humanistic psychologists emphasized the self as the integrative control center of the personality. Further, all humanistic psychologists postulated a continuous personality growth and selfactualization. It was Kurt Goldstein (1939) who introduced this last concept as the basic drive in the make up of a healthy, organism. This basic drive was given several different technical names by humanistic psychologists, such as: self-actualization, self-realization, or individuation. When personality growth was stunted there was an impediment to self-actualization, and this, it was alleged, caused mental illness.

Abraham Maslow (1908-1970) (1954, 1962) presented the version of self-actualization theory which may be described as Aristotelian. His notion of self-actualization presupposed a developmental potency, similar to the Aristotelian notion of *entelechy*, which was aiming at the attainment of the developmental goal. This goal was the achievement of the essence of humaness (the perfect mature man). According to Maslow, fully self-actualized people were mature. They were characterized by a clear perception of reality, openess to experience, personality integration, spontaneity, and expressiveness. Further, they displayed self-acceptance, autonomy, uniqueness, and the acceptance of others. Self-actualized individuals were creative, original, and had a democratic character structure. They were problem centered rather than self-centered. They had a capacity to give and to receive love. Finally, they were characterized by self-transcendence and a high frequency of "peak experiences."

Maslow compiled the above list of character traits and values from his observation of mature, superior persons who, he believed had achieved self-actualization. During "peak experiences," which had a profound mystical quality, the state of self-actualization became enhanced. The self-actualizing persons enjoyed superior mental health and had higher moral standards. They came close to being perfect specimens of human species, and came close to the realization of the human essence. Maslow, of course, did not minimize the importance of unique characteristics or the idiosyncrasies of each individual personality, but he focused on general properties of humaness. The latter was the essence of man, which Maslow defined as "fulfilling the concept of human being" (1962). A person was born with the potential to attain full humaness, in the same way that an acorn had the potential of becoming an oak tree. Like Aristotle, Maslow believed that the purpose of each man was to actualize his potential, to be himself, and to achieve the state of *eudaimonia* or self-fulfillment. This state was synonymous with one of attaining goodness and happiness. However, there was an important difference. Aristotle had a static conception of human nature. He identified the fulfillment of man with the fulfillment of his function which was, he believed, that of playing his social role. His fulfillment depended on how effectively he performed it. Therefore the fulfillment of a free man was different from that of a slave. For Maslow self-fulfillment or self-actualization meant attaining certain personality characteristics and a type of cognition which were independent of one's social role and culture.

A further difference between Maslow's and Aristotle's conception of self-actualization needs to be mentioned. The Aristotelian form of self-realization referred to the realization of the human intellectual potential through reason. Maslow's concept of self-actualization comprised the realization of both intellectual and emotional potentials. For Maslow, the emotions and feelings were of the same importance as the intellect. However, it seems that Maslow came close to the Aristotelian interpretation of self-actualization when he described the chief characteristics of the self-actualizing man as the ideal to be aimed at and the final goal of personality development. This also represented the ideal of mental health.

Maslow (1954) postulated a hierarchy of human needs. At the bottom of the hierarchy, were the biological deficiency needs. Further up the ladder, were the social deficiency needs. At the apex was the self-actualization need of the psyche. Maslow associated deficiency needs with striving to fulfill them and self-actualization with the final state of being. The state of self-actualization was synonymous with the state of positive mental health. He emphasized the importance of positive mental health instead of focusing on disease. Maslow believed that people could be ranked along a continuum which stretched from the state of severe mental illness to that of maximum positive mental health. At one extreme were those grossly deficient in mental health. Their deficiency needs remained unsatisfied. Then came those who were less grossly deficient but were not actualizing their potential. Thus they were not attaining the state of positive mental health. Finally, there were those who reached various degrees of self-actualization. Complete self-actualization remained an ideal which was approached only by a few exceptionally mature, autonomous and creative individuals. These individuals were also subject to frequent peak experiences. The vast majority of the population were not grossly deficient in need attainment, but had not achieved complete self-actualization nor perfect mental health.

Another important humanistic psychologist was an Austrian transplanted to America, Charlotte Buehler (1962), the wife of Karl Buehler. She was interested in the psychotherapy of adolescents who, according to her, suffered often from value disorientation. Hence, she stressed the importance of values in psychotherapy.

The philosophical idea of Becoming, had been regarded for a long time by American intellectual historians as essential to the understanding of the development of Western thought in general (Baumer, 1977). The process of Becoming and of the unfolding or continuous growth of human personality was also a characteristic feature of the theories of many humanistic psychologists. These included Gordon Allport (1897-1967) (1955), Carl Rogers (1902-1987) (1965), and Rollo May. The tenor of the argument remained the same from Allport's Terry lectures on "Becoming" in 1955 to Carl Rogers' conception of *A Way of Being* (1980). Rollo May, too, has emphasized it in his *Existential Psychology* (1969) and *The Discovery of Being* (1983). Thus, while Maslow subscribed to the Aristotelian notion of a final state in personality growth, an idea which implied the Parmenidean idea of an unchanging ultimate reality, Allport and Rogers viewed personality development in terms of a Heraclitean notion of contant change and flux (*pantarei*). They came closer than Maslow to the existentialist idea of man as being involved in the project of his creation, oriented towards the future and creating his *essence* instead of being determined by it. (According to the Sartrean version of existentialism, "existence preceded essence," and not the other way around). In addition, Rogers and Allport stressed individuality, uniqueness, and the divergence of human developments. During the "non-directive counselling," the term used by Rogers for psychotherapy, the personality growth of each client was unique and undetermined. This made it impossible to describe universally valid criteria for self-actualization, and for good mental health. The criteria were unique for each client (patient), and unfolded only during the psychotherapeutic process.

In later years Rogers began to focus his attention increasingly on the actual act of experiencing, rather than on its contents, and on interpersonal encounter. Following the tradition of the Wesleyan evangelical brand of American Protestantism, Rogers placed the individual above his society as he emphasized the freedom of man. Under the influence of Eugene Gendlin (1962), Rogers came very close to the European existerntialist point of view.

In spite of the convergence of views of the American Humanistic psychologists and those of the European existentialist ones, an important difference existed in their underlying world views. American Humanistic psychology radiated optimism about human nature and the world. The end to be attained by self-actualization and self-fulfillment was happiness. The existentialists did not share this optimism about the human predicament since theirs was a pessimistic view of the world. Perhaps this was still the influence of the Schopenhauerian and the Nietzschean tradition. To surmount this pessimism, they emphasized the dignity of being human (Weckowicz, 1988). The pessimism of existentialists was shared by Casimir Dabrowski (1964), this author represented the European point of view. He defined psychoneurosis as a positive personality disintegration causing suffering, but necessary to achieve personality growth.

Neo-Kantianism and the Philosophy of Symbolic Forms

The fourth current of German philosophy which had an impact on psychiatry was the neo-Kantian philosophy of symbolic forms developed by Ernst Cassirer. Since this philosophy is concerned with the problems of language and symbolism and hence relates to hermeneutics and linguistics, a few introductory remarks on the historical background of these topics are appropriate. The field of symbolic behaviour and symbolic products has always been an area of great interest to humanistic scholars, and in particular to *geisteswissenschaftliche* philosophers in Germany. This extremely difficult and complex subject has been investigated by linguists, logicians, philosophers, and literary critics. Logicians have developed a formal theory of signs and symbols. Such pioneers of semantics as Gottlieb Frege (1848-1925) (1892) and Charles Peirce (1839-1914) (1955/1897) were concerned with the meaning and reference of linguistic and nonlinguistic symbols. Somewhat later Karl Buehler published an influential work on *Sprachtheorie* (Theory of Speech) (1934).

Meaning tended to be explained in terms of reference and of implications rather than in terms of causality. Outisde the artificial languages, a domain of logic, the search for meaning in such symbolic products as natural language and myth has been the task of the broad domain of hermeneutics. In Germany, there has been a long tradition of linguistic philosophy and the philosophy of other symbolic forms. The names of Johann Gottfried Herder (1744-1803) and of Wilhelm von

Humboldt (1767-1835) may be cited to illustrate the point. Wilhelm von Humboldt described the "inner form" of language and considered it responsible for the deep-rooted, subjective view of the world. It represented a spiritual attitude that controlled the formation of concepts (Isham,1967). His views influenced Dilthey and Ernst Cassirer at the turn of the century, and more recently Heidegger. In his lectures on philosophy of art and of mythology, Friedrich Schelling conceived of mythology as a system of symbols with its own *a priori* categories. This idea had a great influence on the philosophical theories later developed by Cassirer.

Ernst Cassirer (1874-1945) was a German neo-Kantian philosopher. He was a student of Hermann Cohen (1848-1918), a professor at Marburg who was the leading neo-Kantian of his time. Cassirer was independently wealthy. He published much on his own until the end of the first World War and from 1919 to 1933 was a professor of philosophy at Hamburg University. When Hitler came to power he went into exile to teach at Oxford from 1933-35, then at Goteborg in Sweden until 1941. He migrated to the United States in 1941 and from then until 1944 was a professor at Yale. He died while teaching at Columbia University in New York. Cassirer extended the Kantian critique to broader realms of human experience than those encompassed by Kantian pure and practical reason. In contrast to Kant, he regarded the crystallizing experience categories as relative to the mode of symbolic representation. They were non-static, but continually undergoing development (Cassirer, 1944, 1957). According to him, symbolic representation was an essential function of human consciousness. Symbols, the signifiers, were perceived both as different and as identical with the signified objects. Man lived in a symbolic world, or rather in several of them. Cassirer maintained that there are three symbolic systems representing three types of symbolic forms and three corresponding modes of symbolic function. Each of the modes resembles the content of the three stages of Comtean positivism. The first mode was the "expressive function" which represented the primitive world of myth and magic. The second mode was that of "intuitive function" which represented the world of ordinary language and common sense. It was also the world of naive Aristotelian physics, where the property of objects was determined by their class membership. The third mode was that of the "conceptual function" which constituted the world of science. Thus the humanities, sciences, and common sense worlds used different symbolic forms. Their thought processes were distinct too. They employed different languages and their criteria of truth were different.

The methods of inquiry used by human and natural sciences were also different. Cassirer's philosophy had a great influence in English-speaking countries. It was popularized by Suzanne Langer in her *Philosophy in a New Key* (1948). The philosophy of symbolic form influenced the thinking of a number of psychiatrists and psychologists. Thus, M. Edelson (1971) reformulated Freudian psychoanalytical theory in terms of symbolic implications rather than in terms of causal explanations. In the same vein, R. Schafer (1976) proposed a new "action language" for psychoanalysis. In France, Paul Ricoeur used the hermeneutic approach in his *Freud and Philosophy* (1970) and tried to show that psychoanalysis belonged to the humanities rather than to the natural sciences (Weckowicz, 1984).

The most important influence of Cassirer was on his cousin, Kurt Goldstein (1878-1965), a prominent neurologist, but also a psychologist and a philosopher of biology. Goldstein was for many years at the medical faculty of the University of Frankfurt. He was influenced not only by the neo-Kantian philosophy of Cassirer, but also by Gestalt psychology. Max Wertheimer, Wolfgang Koehler, and Kurt Koffka, the founders of the Gestalt school, were conducting their famous experiments on the perception of movement (the "phi phenomenon") at Frankfurt in 1912 when Goldstein was there. A lively exchange of ideas took place between Goldstein and the Gestaltists. Later Goldstein became a member of the editorial board of the *Psychologische Forschung* founded by the *Gestalt* psychologists. Another member of the editorial board was Hans Gruehle (1880-1958), a Heidelberg psychiatrist. Goldstein became a frequent contributor to that journal. However he never identified himself with the Gestalt school. His biological theory of holism went further than that of the Gestaltists. Goldstein took his inspiration from the philosophies of Goethe, Kant, Cassirer, Husserl, and even Aristotle.

During the first World War and in the postwar period, Goldstein together with Adhemar Gelb (1887-1936), investigated brain injured soldiers. On the basis of this study, as well as on those of aphasic patients, Goldstein & Gelb (1920), and Goldstein & Scheerer (1941), also Goldstein (1948), concluded that the basic disorder underlying various abnormalities of speech and behaviour in these patients was a disorder of symbolic functions. This disorder was not related to a localized lesion but was a disorder of the total brain functioning, affecting the functioning of the total organism. It involved "coming to terms" with the environment by a defective organism. According to Goldstein, the brain damaged patients were not capable of assuming the "abstract attitude," and were unable to represent the external world by conceptual categories and symbolic forms. These patients were incapable of manipulating symbols, of shifting perspectives, and of considering all the possibilities implied by the situation. Instead, they were capable only of assuming a "concrete attitude." They were bound to the "here" and "now" of the concrete situation determined by the immediately given display of stimuli. Goldstein's theory implied that a normally functioning individual interposed a system of symbolic forms between himself and the world of concrete objects. A brain injured or aphasic individual interacted directly with concrete objects. Goldstein believed that schizophrenic patients, just like brain injured ones, were not capable of abstract thought. but reacted to the environment and behaved in a concrete manner.

Goldstein's most important book was *Der Aufbau des Organismus* (1934) which K.S. Lashley translated as *The Organism: A Holistic Approach to Biology Derived from Pathological Data in Man* (1939). Goldstein wrote that book after being exiled from Germany to Holland when Hitler came to power. Afterwards he migrated to the United States and taught at Columbia University. In *The Organism*, he presented his holistic theory of organisms. According to him, all functions had to be considered in their totality, in relation to each other, not in isolation. An organism was a *Gestalt* in which the actively engaged process constituted the figure, and the rest the organism, the ground.

An organism tended to equalize its internal tension and to attain an equilibrium. It also strove to come to terms with the environment. In addition, the organism tried to actualize its potential. Thwarting the drive to self-actualization led to illness and maladjustment. The idea of self-actualization influenced the thinking of American psychologists, who followed theories of personality growth, and of humanistic psychologists. These included Abraham Maslow and Carl Rogers.

A parallel work on the thinking and language of schizophrenic patients was carried out by the Russian psychologist Lev Vygotsky (1896-1934) (1987, 1988). Vygotsky was a pioneer cognitive psychologist who focused on the relation between the development of concept formation and that of language. He extended his studies of children to schizophrenic patients, and investigated concept formation in these patients, using an object sorting test.

A different line of approach to the problem of language was taken out by structural linguistics. This approach was exemplified by the work of L. Bloomfield (1933) and particularly by the work of Ferdinand de Saussure (1966). The latter inspired the French psychoanalyst, Jacques Lacan (1966, 1968), who reinterpreted the psychoanalytical theory in terms of structural linguistics. These developments are too recent to be included in a historical survey. The interested reader is referred to Wilden (1968) and Weckowicz (1984).

15

Epilogue

The history of psychiatry may be approached from different perspectives. One can focus on the biographies of important psychiatrists and describe the details of their life histories and significant events which determined their activity. On the other hand, one can also emphasize the historical context, the prevailing social conditions, and the intellectual climate. This would include the prevailing ideas which were responsible for particular thinking about mental illness. Ernst Mayr in *The Growth of Biological Thought* (1982) refers to this approach to the history of science as "cultural-sociological." He also mentions a "problematic" type of historical writing where the historian of science studies problems and perennial controversies. We have taken a problematic approach in the present work which is nevertheless organized as a sequence of historical periods. It has focused on different perspectives or "models" of mental illness such as the organic, the psychological, the sociological, and the patient or disease oriented.

The history of psychiatry which has been presented in the pages of this book plays down the importance of biographical detail. These may be more fully studied in such works as Zilboorg's *A History of Medical Psychology*, Alexander and Selesnick's *The History of Psychiatry*, and Ernest Jones' *The Life and Work of Sigmund Freud*. Instead the authors have attempted to present the history of psychiatry in the context of general history of ideas in the field of medicine, of science, and of philosophy. It is the belief of the authors that the ideas about, and the attitude towards mental illness have been influenced by wider contexts of ideas at different historical periods. We have not attempted to analyze the social conditions which were responsible for the attitudes to, and for the theories of mental illness prevailing at particular periods of history.

The internal transmission of the key ideas would seem to have played a greater role in the achievements of modern psychological and psychiatric thought. We have emphasized, instead, the cross-fertilization of ideas among various disciplines. The authors have deemed it appropriate to relate the history of psychiatry to that of medicine and philosophy, in order to reveal the theoretical and scientific principles, which were in the process of emergence, so that they might be understood and interpreted according to modern professional beliefs.

In his chapter on the history of psychiatry, in *The Comprehensive Textbook of Psychiatry*, George Mora (1967) describes two alternative approaches to the history of psychiatry and generally of science. The first approach is that of "presentism," or "inductivism." The second is that of "continuity theory." The first divides the ideas and theories occurring in the past into (1) those which anticipated important discoveries which revolutionized the discipline, and (2) those which were erroneous and delayed progress. The second approach does not distinguish between true and false theories, but accepts all of those which appeared as part of a continuous process of the development of the discipline. Thus from the Kuhnian view, one might argue that paradigm shifts alone do not account for the transformations of scientific thought. Those ideas cast aside when a new paradigm emerges, would seem to have played a useful role and often provide the material for a reassessment of old theories. At that time, they help prepare the ground for still more advanced discoveries. We have also accepted some of the more positivist ideas that forms of analysis, ideas about causation, and modes of thought about nosological entities change as the cultural level changes to some extent. Yet some of the traditional conceptualizations remain, and continue to play a significant role. This has been particularly true of the richness of the Greek philosophical tradition in medicine as that of Hippocrates.

The authors have taken the continuity theory approach and have drawn attention to certain recurrent themes and perennial controversies in the history of the discipline. They have assumed an approximation of objectivity to be possible, and have not taken sides in any of the modern controversies.

When comparing ideas and issues that occur in one historical period, with those taking place in any other, the historian is confronted with the problem of historical relativism. According to some modern philosophers of history like Leopold Ranke, Jose Ortega y Gasset, and Wilhelm Dilthey, ideas have validity in their own unique historical context. It is meaningless to take them out of context and to compare them with ideas which may at first glance seem to be similar. Especially not if they have occurred in an entirely different historical context. On the other hand, the "covering law" model of historical explanation as developed by Carl Hempel (1942) and Karl Popper (1957), assumes a basic generality of historical conditions as well as a generality of human nature. As a result, it allows comparisons between ideas occurring in different historical periods. The authors share some of the views of both kinds of thinkers. In spite of the overall emphasis on the uniqueness of historical events found in the historicist tradition emanating from Leopold Ranke (1964), even Ranke always assumed the existence of a part-whole relationship between generalizations of which the knowing scientific historian was capable, and what he considered to be a "loving" appreciation of the unique, the original, the once-occurring greatness of a major thinker, and the particularity of the colorful events of living history. The authors have been interested in both perspectives too. Yet they subscribe to the view that certain themes and controversies about mental illness, have recurred, especially in the history of Western thought and Western medicine.

Controversies which often recur may be called antinomies. The most important controversy in the history of medicine and psychiatry is that between the patient and the disease. To follow the terminology of Henry Sigerist (1932), an important historian of medicine, this controversy is between the "ontology of the patient" and the "ontology of the disease." The first point of view regards pathology as intrinsic to the patient. In this sense, it seems to be part of his constitutional make-up or his personality development. The second point of view regards pathology as extrinsic to the patient. It is caused by an alien disease entity. The first view is exemplified by the psychodynamic, constitutional, and personality developmental approaches. Both the nosological approach and the theory of demoniacal possession exemplfy the second view. The nosological approach tries to dellneate disease entities as extrinsic causal agents of pathology. In primitive culture this role is assigned to evil spirits which take possession of a patient. As Cassirer (1957) pointed out in his theory of symbolic forms, mythology does not have a clear idea of causation. However, there is a similarity in the thought schema that underlies the nosological theory and that of demoniacal possession. We have tried to trace the continuity of some of these ancient themes in the diversity of modern theory.

The second important controversy appeared with the emergence of the ancient Greek scientific attitude during the fifth and sixth centuries B.C. This was a controverys between supernatural and natural explanations. The supernatural explanation of mental illness attributes it to supernatural powers which afflict the spiritual condition of man and of his soul. The natural explanation attributes mental illness to natural causes. These may be directly observed or inferred. Recently, philosophers like Bas C. van Fraassen (1985) and Thomas Kuhn (1979) have found the assumptions of empirical science, which such explanations suppose, to be naive (Churchland & Hooker, Eds., 1985). The supernatural schema of explanation has had a strong tradition behind it, and despite the emergence of modern science, continued to exist in many strata of society where access to advanced knowledge was limited. Yet it continued also among practising physicians. The theory of demoniacal possession is a case in point. So is that of Heinroth, a *Psychiker* psychiatrist of the early nineteenth century, who believed that mental illness was caused by sin. This obviously belongs to the first, the supernatural explanation. Some contemporary philosophical approaches to mental illness such as those found in existentialism, invoke the "human predicament" or the "spirituality of man." These might also be classified as representing a supernatural explanation of mental illness.

The third important controversy is the one between the organic and psychological explanations of mental illness. These two contrasting perspectives in the history of Western philosophy and medicine could be discerned as already present at the beginning of the Greek scientific revolution in the sixth century B.C. As a controversy, it has become more acute since Cartesian metaphysics created a polarisation between the mind and body categories of thought. This controversy became known as the mind-body problem. We have tried to show its influence on the subsequent division in psychiatric theorizing. This polarization, which began in the seventeenth century, was responsible for the division of psychiatric thought into organic and psychological orientations.

The fourth important issue which is of importance to the history of psychiatry exists more at the level of the strategy of discipline than at that of the philosophy of science. The issue is whether to focus on the individual or on society in the discussion of mental illness. Those who focus on the individual regard mental illness as caused by personal conflicts and events in the history of the patient. They are concerned with the actual treatment of the patient and place him at the center of attention. Their concerns are with psychoneurosis and with individual psychotherapy. Those who focus on the society are interested in the possible social causes of mental illness. Consequently, they are interested in epidemiology. They tend to focus on psychoses and on the development of treatment facilties in mental hospitals, because psychoses present a serious social problem.

In the section dealing with the history of psychiatry in the early part of the twentieth century, six different approaches were presented to the problem of mental illness and mental health. In particular, the organic explanation of mental illness was contrasted with the psychological one. It has to be pointed out that throughout history, the pendulum has tended to swing between these two explanations, and that this is in part, the result of the continuing persistence of mind-body controversy.

In summary, it might also be mentioned that an important problem in historiography is that of objectivity. Leopold Ranke, (Liebel-Weckowicz, 1976), the founder of modern historiography believed that a historical narrative ought to show what actually happened ("wie es eigentlich gewesen"). More recent historians like R.G. Collingwood (1946) have also envisaged history to be an accurate reconstruction of a chain of past events. Subjectivity enters when attempts are made to interpret the meaning of past events, and more generally, the meaning of historical processes. Such attempts always involve the bias of personal judgment of the kind which is responsible for the relativity of all interpretations. Since the present book has attempted not only to record, but also to interpret the development of ideas in the field of mental illness and mental health, a personal bias could not be avoided. There is always the possibility that a new interpretation might be made from a different epistemic or hermeneutical perspective.

The Present Situation and the Prospects for the Future

As the final comment, a few remarks could be made about the present state of the discipline and its prospects in the near future. In the past ten to twenty years, the pendulum has once again shifted towards organic types of explanation about the nature of mental illness. Biological psychiatry has become the dominant orientation favouring a neurological and nosological model. This development may be attributed to the stupendous advances in neurosciences which include neurochemistry, neuropharmacology, neuroanatomy, immunology and cellular genetics. A veritable Kuhnian (Kuhn, 1962) revolution has occurred which affords new insights into the workings of the brain. Much mapping of the brain's biochemistry has taken place only since the second World War. Recent breakthroughs have been anticipated by mid-twentieth century work on steroid hormones secreted by the suprarenal cortex and on their relations to the etiology of mental illness. This proved to be a blind alley. However, more recent work on biogenic amines has fared much better. In the sixties, Julius Axelrod (1966, 1971) mapped out the metabolic pathways of the catecholamines, dopamine and noradrenaline. For this achievement Axelrod was awarded the Nobel Prize. Others (Barachas & Usdin, 1973; Chase & Murphy, 1973) investigated the metabolic pathways of serotonin. Catecholamines and serotonin were found to be important synanaptic neurotransmitters which were affected by anti-psychotic and anti-depressant drugs. Their deficiency or imbalance came to be regarded as important factors in the etiology of mental illness. Subsequently, it has been discovered that in addition to biogenic amines, several aminoacids and peptides may act as neurotransmitters. Probably there are thirty or more neurotransmitters associated with different neural pathways in the brain. To complicate the matter further, the effects of neurotransmitters vary and depend on the particular receptors affected by them. New receptors are being discovered all the time. In addition, several peptides produced by the pituitary and the hypothalamus play an important role as neurohormones in the regulation of the functioning of neuronal systems in the brain. This state of affairs indicates that normal functioning of the brain may depend on the proper balances of several neurotransmitters and neurohormones (Weckowicz, 1984).

The new neurodiagnostic techniques such as CAT (computerized axial tomography). PETT (positron-emission transaxial tomography), and MNR (magnetic nuclear resonance) allow investigation of brain neuro-chemistry and metabolism *in vivo*. This offers unprecedented possibilities for understanding the biochemical changes accompanying mental illness. These technological breakthroughs followed on the heels of an earlier revolution in the treatment of chronic schizophrenic patients associated with the introduction of phenothiazine drugs in the fifties and the sixties of the present century. The consequence of this revolution was an emptying of mental hospitals with the patients on maintenance drug therapy able to function outside of hospital, in the community.

The therapeutic revolution associated with the introduction of psychotropic drugs in the treatment of chronic mental patients and their consequent mass discharge from mental hospitals, was abetted by the rights of patients movement. (Although this had also existed earlier in the United States, at intervals since the 1860s). In the sixties, the anti-psychiatry group led by Thomas Szasz (1961, 1965), a rebel against the psychiatric establishment, started an agitation for the civic rights of the patients and against their involuntary confinement in mental institutions. This agitation was successful, not only in its appeal to radical circles of society, but also to conservative American state legislators who saw in it, an opportunity to cut down the maintenance costs of mental hospitals.

The earlier enthusiasm about the mass discharge of mental patients and the closing down of mental hospitals, has been somewhat dampened by the necessity of readmitting many of those patients who stopped taking their drugs. The result has been a revolving door situation. Patients have been discharged and readmitted repeatedly. Also, many patients have ended in cheap rooming houses exploited by unscrupulous landlords. They displayed their psychotic symptoms publically. There is no doubt, however, that large strides have been made in treatment of the mentally ill by drug therapy. New discoveries in brain biochemistry also seem to indicate a better understanding of the organic causes of diseases of the sort hoped for in Kraepelin's generation a century ago. Only the future will show whether the present developments have established biological psychiatry firmly, as the generally accepted paradigm. However, one cannot help but wonder whether the pendulum will start swinging back again in the direction of a new kind of psychological approach to the question of mental illness.

References

Ackerknecht,E.H. *A short history of medicine*. New York: Ronald Press, 1968.

Ackerknecht,E.H. *Kurze Geschichte der Psychiatrie*. 3rd Ed. Stuttgart: Ferdinand Enke Verlag, 1985.

Ackerknecht,E.H. Zur Geschichte der Lehr-und Forschungsstaetten fuer Psychiatrie und Neurologie in Europa ausserhalb des deutschen Sprachgebietes.In K. Kolle (Ed.), *Grosse Nervenaerzte* (Vol. 2, pp. 237-244). 3 Vols. 2nd ed. Stuttgart: Georg Thieme, 1970.

Adler,A. *Gesundheitsbuch fuer das Schneidergewerbe. Wegweiser der Gewerbehygiene*. no.5. G. Golebiewski, Ed. Berlin: Carl Heymanns, 1898.

Adler, A. *Problems of neurosis*. New York: Harper & Row, 1964.

Adler, A. *Social interest: A challenge to mankind.* (1933). London: Faber & Faber, 1938.

Adler, A. *Study of organ inferiority and its psychical compensation*. New York: Nervous and Mental Disease Publishing Co. (German original, 1907), 1917.

Adler,A. *Neurotic constitution* (1912). New York: Moffat & Yard, 1917.

Adler, A. *The practice and theory of individual psychology* (1920). Patterson, NJ: Littlefield & Adonis, 1963.

Adler, A. *Understanding human nature.* New York: Greenberg, 1927.

Alexander, F.S. *The psychoanalysis of the total personality*. Trans. B. Glueck. New York: Nervous and Mental Diseases Publisher, 1930.

Alexander, F.S., & Selesnick, S.T. *The history of psychiatry: An evolution of psychiatric thought and practice from prehistoric times to the present.* New York: Harper & Row, 1966.

Allport, G.W. *Becoming, Basic considerations for a psychology of personality.* New Haven: Yale University Press, 1955.

Altschule, M.D.(with the collaboration of Hegedus,E.R.) *Roots of modern psychiatry: Essays in the history of psychiatry.* (2nd ed.) New York: Grune & Stratton, 1965.

Amadur, M.K. & Messinger, E. Jean-Etienne-Dominique Esquirol. His work and importance for modern psychiatry. *American Journal of Psychiatry*, 1939, *96*, 129-135.

Aquinas, St. T. *De anima*. Trans. K. Foster & S. Humphries. London: Routledge, Kegan, Paul, 1951.

Aquinas, St. T. *Introduction to St. Thomas Aquinas*. A.C. Pegis, Ed. New York: The Modern Library, 1948.

Aquinas, St. T. *Summa theologica*. Trans. D.J. Sullivan et al. Great Books of the Western World. (Vols. 19-20). Chicago: Encyclopedia Britannica, 1952/1955.

Arieti, S. & Meth, J.M. Rare, unclassified, collective, and exotic psychotic syndromes. In S. Arieti (Ed.), *American handbook of psychiatry*.(Vol.2). New York: Basic Books, 1959.

Aristotle. *De anima (On the soul)*. W.D. Ross,(Ed). Oxford: Oxford University Press, 1961.

Assagioli, R. *Psychosynthesis: a manual of principles and techniques*. New York: The Viking Press, 1965/1971.

Augustine, St. *The city of God.* Writings of St. Augustine. Trans. G.J. Walsh & D.J. Nonan. Fathers of the Church, 8. New York: Cima, 1954.

Augustine, St. *The confessions of St. Augustine*. Trans. E.B. Pusey. Oxford: Parker, 1843. Reprint, New York: Collier Book, 1961.

Axelrod, J. Methylation reactions in the formation and metabolism of catecholamines and other biogenic-amines. *Pharmacological Review*, 1966, *18*, 95-113.

Axelrod, J. Noradrenaline. *Science.* 1971, *173*, 598-606.

Ayllon,T. & Michael, J. The psychiatric nurse as a behavioural engineer. *Journal of the Experimental Analysis of Behaviour.*, 1959, *2*, 323-334.

Ayllon,T. & Houghton,E. Control of the behaviour of schizophrenic patients by food. *Journal of the Experimental Analysis of Behaviour*, 1962, *5*, 343-352.

Ayllon,T. Some behavioural problems, associated with eating in chronic schizophrenic patients. In L.P. Ullmann & L. Krasner, (Eds.), *Case Studies in Behaviour Modification.* New York: Holt, Rinehart & Winston, 1965.

Babonoix, L. Dementia praecox and syphilis. *Medicine*, 1921, *37*, 118-119.

Bacon, F. *Novum organon.* (1620). T. Fowler,(Ed.) Oxford: Oxford University Press, 1889.

Bacon, R. *The mirror of alchemy*. Los Angeles, n.p., 1975.

Bain, J.A. *Thought control in everyday life*. New York: Funk & Wagnalls, 1928.

Bakan, D. *Sigmund Freud and the Jewish mystical tradition*. New York: Schocken Books, 1965.

Ballard, E.G. *Philosophy at the crossroads*. Baton Rouge: Louisiana State University Press, 1971.

Barachas, J. & Usdin, E. *Serotonin and behaviour.* New York: Academic Press, 1973.

Barnard, C.P. & Corrales, R.S. *The theory and techniques of family therapy.* Springfield, Ill.: C.C.Thomas, 1979.

Baruk,H., Bidermann,M., & Albane,A. Tuberculose et demence precoce: Reactions allergiques et encephalite toxique. *Paris Medical*, 1932, *2*, 166-172.

Battie, W. *A treatise on madness. Remarks on Dr. Battie's treatise on madness. A psychiatric controversy of the eighteenth century.* R. Hunter,(Ed.). London: Dawson of Pall Mall, reprint of 1758 ed., 1962.

Baudelaire, C. *Les paradis artificiels* (1858), In J. de Crepet, (Ed.), *Oeuvres completes des Charles Baudelaire.* Paris: L.Conard, 1923-1939.

Bauman, Z. *Hermeneutics and social science.* London: Hutchinson, 1978.

Baumer, F.L. *Modern European thought.* New York: Macmillan Publishing Co., 1977.

Beck, A.T. *Depression: clinical experimental and theoretical aspects.* New York: Hoeber, 1967.

Becker, E. *The denial of death.* New York: Free Press, 1973.

Beer, Th., Bethe, A., & Uexkull, J.V. Vorschlaege zu einer objektivierenden Nomenklatur in der Physiologie des Nervensystems. *Biologisches Centralblatt*, 1899, *19*, 517-521.

Beers, C. *A mind that found itself.* New York: Doubleday, 1908.

Bekhterev, V.M. *La psychologie objective (1910).* Paris: Alcan, 1913.

Bekhterev, V.M. *General principles of human reflexology: An introduction to the objective study of personality.* (1917). Trans. E. Murphy and W. Murphy. London: Jarrold, 1933.

Bellak, L. *Contemporary European psychiatry.* New York: Grove Press, 1961.

Benedict, R. *Patterns of culture.* New York: Mentor Books, 1959.

Beneke, F.E. *Grundlinien des natuerlichen Systems der praktischen Philosophie.* Berlin, 1837.

Bergman, G. & Spence,K. Operationism and theory of psychology. *Psychological Review*, 1941, *48*, 1-14.

Bergson, H. *Creative evolution.* (1907) Trans. A. Mitchell. New York: Henry Holt & Co., 1911.

Bernal, J.D. *Science in History.* 4 Vols., 3rd ed. Cambridge, Mass.: M.I.T.Press, 1965/1977.

Bernard, C. *An introduction to the study of experimental medicine.* Trans. H.C. Greene. New York: Dover Publications, 1957. (Original, 1865).

Bernard, W. Freud and Spinoza. *Psychiatry*, 1946, *9*, 99-108.

Bernard, W. Psychotherapeutic principles in Spinoza's Ethics. In S. Hessing (Ed.), *Speculum Spinozanum 1677-1977.* Foreword by H. Smith London: Routledge & Kegan Paul, 1978.

Berze, J. Bewusstseinstonus. *Wiener medizinische Wochenschrift*. 1911.

Berze, J. Paranoia oder dementia praecox. *Psychiatrische-neurologische Wochenschrift*, 1904.

Berze, J. & Gruhle, H.W. *Psychologie der schizophrenie*. Berlin: Springer, 1929.

Binet,A. *L'étude experimentale de l'intelligence*. Paris: Schleicher, 1903.

Binswanger, L. *Grundformen und Erkenntnis menschlichen Daseins*. Zuerich: Niehaus, 1942.

Binswanger, L. Dream and existence (1930). In J. Needleman (Trans. & Ed.), *Being-in-the-world*. New York: Basic Books, 1963.

Binswanger, L. *Sigmund Freud: Reminiscences of a friendship*. New York: Grune & Stratton, 1957a.

Binswanger, L. *Schizophrenie.* Pfullingen: Neske, 1957b.

Binswanger, L. *Melancholie und manie*. Pfullingen: Neske, 1960.

Birbaum, K. *Der Aufbau der Psychose: Grundzuege der psychiatrischen Strukturanalyse.* Berlin: J.Springer, 1923.

Bleuler, E. *Dementia praecox: A group of schizophrenias.* (1911). New York: International University Press, 1950.

Blondel, C. *La conscience morbide.* Paris: Alcan, 1914.

Bloomfield,L. *Language.* New York: Holt, 1933.

Boas, F. *Contributions to the ethnology of the Kwakiutl.* New York: Columbia University Press, 1925.

Bockoven, J.S. *Moral treatment in American psychiatry.* New York: Springer Publishing, 1963.

Bockoven,J.S. *Moral treatment in community mental health*. New York: Springer, 1972.

Bodin,J. *De la demonomanie des sorciers aveque la refutation des opinions de Jean Wier.* 1580.

Boring, E.S. *A history of experimental psychology.* New York: Appleton, Century, Crofts, 1950.

Boussard, J. *The civilization of Charlemagne*. New York: McGraw-Hill, 1968.

Bowen,T. *An historical account of the origin, progress, and present state of Bethlehem Hospital: founded by Henry the Eighth for the cure of lunatics and enlarged by subsequent benefactors for the reception and maintenance of incurables.* London, 1783.

Brentano, F. *Psychologie vom empirischen Standpunkt.* Leipzig: Duncker & Humblot, 1874.

Breuer, J. & Freud, S. *Studies of hysteria.* (1895). Trans. J. Strachey. New York: Basic Books, 1957.

Bridgman, P. *The logic of modern physics.* New York: Macmillan, 1927.

Briquet, P. *Traité de l'hystérie*. Paris: J.B.Bailliere, 1859.

Brown, J. *Elementa medicinae*. Edinburgh: C. Elliot, 1780.

Brown, T. *Lectures on the philosophy of the human mind*. Edinburgh, 1840.

Brunner, H. *Altaegyptische Religion. Grundzuege*, (2nd ed.). Darmstadt: Wissenschaftliche Buchgesellschaft, 1989.

Buber, M. *I and thou.* New York: Scribner, 1958.

Budge, E.A.W. *The gods of the Egyptians; or, Studies in Egyptian mythology.* New York: Dover Publications, 1969.

Buehler, C. *Values in psychotherapy*. New York: The Free Press of Glencoe, 1962.

Buehler, K. *Sprachtheorie: Die Darstellungsfunktion der Sprache*. Jena: Fischer, 1934.

Bullough, D.A. *The age of Charlemagne*. London: Elek Books, 1965.

Burnham, W. *The normal mind: An introduction to mental hygiene and the hygiene of school instruction.* New York: Appleton, 1924.

Burton, R. *The anatomy of melancholy.* F. Dell & P. Jordan, (Eds.) New York: Tudor Publishing, 1948.

Burtt, E.A.(Ed.) *The English philosophers from Bacon to Mill.* New York: The Modern Library, 1939.

Buscaino, V.M. Production of hallucinations, catatonia and Parkinsonism by action of amines (Indol). *Revista de Patalogia Nervosa e Mentale,* 1929, *34*, 162-165.

Byrd, M. *Visits to Bedlam; madness and literature in the eighteenth century.* Columbia: University of South Carolina Press, 1974.

Campeau, L. *La mission des Jesuites chez les Hurons, 1634-1650.* Montreal: Editions Bellarmin, 1987.

Cannon, W.B. *The wisdom of the body.* New York: Norton, 1932.

Carnap, R. Psychology in physical language. Trans. G. Schick. In A.J. Ayer (Ed.), *Logical positivism*. Glencoe,.Ill.: Glencoe Press, 1959.

Carnegie, D. *How to stop worrying and start living.* New York: Simon & Schuster, 1948.

Carus, C.G. *Physis: zu Geschichte des leiblichen Lebens*. Stuttgart, 1851.

Carus, C. G. *Psyche, zur Entwicklungsgeschichte der Seele*. Pforzheim: Plammer & Hoffmann, 1846.

Cassirer, E. *An essay on man.* New Haven: Yale University Press, 1944.

Cassirer, E. *Die Philosophie der Aufklaerung*. Tuebingen: Verlag J.C.B.Mohr (Paul Siebeck), 1932.

Cassirer, E. *Philosophy of symbolic forms.* 3 vols. Trans. R. Manheim. New Haven: Yale University Press, 1957.

Chase, T.N.,& Murphy, D.L. Serotonin and central nervous system function. *Annual Review of Pharmacology*, 1973, *13*, 181-197.

Cheyne,G. *An essay on regimen*. London: C. Rivington, 1740.

Cheyne,G. *The English malady, or a treatise on nervous disease of all kinds, as spleen, vapours, lowness of spirits, hypochondriacal and hysterical distempers*. London: G. Strahan in Cornhill,1733.

Churchland, P.M. & Hooker, C.A. *Images of science: Essays on realism and empiricism, with a reply from Bas C. Fraasen*. Chicago: University of Chicago Press, 1985.

Cicero, M.T. *The academic questions: Treatise de finibus, and Tusculan disputations.* Trans. C.D. Yonge. London: George Bell, 1878.

Clements, F.E. Primitive concepts of disease. *University of California Publications in Archaeology and Ethnology*, 1932, *32*, 185-252.

Cleve, T.C. van. *The emperor Frederick II Hohenstaufen*. Oxford: The Clarendon Press, 1972.

Cohen, D. *J.B. Watson, the founder of behaviorism. A biography*. London: Routledge & Kegan Paul, 1979.

Collingwood, R.S. *The idea of history.* Oxford: Clarendon Press, 1946.

Cooley, C.H. *Social organization*. New York: Scribner, 1929.

Combe, G. *Constitution of man considered in relation to external objects.* Boston: Marsh, Capen, Lyon & Webb, 1839.

Comte, A. *Cours de philosophie positive.* 6 vols. Paris: Schleicher Freres, 1908.

Cotton, H.A. *The defective, delinquent and insane.* Princeton: Princeton University Press, 1921.

Cotton, H.A. The relation of chronic sepsis to the so called functional disorder. *Journal of Mental Science*, 1923, *69*, 334-365.

Coue, E. *The practice of autosuggestion.* New York: Doubleday, 1922.

Cullen, W. *First lines of the practice of physic, with practical and explanatory notes by John Rotheram*. Edinburgh: Bell & Bradfute, 1769.

Cullen, W. *Synopsis nosologiae methodicae*. Hartford: I. Thomas, 1792.

Dabrowski, K. *Positive disintegration*. Boston: Little, Brown, 1964.

Darwin, C. *The expression of the emotions in man and animals.* London: Murray, 1872.

Darwin, C. *The origin of species by means of natural selection, or the preservation of favored races in the struggle for life.* London: Murray, 1859.

Davenport,C. *Heredity in relation to eugenics.* New York: F. Holt, 1911.

Dawson, C. *The making of Europe; an introduction to the history of European unity.* New York: Sheed & Ward, 1945.

Deferrari, R.J. et al. *A lexicon of St. Thomas Aquinas based on the Summa theologica and selected passages of his other works*. Washington, D.C.: Catholic University of America Press, 1948.

Defoe, D. *Augusta triumphans, or the way to make London the most flourishing city in the universe*. London: Roberts, 1728. [Quoted by R. Hunter & J. Macalpine, *Three hundred years of psychiatry 1535-1860.* London: Oxford University Press, 1963.]

De Giovanni,A. *Clinical commentaries deduced from the morphology of the human body* (1877). Trans. J.J. Eyre. New York: Rebman Co., 1910.

Depue, R.A. & Monroe, S.M. The unipolar-bipolar distinction in the depressive disorders. *Psychological Bulletin*, 1978, *85*, 1001-1030.

Descartes, R. *The philosophical works of Descartes*. Trans. & Eds. E.S. Haldane & G.T. R. Ross. 2 vols. Revised Ed. 1st Ed. 1911. Cambridge: Cambridge University Press, 1979.

Deutsch, A. *The mentally ill in America; a history of their care and treatment from colonial times*. 2nd Ed. New York: Columbia University Press, 1960.

Dewey, J. *Democracy and education.* New York: Macmillan, 1916.

Dewey, J. *Human nature and conduct.* New York: Holt, 1922.

Dewhurst, K. *Hughlings Jackson on psychiatry*. Oxford: Sandford Publications, 1982.

Diethelm, O. *Adolf Meyer, 1866-1950. Grosse Nervenaerzte*. K.Kolle, (Ed.) 3 Vols. (2nd ed.) Stuttgart: Georg Thieme, (Vol. 2, 129-138) 1970.

Dilthey, W. *Descriptive psychology and historical understanding*. Includes: The understanding of other persons and their expressions of life. Rudolf A. Makkreel, (Ed.) Trans. R.M. Zaner, K.L.Heiges. The Hague: M. Nijhoff, 1977.

Dilthey, W. *The essence of philosophy.* Trans. S.A. Emery & W.T. Emery. Chapel Hill: University of North Carolina, 1954.

Dilthey, W. *The meaning in history*. Trans. & Ed. H.S. Rickman. London: Allen & Unwin, 1961.

Dilthey, W. Typologie der Weltanschauungen. In: *Gesammelte Schriften.* 2nd Ed. Vol. 9. Stuttgart & Goettingen: B.G. Teubner, 1957-1960.

Dreikurs, R. *Fundamentals of Adlerian psychology*. New York: Greenberg, 1950.

Durkheim, E. *Suicide*. Trans. J.A. Spaulding & G. Simpson. New York: The Free Press of Glencoe, 1951. Originally published in French, 1894.

Draper, G. *Human constitution in clinical medicine*. New York: Saunders, 1924.

Dubos, R. & Dubos, J. *The white plague*. Boston: Little, Brown, 1952.

Dunlap, K. *Habits: Their making and unmaking*. New York: Liveright, 1932.

Ebbinghaus, H. Ueber erklaerende und beschreibende Psychologie. *Zeitschrift fuer Psychologie und Physiologie der Sinnesorgane*, 1896, *9*, 161-205.

Edelson, M. *The idea of mental illness*. New Haven: Yale University Press, 1971.

Einhard. *The life of Charlemagne*. Trans. S.E. Turner. Ann Arbor:University of Michigan Press, 1960.

Ellenberger, H.F. *The discovery of the unconscious: The history and evolution of dynamic psychiatry*. New York: Basic Books, 1970.

Ellenberger, H.F. Fechner and Freud. *Bulletin of the Menninger Clinic,* 1956, *20*, 201-214.

Erikson, E.H. *Childhood and society*. New York: Norton & Co., 1963.

Erikson, E.H. *Young man Luther*. New York: Norton & Co., 1958.

Esquirol, J.E.D. *De maladies mentales considerees sous les rapports medical, hygieniques et medico-legal*. (2 Vols). Paris, 1838.

Ey, H. Outline of an organic-dynamic conception of the structure, nosography and pathogenesis of mental diseases. In E. Straus, M. Natanson & H. Ey (Eds.), *Psychiatry and philosophy*. New York:Springer Verlag, 1969.

Eysenck, H.J. The effects of psychotherapy: An evaluation. *Journal of Consulting Psychology*, 1952, *16*, 319-324.

Eysenck, H.J. *Behaviour therapy and the neuroses; readings in modern methods of treatment derived from learning theory*. New York: Pergamon, 1960.

Eysenck, H.J. Learning theory and behaviour therapy. *Journal of Mental Science,* 1959, *105*, 61-75.

Fairbairn, W.P.D. *The object relation theory of personality*. New York: Basic Books, 1954.

Faris, R.E. L. & Dunham, W.H. *Mental disorders in urban areas*. Chicago: University of Chicago Press, 1939.

Farmer, D.H. (Ed.) *The rule of St. Benedict*. Early English manuscripts in facsimile, 15. Copenhagen: Rosenkilde & Bagger, 1968.

Fechner, G.T. *Nanna, oder ueber das Seelenleben der Pflanzen*. Leipzig: Voss, 1848.

Fechner, G.T. *Zend-Avesta oder ueber die Dinge des Himmels und des Jenseits.* Leipzig: Voss, 1851.

Fechner, G.T. *Elemente der Psychophysik.* Leipzig: Voss, 1951.

Fechner, G.T. *Vorschule der Aesthetik.* Leipzig: Breitkopf & Haertel, 1873.

Felix, R.H. *Mental illness, progress and prospects.* New York: Columbia University Press, 1967.

Ferenzi, S. *Further contributions to the theory and technique of psychoanalysis.* Trans. J.I. Suttie. London: Hogarth Press, 1926.

Ferenczi, S. & Rank, O. *The development and goals of psychoanalysis.* (1924). New York: Nervous and Mental Diseases Publishing Co., 1925.

Feuchtersleben E. von. *The principles of medical psychology, Being the outline of a course of lectures.* Trans. H. Evans Lloyd. London: Syndenham Society, 1847 (Original, 1845).

Fichte, J.S. *The science of knowledge.* New York: Appleton, Century, Crofts, 1969.

Fish, F.J. *Schizophrenia.* Bristol: John Wright, 1962.

Flournoy, T. *From India to the planet Mars. A study of a case of somnabulism with glossalia.* New York: Harper, 1900.

Foucault,M. *Madness and civilization: A history of insanity in the age of reason.* Trans. R. Howard. New York: Pantheon Books, 1965/1973.

Fraasen, B.C. van. Empiricism in the philosophy of science; B.C. van Fraasen replies to his critics. In P.M.Churchland & C.A.Hooker,(Eds.), *Images of science.* Chicago: The University of Chicago Press, 1985.

Franke, H. et al. *Saeculum Weltgeschichte.* 7 Vols. Freiburg/Br.,Basel,Vienna: Herder,1965-1975.

Frankfurt, H. (Ed.) *Leibniz.* Garden City, N.Y.: Doubleday, 1972.

Frankl, V. *Man's search for meaning: An introduction to logotherapy.* New York: Washington Press, 1963.

Franklin, B. *Some account of the Pennsylvania Hospital.* Baltimore: Johns Hopkins, 1954.

Frege, G. Ueber Sinn und Bedeutung. *Zeitschrift fuer Philosophie und Philosophische Kritik,* 1892, *100*, 25-50.

Freind, J. *The history of physick from the time of Galen, to the beginning of the sixteenth century.* 2 Vols. London: J. Walther, 1727.

French, T.M. The reintegrative process in a psychoanalytical treatment. In: *The integration of behavior.* Chicago: University of Chicago Press, 1958.

Freud, Anna. *The ego and the mechanisms of defense.* Trans. C. Beines. London: Hogarth Press, 1937.

Freud, S. *On aphasia.* (1891) Trans. E. Stengel. New York: International Universities Press, 1891/1953.

Freud, S. The interpretation of dreams (1900). In: *The complete psychological works of Sigmund Freud.* J. Strachey, (Ed.) (Vol. 18). London: The Hogarth Press, 1955.

Freud, S. Three essays on the theory of sexuality (1905). In: *The complete psychological works of Sigmund Freud.* J. Strachey, (Ed.) (Vol. 7). London: Hogarth Press, 1953.

Freud, S. Psychopathology of everyday life (1904). In J. Strachey, (Ed.), *The complete psychological works of Sigmund Freud,* (Vol. 6). London: The Hogarth Press, 1960.

Freud, S. Jokes and their relation to the unconscious (1905). In J. Strachey, (Ed.), *The complete psychological works of Sigmund Freud* (Vol. 8). London: The Hogarth Press, 1960.

Freud, S. Analysis of phobia in a five year old boy (1909). In J. Strachey, (Ed.), *The complete psychological works of Sigmund Freud,* (Vol. 10). London: The Hogarth Press, 1955.

Freud, S. Psychoanalytic notes on an autobiographical account of a case of Paranoia (1911). In J. Strachey, (Ed.) *The complete psychological works of Sigmund Freud,* (Vol. 12). London: Hogarth Press, 1958.

Freud, S. Totem and taboo (1912). In J. Strachey (Ed.), *The complete psychological works of Sigmund Freud,* (Vol. 13). London: The Hogarth Press, 1955.

Freud, S. *The history of the psychoanalytic movement and other papers* (1914). New York: Collier Books, 1963.

Freud, S. Mourning and melancholia (1917). In J. Strachey (Ed.), *The complete psychological works of Sigmund Freud,* (Vol. 14). London: The Hogarth Press, 1957.

Freud, S. Beyond the pleasure principle (1920). In J. Strachey, (Ed.), *The complete psychological works of Sigmund Freud,* (Vol. 28). London: The Hogarth Press, 1955.

Freud, S. Group psychology and the analysis of the ego (1921). In J. Strachey (Ed.), *The complete psychological works of Sigmund Freud.* (Vol. 18, pp. 65-172). London: Hogarth Press, 1961.

Freud, S. The ego and the id (1923). In J. Strachey, (Ed.), *The complete psychological works of Sigmund Freud,* (Vol. 19). London: The Hogarth Press, 1961.

Freud, S. The future of an illusion (1927). In: *The complete psychological works of Sigmund Freud.* J. Strachey, Ed. (Vol. 21). London: The Hogarth Press, 1961.

Freud, S. Civilization and its discontents (1930). In: *The complete psychological works of Sigmund Freud*. J. Strachey, Ed. (Vol. 21). London: The Hogarth Press, 1961.

Freud, S. Moses and monotheism (1939). In: *The complete psychological works of Sigmund Freud.* J. Strachey Ed. (Vol. 22). London: The Hogarth Press, 1964.

Freud, S. *The origins of psychoanalysis: Letters, drafts and notes to Wilhelm Fliess*. M. Bonaparte, E. Mosbacher, & J. Strachey, Eds. Garden City, N.Y.: Doubleday, 1957.

Friedreich, J. *Historisch-kritische Darstellung der Theorien ueber das Wesen und den Sitz der psychischen Krankheiten*. Leipzig, n.p. 1836.

Fromm, E. *Escape from freedom.* New York: Holt, Rinehart & Winston, 1941.

Fromm,E. *Man for himself.* New York: Holt, Rinehart & Winston, 1947.

Fromm, E. *The sane society.* New York: Holt, Rinehart & Winston, 1955.

Fromm, E. *Marx's concept of man.* New York: Frederick Ungar, 1961.

Gall, F. J. *The Nervous system in general and of the brain in particular* (1810). Reprint 1980. Boston: March, Capen & Lyon, 1835.

Galton, F. *Hereditary genius.* London: Macmillan, 1869.

Gantt, W.H. *Experimental basis for neurotic behaviour: origin and development of artificially produced disturbances of behaviour in dogs.* New York: Paul H. Hoeber, 1944.

Gardiner, Sir Alan. *Egypt of the pharaohs. An introduction*. London: Oxford University Press, 1961.

Garrison, F.D. *An introduction to the history of medicine, with medical chronology, Suggestion for study and bibliographic data*. 4th ed. Philadelphia: Saunders, 1929.

Gaskin, E. B. *The rise of experimental biology.* New York: Random House, 1970.

Gay, P. *Freud. A life for our time.* New York: W.W. Norton, 1988.

Gebsattel von, V. *Prolegomena zu einer Medizinischen Anthropologie.* Berlin: Springer, 1954.

Gebsattel von, V. *The world of the compulsive.* Trans. S. Koppel & E. Angel. In: *Existence*, eds. R. May, E. Angel, & H.F. Ellenberger. New York : Basic Books, 1958.

Gendlin, E.T. *Experiencing and creation of meaning*. Glencoe, Ill.: Free Press, 1962.

Ghalioungui, P. *Magic and medical science in ancient Egypt.* London: Hodder & Stoughton, 1963.

Ghalioungui, P. *The physicians of pharaonic Egypt.* Al-Ahram Center for Scientific Translations. Cairo: A.R.E., 1983.

Gjessing, R. Biological investigation in endogenous psychoses. *Acta Psychiatrica* (Kfh) 1947, *93*, Suppl. 47.

Gjessing, R. Disturbances of somatic functions in catatonia with a periodic course and their compensation. *Journal of Mental Sciences,* 1938, *84*, 608-621.

Goethe, J.W. *Versuch die Metamorphosen der Pflanzen zu erklaeren*. Gotha: C.W. Ettinger, 1790.

Goldstein, K. *The organism: A holistic approach to biology derived from pathological data in man* (1934). New York: American Book, 1939.

Goldstein, K. *Language and language disturbances: Aphasic symptoms and their significance for medicine and theory of language.* New York: Grune & Stratton, 1948.

Goldstein, K. & Gelb, A. *Psychologische Analysen hirnpathologischer Faelle.* Leipzig: Barth, 1920.

Goldstein, K. & Scheerer, M. Abstract and concrete behaviour, an experimental study with tests. *Psychological Monographs*, 53. No. 2. 1941.

Gottfried, R.S. *The black death: natural and human disaster in medieval Europe*. New York: Collier, Macmillan, 1983.

Griesinger, W. *Mental pathology and therapeutics.* (1845) Trans. C. L. Robertson & G. Rutherford. London: New Sydenham Society, 1867.

Grimal, P. *The dictionary of classical mythology.* Trans. A.R.Maxwell. New York: Blackwell, 1987.

Grinspoon, L. *Marihuana reconsidered.* Cambridge, Mass.: Harvard University, 1971.

Grob, G.N. *Mental illness and American society, 1875-1940.* Princeton: Princeton University Press, 1983.

Grob, G.N. *Mental institutions in America; social policy to 1875*. New York: Free Press, 1973.

Grob, G.N. *The state and the mentally ill; A history of Worcester State Hospital in Massachusetts, 1830-1920*. Chapel Hill: University of North Carolina Press, 1966.

Groddeck, G. *The book of the id.* (1923) New York: Nervous and Mental Disease Publishing, 1928.

Groos, F. *Entwurf einer philosophischen Grundlage fuer die Lehre von den Geisteskrankheiten*. Heidelberg, n.p. 1828.

Gross, O. *Die cerebrale Sekundaerfunktion.* Leipzig: F.C.W.Vogel,1902.

Gruehle, H.W. *Verstehende Psychologie.* Stuttgart: Thieme, 1948.

Gruenthal, E. Bernard von Gudden, 1824-1886. In Kurt Kolle, (Ed.) *Grosse Nervenaerzte.* (3 Vols. 2nd ed.) Stuttgart: Georg Thieme Verlag, 1970. 1:128-134.

Guardini, R. *The conversion of St. Augustine*. Trans. Elinor Briefs. Chicago: Henry Regnery Co., 1960.

Guthrie, E.R. *The Psychology of human conflict.* New York: Harper & Row, 1938.

Guthrie, E.R. *The psychology of learning (revised).* New York: Harper, 1952.

Haenel, T. *Zur Geschichte der psychiatrischen Gedanken zur allgemeinen und Basler Psychiatriegeschichte*. Basel: Birkenhaeuser Verlag, 1982.

Haindorf, A. *Versuch einer Pathologie und Therapie der Gemueths und Geisteskrankheiten*. Heidelberg: n.p., 1811.

Hall, A.R. *The scientific revolution, 1500-1800; the formation of the modern scientific attitude*. Boston: Beacon Press,1956. (2nd rev. ed.) 1962.

Hall, Marshall. On the reflex function of the Medulla Oblongata and the Medulla Spinalis. *Philosophical Transactions*. 1833, *123*, 635-665.

Harms, E. *Origins of modern psychiatry.* Springfield, Ill. C. C. Thomas, 1967.

Harrington, A. *Medicine, mind, and the double brain. A study in nineteenth century thought*. Princeton: Princeton University Press, 1987.

Hartmann von, E. *Philosophie des Unbewussten.* (Philosophy of the unconscious), Berlin: Duncker, 1869.

Hartmann, H. *Ego psychology and the problem of adaptation.*New York: International University Press, 1958.

Haslam, J. *Observations on insanity with particular remarks on the disease and an account of the morbid appearance on disection.* London: n.p., 1798.

Haslam, J. *Medical jurisprudence as it relates to insanity*. New York: Garland, reprint of the 1817 edition, 1979.

Hegel, G.W.F. *Phenomenology of mind.* (1807) Trans. J.B. Baillie. New York: Macmillan, 1949. (Original 1807).

Hegel, G.W.F. *Philosophy of right*. Trans. T.M.Knox. Oxford: Clarendon, 1942.

Heidegger, M. *Sein und Zeit.* Halle: Niemeyer,1927. English trans. J.Macquarri & E. Robinson. New York: Harper,1962.

Heinemann, E. *Hexen und Hexenglaube. Eine historisch-sozial-psychologische Studie ueber den europaeischen Hexenwahn des 16. und 17. Jahrhunderts*. Frankfurt a. M.: Campus Verlag, 1986.

Heinroth, J.C.H. *Lehrbuch der Stoerungen des Seelenlebens oder Seelenstroemungen und Ihrer Behandlung.* 2 Vols. Leipzig: F.C.W.Vogel, 1818.

Hempel, C.G. The function of general laws in history. *Theories of history.* P. Gardiner, (Ed.) Glencoe, Ill.:The Free Press, 1959. (pp. 344-356).

Henderson, D.K. & Gillespie, R.D. *Textbook of psychiatry.* 9th edition. London: Oxford University Press, 1963.

Henry, G. W. Organic mental diseases. In: G. Zilboorg, *A History of medical psychology* (pp. 526-551). New York: Norton, 1941.

Herbart, J.F. *Allgemeine practische Philosophie*. Goettingen: J.H. Danckwerth, 1808.

Herbart, J.F. *Psychologie als Wissenschaft, neugegruendet auf Erfahrung, Metaphysik und Mathematik* (1824). In: Saemtliche Werke. Leipzig: Voss, 1850.

Herder, J.G. *Ideen zur Philosophie der Geschichte der Menschheit.* 4 Vols. Riga: Hartknoch, 1784-1791. English trans. T.O. Churchill, *Outline of a philosophy of the history of man*. New York: Bergman Publishers, 1966.

Hettner, H. *Geschichte der deutschen Literatur im Achtzehntenjahrhundert.* Vol. 3/3. (5th ed.) Braunschweig: F. Vieweg & Sohn, 1909.

Hirsch, A. *Geschichte der Medizinischen Wissenschaften in Deutschland.* Munich, Leipzig: Verlag Oldenburg, 1893.

Hoff, H. & Arnold, O.H. Germany and Austria. Trans. R. Spielmeyer. In: *Contemporary European Psychiatry.*L. Bellak, ed. New York: Grove Press, 1961.

Hollingsworth, H.L. *Abnormal psychology*. New York: Ronald, 1930.

Holmes, G. John Hughlings Jackson, 1835-1911. In: K. Kolle, Ed. *Grosse Nervenzaerzte*. (Vol.1:135-144, 2nd ed.) Stuttgart: G.Thieme Verlag, 1970.

Holt, E.B. Response and cognition. *Journal of Philosophy.* 1915, *12*, 365-409.

Horn, W. & Born, E. *The plan of St. Gall: a study of the architecture and economy of a life in a paradigmatic Carolingian monastery.* 3 Vols. Berkeley: University of California Press, 1979.

Horney, K. *New ways in psychoanalysis.* New York: W.W. Norton, 1939.

Horney, K. *Our inner conflict.* New York: W.W. Norton, 1945.

Horney, K. *Neurosis and human growth.* New York: W.W. Norton, 1950.

Horney, K. *The Neurotic personality of our time*. New York: W.W. Norton, 1937.

Horney, K. *Self analysis*. New York: W.W. Norton, 1942.

Hoskins, R.G. *Biology of schizophrenia*. New York: W.W. Norton, 1946.

Hull, C.L. *Principles of behaviour.* New York: Appleton-Century-Crofts, 1943.

Hunter, R. & Macalpine, I. *Three hundred years of psychiatry, 1536-1860.* London: Oxford University Press, 1963.

Husserl, E. *Logische Untersuchungen.* 2 Vols. Halle: Niemeyer, 1900-1901.

Husserl, E. *Ideen zu einer reinen Phaenomenologie und phaenomenologischen Philosophie* (1913, 1930). 3 Vols. The Hague: M. Nijhoff, 1950-1952. English trans. F. Kerste. Hague: M. Nijhoff, 1982.

Husserl, E. *Cartesian meditations.* The Hague: M. Nijhoff, 1960.

Husserl, E. *Die Krisis der Europaeischen Wissenschaften und die Transzendentale Phenomenologie.* The Hague: M. Nijhoff, 1954.

Husserl, E. *Phaenomenologische Psychologie. Vorlesungen Sommersemester 1925.* Walter Biemel, Ed. Husserliana, Gesammelte Schriften, *9*. The Hague: M. Nijhoff, 1962.

Husserl, E. Philosophy as a rigorous science (1911). In *Phenomenology and the crisis of philosophy.* Trans. & Ed. A. Lauer. New York: Harper & Row, 1965.

Ideler, K.W. *Grundriss der Seelenheilkunde.* 2 Vols. Berlin: T.C.F. Enslin, 1835.

Isham, H. Wilhelm von Humboldt. In: *The Encyclopedia of Philosophy.* P. Edwards, (Ed.) Vol. *4, pp.* 72-74. New York: Macmillan, 1967.

Jackson, H.J. Croomian lectures. (1884) Reprinted in *Selected Writings.* London: Hodder & Stoughton, 1932.

Jacobi, J. *The psychology of C.G. Jung.* New Haven: Yale University Press, 1962.

Jacobson, E. *Progressive relaxation.* Chicago: University of Chicago Press, 1938.

James, W. *The principles of psychology.* 2 Vols. (1890). New York: Dover Publications, 1950.

James I. *Demonologie, In Form of a Dialogue Divided into Three Books: Written by the High and Mighty Prince James, By Grace of God, King of England, Scotland, France and Ireland, Defender of the Faith, etc.* London: Waldgrave, 1603.

Janet, P. *L'automatisme psychologiques: essai de psychologie experimentale sur les formes inferieures de l'activité.* Paris: Alcan, 1889.

Janet, P. *Les obsessions et la psychasthénie.* 2 Vols. Paris: Alcan, 1903.

Janet, P. *Les nevroses.* Paris: Flammarion, 1909.

Janet, P. *Les medications psychologiques; études historiques, psychologiques et cliniques sur les methodes de la psychotherapie.* Paris:Alcan, 1919.

Janet, P. *De l'angoise à l'extase.* Paris:Alcan, 1926.

Jaspers, K. *General psychopathology (1913).* Trans. J. Hoening & M.W. Hamilton. Manchester: Manchester University Press, 1963.

Jaspers, K. The phenomenological approach in psychopathology. *British Journal of Psychiatry.* 1968, *114*, 1313-1323. Trans. from the German original: *Zeitschrift fuer die Gesamte Neurologie und Psychiatrie.* 1912, *9*, 391-408.

Jaspers, K. *Psychologie der Weltanschauungen.* Berlin: J. Springer, 1919.

Jaspers, K. *Reason and Existenz.* New York: The Noonday Press, 1955.

Jaspers, K. Mein Weg zur Philosophie. In: *Rechenschaft und Ausblick.* Munich: Piper, 1958.

Jaspers, K. *Schelling: Groesse und Verhaengnis*. Munich: Piper, 1955.

Jaspers, K. *The Way to Wisdom*. New Haven: Yale University Press, 1951.

Jaynes, J. *The origin of consciousness in the breakdown of the bicameral mind.* Boston: Houghton, Mifflin, 1976.

Johnson, R.H. *The concept of existence in the Concluding Unscientific Postscript*. Hague: Martinus Nijhoff, 1972.

Johnston, W.M. *The Austrian mind. An intellectual and social history, 1848-1938.* Berkeley, Los Angeles, London: University of California Press, 1972.

Jones, E. *The life and work of Sigmund Freud.* 3 Vols. (Vol. 1). New York: Basic Books, 1953.

Jones, M.C. The elimination of children's fears. *Journal of Experimental Psychology.* 1924, *7,* 382-390.

Jung, C.G. *Psychology of Dementia Praecox (1907).* New York: Nervous and Mental Disease Monograph Series, No. 3, 1909.

Jung, C.G. Wandlungen und Symbole der Libido. Beitraege zur Entwicklungsgeschichte des Denkens. *Jahrbuch fuer Psychoanalytische und Psychopathologische Forschungen, 1911, 3*, 120-227; 1912, *4*, 169-464. English Trans. *Psychology of the unconscious.* New York: Moffat Yard, 1916.

Jung, C.G. *Studies in word association.* 2 Vols. New York: Moffat Yard, 1919.

Jung, C.G. *Psychological types.* Trans. H.G. Baynes. New York: Harcourt Brace, 1923.

Jung, C.G. *Contributions to analytical psychology*. Trans. C.F. Baynes & H.G. Baynes. New York: Harcourt, Brace, 1928.

Jung, C.G. *Modern man in search of a soul*. Trans. W.S. Dell & C.F. Baynes. New York: Harcourt & Brace, 1933.

Jung, C.G. *Psychology of religion*. New Haven: Yale University Press, 1938.

Jung, C.G. *Modern man in search of a soul*. New York: Harcourt & Brace, 1939a.

Jung, C.G. *The integration of personality.* Trans. S. Dell. New York: Farrar & Rinehart, 1939 b.

Jung, C.G. The psychology of alchemy: Alchemic studies. In: *Collected works of C.G. Jung,* Vols. 12-13. Trans. R.F.C. Hall. London: Routledge & Kegan Paul, 1953.

Jung, C.G. Paracelsus. In: *Collected works of C.G. Jung*. Vol. 15. Trans. R.F.C. Hall. London: Routledge & Kegan Paul, 1957.

Jung, C.G. *Man and his symbols.* Garden City, N.Y. Doubleday, 1964.

Jung, C.J. Introduction to the religious and psychological problems of alchemy. *The Basic Writings of C.J. Jung*. V.S. de Laszlo, Ed. New York: The Modern Library, c1959. Pp. 433-468.

Kamal, H. *Dictionary of pharaonic medicine*. Cairo: The National Publications House, 1967.

Kant, I. *Anthropologie in Pragmatischer Hinsicht Abgefasst. (Anthropology from the Pragmatic Point of View)*. Koenigsberg: Friedrich Nicolovius, 1789.

Kant, I. *Critique of pure reason* (1781). New York: Anchor Books, 1966.

Kant, I. *Foundations of the metaphysics of morals. (Grundlegung zur Metaphysik der Sitten,* 1785*). Trans. L.W. Beck. In: Critique of practical reason and other writings in moral philosophy.* Chicago: University of Chicago Press, 1949.

Kant, I. *The critique of judgement*. (*Kritik der Urteilskraft,* 1790). English trans. J.H. Bernard. London, New York:Macmillan, 1892.

Kant, I. *Traueme eines Geistersehers* (*Dreams of a spiritist*, 1766). In: I. Kant, *Werke*, Ed. E. Cassirer. Vol. 1, pp. 923 ff. Berlin, 1912.

Kardiner, A. *The individual and his society.* New York: Columbia University Press, 1939.

Kardiner, A. *Culture and mental disorders*. Springfield, Ill.:C.C.Thomas, 1956.

Kazdin, A.K. *History of behaviour modification.* Baltimore: University Park Press, 1978.

Kerferd, G.B. Apeiron. In *The Encyclopedia of Philosophy*. (Vol. 1, p. 133) Paul Edwards, (Ed.) New York: Macmillian, 1967.

Kierkegaard, S.A. *Concluding unscientific postscript of philosophical fragments*. Trans. D.F. Swanson & W. Lowrie. Princeton: Princeton University Press, 1941.

Kierkegaard. S.A. *The concept of dread*. Trans. W. Lowrie. Princeton: Princeton University Press, 1944.

Kierkegaard, S.A. *Fear and trembling*. Trans. W. Lowrie. Princeton: Princeton University Press, 1954a.

Kierkegaard, S.A. *The sickness unto death*. Trans. W. Lowrie. Princeton: Princeton University Press, 1954b.

Kierkegaard, S.A. *Johannes Climacus or, de omnibus dubitandum est and a Sermon.* Trans. T.H. Croxall. London: A. & C. Black, 1958.

Kierkegaard, S.A. *Either/or: A fragment of life*. Trans. D.F. Swanson, L.M. Swanson, W. Lowrie. Garden City, N.Y.:Doubleday, 1959.

Kiefl, F.X. *Leibniz*. Mainz:Verlag von Kirchheim, 1913.

Kirchhoff, T. *Deutsche Irrenaerzte. Einzelbilder ihres Lebens und Wirkens*. 2 Vols. Berlin: Springer, 1921-1924.

Kirchhoff, T. *Geschichte der Psychiatrie*. Handbuch der Psychiatrie. G. Aschaffenburg, ed. Allgemeiner Teil. Abt. 3. Leipzig, Vienna: F. Deutike, 1912.

Klein, Melanie. *The psychoanalysis of children*. London: Hogarth Press, 1949.

Kleist,K. Carl Wernicke, 1848-1905. *Grosse Nervenaerzte* (Vols. 2, pp. 106-128). In K. Kolle, (Ed.) 3 Vols. 2nd ed. Stuttgart: Georg Thieme Verlag, 1970.

Kleist, K. Schizophrenic symptoms and cerebral pathology. *Journal of Mental Science*. 1960, *106*, 246-255.

Knittermeyer, H. *Schelling und die romantische Schule*. Munich: E. Reinhardt, 1929.

Koch, I.L.A. *The psychopathic inferiority*. Ravensburg: n.p.,1891.

Kolle, K. Emil Kraepelin, 1856-1926. *Grosse Nervenaerzte*. K. Kolle, (Ed.) 3 Vols. (2nd ed.) Stuttgart: Georg Thieme, 1970, *1*, 175-186.

Kraepelin, E. *Dementia Praecox and paraphrenia*. Trans. R.M. Barclay. Edinburgh: Livingstone, 1919.

Kraepelin, E. Die Erscheinungsformen des Irreseins. *Zeitschrift fuer die gesamte Neurologie und Psychiatrie*, 1921. *62*, Heft 1/5, 1-20.

Kraepelin, E. *Lebenserinnerungen*. Berlin: Springer Verlag, 1983.

Kraepelin, E. *Lectures on clinical psychiatry*. Trans. & Ed. J. Johnston. London: Bailliere, Tindall & Cox, 1913.

Kraepelin, E. *Manic depressive insanity and paranoia*. Trans.R.M. Barclay. Edinburgh: Livingstone, 1921.

Kraepelin, E. *One hundred years of psychiatry*. Trans. W. Baskin. New York: Philosophical Library, 1962.

Kraepelein, E. *Psychiatrie. Ein Lehrbuch fuer Studierende und Aerzte*. (8th edition). 4 Vols. Leipzig: Barth, 1909-1915.

Kraepelin, E. Wilhelm Wundt. *Zeitschrift fuer die gesamte Neurologie und psychiatrie*, 1921, *61*, 351-362.

Krafft-Ebing, R. *Psychopathia sexualis* (1886). Transl. S. Klaf. New York: Stein & Day, 1965.

Kramer, H. & Sprenger, J. *Malleus maleficarum* (1494). Trans. M. Summers. London: Arrow Books, 1971.

Krasnogorski, N.I. The conditioned reflexes and children's neuroses. *American Journal of Diseases in Children*. 1925,. *30*, 735-768.

Kretschmer, E. *Der Sensitive Beziehungswahn: Ein Beitrag zur Psychiatrischen Chracterlehre.* Berlin: J.Springer, 1918.

Kretschmer, E. *Hysterie, Reflex und Instinkt.* Stuttgart: G.Thieme, 1923/1948. English trans. O.H. Boltz, New York: Nervous and Mental Disease Publishing Co., 1926.

Kretschmer, E. *Physique and character.* (1921) Trans. W.J.H.Sprott. New York:Harcourt & Brace, 1925.

Kretschmer, E. *Medizinische Psychologie.* (2nd ed.). Stuttgart: G.Thieme, 1950. English trans. E.B.Strauss, *Textbook of medical psychology.* London: Hogarth Press, 1952.

Kretschmer,E. *Genius of man.* Trans. R.B. Cattell. London: Kegan, Paul, Trench, Trubner & Co., 1931.

Kretschmer, E. & Enke, W. *Die Persoenlichkeit der Athletiker.* Leipzig:G.Thieme, 1936.

Kris, E. *Psychoanalytic exploration in art.* New York: International University Press, 1952.

Krug, A. *Heilkunst und Heilkult. Medizin in der Antike.* Munich: C.H. Beck, 1985.

Kuhn, T.S. *The structure of scientific revolutions.* Chicago: University of Chicago Press, 1962.

Kuhn, T.S. Second thoughts on paradigms. In: F. Suppe, Ed. *The structure of scientific theories.* Urbana: University of Illinois Press, 1977.

Lacan, J. *Ecrits.* Paris: Senil, 1966.

Lacan, J. *The language of the self: The function of language in psychoanalysis.* Baltimore: John Hopkins Press, 1968.

La Mettrie, J.O. de. *Discours sur le bonheur.* In: *Oeuvres philosophiques* (1796). 3 Vols. Hildesheim: Olms, 1970.

La Mettrie, J.O. de. *Man a machine.*(1748) Trans. G.C. Bussey. Chicago: Open Court, 1961. Hildesheim: Georg Olms, repr. 1774 Ed., 1970.

Langer, S. *Philosophy in a new key.* New York: Penguin Books, 1948.

Lassek, A.M. *The unique legacy of Doctor Hughlings Jackson.* Springfield, Ill: C.C.Thomas, 1970.

Laycock, T. *Mind and brain.* New York: Appleton, 1860.

Lehmann, H.E. Classification of depressive states. *Canadian Psychiatric Association Journal.* 1977, *22*, 381-390.

Leibbrand, W. *Der goettliche Stab des Aeskulap.* 3rd edition. Salzburg: O. Mueller Verlag, 1939.

Leibbrand, W. & Wettley, A. *Der Wahnsinn: Geschichte der abendlaendischen Psychopathologie.* Freiburg/Muenchen: Karl Alber, 1961.

Leibbrand, W. & Leibbrand-Wettley, A. *Kompendium der Medizingeschichte*. Munich: Dr. Edmund Banaschewski Verlag, 1964.

Leibniz, G.W. *Discourses on Metaphysics. Correspondence with Arnauld. Monadology*. G.K.Montgomery, Ed. Intro. Paul Janet. La Salle,Ill.: Open Court, 1973.

Leibniz, G.W. *New essays concerning human understanding* (1765). Trans. A.G. Langley. Chicago, 1949.

Leonhard, K. *The classification of endogenous psychoses.* (1957) Trans. R. Berman. New York: Irvington, 1979.

Leonhard, K. *Defektschizophrenen Krankheitsbilder*. Leipzig: Thieme, 1936.

Lesky, E. Heilkunde und Gesundheitswesen. In: *Maria Theresia und Ihre Zeit.* W. Koschatzsky, ed. S.192-196. Salzburg: Residenz Verlag,1979.

Leveque, P. *The Greek adventure*. Trans. M. Kochan. Cleveland, New York: The World Publishing Co., 1968.

Lewis, Nolan. American psychiatry from its beginnings to World War Two. In: *American handbook of psychiatry*. Vol. 1. New York: Basic Books, 1959.

Liebel-Weckowicz, H. The place of antiquity in Ranke's philosophy of history. *Clio*, 1976, *5/2*, 211-231.

Liebel-Weckowicz, H. Was Vico's theory of history a true social science? *The Historian. A Journal of History*, 1982, *44/4*, 466-482.

Liebel-Weckowicz, H. & Weckowicz, T.E. Kant's theory of mental illness. In: *Akten des 11. Internationalen Leibniz Kongress*. Hanover. July, 1972. Wiesbaden: Franz Steiner, G.m.b.H., 1973.

Lindener, G.A. *Lehrbuch der empirischen Psychologie nach genetischer Methode*. Graz: Wiesner, 1858.

Linton, R. *Culture and mental disorders*. Springfield, Ill.:Charles C. Thomas, 1956.

Liddell, H.S. *Emotional hazards in animals and man.* Springfield, Ill.: C.C. Thomas, 1956.

Lief, A. Ed. *The commonsense psychiatry of Adolf Meyer.* New York: McGraw Hill, 1948.

Locke, A.E. Is "Behaviour therapy" behaviouristic? (An analysis of Wolpe's psychotherapeutic methods). *Psychological Bulletin*, 1971, *76*, 318-327.

Locke, J. *An essay concerning human understanding* (1700). J.W. Yolton, Ed. 2 Vols. New York: Dover Publications, 1959.

Loeb, J. *Comparative physiology of the brain and comparative psychology*. New York: Putnam, 1900.

Loewenstein, E. Suggestions for a new therapy in Dementia Praecox. *Journal of Nervous and Mental Diseases*, 1944, *99*, 629-639.

Lombroso, C. *L'uomo delinquente in rapporto alla antropologia, alla giurisprudenza ed alla discipline carcerarie*, Milan, n.p. 1876.

Lovejoy, A.O. *The great chain of being.* Cambridge,Mass.: Harvard University Press, 1936/1964.

Lovejoy, A.O. *The revolt against dualism.* LaSalle, Ill.: The Open Court Publishing Co., 1955.

Lukacs, G. *Der Junge Hegel und die Probleme der Kapitalistischen Gesellschaft*. Berlin: Aufbau Verlag, 1948.

Macdonald, M. *Mystical Bedlam; madness, anxiety, and healing in seventeenth century England*. Cambridge: Cambridge University Press, 1981.

Mace, C.A. Some implications of analytical behaviourism. *Proceedings of the Aristotelian Society*, 1948, *49*, 1-16.

Mach, E. *The analysis of sensations* (1906). Trans. C.M.Williams and S.Waterlow. Chicago: University of Chicago Press, 1914.

Magnan, V. *Alcoholism*. Paris,n.p. 1874.

Makkreel, R. *Dilthey. Philosopher of the human studies*. Princeton: Princeton University Press, 1975.

Malinowski, B. *Magic, science and religion, and other essays*. R. Redfield, (Ed.) Boston: Beacon Press, 1948.

Malinowski, B. *Sex and repression in savage society*. London: Routledge & Kegan Paul, 1953.

Mann, T. *Freud und die Zukunft*. Vienna: Bermann-Fischer, 1936.

Marie, A. & Toporkoff, N. Demence precoce et syphillis. *Archive Internationale de Neurologie,* 1929, *1*, 163-178.

Martin, H. *Kierkegaard, the melancholy Dane*. New York: Philosophical Library, 1950.

Marx, K. *Early writings.* Trans.& ed. T.B. Bottomore. New York: McGraw-Hill, 1963.

Maslow, A. *Motivation and personality*. New York: Harper, 1954.

Maslow, A.H. *Towards a psychology of being*. Princeton: Van Nostrand, 1962.

Masserman, J.H. *Behaviour and neurosis: An experimental psychoanalytic approach to psychobiologic principles.* Chicago: University of Chicago Press, 1943.

Maudsley, H. *The physiology and pathology of the mind.* New York: Appleton, 1867.

May, R. *Existential psychology.* Studies in psychology, Vol. 19 (2nd ed.) New York: Random House, 1969.

May, R. *The discovery of being in writings in existential psychology.* 1st Ed. New York: W. W. Norton, 1983.

May, R. The origins and significance of the existential movement in psychology. In: *Existence*. R. May, E. Angel, & H. F. Ellenberger, Eds. New York: Basic Books, 1958.

Mayer-Gross, W.A. Zur Phenomenologie Abnormer Gluecksgefuehle. *Zeitschrift fuer Pathopsychologie*, 1914, *2*, 588-601.

Mayer-Gross, W. *Selbstschilderung der Verwirrtheit: Die Oneiroide Erlebnisform*. Berlin: Springer, 1924.

Mayr, E. *The growth of biological thought*. Cambridge, Mass.: The Belknap Press of Harvard University Press, 1982.

Mead, G.H. *Mind, self, and society from the standpoint of a social behaviorist*. Chicago: University of Chicago Press, 1934.

Mead, M. *Coming of age in Samoa*. New York: Morrow, 1928a.

Mead, M. *Growing up in New Guinea*. New York: Morrow, 1928b.

Mead, M. *Male and female*. New York: New American Library, 1953.

Menninger, K. Influenza and schizophrenia: Analysis of post-influenzal dementia praecox as of 1918 and 5 years later. *American Journal of Psychiatry*, 1926. *5*, 469-524.

Menninger, K. *The vital balance*. New York: Viking Press, 1963.

Merton, R.K. Social structure and anomie. In: *Social theory and social structure*. New York: Macmillan, 1968.

Mesmer, A.F. *Memoire sur la decouverte du magnetism animal*. Paris: Didot, 1779.

Meyer, A. *Collected works of Adolph Meyer*. E.E. Winters, Ed. Baltimore: Johns Hopkins Press, 1950-52.

Meyer, A. *Psychobiology: A science of man*. Springfield,Ill.: C.C. Thomas, 1957.

Meyer-Steinegg, T. & Sudhoff, K. *Geschichte der Medizin in Ueberblick mit Abbildungen*. B. von Hagen, Ed. Jena: Gustav Fischer, 1950.

Minkowski, E. *La Schizophrenie: Psychopathologie des schizoides et des schizophrenes*. 2nd Ed. Paris: Desclee de Brouwer, 1953.

Minkowski, E. *Lived time (1933)*. Evanston: Northwestern University Press, 1970.

Minkowski, M. Iwan Petrowitsch Pawlow 1849-1936. K.Kolle, Ed. *Grosse Nervenaerzte.* 2nd edition. Vol.1, 200-215. 3 Vols. Stuttgart: G.Thieme Verlag, 1970.

Mora, G. Historical antecedents of modern psychopharmacology. *Psychiatric Journal of the University of Ottawa*, 1989, *14*, 279-281.

Mora, G. History of psychiatry. In *Comprehensive textbook of psychiatry.* A.M. Freedman, H.I. Kaplan & H.S. Kaplan, eds. Baltimore: Williams & Wilkins, 1967.

Moreau de Tours, J.J. *La psychologie morbide dans ses rapports avec la philosophie de l'histoire, et de l'influence des neuropathies sur le dynamism intellectual.* Paris: Libraire Victor Masson, 1859.

Morel, B.A. *Traite des degenerescences physiques intellectuelles et morales de l'espece humaine.* Paris: J.B. Balliére, 1857.

Morgan, L. *An introduction to comparative psychology.* London: Scott, 1894.

Mowrer, O.H. & Mowrer, W.M. Enuresis, a method for its study and treatment. *American Journal of Orthopsychiatry.* 1938, *8,* 436-459.

Munci, W. *Psychobiology and psychiatry.* St. Louis, Mo.: Mosby, 1939.

Murphy, J.M. Psychiatric labelling in cross-cultural perspective. *Science,* 1976, *191,* 1019-1028.

National Geographic Society,(U.S.) eds. *Ancient Egypt. Discovering its splendors.* Washington, D.C.: National Geographic Society, 1978.

Neuburger, M. *History of medicine.* Trans. E. Playfair. London:Froude, 1910-1925.

Neumann, H. *Lehrbuch der Psychiatrie.* Erlangen, 1859.

Neurath,O. Carnap, R. & Morris, C. *International encyclopedia of unified science.* Chicago: Chicago University Press, 1955/ 1970.

Nietzsche, F. The birth of tragedy. In: *Basic writings of Nietzsche.* W. Kaufman, Ed. New York: Modern Library, 1966.

Nietzsche, F. Beyond good and evil. In: *Basic writings of Nietzsche.* W. Kaufman, Ed. New York: Modern Library, 1966.

Nietzsche, F. The genealogy of morals. In: *Basic writingsof Nietzsche.* W. Kaufman, Ed. New York: Modern Library, 1966.

Nietzsche, F. Ecco homo. In: *Basic writings of Nietzsche.* W. Kaufman, Ed. New York: Modern Library, 1966.

Nietzsche, F.W. *The birth of tragedy* (1872); *and the case of Wagner.* Trans. W. Kaufmann. New York: Vintage Books, 1967.

Nietzsche, F. *The will to power.* Trans & Ed. W. Kaufmann & R. Hollingsdale. London: Weidenfeld & Nicolson, 1968.

Nietzsche, F. Thus spake Zarathustra. In: *The portable Nietzsche.* Trans. & Ed. W. Kaufmann. New York: Viking Press, 1966.

Noizet, G. *Memoire sur le somnabulism et le magnetism animal.* Paris: Plon, 1854.

Oesterlen, F. *Medical logic.* Trans. G. Whitley. London: Sydenham Society, 1855.(Original, 1852).

Oesterreich, T.K. *Possession. Demonical and other, Among primitive races in antiquity, the middle ages and modern times*. New York: R.R. Smith, 1930.

Oppenheim, A.L. The interpretation of dreams in the ancient Near East - with the translation of an Assyrian dream book. *American Philosophical Society: Transactions*. 1956, *46*, 170-373.

Ostenfeld, B. *Soren Kierkegaard's psychology*. Trans. A. McKinnon. Waterloo, Ont.:Wilfried Laurier University Press, 1978.

Pagel, J. Ed. *Biographisches Lexikon hervoragender Aerzte des neunzehnten Jahrhunderts*. Berlin, Vienna: Urban & Schwarzenberg, 1901.

Painter, S. *A history of the middle ages*. New York: A.Knopf, 1953.

Paracelsus, T.B.v.H. *Paracelsus Saemtliche Werke*. B.Aschner, Ed. 4 Vols. Jena: Gustav Fischer, 1926-1932. Reprint Munich: Karger, 1976-1981.

Park, R.E. & Burgess, E.W. *The city*. Chicago: University of Chicago Press, 1925.

Parsons, T. *Social theory and modern society*. New York: Free Press, 1967.

Parsons, T. *The social system*. Glencoe, Ill.:Free Press, 1951.

Pascal, B. *Pensees*. Trans. H.F. Stewart. New York: Modern Library, 1967.

Patrick, R. *Book of Egyptian mythology*. Margaret Drower, Ed. London: Octopus Books, 1972.

Pavlov, I.P. *Conditioned reflexes. An investigation of the physiological activity of the cerebral cortex*. Trans. S.V. Anrep. London: Oxford University Press, 1927.

Pavlov, I.P. *Lectures on conditioned reflexes*. Vol. 2. *Conditioned reflexes and psychiatry*. Trans. W.H. Gantt. New York: International Publishers, 1941.

Pegues, R.P.T. *Commentaire francais litteral de la Somme Theologique de Saint Thomas d'Aquin*. 8 Vols. Toulouse: E. Privat and Paris: P. Tequi, 1907-1918. Vols. 4, 9.

Peirce, C.S. Logic as semiotic: The theory of signs (1897). In: *Philosophical writings of Peirce*. J. Buchler, Ed. New York: Dover Publications, 1955.

Penrose, L.S. *The biology of mental defect*. London: Sidwick & Jackson, 1949.

Pfaender, A. *Phenomenology of willing and motivation* Trans. H.Spiegelberg. Evanston, Ill.: Northwestern University Press, 1967. (Original, *Phenomenologie des Wollens*, 1900).

Pick, A. *Die grammatischen Sprachstoerungen. Studien zur psychologischen Grundlegung der Aphasielehre*. Reprint of 1913 edition. Berlin: Springer Verlag, 1986.

Piers, G. & Singer, M.B. *Shame and guilt*. Springfield, Ill.: Charles C. Thomas Co., 1953.

Pinel, P. *Nosographie philosophique ou la méthode de l'analyse applique à la médicine* (5th ed.) Paris: J.A. Brosson, 1813.

Pinel, P. *A treatise on insanity.* (1801) Trans. D.D. Davis. London: Cadell Davis, 1806.

Plato. *The republic*. In: Great dialogues of Plato. Trans. W.H.D.Rouse. Toronto: Mentor Books (The New American Library of Canada), 1963.

Poetzl, O. *Die Aphasielehre vom Standpunkte der klinischen Psychiatrie*. Handbuch der Psychiatrie. G. Aschaffenburg, ed. 3 Abt. 2 Haelfte. 2 Teil. 1 Bd. Leipzig, Vienna: F. Deutike, 1928.

Poetzl, O. *Zur Klinik und Anatomie der reinen Worttaubheit*. Berlin: Verlag S. Karger, 1919.

Popper, K.R. *The poverty of historicism*. London: Routledge, & Kegan Paul, 1957.

Price, L. *The plan of St. Gall in brief*. Berkeley: University of California Press, 1982.

Prichard, J.C. *A treatise on insanity and other disorders affecting the mind*. London: Sherwood, Gibberts & Piper, 1835.

Prince, M. *The dissociation of a personality*. New York: Longman's Green, 1906.

Rank, O. The myth of the birth of the hero. New York: *Journal of Nervous and Mental Diseases*. Monograph, 1914.

Rank, O. *Art and artist.* New York: Alfred Knopf, 1932.

Rank, O. *The trauma of birth.* New York: R. Brunner, 1952.

Rank, O. *Will therapy and truth and reality.* New York: R. Brunner, 1950.

Rank, O. *Beyond psychology.* New York: Dover, 1958.

Rank, O. *The myth of the birth of the hero, and other writings*. P. Freund, Ed. New York: Alfred Knopf, 1964.

Ranke, L. von. *Aus Werk und Nachlass*. W.P. Fuchs & P. Schieder, eds. 4 Vols. Munich: R. Oldenbourg, 1964-

Ranke, L. von. *The secret of world history: selected writings on the art and science of history.* R. Wines, Ed. New York: Fordham University Press, 1981.

Rapaport, D. The structure of psychoanalytical theory. *Psychological Issues*. Monograph 6. Vol. 2/2. New York: International University Press, 1960.

Rather, L.J. Towards a philosophical study of the idea of disease. *The historical development of physiological thought*. C. McC. Brooks & P. F. Cranefield, Eds. New York: Hafner, 1959.

Ray, I. *A treatise on the medical jurisprudence of insanity*. 4th edition. Boston: Little Brown, 1838/1860.

Redondi, D. *Galileo heretic*. Trans. R. Rosenthal. Princeton: Princeton University Press, 1987. (Original Italian 1983).

Reeves, J.W. *Body and mind in western thought. An introduction to the origins of modern psychology*. Harmondsworth: Penguin Books, 1958.

Reich, W. *Character analysis*. Trans. T.P. Wolff. New York: Orgone Institute Press, 1945.

Reil, J.C. *Rhapsodien ueber die Anwendung der psychischer Curemethode auf Geisteszerruettungen*. Halle: Curt, 1803.

Richards, R. *Darwin and the emergence of evolutionary theories of mind and behavior*. Chicago, Ill.: University of Chicago Press, 1987.

Rickert, H. *Science and history*. Trans. G. Reisman. Princeton: Van Nostrand, 1962.

Ricoeur, P. *Freud and philosophy. An essay on interpretation*. Trans.A. Savage. New Haven: Yale University Press, 1970.

Rieber, R.W. ed. *Insanity and the law: two nineteenth century classics*. New York: Da Capo press, 1981.

Rogers, C. *A way of being*. Boston: Houghton Mifflin, 1980.

Rogers, C. *Client-centered therapy*. Boston: Houghton-Mifflin, 1965.

Roheim, G. *The origin and function of culture*. Monograph No.6. New York: Nervous and Mental Diseases Monographs, 1943.

Rosenow, E.C. Specific types of alpha streptococi in the etiology of streptococal thermal antibody in diagnosis and treatment of diverse diseases. *Journal of Nervous and Mental Disease,* 1955, *122*, 238-247.

Rousseau, J.J. *Emil, ou de l'education*. P. Richard, Ed. Paris: Garnier, 1964.

Rothschuh, K. *History of physiology*. Trans. & Ed. G.B.Risse Huntington, N.Y.:Krieger, 1973.

Roux, G. *Ancient Iraq*. 2nd edition. Middlesex, Eng.: George Allen & Unwin Ltd., 1964.

Ruedin, E. *Studien ueber Vererbung und Entstehung geistiger Stoerungen.* Vol. 1. *Zur Vererbung und Neuentstehung der Dementia Praecox*. Berlin: Julius Springer, 1916.

Ruemke, H.C. *Zur Phenomenologie und Klinik des Gluecksgefuehls*. Berlin: Springer, 1924.

Rush, B. *Two essays on the mind: An enquiry into the influence of physical causes upon the moral faculty, and on the influence of physical causes in promoting an increase of the strength and activity of the intellectual faculties of man.* New York: Brunner/Mazal, 1972.

Rush, B. *Benjamin Rush's lectures on the mind.* American Philosophical Society. Memoirs. *Vol. 144.* Philadelphia: American Philosophical Society, 1981.

Russell, W.L. ed. *A psychiatric milestone. Bloomingdale hospital centenary, 1821-1921*. New York: The Society of the New York Hospital, 1921.

Ryle, G. *The Concept of Mind.* Hammondsworth: Penguin Books, 1949.

Saint Thomas Aquinas. See Aquinas, St. T.

Salter, A. *Conditioned reflex therapy: The direct approach to the reconstruction of personality*. New York: Creative Age Press, 1949.

Saggs, H.W.F. *The greatness that was Babylon*. New York: Hawthorn Books, 1962.

Saint-Simon, H. *Selected writings.* Trans. F.M.H. Markham. Oxford: Oxford University Press, 1952.

Saussure, F. de. *Course in general linguistics.* Eds. C. Balley & A. Sechehaye. Trans. W. Baskin. New York: McGraw Hill, 1966.

Schacht, R. *Alienation*. Garden City, N.Y.: Doubleday, 1970.

Schafer, R. *A new language for psychoanalysis.* New Haven: Yalc University Press, 1976.

Scheler, M. *The nature of sympathy.* New Haven : Yale University Press, 1954.

Schelling, F.W.J. *Ideas for a philosophy of nature as introduction to the study of this science,* (1797). Trans. E.E. Harris, P. Heath. Foreword by R. Stern. 2nd Ed. 1803. New York: Cambridge University Press, 1988.

Schelling von, F.W. *Werke.* Vol.1. Leipzig: Fritz Eckard, 1907.

Schilder, P. *Medical psychology* (1924). Trans. D. Rapaport. New York:International Universities Press, 1953.

Schilder, P. *The image and appearance of the human body.* New York: International Universities Press, 1935.

Schmidt, J. Ed. *Aufklaerung und Gegenaufklaerung in der europaeischen Literatur, Philosophie und Politik von der Antike bis zur Gegenwart.* Darmstadt: Wissenschaftliche Buchgesellschaft, 1989.

Schneider, K. Die Schichtung des emotionalen Lebens und der Aufbau der Depressionzustande. *Zeitschrift fuer die gesamte Neurologie und Psychiatrie*, 1921a, *49*, 281-286.

Schneider, K. Pathopsychologische Beitraege zur Phenomenologischen Psychologie von Liebe und Mitfuehlen. *Zeitschrift fuer die gesamte Neurologie und Psychiatrie*, 1921b, *65*, 281-286.

Schneider, K. *Psychopathic personalities.* London: Cassel, 1958.

Schneider, K. *Clinical psychopathology.* New York: Grune & Stratton, 1959.

Scholz, W. (Ed.) *50 Jahre Neuropathologie in Deutschland, 1885-1935*. Stuttgart: Georg Thieme Verlag, 1961.

Schopenhauer, A.S. *Die Welt als Wille und Vorstellung.* (World as Will and Representation). Leipzig: Brockhaus, 1819/1873.

Schubert von, G. *Die Symbolik des Traumes.* Leipzig: Brockhaus, 1837.

Schuetz, A. *Der Sinnhafte Aufbau der Sozialen Welt*. Vienna: Springer, 1932.

Schultz, D.P. *A history of modern psychology*. New York: Academic Press, 1960.

Schumpeter, J. *History of economic analysis.* New York: Oxford University Press, 1954.

Scot, R. *Discoverie of witchcraft*. London: Elliot Stock, 1886. Sechenov, I.M. *Reflexes of the brain: An attempt to establish the physiological basis of psychological processes.* (1863) Trans. S. Belsky. Cambridge, Mass.: MIT Press, 1965.

Sheldon, W.H. *The varieties of human physique: An introduction to constitutional psychology*. London: Harper & Brothers, 1940.

Sheldon, W.H. *The varieties of temperament: A psychology of individual differences*. London: Harper, 1942.

Sher, R.B. *Church and university in the Scottish enlightenment. The moderate literati of Edinburgh*. Princeton: Princeton University Press, 1988.

Sherrington, C.S. *The integrative action of the nervous system*. New Haven: Yale University Press, 1906.

Shorter, P. Personal communication, 1985.

Siegler, M. & Osmond, H. *Models of madness, Models of medicine*. New York: Macmillan, 1974.

Sigerist, H.E. *The great doctors. A biographical history of medicine*. Trans. C. Paul. New York: Norton, 1933.

Sigerist, H.E. *A history of medicine*. New York: Oxford University Press, 1951.

Sigerist, H.E. *Man and medicine: An introduction to medical knowledge*. Trans. M.G. Boise. London: Allen and Unwin, 1932.

Simon, B. *Mind and madness in ancient Greece*. Ithaca: Cornell University Press, 1978.

Skinner, B.F. *The behaviour of organisms: an experimental analysis*. New York: Appleton-Century, 1938.

Skinner, B.F. *Science and human behaviour*. New York: Macmillan, 1953.

Skinner, B.F. What is psychotic behaviour? In F. Gildea, (Ed.) *Theory and treatment of the psychoses, some newer aspects; papers presented at the dedication of the Renard Hospital, St. Louis. October, 1955*. St. Louis: Washington University Studies, 1956.

Skinner, B.F. *Walden two*. New York:Macmillan, 1962. Solomon, D. ed. *The Marihuana Papers*. Indianapolis: Bobbs-Merill, 1966.

Spiegelberg, H. *The phenomenological movement, A historical introduction.* 2 Vols. The Hague: Nijhoff, 1960.

Spiegelberg, H. *Phenomenology in psychology and psychiatry.* Evanston: Northwestern University Press, 1972.

Spielmeyer, W. Die Anatomie im Dienste der Psychiatrie. *Die Naturwissenschaften*, 1920, *18*, 1-8.

Spinoza, B. *Ethics, proved in geometrical order.* Trans. A. Byle. New York: Dutton, 1910.

Spranger, E. *Types of men*. Trans. J.W. Pigors. Halle: Max Niemeyer Verlag, 1928.

Sprenger, J., Insistoris, H., Spee, F., Thomasius, C. *Von Zauberei und Hexenwahn. Grundschriften zur Geschichte der Hexenprozesse in Deutschland*. 3 Vols. Munich: Deutscher Taschenverlag, 1986

Stahl, G.E. *Theoria medica vera.* Halle, 1708.

Stekel, W. *Das liebe Ich: Grundriss einer Neuen Diatetik der Seele*. Berlin: Otto Stalle, 1927.

Stekel, W. *Technique of analytical psychotherapy*. New York: Liveright, 1950.

Straus, E. *The primary world of senses: A vindication*. Glencoe, Ill.: Free Press, 1963.

Straus, E. *Phenomenological psychology: Selected papers*. Trans. E. Eng. New York: Basic Books, 1966.

Sullivan, H.S. *Interpersonal theory ofpsychiatry*. New York: W.W. Norton, 1953.

Sydenham, T. *Medical obervation concerning the history and the cure of acute diseases*. Trans R.G. Latham. London: Sydenham Society, 1848.

Szasz, T.S. *The myth of mental illness. Foundations of a theory of personal conduct*. New York: Harper & Row, 1961.

Szasz, T.S. *Psychiatric justice*. New York: Macmillan, 1965.

Talbott, J.A. *The chronic mentally ill. Treatment, programs, systems.* New York, London: Human Sciences Press, 1981.

Thiele, R. Wilhelm Griesinger, 1817-1868. K. Kolle, (Ed.) *Grosse Nervenaerzte*. (Vol. 1, pp. 115-127) 3 Vols. (2nd ed.). Stuttgart: Georg Thieme, 1970, *1*, 115-127.

Thiselton, A.C. *The two horizons: New Testament hermeneutics and philosophical description with special reference to Heidegger, Bultmann, Gadamer, and Wittgenstein.* Exeter: Paternoster Press, 1980.

Thompson, C. *Psychoanalysis. Evolution and Development*. New York: Hermitage House, 1950.

Thorndike, L. *A history of magic and experimental science*. 8 Vols. New York: Macmillan, 1923-1958.

Thorndike, E.L. *Animal intelligence:Experimental studies*. New York: Macmillan, 1911.

Thorndike, L. *The place of magic in the intellectual history of Europe*. New York: AMS Press, 1967.

Thwaites, R.G. ed. *The Jesuit relation and allied documents; travels and explorations of the Jesuit missionaries in New France, 1610-1791*. 73 Vols. Cleveland: Burrows, 1896-1901. Ottawa: Canadian Institute for Historical Microreproductions, 1980.

Tolman, E.C. *Purposive behaviour in animals and men*. New York: Century, 1932.

Totok, W. & Haase, C. Eds. *Leibniz*. Hanover:Verlag fuer Literatur und Zeitgeshehen, 1966.

Tredgold, A.F. *A textbook of mental deficiency*. London: Bailliere, Tindell & Cox, 1929 (1909).

Troxler, I. *Blicke in das Wesen des Menschen*. Aarau: Sauerlaender, 1812.

Tuke, D.H. *A manual of psychological medicine*. New York: Hafner, 1968.

Tuke, D.H. *Chapters in the history of the insane in the British Isles*. Amsterdam: E.J. Bonset, 1968. (Reprint of London: Kegan, Paul & Trench, 1882).

Tuke, D.H. *The insane in the United States and Canada*. London: H.K.Lewis, 1885.

Tuke, S. *Description of the Retreat, an institution near York, for insane persons of the Society of Friends*. London:Dawsons of Pall Mall, repr. 1813 Ed., 1964.

Twardowski, K. *Zur Lehre vom Inhalt und Gegenstand der Vorstellungen*. Vienna: W. Hoelder, 1894. English trans. R. Grrossmann. *On the content and object of presentations*. The Hague: M.Nijhoff, 1977.

Ungar, F. (Ed.) *Goethe's world view presented in his reflections and maxims*. Trans. H. Norden. New York: F. Ungar, 1963.

Vaihinger, H. *Philosophy of the as if. (Die Philosophie des als Ob)*. Berlin: Reuther & Reichard, 1911.

Veith, I. *Hysteria:The history of a disease*. Chicago: University of Chicago Press, 1965.

Vico, G. *The new science of Giambattista Vico*. T.G. Bergin & M.H. Fisch, (Eds.) Ithaca: Cornell University Press, 1948.

Vietor, K. *Goethe the thinker*. Trans. B.Q. Morgan. Cambridge, Mass.: Harvard University Press, 1950.

Virchow, R. *Cellular pathology*. Trans. F. Chance. London: Churchill, 1860.

Virchow, R. Ueber die Standpunkte in der Wissenschaftlichen Medizin. (Points of view in scientific medicine). Trans. L.J. Rather. *Bulletin of the History of Medicine. 1956, 30*, 436.

Voegthin, W.L. The treatment of alcoholism by establishing a conditioned reflex. *American Journal of Medical Sciences*. 1940, *199*, 802-810.

Vygotsky, L.S. *The collected works of L.S. Vygotsky*. Trans. R.W. Rieber & A.S. Carton. Vol.1 New York: Plenum Press, 1987a.

Vygotsky, L. *Thought and Language*. A.Kazulin, Ed. & trans. Cambridge,Mass.:The MIT Press, 1987b.

Wach, J. *Das Verstehen. Grundzuege einer Geschichte der hermeneutischen Theorie im Neunzehnten Jahrhundert*. 3 Vols. Tuebingen: J.C.B. Mohr (Paul Siebeck), 1926.

Watson, J.B. *Behaviorism*. New York: W.W. Norton, 1930.

Watson, J.B. Psychology as the behaviourist views it. *Psychological Review*, 1913, *20*, 158-177.

Watson, J.B. & Rayner, R. Conditioned emotional reactions. *Journal of Experimental Psychology*, 1920, *3*, 1-14.

Weber, M. *The methodology of social sciences.* Trans. E.A. Shils & H.A. Finch. New York: The Free Press, 1949.

Weckowicz, T.E. The impact of phenomenological and existential philosophies on psychiatry and psychotherapy. In: *Humanistic psychology: Concepts and criticisms*. (pp. 49-74). J.R. Royce & L.P. Mos, Eds. New York: Plenum Press, 1981.

Weckowicz, T.E. "Kazimierz Dabrowski's theory of positive disintegration and the American humanistic psychology." *Counseling and Values*, *32/2*, 124-134, 1988.

Weckowicz, T.E. *Models of mental illness, Systems and theories of abnormal psychology*. Springfield, Ill.: C. C. Thomas, 1984.

Weckowicz, T.E. & Liebel-Weckowicz, H. Typologies of the theory of behaviourism since Descartes. *Sudhoffs Archiv*., 1982, *66*, 129-151.

Weiss, A.P. *A theoretical basis of human behaviour*. Columbus, Ohio: R.G. Adams, 1925.

Wernicke, C. *Der aphasische Symptomenkomplex*. Breslau: M.Cohn & Weigert, 1874.

Wernicke, C. *Grundriss der Psychiatrie in Klinischen Vorlesungen*. Leipzig: G.Thieme, 1894.

Wernicke, C. *Lehrbuch der Gehirnkrankheiten fuer Aerzte und studirende*. 3 Vols. in 2. Kassel: T. Fischer, 1881-1883.

Weyer, J. De praestigiis daemonum et incantionibus ac veneficis (1563). In: *Joannis Wieri Illustrissimi Ducis Cleviae et Quondam Archiatri: Opera Omnia*. Amsterdam: Vanden Berg, 1660.

Whytt,R. *An essay on the vital and other involuntary motions of animals*. Edinburgh: J. Balfour, 1763.

Whytt, R. *Observations on the nature, causes and cure of those disorders which have been commonly called nervous, hypochondriac, or hysteric, to which are prefixed some remarks on the sympathy of the nerves*. Edinburgh:J.Balfour, 1767.

Wilden, A. Lacan and the discourse of the other. In: J. Lacan, *The language of the self: The function of language in psychoanalysis*. Trans. A. Wilden. Baltimore: John Hopkins University Press, 1968.

Wilhelm, R. & Jung, C.G. *The secrete of the golden flower*. Trans. C.F. Baynes. New York: Harcourt Brace, 1931.

Windelband, W. Geschichte und Naturwissenschaft. Reprinted in *Praeludien*, 2. Tuebingen: J.C.B.Mohr, 1924.

Windelband, W. *History of philosophy*. Trans. J.H. Tufts. New York: Macmillan, 1901.

Wolpe, J. Experimental neuroses as learned behaviour. *British Journal of Psychology*, 1952, *43*, 243-268.

Wolpe, J. Reciprocal inhibition as the main basis of psychotherapeutic effects. *Archives of Neurology and Psychiatry*, 1954, *72*, 205-226.

Wolpe, J. *Psychotherapy by reciprocal inhibition*. Stanford: Stanford University Press, 1958.

Wolpe, J. & Theriault, N. Francois Leuret: A progenitor of behaviour therapy. *Journal of Behaviour Therapy and Experimental Psychiatry*, 1971, *2*, 219-221.

Wundt, W. *Grundzuege der Physiologischen Psychologie* (1874). 3 Vols. Leipzig: Engelmann, 1911.

Wundt, W. *Voelkerpsychologie: Eine Untersuchung der Entwicklungsgesetze von Sprache, Mythus und Sitte*. 10 Vols. Leipzig: Engelmann, 1910-1920.

Wyrsch, J. *Ueber Akute Schizophrene Zustaende, Ihren Psychopathologischen Aufbau und Ihre Praktische Bedeutung*. Basel: Karger, 1937.

Zabarella, J. *De rebus naturalibus in Aristotlis libros de Anima*. Frankfurt a. M. Minverva, reprint of 1606/07 Ed., 1966.

Ziehen, T. *Die Grundlagen der Psychologie*. 2 Vols. Leipzig, Berlin: B.G. Teubner, 1915.

Zilboorg, G.(In Collaboration with G.W. Henry). *A history of medical psychology*. New York: Norton, 1941.

Author Index

Subject Index